*f*P

ALSO BY MICHAEL KNOX BERAN

The Last Patrician: Bobby Kennedy and the End of American Aristocracy

Jefferson's Demons

Portrait of a Restless Mind

MICHAEL KNOX BERAN

FREE PRESS

New York   London   Toronto   Sydney   Singapore

ƒP

FREE PRESS
A Division of Simon & Schuster Inc.
1230 Avenue of the Americas
New York, NY 10020

FREE PRESS and colophon are
trademarks of Simon & Schuster, Inc.

For information about special discounts for bulk purchases,
please contact Simon & Schuster Special Sales:
1-800-456-6798 or business@simonandschuster.com

Designed by Jan Pisciotta

Manufactured in the United States of America

1   3   5   7   9   10   8   6   4   2

Library of Congress Cataloging-in-Publication Data

Beran, Michael Knox.
Jefferson's demons : a portrait of a restless mind / Michael Knox Beran
p.   cm.
Includes bibliographical references (p.   ) and index.
1. Jefferson, Thomas, 1743–1826—Mental health
2. Jefferson, Thomas, 1743–1826—Psychology
3. Presidents—United States—Biography. I. Title.
E332.2.B427 2003
973.4'6'092—dc21
[B]
2003052760
ISBN 0-7432-3279-8

To my wife,
and my daughter

Yet a little while is the light with you.

Contents

A Note on Terms		xi
Prologue		xiii
PART ONE	SPRING	I
PART TWO	SUMMER	27
PART THREE	FALL	109
PART FOUR	WINTER	149
Epilogue		199
A Note on Designs		205
Notes and Sources		206
Acknowledgments		255
Index		256

A Note on Terms

A *Tory* is a searcher, a finder out of things. The name comes from the Gaelic word for "pursuer," for the Tories were originally Irish outlaws who had been stripped out of their lands, bog-crawling men who lived by plundering the English invader. But the word has come gradually to denote, not merely a narrow and factious tribe, but a universal state of mind. There have been Tories in every age, and in every civilization. The Tory believes that the world appears chaotic only to those whose sight is too dim to perceive its more exquisite unities; and he pursues always his ideal of a society in which man's different endeavors—the long extent of his works and loves—can be made to form a coherent whole. The Tory is an exile from the close-blooded brotherhoods of the classical city-state; is a refugee from the delicious intimacies of old Christendom; is unwillingly estranged from the moral certitudes of Abraham, of Moses, and of David.

The term *Whig* comes from southwestern Scotland, where country people called Whiggamores drove their horses with the exclamation *"Whiggam!"* But this word, too, has come to denote an attitude of soul that may be met with in any time or place. The Whig is impressed by the vastness and intricacy of the universe. So gigantic has the world become, the Whig thinks, that it is no longer possible to wrap up man's different endeavors in such a neat exemplary bundle as once was found in the tents of the Israelites, in the Greek polis, in the Early Church, and in the Christian Middle Ages. In the Whig view people must take their politics, and even their religion and their private morality, much as they take their other household goods—by going to the marketplace and seeing what is on sale, and at what price. In 1688 the

Whigs came to power in England and imposed a revolutionary settlement that contained the seed of Thomas Jefferson's own program of liberation. The Whig Bill of Rights (1689) liberated the individual from the tyranny of the state; the Toleration Act (1689) protected certain categories of religious dissent; the Triennial Act (1694) reformed the Parliament; and the decision to allow the Licensing Act to expire (1695) emancipated the press.

Prologue

"I am burning the candle of life," he told a friend, "without present pleasure, or future object." "A dozen or twenty years ago this scene would have amused me," he said. "But I am past the age for changing habits." Under the perpetual dullness of the winter sky, Jefferson contemplated the "empty bustle" of Paris and studied the means by which the beautiful people in that city sought to escape their demons.

He drew, in a letter to one of his American friends, a picture of the pointlessness of a Parisian existence. It is an elaborate letter, written to a rich and, as it happens, pretty lady called Mrs. Bingham, a great hostess in Philadelphia. The high Parisians, Jefferson told Mrs. Bingham, sought always to escape from the *"ennui"* (literally, the annoyance) of the "present moment." But they inevitably failed. We are, he said, "ever flying from the *ennui* of that [i.e., the present], yet carrying it with us." We—and here Jefferson means *we;* he is no longer talking simply about morally decayed Parisians—are "eternally in pursuit of happiness which keeps eternally before us."

Odd, disconcerting even, to find Jefferson dredging up, in the depths of his distemper, the famous words, the brighter faith of the Declaration of Independence. He was quoting himself, alluding to the person he had been eleven years before, when he wrote out his draft of the Declaration during the heat of a Philadelphia summer. But there is in the letter nothing like the younger man's joy. In the darkness of a Paris winter, an older Jefferson—he would turn forty-four in April 1787—questioned the promise of the earlier springtime.

We figure him as a man heroically active, prodigiously vigorous, but Jefferson's grandest acts and his most illuminating experiences were always preceded by muddy stretches, periods in which he was at once dull spirited and full of trepidation. It was in such a ragged condition that he lay, invalid-like, in April 1776, not long before the happy inspiration under which he composed the Declaration of Independence. It was in such a state that he now surveyed the dreariness of his Paris life, oblivious of the approach of the dry light that was for a time to dispel the mists. It was in such a state that he would later find himself during the barren periods of the 1790s, when he tried to reconcile his dream of an ideal republic with the imperfect reality.

"My temperament," Jefferson said,

> is sanguine. I steer my bark with Hope in the head, leaving Fear astern. My hopes indeed sometimes fail; but not oftener than the forebodings of the gloomy. There are, I acknolege, even in the happiest life, some terrible convulsions, heavy set-offs against the opposite page of the account. I have often wondered for what good end the sensations of Grief could be intended.

He chose his words, as always, with care. He spoke not only of his "sensations of Grief," that sensitivity to the tears in things that formed so unexpected a part of his mental equipment, but also of his "forebodings of the gloomy," the burden of presentiment that lay heavily upon him, an apprehension of possible futures that enabled him to become a great man, but that also made him a nervous and often an indecisive one.

To bring order to this interior confusion, Jefferson carefully devised rules of conduct. Indolence was to be avoided at all costs. When the mind was indolent, Jefferson told his daughter Martha, or "Patsy"—given up to "snaggle-toothed laziness"—one's "being becomes a burthen, and every object about us loathsome." Idleness, Jefferson warned, "begets *ennui*," and "*ennui* the hypochondria." (The word *hypochondria* was not limited, in the eighteenth century, to the morbid apprehension of imaginary diseases; the term was more often used to indicate an habitual melancholy, thought in those days to be caused by a defect in the nervous system or by the epigastric juices of the abdomen, those "hypochondrial" regions of the body where the liver, the spleen, and the gallbladder are found.) Hypochondria led to hysteria. "No laborious person," Jefferson said, "was ever yet hysterical."

Exercise was especially important in the struggle to preserve sanity. "Not less than two hours a day should be devoted" to it, Jefferson believed. Of all the exercises, he maintained, "walking is best." "I have known some great walkers," he said, "and had particular accounts of many more; and I never knew or heard of one who was not healthy and long lived." A brisk walk, according to Jefferson, "shakes off sleep, and produces other good effects in the animal œconomy." The "object of walking," he said, "is to relax the mind." "You should not permit yourself even to think when you walk," he advised. "Never think of taking a book with you."

Labor, discipline, a scrupulous avoidance of the dark places of the mind—these were, for Jefferson, the principles of a healthy life, precepts by which a man might hope to be guided to a serene old age. The consequences of not following so prudent a course were likely to be grave: a descent into the abysses of ennui and hypochondria, perhaps even into madness. For Jefferson even so simple a thing as staying up late with a book was a bad idea, a transgression of salutary limits. The night has often been the nursery of genius; but Jefferson had an almost superstitious abhorrence of its power. "Rise at a fixed and an early hour," he advised, "and go to bed at a fixed and early hour also." "Sitting up late at night is injurious to the health," he maintained, "and not useful to the mind." The night was a dangerous time, a time when the mind's discipline was relaxed, and dreams came. That is why, Jefferson explained, he never went "to bed without an hour, or half hour's previous reading of something moral, whereon to ruminate in the intervals of sleep." Even the sleeping mind had to be coaxed into submitting to a Jeffersonian discipline.

Jefferson walked fast; his unremitting labors kept him exceedingly busy; he read moral literature before bedtime. But still the shadows came. He was not, like his father, a work of natural simplicity, a stout man of action, a vestige, it seemed, of a more vigorous epoch in human development—a throwback to the Bronze Age. In the constitution of the son's mind there were complications; there were refinements of spirit; there were depths.

In order to invent America, he had first to invent himself. He was called to be an architect of a liberating (Whig) revolution, but it is a paradox of the Whig system that it cannot be built without a resort to the very materials it is supposed to render obsolete. Jefferson dedicated his life to freeing men, not only from the forms of oppressive authority, but also from the varieties of mystic craft. For according to the Whig, it is precisely this mystic craft that enables the tyrant to perpetuate his primacy. "I have," Jefferson said, "sworn upon the altar of God, eternal hostility against every form of tyranny over the mind of man." Superstitious faith—the awe of things that "stand above"—was, Jefferson believed, the most potent form of mental tyranny. He stood, he said, for common sense, and he was skeptical of any claim that could not be verified by it. But no more than other people could Jefferson live without those *un*common trumpets, mystic and nonsensical, that bid a man rise from his moperies and act with an heroic creativity.

Jefferson was, in his philosophy, a materialist, and he was devoted to the rational interpretation of empirical facts. But his theories were unequal to his perceptions, and his yearnings outstripped his philosophy. It is because he understood the inadequacy of his theories before the great mysteries of existence that he resorted, on occasion, to a language stained in mysticism, and truer to the strangeness. It is one of the principal oddnesses of his life. If he was to be a model Whig, he could not be *wholly* a Whig. To build the modern (Whig) world he dreamed of building, he would have to do more than act commonsensically in the universe his heroes—Bacon, Newton, and the other grandpas of the Enlightenment—had painted for him. To be a complete Whig, Jefferson would have to be at least partly a Tory. He might pace the pillared spaces of his villa entranced by the reasonableness of Locke's intelligence, or Voltaire's wit, or Gibbon's history; he might adorn his house with the rational luxuries of an eighteenth-century taste; but if he were to succeed in rousing himself from his lassitudes and show himself capable of action, he would have to descend to the Tory crypts and assemble, in those strange vaults, in the light of those dim candles, a philosophy that did more than reason and common sense could to facilitate the expedition of the will.

This book is a portrait of Jefferson descending. In those secret laboratories we find him melting down strangely *un*enlightened creeds, orthodoxies, patterns of thought and belief. We find him mixing the molten materials together and anxiously pouring the glowing liquid into the cast of a livable life. Ever since Garry Wills published, in 1978, his book *Inventing America,* it has ceased to be possible to think of Jefferson as simply a good Whig, dedicated to an unbinding of the chains, a liberation of the spheres. Wills showed that Jefferson's Whig ideas were colored by a form of sentimental faith highly fashionable in the eighteenth century. These sentimental canons were a secular edition—revised and corrected for the eighteenth-century press—of an older European mysticism. This was the medieval language of love, and the revivified love song appealed to lapsed Christians who, if the truth were confessed, found themselves bored by the wit and enlightenment of Voltaire. Sentimentality touched them in the depths of their blood, in the agony of their stony places, in a way Voltaire never could; it endowed with coherence a universe tottering on the edge of anarchy.

But sentimentality was not the only mystic fabric Jefferson took up, fondled, intellectually caressed. The modern man's life is, Jefferson said, a continual *pursuit* of happiness, a perpetual chase; amid the plenitude of possibility, the infinity of choice—the superabundance of creeds and destinies on sale in the Whig markets—the modern man must find his way, through trial and error, to a faith, or at least to an éclaircissement. Jefferson did, although he was always a little mysterious about its character. "I am of a sect by myself, as far as I know," he told Ezra Stiles in the decade before he died.

Just now we are between Jeffersons. Older editions of the man have been put aside. No new volume has yet been issued to take its place. "All honor to Jefferson," Abraham Lincoln said,

> to the man who, in the concrete pressure of a struggle for national independence by a single people, had the coolness, forecast, and capacity to introduce into a merely revolutionary document, an abstract truth, applicable to all men and all times, and so to embalm it there, that to-day, and in all coming days, it shall be a rebuke and a stumbling-block to the very harbingers of re-appearing tyranny and oppression.

Lincoln believed Jefferson to be the greatest teacher of liberty in the American tradition; but by the 1930s, Lincoln's Jefferson had given way to another Jefferson, that of Franklin D. Roosevelt. Inspired by Claude Bowers's pungently partisan *Jefferson and Hamilton* (1925), F.D.R. invoked the third president as a fellow struggler against the "economic royalists" who, in the tradition of Hamilton, had erected the "dynasties" which the New Deal was intended to destroy. "I have a breathless feeling as I lay down this book," Roosevelt wrote in a review of *Jefferson and Hamilton* in the *Evening World*. (It was the only book Roosevelt ever reviewed for publication.) "Hamiltons we have today," the future president said. "Is a Jefferson on the horizon?" After he won the White House, F.D.R. laid the cornerstone for the Jefferson Memorial in Washington, and he watched with approval as John Russell Pope's dish of neoclassical vanilla ice cream rose on the banks of the Potomac. Each April, on the anniversary of his hero's birth, the president dispatched a courtier to Monticello to lay a wreath at Jefferson's tomb.

Roosevelt's Jefferson, a New Deal tribune of the plebs, was succeeded by the Jefferson of the postwar imperial republic, the idol of the bright confident men who made the American Century. Unsurprisingly, this Jefferson possessed many of the virtues which the makers of the American Century attributed to themselves. They discovered, in the master of Monticello, a cool, rational, somewhat technocratic genius—a man who might without incongruity grace a cover of *Time* magazine. This was the Jefferson John F. Kennedy invited the Nobel laureates to feast upon at a famous dinner in 1962. The Nobels, Kennedy said, represented "the most extraordinary collection of talent, of human knowledge, that has ever been gathered together at the White House, with the possible exception of when Thomas Jefferson dined alone." Kennedy's Jefferson was a supertalented New Frontiersman, a shade more versatile than McGeorge Bundy, a more masterly version of Robert McNamara. It is this Jefferson—the forerunner of the best and the brightest—who is enshrined in the greatest work of Jeffersonian hagiography which the last century produced: Dumas Malone's *Jefferson and His Time.* But the placidly rational Jefferson of Malone and John Kennedy is dead, killed off by exposure to scandal and DNA testing. Can we find another Jefferson to take his place?

Jefferson once wrote that he envied a young man who was embarking on "his classical voyage to Rome, Naples and Athens." *A classical voyage*—it's not a bad way to envision Jefferson's own life. His mental odyssey took him to curious and splendid ports: to the brutish ecstasies of the old pagan cults, to the piety and rage of the Hebrew prophets, to the charity of the Christian Gospels.

Think of him as a man beguiled by the old virtues and ideals, but one who did not wish to be enslaved by them. Shopping in the grandest marts of his civilization, Jefferson brought back with him what he thought could be useful. (The library at Monticello was never merely ornamental; it was here that the intellectual pirate hoarded his cultural treasures.) Jefferson tried to translate what was useful in the archaic forms into the American vernacular, and through this fruitful sorcery to raise the tone of the young republic's civilization. A large ambition, to be sure, perhaps an impossible one. Jefferson hoped to influence, not just America's public culture (its politics and governing traditions), but also the private culture of the individual citizen, as revealed in those little communities (the family, the village, the neighborhood, the school) in which so much of American life is actually lived. His ideas about what causes these modest gardens to flourish have been too often neglected, which is a pity, for it is in these places that he can most directly touch our own lives.

He lived a large part of his life in his books. To understand what he became, it is necessary to understand the esoteric intellectual rites that made him what he was. He was born on the remote frontier of a great empire, but although he grew up in a British province, his mind was not provincial. Modern scholarship too often is. Bereft of the comprehensive visions of Bowers and Malone, contemporary historians tend either to confess their bafflement before the sphinx or to involve themselves in small-beer controversies about the great man's sexual proclivities—history as gossip, a literary style dear to our epoch. Oddly (Jefferson might say predictably) the people who line up at the gates of Monticello to tour his house have a more sympathetic insight into the value of his secret studies. The tourists might not, for the most part, have been bred up in scholarly arts; but their perceptions are in some ways truer than those of the professionals. They sense what the higher learning has failed to see, or forgotten how to appreciate. The people gather to glimpse the sanctuary of a (mostly) benign wizard, a Virginia Prospero—a prime author of the American pageant. They feel the enchantment of his spirit, in spite of its perversities and hypocrisies, while the professors, with their academic squabbles, massage the flesh of the corpse.

Jefferson grew old learning new things, and this suppleness of mind made it possible for him to become something more than a statesman: he was also an educator. Jefferson conforms to an historic type of visionary leadership, the statesman who possesses certain qualities of the artist, qualities that enable him to adapt the older mystic intuitions of his civilization to the altered conditions of the present. These qualities, if they did not always make Jefferson attractive as a man, allowed him to be effective as a teacher, one who showed how the meat of his civilization's obsolescent carcasses could be used to nourish new patterns of cultivated order. The ancient Greeks, whom Jefferson read closely during the greater part of his life, believed that a nation is forged not only by force of arms and structures of law but also by acts of poetic will. Think of Lincoln's Gettysburg Address, which helped to form the American character, or the oratory of Churchill, which defined the fighting spirit of the British. Jefferson's achievement is of that kind, and on that order: he wrote the Declaration of Independence.

Those whose minds, like so many in our own age, have been formed in a school of disenchantment need to work a little harder to perceive the reach of his statesmanship. Great republics are not founded on common sense alone: they flourish only where their founders, with their common sense and common faults, possess also the uncommon ability to reach into the auger hole of time and impose their ideals on the future. The state-making man, according to the poet Virgil, must seek out the Sibyl in her prophetic cave before he can found his city; but our contemporary historians, preoccupied with Sally Hemings, fail to perceive the lawgiver's descent:

> *thus in the wind, on the light leaves,*
> *the Sibyl's oracle was lost.*

Of course his sins matter: nor can human nature forbear to peep into the closets of the great. But if we end by becoming a nation of valets, so also will we be a nation destitute of heroes. Stripped of our teachers, we will be left with nothing more than an "odor of phrases."

The oracular splendor of Jefferson's state-making work was not without a psychological cost: his creative activity was rooted in the peculiarities of his nervous organization. The exquisite sensitivity that enabled Jefferson to attain, in his highest work, a prophetic strain was closely connected to his struggle with ennui, those sensations of *"tedium vitae"* which he called the "most dangerous poison of life." *Ennui* was what the French psychologists called soul error (*erreur d'âme*), a man's inability to be satisfied with his situation in the one and only moment he has within his power, the present. As a man grows older, Jefferson observed, time becomes more precious to him, but the man in the griping hand of *ennui* is careless of his temporal blessings. He laments the shortness of the time even as, a half dozen times a day, he finds himself dissatisfied by its dullness and wishes he could transfer himself to one of eternity's happier shores. He comes to resent the time; possibly he tries to kill it—smother it, as, Jefferson observed, the grand Parisians did, in gossip and card games; certainly he is unable to do justice to its greatest gift, the present moment, to get the most out of it and act creatively and usefully in it.

Ah, but to do that, to take up the time and wring from it its deepest revelation, to do it the exquisite justice of action, one must put the whole of one's self into its arms. One cannot, in the manner of an eighteenth-century gentleman, offer up only one's surfaces; one must hold some communication with one's depths. Jefferson, after his periodic inward struggles, was ready to heed his own oracles, to draw on his depths. But it is difficult to be a suppliant—a suppliant even to one's self—when one is wearing silk stockings, and has powder in one's hair, and is resolved to be in all things smooth and gentleman-like. Some mystic drapery is requisite, and Jefferson was always trying on different robes. The man who confessed, in the emptiness of a Paris winter, to a dissatisfaction with his life was yet determined to squeeze out of it the last enchantment of its mystery. He wrung it more fiercely than we know or have cared to see.

PART ONE

SPRING

I
Decay

*There's not the smallest orb which thou behold'st
But in his motion like an angel sings,
Still quiring to the young-eyed cherubins;
Such harmony is in immortal souls,
But whilst this muddy vesture of decay
Doth grossly close it in, we cannot hear it.*

—SHAKESPEARE

HE WAS BORN in the Virginia backcountry, where his father, large-limbed Peter Jefferson, cleared the forest to make a farm he called Shadwell. But although Thomas Jefferson was born on the rugged ground of the Virginia frontier, he passed much of his boyhood on flatter land closer to the coast. His father had agreed to manage Tuckahoe, one of the Randolph plantations on the James, and before his third birthday little Thomas was brought east, closer to the tidewater lowlands. His first memory was of being carried on a pillow by a mounted slave during the journey from his father's lands at Shadwell to the porches and paneled salons of his mother's kinsmen, the Randolphs.

These transits between the high lands and the smooth lands continued through his youth. Brought east in infancy, the boy returned to western Virginia at the age of nine, when his father took the family back to Shadwell. Eight years later, three years after his father's death, Jefferson, by this time almost seventeen, again went east. It was the father's wish that his son should receive a classical education, and in March 1760 Jefferson and his slave, Jupiter, packed a wagon and drove 150 miles east to Williamsburg, where the young man took up his studies at the College of William and Mary.

He was, by his own confession, a "hard student," but he nevertheless found time to taste the pleasures of a provincial capital. He danced with the young ladies at the Raleigh Tavern, and in rooms heavy with the fumes of tobacco and arrack punch he became acquainted with lawyers and scholars, as well as with "horse racers, card players, fox hunters." The racecourse beckoned, and so did the stage. He went, during race week, to see the heats, and he made his way among the carriages and bullock carts to the theater in Waller Street, where he saw Wycherley and Congreve performed, as well as Shakespeare. In the company of his teachers, Dr. Small and Mr. Wythe (pronounced *with*), the young squire dined in splendor with the viceroy, Governor Fauquier; it was in the glow of the governor's chandeliers that he first learned the art of worldly talk. Jefferson later said that he heard "more good sense, more rational and philosophical conversation" at these intelligent soirees than "in all my life besides."

Beyond the limits of Williamsburg lay the great tidewater plantations, and Jefferson visited them often. In those enchanted zones of tranquillity and order, adorned with every ornament and convenience, he spent languid days immersed in the pursuits of the tidewater gentry. In the mornings he would go foxhunting with his friends, scions of the old planter families; in the afternoons he could be found listening, in a painted parlor, to the music of their sisters' singing.

So pleasant a life might easily have been fatal to the development of the intellect. The elegant cycles of a gentry existence, calculated rather to amuse than to stimulate the mind, would seem to have supplied little that could

awaken, in a young man's imagination, those nourishing disgusts, those re-
vulsions and antipathies, in which large ambitions begin. The mind, diverted at different times by the alternating sensations of the chase and the
hunt, the dance and the ball, the horse race and the card game, was relieved
even of the most rudimentary burdens of introspection. The effect on the
imagination of so elaborate a machinery of pleasure was likely to be unfortunate; the methods of aristocracy, Jefferson would later reflect, like those
of royalty, encouraged a carnal flabbiness in the pampered few. Aristocrats,
like kings, became, he said, "all body and no mind," and he remarked on
how "worthless" many of his youthful friends among the gentry ended up
becoming. He was astonished, he said, that he did not "turn off" with some
of these characters and find himself, like them, caught up in a narrow middle age.

He did not turn off; he adhered, with only minor deviations, to the path
of duty and destiny. For although he yielded to the pressure of tidewater
pleasures, the capitulation was never complete; the frontier-bred boy was re-
strained by the sense that something pernicious lurked behind the tidewater
facades. There was, Jefferson confided to his good friend John Page, too
much powder, too much embroidery, too much perfume in his well-bred
world. He took to calling Williamsburg "Devilsburgh," and he faulted himself for having involved himself too intimately in its stains and defilements.
There is a tradition that the young man, reviewing one of his years at college, was mortified by his profligacy, the sums casually spent on clothes,
horses, revels. When he returned home to Shadwell for the vacation, Jefferson forced himself to perform a severe penance, and in the effort at expia-
tion he shut himself up with his books.

The bad qualities he detected at Williamsburg were heightened by the
climate of the tidewater. All his life Jefferson retained an aversion to it.
There was an unhealthiness in the lowlands, a sultriness not merely of situation but of mind, the overripeness bred by the southern summer. In the hot
months the tidewater shallows became fetid pools: they stank in the sunlight, and from them rose unwholesome vapors productive of disease—ty-
phoid, malaria, the bloody fluxes of dysentery and enteritis. Visitors to those
fragrant deltas remarked upon the sickliness of the men and women they encountered there; their pallid complexions, their incorrigible indolence, their
strange and scented lassitudes—all proclaimed them less vigorous than their
cousins who lived in the cleaner air of the up-country.

In the lurid light of the tidewater, the unhealthiness of the Virginia oligarchy appeared especially grotesque, but the derelictions that provoked Jef-

ferson's disgust were not limited to the lowland barons he encountered around Devilsburgh. They were faults shared, in greater or lesser degrees, by the whole of the Virginia gentry. It was the class to which he himself belonged. Jefferson's father, Peter Jefferson, might, as a new man, have been exempt from some of the viciousness of the oligarchs, but Jefferson himself was not. He was not—and knew that he was not—a new man. His mother, Jane, was Captain Isham Randolph's daughter, a descendant of William Randolph of Turkey Island, as the Randolphs' lands below Richmond were called. William Randolph was one of the founders of his family's fortunes in Virginia; together with the Byrds and the Ishams, the Carters and the Lees, he was an architect of the primordial oligarchy of the province. Like other opulent families who sought to preserve the plumage of their caste unsullied in a dense colonial undergrowth, the Randolphs sanctioned frequent intermarriage among the members of a compact cousinage and bred a bloodline in which qualities of intelligence, pride, and eccentricity were preeminent.

No scion of such a house could be unaware of the mental wreckage associated with it. Long before the intuitions of Darwin, the Virginians knew the truth of inherited traits. Family character was, in Virginia, "traced thro' many generations." Fitzhughs had "bad eyes." Every Thornton "hears badly." Winslows and Lees "talk well." Carters were "proud and imperious." Taliaferros were "mean and avaricious." Fowkses were "cruel." As for the Randolphs, they were "indolent," "impatient of reproof," and "irritable." They were also melancholy, and they possessed what one of them called a "sublunary" genius. The family traditions were full of horrors, and every one in them was morbid. There were tales of child murder, of desperate insanities, of young manhood dissipated in drink, of promising life extinguished in the prime.

Jefferson took no satisfaction, he said, in this high and complicated descent, and doubtless this was true. He liked to dwell instead on all that distinguished him from the aristocracy into which he had been born. The embroidery, the powder, the perfume of the best-blooded Virginians bothered him, not because he had any intrinsic contempt for pleasant surfaces— quite the contrary—but because he suspected, as Westerners do when they look east, that the splendid exteriors concealed a deficiency of character. The Virginia grandees were, Jefferson observed, "aristocratical, pompous, clannish, indolent." They possessed "some good traits"—few people were more generous or hospitable—but also many "feeble ones." The young squire taught himself to look down on men who slatterned away their time in cards, gaming, the chivy and halloo of the hunt, and he prided himself on having the energy of mind to tear himself away from such pursuits.

Jefferson frowned upon the idleness of the gentry; and we may guess—it is a fair bet—that he was disturbed, too, by the amount of loose wenching that went on. We know, from his later letters, that he disapproved of people who strayed from the marriage bed, though on at least two occasions, once as a bachelor and once as a widower, he talked love to a married woman. We have all heard how, later in life, he may have fathered children by a woman who was not his wife. But of course it is possible to make mistakes in one's own life—or to countenance in one's own behavior a quantity of depraved pleasure seeking—and still be disgusted by the character of other people's debaucheries. And there *was* a sordidness in the peccadilloes of the Virginia master class; they might have provoked even a less fastidious man. The *cavalieros* could romp and roister like animals in rutting. When not engaged in the manage of his horses, or enchanted by the prospect of killing a fox, the Virginia chevalier could always be tempted into an indulgence of the pleasures of the flesh. William Byrd II, living, it is true, in an earlier part of the century, left in his diary a record that allows us to form some idea of the seigneurial lusts of old Virginia: "Jenny, an Indian girl, had got drunk," Squire Byrd wrote in his entry for October 20, 1711, "and made us good sport." "At night I asked a negro girl to kiss me," he wrote in his entry for the following day. "Then came Mrs. Johnson with whom I supped and ate some fricasse of rabbit and about ten went to bed with her and lay all night and rogered her twice." A few days later, Squire Byrd wrote, he "went to Mrs. FitzHerbert's where I ate some boiled pork and drank some ale. About nine I walked away and picked up a girl whom I carried to the bagnio [a bathhouse or brothel] and rogered her twice very well. It rained abundance in the night." Occasionally the master of Westover confessed to a pang of remorse: "16 October picked up a woman and went to the tavern where we had a broiled fowl and afterwards I committed uncleaness for which God forgive me. About eleven I went home and neglected my prayers." But a month later he was again in the stews, writing that he "went away to Will's where a woman called on me . . . then went to a bagnio where I rogered my woman but once. Her name was Sally Cook. There was a terrible noise in the night like a woman crying."

The lewd sallies of the planters were only one symptom of a deeper moral disorder, a decadence that Jefferson was later to attribute in part to the bad effects of slavery. "The whole commerce between master and slave," he said, "is a perpetual exercise of the most boisterous passions, the most unremitting despotism on the one part, and degrading submissions on the other." In his own mind, however, he was better than this: he possessed the virtues of his caste, the outwardly polished manner, the gracefulness of address, the flowing courtesy, the sensitivity of personal honor, but he was, he believed, less stained by the vices, and so less likely to make slovenry work of life. A conviction true enough, so far as it went. But not entirely true. Jefferson was more deeply implicated in the unhealthiness of the place than he knew, or at any rate than he cared to confess.

The Virginia into which he was born was unhealthy in another way. Its wealth rested on an illusion. The prosperity of the province was founded on tobacco, but by the 1760s tobacco could no longer support the palatial aspirations of the planters. The rapacious plant rapidly exhausted the soil in which it was sown; at the same time the prices it fetched had begun to fall. And yet aristocracy, with all its strange pathologies, resists the discipline of retrenchment; and perversely enough the life of the magnificoes became, in the face of ruin, ever more extravagant. Men of old families were declared bankrupts; the Byrds themselves were not free from the dread of penury. William Byrd III, son of William of Westover, was to become one of Jefferson's law clients; at one time he owed his creditors in the mercantile houses of London the then fantastic sum of one hundred thousand pounds.

There was splendor in the provincial world in which Jefferson grew to manhood; but it was an autumnal splendor. The processes of decay were well advanced by the time he reached Williamsburg. He was sensitive to the rot. We like to think of Jefferson's early career as passed in the freshness of a Revolutionary dawn; but this is fanciful. It was in an uncertain twilight, amid the guttering candles of a declining order, that he first began to look around him.

2

Anxiety

Vexed I am
Of late with passions of some difference,
Conceptions only proper to myself.

—Shakespeare

Jefferson suffered, during the course of his life, from periodic bouts of apathy and dejection. The lapses occurred for the most part during anxious times, periods when the vexations of private life or the pressures of public business weighed heavily upon him. Sometimes, though not always, the sluggish moods were accompanied by violent headaches.

The curious thing about the breakdowns is that they were often followed by stretches of extraordinary creative activity. Often, but not every time. So far as we can tell, the first of his crises—the first, at any rate, for which there is any evidence—did not result in any heightened clarity or revelatory light. But the first breakdown has an interest of its own, for though it incubated no noble political work, no pregnant phrase or idea, no act of creative artistry, it reveals something of the oddness of a sensitive young man who would go on to achieve things most sensitive young men never do.

The crisis culminated in the spring of 1764, the year in which Jefferson turned twenty-one. Two years earlier he had completed his studies at the College of William and Mary, and he had begun to read law in Mr. Wythe's office. (Mr. Wythe was among the most prominent advocates in Williamsburg.) At sea in the law, as the beginner is bound to be, the young man found himself disoriented in other ways as well. He still felt the poignance of his father's passing seven years before; historians speculate that his relations with his mother were strained. The course of his reading in the late 1750s and early 1760s reflected the morbidity of his preoccupations. He covered the leaves of his commonplace book with maxims of the sages, savoring especially their reflections on the brevity of life and the faithlessness of women. Even sympathetic critics, impressed by Jefferson's copious extracts from Greek, Latin, and French literature, have wondered at the violent language he selected in assembling the strange catalog of feminine iniquity to which a portion of the book is devoted. Once their "loose desires" got dominion, Jefferson wrote, no hungry churl "fed coarser at the feast."

Such language, if it did not accurately reflect the young man's convictions, betrayed his passing moods, and perhaps concealed his real desires. Certainly he would not have been the first young man to disguise his tremulous hopes of love with the convenient cloak of misogyny. Jefferson's motives in making death a principal theme of the commonplace book were more straightforward: he had watched his father die. The son copied out Cicero's words. "What satisfaction can there be in living," that disappointed Roman had asked, "when day and night we have to reflect that at this or that moment we must die?" Jefferson looked to the meditations of the philosophical Cicero for consolation; in his letters he toyed with the Stoic mask that the great statesman wore in the last days of his own life, before Mark Antony's thugs came for him. But it was in vain; not even the *Tusculan Disputations* could assuage the rooted sorrow.

From the entries in his commonplace book, one might deduce that women, unfaithful, *méchantes,* and cruel, were to be avoided at all costs, and yet not long after Jefferson inscribed these sentiments in the pages of his book, he proclaimed an intense and undying love for Miss Burwell.

Rebecca Burwell was not an otherwise memorable character. Had Jefferson not loved her, and had the future chief justice John Marshall not later loved (and married) her daughter, Miss Burwell would undoubtedly lie forgotten by history. But to the young Jefferson, Miss Burwell embodied an absolute perfection; and his anxious passions, his morbid fears, and his uncertain desires, imperfectly concealed beneath the mask of stoicism or indifference, all conspired to inflame his love for the ordinary girl. "Was SHE there?" he asked his friend Page in a letter in which he sought an account of a recent marriage. "Because if she was I ought to have been at the devil for not being there too." "How does R.B. do," Jefferson asked Page a few weeks later. "What do you think of my affair, or what would you advise me to do?"

Miss Burwell, for her part, seems to have had little interest in so diffident and indeed so unskillful a lover, and while Page urged his friend to sally forth in a spirit of conquest and "lay siege" to her, Jefferson found excuses for not doing so. At last, however, a momentous interview took place at Williamsburg; Jefferson danced with Miss Burwell in the Raleigh Tavern; he there attempted to woo her with carefully meditated words of love. But he discovered, as soon as he began to speak, that the love poetry he had inwardly rehearsed could not survive the spontaneity of conversation. "I was prepared," Jefferson said, "to say a great deal. I had dressed up in my own mind such thoughts as occurred to me, in as moving language as I knew how, and expected to have performed in a tolerably creditable manner." But "good God! When I had an opportunity of venting them, a few broken sentences, uttered in great disorder, and interrupted with pauses of uncommon length, were the too visible marks of my strange confusion."

Not long after this Miss Burwell became engaged to marry another man. "With regard to the scheme which I proposed to you some time since," Jefferson wrote his friend Will Fleming in March 1764,

> I am sorry to tell you it is totally frustrated by Miss R. B.'s marriage with Jacqueline [sic] Ambler which the people here tell me they expect daily. I say, the people here tell me so, for . . . I have been so abominably indolent as not to have seen her since last October.

In the same letter in which he confessed the misadventure of his love, Jefferson mentioned, for the first time in his surviving correspondence, that he was suffering from a "violent head ach," one with which he had "been afflicted these two days." "My head achs," he complained to Fleming, and he explained that the intense pain made letter writing difficult. It may be that the sensitivity of his eyes contributed to the headache; his methodical absorption in his studies had in the past led to eyestrain. In a letter of the previous year, Jefferson had written that the whites of his eyes had become red from excessive application to books; his eyestrain left him, he said, in "such exquisite pain that I have not attempted to read anything since a few days after Jack Walker went down, and God knows when I shall be able to do it" again. In later descriptions of his "periodical head ach," Jefferson would note particularly this inability to read as one of its least happy symptoms.

Was the headache a migraine? *Hemicrania,* the Latin word from which *migraine* derives, means a headache limited to one side of the head. But both words, *hemicrania* and *migraine,* had by the eighteenth century acquired a neurasthenic coloring, which rendered their meaning ambiguous; to say that Jefferson suffered from migraine is merely to perpetuate the mystery of his complaint and leave unanswered the question of whether its ultimate causes were physiological or psychological. Was the headache related to the "melancholy fit," as Jefferson called it, into which his amorous exertions had plunged him? Or were his chronic late-adolescent complaints—his confusions, his despairs, what he called his "solemn notions"—rather to blame for provoking the malady in his head?

In the absence of evidence, the "violent head ach" must remain, like other aspects of the April periods in Jefferson's life, shrouded in obscurity. Later crises would issue in illumination and insight, but there is no evidence that this one did. No candles were lit, or if they were, they were put under the bed and not set out in candlesticks for later generations to see. But the eruption of the forgotten springtime, whatever might have been its cause, hints at a strangeness within him, not easy to figure out.

3
Exhilaration

They are happy men whose natures sort with their vocations.

—Bacon

In the summer of 1765, a little more than a year after his "violent head ach," Jefferson passed his law examinations and was duly called to the bar. He began at once to practice, and he was soon riding over the slough roads of the Virginia up-country, helping clients secure claims to the western lands.

By specializing in land patents, the young lawyer found a way to involve himself in the fresh energies at work in the land. He was able to play a part in the opening of the West—to serve the unseen forces that were pushing men through the Cumberland Gap into Kentucky and drawing them down the Holston River toward Tennessee. A new world had begun to take shape on the frontier; in the shadow of the Shenandoah Mountains Jefferson saw the smoking fires of settlers who had come south from Pennsylvania in search of fresh soil. The Virginia squirealty was, as a rule, hostile to the in-cursions of the Scotch-Irish newcomers. William Byrd III, loaded with the debts and defensiveness of a degenerate order, saw in the immigrants the threat of a barbarian strain. They were, he said, like the "Goths and Vandals of old." Jefferson, however, perceived a greater promise in the struggle of the pioneers. He saw in them the genesis of a civilization that would one day overspill the Blue Ridge and cover a continent—an empire in embryo.

So much for the New World he encountered in his practice on the western circuit. What of the Old World that he had studied in college? He had come into contact with the new energies of the borderlands and the frontier; but what of the *old* energies? Was the young barrister who now rode the western marches of his civilization to forsake its eastern strongholds, the lamps of the dawn? No, it was out of the question. The American West was like a blank book, pretty—and empty. Unwritten and as yet even unconceived. There was, to be sure, a quantity of dirty poetry in the language of the frontier, poetry more genuine, some would say, than the polished couplets of Pope and Dryden, so labored, so affected, so *maniéré*. But frontier poetry was not just the sort of poetry Jefferson loved: he was drawn to a complexity of masks and manners; he had a craving for the elaborate, the "turnings intricate of verse," and it was not to be satisfied by what he called the "semi-barbarous" culture of the borderers.

He continued his west ridings—but he never forsook his search for truth in the classical texts of the East. Reading was the principal means by which he conducted his investigations; he spent large sums on books brought west across the Atlantic. As often as not the volume in his hand was a Greek or Roman one; Homer was a particular favorite. "I enjoy Homer in his own language infinitely beyond Pope's translation of him," Jefferson later told a friend. "I thank on my knees him who directed my early education, for having put into my possession this rich source of delight."

He loved books, especially old ones, and more especially classical ones. Yet he was not bookish. He had grown into a big-boned man who was as at home on horseback as he was in a cream-and-gilt library. He passed from the poetry of Homer or Anacreon to the mud and manure of the stables as though it were the most natural thing in the world; and the squire who sat rapt over the beauties of Virgil's verses in the morning might be seen, later in the day, superintending the foaling of a colt, or giving orders for the slaughter of pigs, or engrossed in the arcana of his studbook. These qualities of self-assurance—they are often found in heavy-booted men with property to command—spilled over into the other departments of Jefferson's life. Vanished forever was the boy who had blushed bashfully in the presence of Miss Burwell. Jefferson was now perfectly at ease in the company of pretty women; perhaps too much at ease. When, many years later, his political opponents threatened a disclosure of his unauthorized kisses, Jefferson confessed that in the summer of 1768, as a "young and single" lawyer, he had "offered love to a handsome lady."

This was Mrs. Walker, who happened, inconveniently, to be married to Jefferson's old friend Jack Walker. Mrs. Walker neglected to say anything to her husband at the time, and the twenty-five-year-old Jefferson, his reputation unsullied, was duly elected to the Virginia legislature a few months later. The next year the governor, Baron de Botetourt, made him lieutenant of Albemarle, a place of honor modeled on the English office of the territorial lord lieutenant. Jefferson was entitled to be called colonel, and as a notable landowner he was of course made commander of his majesty's militia in the county, both horse and foot.

He was intensely idealistic. As a young legislator he made, he said, an "effort" for the "emancipation of slaves." The procedures for freeing a slave in Virginia were cumbersome; Jefferson proposed to simplify them. The measure was rejected; in the days before the Revolution, he said, "nothing liberal could expect success." Yet his own liberality was even at this time in his life nicely counterbalanced by a sense of personal interest; in the same year he took his seat in the Virginia legislature with hopes of emancipating blacks, Jefferson offered a reward for the return of a "mulatto slave called Sandy" who had slipped his shackles. Jefferson portrayed the runaway slave as the kind of charmless servant-monster another master might well wish to be rid of. "Rather low" in stature and "inclining to corpulence," Sandy was "greatly addicted to drink," Jefferson wrote, and when drunk, he was "insolent and disorderly." As if this were not enough, the shoemaking slave swore a great deal and was "artful and knavish" in his behavior.

Sandy was eventually dragged back to Albemarle County; he was put again to his cobbling work just as his master's own life began to assume a new and more mature shape. It was for Jefferson a time of multiple exhilarations. There was, first, Monticello, which he began to build in the summer of 1769. And there was Martha Wayles Skelton, whom he began to court in 1770 and whom he married on New Year's Day 1772. As for the house, it was not large, especially when compared with the Monticello we see today; Jefferson would rebuild it almost completely in later years. Like the house, the woman, too, was small, especially when compared with her husband, who stood some six feet, two inches tall. But her eyes, like his in some lights, were hazel, and like the house she was "exquisitely formed." She was a widow when Jefferson began to court her; her first husband, Bathurst Skelton, had died in 1768 after two years of marriage. And she was an heiress: her father, John Wayles, was a lawyer who, in the course of a long career, had acquired a great deal of land. At his death, in 1773, his daughter inherited eleven thousand acres from him and more than a hundred slaves. Among those she brought to Monticello were a family of "bright" mulattoes, the Hemingses.

He did not, at the beginning of the 1770s, seem especially marked for greatness; he was a rich gentleman farmer who appeared, at times, to be more interested in pursuing the sweet life of Monticello than in pressing on with an arduous law practice. But his orchards, his gardens, his horses, and his wines could not entirely distract Jefferson from the momentous questions of the day. In 1765, at the time of the Stamp Act Crisis, he had stood at the door of the Virginia legislature and heard Patrick Henry denounce the infamous statute. "He appeared to me to speak as Homer wrote," Jefferson said. "Tarquin and Caesar each had his Brutus," Henry declared before the burgesses, "Charles the First his Cromwell, and George the Third . . ." Here Henry broke off his discourse; in his scarlet robes the speaker of the house, old John Robinson, cried out the dread word *treason*. "I well remember the cry of treason," Jefferson later wrote, "the pause of Mr. Henry at the name of George III and the presence of mind with which he closed the sentence and baffled the charge vociferated." George III, Henry said, "may profit by their example."

The problems that now started Jefferson from his luxurious repose at Monticello were the fruit of overreaching empire. Ever since the end of the Seven Years' War in 1763, successive British ministries had, in their quest for revenue, pursued schemes for making the American colonies contribute more to the cost of maintaining his majesty's overseas dominions. The shortsighted policy of George Grenville, the author of the Sugar Act and the Stamp Act, and the equally myopic legislation of Charles Townshend, who devised a set of duties on glass, lead, paper, and tea, risked the peace of an empire in order to raise a few hundred thousand pounds for the treasury. Their measures, impotent to beget revenue, bred vexation instead; and although the stupidity of the policy was pointed out by men like Chatham and Edmund Burke, the King's ministers obstinately pursued their destructive course, and they soon drove the Americans into open rebellion.

Some colonists rebelled more fiercely than others. Jefferson later said that his own sympathies lay with Virginia's radicals, with Patrick Henry and Richard Henry Lee, men who talked fire, and who were impatient with the lethargic leadership of the old guard. Some have questioned the closeness of Jefferson's association with the radicals; he was perhaps more intimately connected to steadier hands like Peyton Randolph, who was his kinsman, and who had served as Virginia's attorney general. But although Jefferson was attached, by ties of blood and friendship, to the silver-haired patricians of the province, he was nevertheless determined to show what he called "forwardness & zeal" in the struggle to resist the usurpations of the Parliament at Westminster.

In 1774 Lord North, the prime minister, brought a bill to close the port of Boston. The bill was duly passed. This was London's retaliation for the Tea Party. A short time later, on a Monday morning in May, Jefferson went to the Virginia capitol and followed the colony's radicals into the council chamber. There was a library in the room, rich in constitutional precedents, and after rummaging through the old books the men "cooked up" a resolution protesting the actions of the government. The paper which they drew called for a day of fasting, humiliation, and prayer, in order that his majesty's subjects in Virginia might beseech God "to avert from us the evils of civil war, to inspire us with firmness in support of our rights, and to turn the hearts of the King & parliament to moderation and justice."

Their work done, Virginia's leaders went back to their home counties to rally the people against the tyranny of the ministry. Jefferson himself spent much of the next two months at Monticello, closely engaged in drafting a memo. A great and unprecedented congress was to convene, in September at Philadelphia, for the purpose of ascertaining the collective mind of a continent; Jefferson's paper was a petition to the king, presented in the form of instructions to the Virginia delegates who were to be in attendance at the assembly. It turned out to be the most elaborate piece of polemical prose he had yet written, and the laborious effort of composition left him exhausted. Finishing it at the end of July 1774, Jefferson headed east toward Williamsburg, but he collapsed in the heat before he reached the capital. As he lay languishing with a dysentery along the Williamsburg road, the essay went ahead by courier; in the capital cousin Peyton, the former attorney general, laid the paper on the table. The intelligence of the thing impressed people who mattered, and it was soon printed as a pamphlet, *A Summary View of the Rights of British America*. The chances of empire and the vagaries of imperial tax policy had discovered to Jefferson territory in himself previously unvisited, though not perhaps unsuspected. Working in prose, he was able to impose literary form on the chaotic slops of politics. He had thought to be a lawyer and a politician, but he now found that he was something more: he was an artist, one who could change things by throwing over them a broidery of words.

The year after his *Summary View* was published, Jefferson was himself a delegate to the Continental Congress; he arrived in Philadelphia in June 1775 in a phaeton drawn by four horses. At thirty-two he found himself looked upon as a revolutionary leader, possessed already of an influence on account of his talent for composition, the high seriousness of his polemical tone, and the extensiveness of his Virginia connections. "Yesterday the famous Mr. Jefferson . . . arrived," Governor Ward wrote his brother in Rhode Island. "He looks like a very sensible, spirited, fine Fellow and by the Pamphlet he wrote last Summer, he certainly is one."

But the young political poet who now took rooms in Philadelphia had attracted the gaze of eyes less sympathetic than those of Governor Ward. Across the ocean, in Westminster, Jefferson's name was inserted, along with those of other men, now famous, in a bill of attainder being prepared by members of Parliament. The three words had, at that time, a terrible significance: a bill of attainder was a legislative declaration of guilt that, if enacted, would render the proscribed traitors "attaint, *attinctus,* stained, or blackened." For a person attainted of high treason was, in the eyes of the English law, "no longer fit to live upon the earth." He was to be "exterminated as a bane and a monster." The attainder set a "note of infamy upon" him and put him out of the law's protection entirely: the law now took "no farther care of him than barely to see him executed" and to ensure, through the corruption of his blood, that all his lands, goods, and chattels were forfeited to the crown.

4

*A*ction

Plutarch's heroes are my friends & relatives.

—Emerson

Like other peoples involved in revolutionary movements, the Americans of the 1770s cherished an ideal of bold activity. They piqued themselves on their "virtue"—by which they meant their public-spirited toughness—and contrasted it with the enervated spirits of the stay-at-home British, corrupted by the fruits of luxury and empire. Jefferson shared his countrymen's faith in their patriotic competence; he believed in the superiority of American virtue. As a young lawmaker who possessed what he later called the "little spice of ambition," he longed for opportunities to display his own hidden worthiness.

The outward swagger of the Americans concealed their deeper doubts. Jefferson knew that his countrymen sometimes faltered in their virtuous audacity; they too readily stopped at the "half-way house" of unsatisfactory compromise; they had frequently to be aroused from their juiceless torpor by leaders who could dose them with a salutary "shock of electricity." These lapses in virtue might be temporary, but they were still troubling. Could a citizenry that sank into lethargy the moment the immediate danger passed sustain an army in the field? Could it create a set of political institutions from scratch and overmaster an empire that, with all its delinquencies, was still the most formidable military power on earth?

For Jefferson the problem of virtuous action was not only a political one; it was also a personal one. He happened to *like* luxury; and luxury, according to the prevailing theories, was the nemesis of virtue. He reveled in the softer world of the aesthete, in slim duodecimos of obscure classical poets, in the gorgeous confections of modern prose stylists. Nor was his tender feeling for the deliciousness of style, his sensitivity to the subtler nuances of crafted proportion, limited to books. It betrayed itself, too, in the pretty objects and beguiling surfaces with which the young squire loved to surround himself. Jefferson was drawn, as by instinct, to beauty and to opulence, to pillared porticoes, to curiously wrought silver, to the rarer and more singular wines; his favorite recreation lay in drawing the plans of magnificent buildings.

The desire for action was further complicated by his contempt for the hurly-burly of politics. In council chambers and committee rooms he was a quiet figure, slim, cool, detached; he had little patience for the extroverted political arts, for speechmaking, arm twisting, coalition building. In the press of affairs, he was visited by distressing visions of book-lined studies. Add to this his spells of melancholy, of world-weariness, of ennui—the stoic spleen of which his youthful letters are full—and the nature of his predicament becomes clear. Could he act in a crisis? Did he have dagger and nerve enough to carry on enterprises of pith and moment? Was he up to the "mark of the times"? He had, it is true, composed the *Summary View,* a bold piece of work, yet when the storms of composition were over, what had he done but promptly proceed to collapse?

Jefferson was not alone in the uneasiness with which he contemplated the name of action. For all their talk of virtue, the Americans of the 1770s were as bewildered as they were virtuous; they were not always sure how they should act, or whether indeed they *could* act in ways that would make them masters of the historic moment. They looked constantly, a trifle nervously, to the great men of the past for a model and a muse. Plutarch, that profound psychologist of public virtue, had analyzed the mental processes that underlay the civic feats of the Greeks and the Romans; Americans anxiously turned the pages of Plutarch's "lives"—his studies of antique character—in the hope that they, too, might learn how to transform base passions into beautiful deeds.

The fabric of public virtue had been cut out of Roman cloth, and old Greek linen, a magic web of pure patriotism and ideal community sewn up in the prophetic fury of an ancient religious mysticism, and cast at the feet of the archaic civic gods. How were those primitive threads to be woven into the moral tapestry of a modern Whig revolution? The Whig principle—the Whig right—for which Jefferson and his patriot brothers now contended was not in the least mystical; it was hardly even patriotic; it was certainly not civic. The right for which they contended was the right to be left alone and to be allowed to cultivate one's garden in peace. A worthy ideal, one by which most of us now live. Yet private devotion does not win wars. It was the paradox of their revolution that, in order to win it, the Americans were forced to develop qualities of character that were anathema to their ends. To prevail, the provincial rebels were required to study, and master, those forms of civic heroism that their revolutionary efforts were intended to render obsolete.

The question of how to act and what to do came to a head in 1775. The first fighting broke out in Massachusetts in the spring; there were battles at Lexington and Concord, as well as at Bunker Hill. The snows came early that winter; one morning in September 1775 Jefferson looked out from Monticello to see the Blue Ridge fringed with white. In the same month his daughter Jane died, not yet two years old.

In late September, Jefferson parted from his wife and surviving daughter, Patsy, to return to his congressional duties in Philadelphia. The soreness of this separation from his family soon grew rawer, for the advancing autumn brought the sound of trumpet and kettledrum to the Chesapeake. Lord Dunmore, the royal governor, declared martial law in Virginia; British warships menaced the coastal ports. The governor, who had taken refuge on the man-of-war *Fowey* off Yorktown, tenderly probed the most sensitive parts of the Virginia body politic. He invited disaffected slaves to join his standard under the name Lord Dunmore's Ethiopians. British squadrons attempted to burn the town of Hampton, and a detachment of royal grenadiers and marines marched on a patriot redoubt at Great Bridge, near Norfolk. The troops were repulsed, with much loss of life; after the fighting was over, dozens of British soldiers lay dead or wounded, although only a single American was wounded, "slightly injured by a grapeshot." Jefferson, in Philadelphia, learned that his home country had been whipped into a "perfect phrensy," but to his dismay he had no news of his family. "The suspense under which I am is too terrible to be endured," he wrote to his brother-in-law. "If anything has happened, for god's sake, let me know."

At last he was able to return to Virginia; he withdrew to Monticello and passed the remainder of the winter in seclusion with his family. In March 1776 his mother died of an apoplexy, and shortly thereafter Jefferson began to suffer from an unspecified "malady," as he called it, accompanied by one of his violent headaches. This left him unable to work during much of April, and for six weeks he lay in idleness and ill health at Monticello. The origin of the indisposition remains a mystery and one that exercised the ingenious speculation of historians. One biographer ascribed the funk to Jefferson's "order-loving, rigid" qualities, while another supposed it to have been "triggered" by, among other things, his anxious concern for his wife's health. Still another historian suggested that the malaise was one that tended to claim "perfectionists" as its victims.

A number of scholars have wondered at how indifferent to his mother Jefferson had by this time become; a coolness seems to have existed between them to the very hour of her death. But even a withered grief may have its effect on a man's health. Perhaps more disturbing to the peace of Jefferson's mind was the question of action that now lay decisively before him. He had, during the previous fall, grown steadily bolder in his thinking, and toward the end of 1775 he had been especially daring in his utterances. The "successes of our arms," he had written to his cousin John Randolph in November, "have corresponded with the justice of our cause." Cousin Randolph was by that time in England, for he had remained loyal to the crown, but Jefferson did not shrink from telling him that the king was provoking civil war. George III, he said, would live to regret the bloody issue of his obstinacy. "To undo his empire," Jefferson wrote, the king had "but one truth more to learn, that after colonies have drawn the sword there is but one step more they can take." That step was "now pressed upon us," he said, "by the measures adopted" by the British.

The time had come, Jefferson told his cousin, for a swearing out of oaths. "Believe me Dear Sir," he wrote,

> there is not in the British empire a man who more cordially loves a Union with Gr. Britain than I do. But by the god that made me I will cease to exist before I yield to a connection on such terms as the British parliament propose and in this I think I speak the sentiments of America. We want neither inducement nor power to declare and

assert a separation. It is *will alone which is wanting* and that is growing apace under the fostering hand of our king.

But the mounting spirit, the "will" that Jefferson believed so essential to the
preservation of American liberty, was more difficult to foster than he knew.
States of mind are notoriously difficult to interpret, but what the young
rebel experienced in these months seems to have been in the nature of a crisis of the will.

It may be that he realized, as the wintertime swept over Monticello, just
how high a cost he might be required to pay. During the quiet months he
tended, in the hoarfrost mornings, to the stocking of his deer park, and he
had the five-year-old Madeira brought up from the cellar, that he might sip
it beside the fire in the afternoons. A glass of sweet wine; a sensation of the
order of his house; a perception of the frigid perfection of the landscape that
lay beyond the windows—he must at such moments have been something
more, or something less, than a man if he did not reflect on the dangers he
would soon encounter. He was on the verge of mortgaging, to the uncertain
chances of a revolutionary struggle, not just Monticello itself, and his own
life. Other fates besides his own were saddled to his gamble and would ride
upon the outcome of the wager. The ardor even of the fiercest Whig—wild
for liberty and zealous for his charters, his laws, his blots and smears of
right—will sometimes flag when he is the husband of a young wife, and the
father of a daughter just three years old.

At all events his health gave way. An opening in time loomed in the near
distance, a portal in that god-built wall; and Jefferson trembled on the
threshold of a world-historical doorway. Others, he told John Randolph,
might revel in the "confusion" that civil tumults create, "but to me," he said,
"it is of all states, but one, the most horrid." In his *thinking* Jefferson had
long been ready to take the decisive step that would clear up this confusion:
he was, as a purely intellectual matter, prepared to make the crossing that
would bring the clarity of either revolutionary success or ruin. But thinking
and acting are different things, and Jefferson knew that in the coming
months he would have to *act* on questions that up to this time had been for
him largely a matter of theory. He would have to act on them, moreover, in
ways that would never be accepted, and could never be forgiven, by the
Crown. In 1775 Jefferson had, he said, still looked "with fondness towards a
reconciliation with Great Britain." But he was now contemplating a course
of conduct that must destroy whatever slender possibility of compromise or
accommodation with Westminster still existed.

When at last he rose from his sickbed that spring, he behaved like a man who had made his peace with destiny; he would not resist history; it was perhaps inescapable anyway. Yet however reconciled to his decision he now was, Jefferson knew that his crossing into history would inevitably involve the destinies of others besides himself, among them those to whom he was closest. The tears of these hostages to his fortune (for tears there must have been, though the formal record is blank) must have salted whatever imaginations of their futures broke his sleeps to perplex him in the night.

By May he was well enough to return to Philadelphia, and feeling, he said, "almost a new man," he and the other revolutionaries prepared to act. He was, he confessed, in an "uneasy anxious state" about Mrs. Jefferson, who remained with their daughter in Virginia. But he did his best not to allow his private worries to interfere with his public duties.

On Friday, June 7, 1776, Richard Henry Lee, speaking for the Virginia delegation, moved "that the Congress should declare that these United colonies are & of right ought to be free & independent states." A long and tempestuous debate followed, while at the same time a committee was formed to prepare the instrument that, in the event the motion passed, would formally effect the separation. Jefferson was appointed to the committee, together with John Adams, Roger Sherman, Robert Livingston, and Benjamin Franklin. To Jefferson was entrusted the task of preparing the draft.

He retired to his rented rooms on Market Street and in a few days produced the draft. He showed it to the committee, which approved it, and on Friday, June 28, he presented it to the house. The draft was read to the delegates and laid upon the table. On Monday, July 1, Congress resolved itself into a committee of the whole, and debate resumed on the resolution that the Virginians had moved. At the end of that day, the delegations of nine colonies voted for the resolution; those of South Carolina and Pennsylvania voted against it. The deputies from Delaware were divided, and those from New York uncertain. Edward Rutledge, of South Carolina, rose, and requested that a final determination be put off until the next day. When, the next morning, the house assembled, the South Carolina delegation changed its vote. Shortly thereafter another delegate, who had ridden posthaste from Delaware to take his seat, was admitted to the chamber and "turned the vote of that colony in favor of the resolution." All hinged now on Pennsylvania and New York; but by this time the advocates of an immediate separation from Great Britain possessed all the momentum, and the resolution was passed.

"Yesterday," John Adams wrote to his wife, Abigail, on July 3, "the greatest Question was decided, which ever was debated in America, and a greater perhaps, never was or will be decided among Men." (To forestall any spousal skepticism, he added, "You will think me transported with Enthusiasm but I am not.") Congress turned next to the wording of the decision. Young men who dream of undertaking beautiful deeds and golden actions in the service of a republican cause seldom reckon, in their ambitious calculations, with the doubts and quibbles of a legislature. All labor creates its own form of heartbreak, those labors that we despise and, still more, those that we love, and Jefferson watched with wounded pride as the congressmen fingered his prose and chawed at his paragraphs. Dr. Franklin attempted to console him as the cruel audit dragged on, but Jefferson remained sullen. He grew especially indignant when his critics, in their politic siftings, struck out the passage in which he denounced King George for "captivating" innocent Africans and "carrying them into slavery in another hemisphere." Jefferson's outrage at the king might seem misdirected in the light of his own extensive commerce with slaves; but the young lawgiver had by this time given many proofs of a singular dexterity in the manipulation of his conscience.

Cavil though succeeding generations might—and people will for centuries to come debate the contradictions and hypocrisies in Jefferson's performance—he had yet managed to act. The famous phrases of the Declaration of Independence—"all men are created equal," "life, liberty, and the pursuit of happiness"—have, it is true, no exact legal or technical meaning; they are full of ambiguity, closer to poetical ideals than to the clipped and circumspect language usually found in state papers. Nor was any one of the words or ideas in the text original to Jefferson; only their combination and arrangement were novel. But the words will survive even after many of the circumstances of their creation are forgotten. They will linger in the human imagination even into a time, it may be, when the United States itself shall have ceased to exist.

Whatever else the words might be, they are cockades of the Whig revolution. In composing the Declaration, Jefferson labored, he said, to "place before mankind the common sense of the subject, in terms so plain and firm as to command their assent." The universe had changed; the old laws—"the laws of nature and of nature's God"—are invoked, but in a novel way. The

New World is cleaner and more transparent than the old one, is in many ways freer and less fearful—but is also less mysterious, less sensuous in its unities, less luxuriant in its fancy. In the New World the individual had to make his own unities—pursue his own happiness. He did so with a new set of tools, called inalienable rights, implements that he was free, for the most part, to use as he saw fit, and not on condition that he bow down before some designated idol, or strive toward some appointed end. Among the rights enunciated in the Declaration are the right to life and (implicitly) to property, as well as the right to liberty. (Jefferson himself was especially zealous for liberty of trade, liberty of conscience, and liberty of the press.) Only once in Jefferson's draft of the Declaration does a vestige of the older world appear in all its aboriginal strength—when he makes the signers pledge to one another their "sacred honor." Honor is a feudal idea, dark with meanings and obligations that have almost ceased to be comprehensible to us.

Action, by a mysterious replicative process, begets itself, and when he returned to Virginia, Jefferson threw himself into the work of reforming that semifeudal state. His labors were prodigious: he drafted legislation to abolish the laws of primogeniture and entail, disestablish the Anglican church, reform the criminal code, create a system of public education, and move the capital to Richmond. How had he come through it? How had he managed to act so gloriously when, not long before, he had been prostrate with agony at Monticello, lying (one supposes) in a blackened room, the blinds drawn tight against the daylight? We do not know; he may not have known himself. It is important to remember, however, that he was still a young man in 1776, with all the resilience of his thirty-three years. When, in a more advanced stage of middle age, he found himself emboweled in another of his complicated glooms, he would discover that mind and body were less elastic, and that all his considerable ingenuity would be needed if he were to spring from the rut.

PART TWO

SUMMER

I

Distress

Miranda: *Alack, what trouble*
Was I then to you!
Prospero: *O, a cherubin*
Thou wast that did preserve me. Thou didst smile.

—SHAKESPEARE

THE WINTER CAME. The Seine stank; the smoke of the city could not rise. It was blocked by the low-hanging grayness—the *grisaille*—of the Parisian winter sky. The air, Jefferson complained, was "extremely damp, and the waters very unwholesome." In the winter in Paris, the sun—when it shines at all—shines for only a small part of the day; Jefferson, at his northernmost extreme, called the city "sunless."

The unanticipated sterility of this scenery was the latest in a succession of blows; in the years that followed the springtime work of declaring America's independence and reforming Virginia, Jefferson had suffered through a series of crises and disappointments. In 1779 he became governor of Virginia, but unlike his legislative labors, Jefferson's record as the state's chief executive was little more than a register of misfortunes and mistakes. He was not entirely to blame for the blunders of his administration. The British generals chose at this time to take the war to the South. At the end of December 1780, a flotilla under the command of Benedict Arnold appeared in the Chesapeake. Foaming with the fury of the turncoat, Arnold pushed rabidly up the James with his dragoons and sacked Richmond. Five months later Lord Cornwallis arrived at Petersburg, on the Appomattox River, and was soon at the head of seven thousand British troops. He, too, menaced Richmond, and he dispatched a raiding party to Monticello with orders to seize the governor.

Jefferson was warned in time to boot and saddle for an escape, but the war had by this time taken its toll. For month upon unspeakable month, Martha Jefferson lay in fear and fragile health; Jefferson was constantly moving her and the children, Patsy and Maria, or Polly, born in 1778, to hiding places in the Virginia countryside. Often on short notice they would be bundled up and taken to a different plantation for safety. He brought them, at strange hours, in desperate moods, to places like Tuckahoe, Fine Creek, Blenheim, Enniscorthy, and Poplar Forest. He had known them, some of these places, from the time he was a boy, but he came to them now in the changed world of war, as a revolutionary governor, often only a step ahead of the king's dragoons.

It got worse. Jefferson's want of chivalry provoked angry criminations in a state that still valued the prowess of the cavalier. After he relinquished his office, the former governor was called upon to account for his ungallant conduct. Why had the commander in chief failed to rally Virginia against the enemy? In December 1781, two months after General Washington's victory over Cornwallis at Yorktown, Jefferson rose in the House of Delegates to defend himself. He acquitted himself well, and the matter was eventually dropped, but it "inflicted a wound on my spirit," he told James Monroe, "which will only be cured by the all-healing grave."

He suffered, but the wheel had still to turn. In May 1782 Martha Jefferson, who with her husband had watched three of their five children go to their graves, gave birth to a sixth, a girl they named Lucy Elizabeth. This time, however, it was Martha's vitality that failed, and over the course of the summer Jefferson watched her decline. He nursed her himself and gave her her medicines. At the beginning of September, she sank rapidly. Near the end she wrote out a passage from *Tristram Shandy*, Laurence Sterne's novel and one of her husband's best-loved books: "Time wastes too fast: every letter I trace tells me with what rapidity life follows my pen. The days and

hours of it are flying over our heads like clouds of windy day never to return—more. Every thing presses on—" Jefferson completed the passage in
his own hand: "and every time I kiss thy hand to bid adieu, every absence
which follows it, are preludes to that eternal separation which we are shortly
to make!"

The paper on which this was written, together with a lock of Martha Jefferson's hair and other remembrances of her life, was found, after Jefferson's
death, "in the most secret drawer" of his private cabinet. Martha Jefferson
died on September 6, 1782.

At first he kept his room. Then, when he emerged, he walked. His daughter
Patsy watched him. She had just turned ten. He "walked almost incessantly," she later said, "day and night," and lay down only when "completely
exhausted." He walked, and he rode, "rambling about the mountain, in the
least frequented roads, and just as often through the woods." "In those
melancholy rambles," Patsy said, "I was his constant companion, a solitary
witness to many a violent burst of grief, the remembrance of which has consecrated particular scenes of that lost home beyond the power of time to
obliterate."

Paris would do him good, James Madison thought. Madison knew that his
friend was tired in spirit, worn out by a succession of trials "really too burthensome to be borne." In May 1784 the appointment finally came
through; John Jay was coming home, and Congress wanted Jefferson to take
his place. He was to join Benjamin Franklin and John Adams in France,
where, as an American minister plenipotentiary, he would represent the
United States in Europe.

They arrived—he and Patsy—at the quay of Le Havre in the summer of
1784; were cheated by the porters; and as "papa spoke very little French and
me not a word," would have "fared badly," Patsy remembered, "if an Irish
gentleman, an entire stranger to us, who seeing our embarrassment, had not
been so good as to conduct us to a house and was of great service to us." After vicissitudes, father and daughter reached Paris. Jefferson strolled in the

Jardin du Luxembourg; he took in the shops in the Palais-Royal; he ordered new clothes, both for himself and for his daughter. They "were obliged to send immediately," Patsy said, "for the staymaker, the mantua [a scarf or mantilla worn about the head and shoulders] maker, the milliner and even a shoe maker, before I could go out." Having seen to it that his daughter was properly fitted with stay and manteau, ribbon and glove, Jefferson went to call on Dr. Franklin at Passy, where that wise old man maintained the simple state of a philosopher in the baroque splendor of the Hôtel de Valentinois. He visited, too, the Adamses in their suburban villa at Auteuil, and the two families soon became intimate. He liked to ride out at midday, for exercise, to the Bois de Boulogne, still a rural garden in those days; in the afternoons he would walk among the fruit trees of the Tuileries.

Paris offered a change of atmosphere, a chance to escape places that provoked painful memories. But the city was in its own way a source of distress. During the first months he was often sick. "I have had a very bad winter," he confessed to James Monroe. "A seasoning as they call it is the lot of most strangers," he said, "and none I believe have experienced a more severe one than myself." "Patsy," he told another correspondent, "enjoys perfect health; but I cannot recover mine." He clung to the company of his fellow Americans John and Abigail Adams before they were transferred to London by Congress in the spring of 1785. "The departure of your family," Jefferson wrote to Adams, "has left me in the dumps." "My afternoons," he said, "hang heavily on me."

But it was not only the absence of his Massachusetts friends that made him sad. Not long before the Adams family left France, Jefferson learned that his youngest daughter, little Lucy Elizabeth, was dead. Her birth had cost her mother her life, and now she herself was gone, of a whooping cough in Virginia, where she and her older sister, Maria (sometimes called Mary and nicknamed Polly), were being cared for by their dead mother's family. "It is in vain to endeavor to describe the situation of my mind," Jefferson wrote to his brother-in-law in February; "it would pour balm neither into your wounds nor mine."

2

The Faubourg Saint-Germain

We come quite fresh to the different stages of life, and in each of them we are usually quite inexperienced, no matter how old we are.

—La Rochefoucauld

IN TIME HE put aside his grief. There was much in his new life that pleased him. After Dr. Franklin returned to Philadelphia, Jefferson took on an additional duty: he became his country's emissary to the court of Versailles. But the appointment added little to the easy burdens of his office; his diplomatic duties remained light, and he was surrounded by the luxuries he loved. In a capricious moment he took a house called the Hôtel de Langeac. This *hôtel particulier,* or private mansion, had been built for a mistress of one of Louis XV's ministers, and it sat in neoclassical splendor on the corner of the rue de Berry and the Champs-Élysées. Jefferson told Abigail Adams that the *hôtel,* with its "clever garden," suited him "in every circumstance but the price."

He was well cared for there. In addition to Monsieur Petit, who served as his maître d'hotel, Jefferson kept a *valet de chambre,* a coachman, a gardener, and a *frotteur* (to polish the parquet floors). James Hemings—one of Jeffer-son's Monticello slaves—crossed the Atlantic to learn how to cook in the French style for his master; in time he became Jefferson's *chef de cuisine.* It was an impressive establishment for a household in which a single widower and a confidential secretary or two lived. (Patsy did not live with her father in the Hôtel de Langeac; she boarded at a convent school, the Abbaye Royale de Panthemont, under the supervision of the nuns of Saint Bernard.) In the Hôtel de Langeac, Jefferson could feel almost at ease.

Almost, but not quite at ease, for Paris itself continued to disturb, and Jefferson's response to the city continued to be full of suppressed foreboding. He was a farmer and a citizen of a freshly liberated republic; Paris was a city in the shadow of a monarchy. He dreamed of an ideal republican commu-nity filled with prosperous yeomen living lives that possessed something of the bucolic beauty of Virgil and Theocritus; Paris was crowded with cynical aristocrats. The men dressed like strutting peacocks, and wore coats the color of ripe fruit; the women were dangerous. They even played cards—something, Jefferson observed, "genteel" American ladies never did. He worried that the "voluptuary dress and arts" of these treacherous nymphs might seduce innocent young men, especially visiting Americans.

He was a good Whig who now found himself in a decidedly un-Whiggish place. France was the antithesis of a Whig state. In the century be-fore Jefferson was born, statesmen like Cardinal Richelieu had labored to create, in the environment of the modern state, a semblance of the shattered medieval coherence. Here was a state in which, by the end of the seven-teenth century, the political, spiritual, and economic life of the people re-volved around the person of the king. Louis XIV was the Roi Soleil at the center of the new universe. Bossuet, the court preacher, believed that monarchy, a "sacred institution," was central to the spiritual meaning of France; Colbert, the finance minister, showed that Versailles could play a no less vital role in superintending the economic development of the realm.

Just how strange such a place must have seemed to Jefferson may be imagined. He was like a staunch Protestant who goes into Saint Peter's in Rome—with this difference: it is the massive solidity of the Roman basilica that, however alien it may be to him, is likely to impress the Protestant visi-tor to the throne of Peter. Jefferson, however, beheld in the Bourbon regime a feeble and tottering structure. By the time he arrived in Paris, the edifice was on the verge of collapse. The glorious reign of Louis XIV had long since ended. Statesmen of the caliber of Richelieu and de Retz had passed from the scene. In the Seven Years' War—the most significant clash between

English Whiggery and French absolutism before the rise of Bonaparte—the French were routed by Wolfe at Quebec, by Boscawen off Lagos, by Hawke in Quiberon Bay, by Clive in India. Jefferson, analyzing the health of the kingdom two decades later, found the treasury exhausted, the trade sluggish and monopolized, the mass of the people poor.

The cumbrous system of Richelieu and the Sun King was no match for the efficiency of England's Whig machine designed by the heroes of its Glorious Revolution in 1688. Jefferson saw this at once. "If any body thinks that kings, nobles, or priests are good conservators of the public happiness," he wrote to George Wythe in Virginia, "send them here." France, he said, was the "best school in the universe to cure them of that folly." The condition of what Jefferson called the *canaille* of Paris—the gutter wretches, poor as dogs—pointed to the larger misery of the kingdom. Much of the landed property of the realm was concentrated in a few aristocratic hands, and the propertyless masses were condemned to hard lives toiling in their masters' vineyards. Those who fled to the towns exchanged one type of misery for an even more degraded kind: in cities like Paris, the newcomers settled down in the vilest kind of squalor. "Of twenty millions of people supposed to be in France," Jefferson wrote to a friend, "I am of opinion there are nineteen millions more wretched, more accursed in every circumstance of human existence, than the most conspicuously wretched individual of the whole United states.—I beg your pardon for getting into politics."

However pronounced a man's republican sympathies might be, when he finds himself swept up in the opulent civilization of the dynastic *hôtels* of Paris, he will be dazzled. Jefferson was. For all his condemnations of the vices of the nobility, he discovered much in the city that pleased him. Few things omit so sweet a fragrance of corruption, possess so seductive a quality of decay, as a doomed aristocracy; and almost against his will Jefferson found himself drawn to the creatures who languished in the golden cages of the Faubourg Saint-Germain, the most aristocratic quarter of the city.

The Marquis de Lafayette opened doors that would otherwise have been closed to a diplomat from a remote and, as the French conceived it a barbarian province. The hero of the French-American alliance, Lafayette was descended from one of the great rich warrior families of France, and he had married into another. He enjoyed the favor of the queen, and he was "well remarked," Jefferson said, by the king. Although he had turned his back on a court life to become a soldier, Lafayette was connected, by ties of blood or friendship, to a large portion of the nobility of France. His friendship with Jefferson could never be a deep one; their tastes and inclinations were too different for a genuine intimacy to develop; and Jefferson was made uneasy by the young man's swashing manners and immoderate ambition. But in spite of these reservations, he praised Lafayette's quick intelligence, his practical energy, his ability, as a man of action, to get things done, and as a diplomat he found Lafayette's aristocratic connections indispensable. He "is a most valuable auxiliary to me," Jefferson told James Madison, and "his weight with those in power great."

Through Lafayette, Jefferson gained entrée to many of the great houses of Paris; but none was to have a greater significance for the American minister than that of the Hôtel de Tessé, where Adrienne-Catherine de Noailles, comtesse de Tessé, presided over a liberal and enlightened salon. She was the aunt of Lafayette's wife, by birth a Grimaldi, by marriage a Noailles, a great invoker and promoter of beauty, the possessor of high but unintimidating manners. Jefferson soon found himself at home with her in a way he never could have been with the jauncing nephew Lafayette. She shared not only Jefferson's political faith but also his aesthetic one; and in her fine old mansion in the Faubourg Saint-Germain, and at her country estate at Chaville, on the road to Versailles, the American minister passed many happy hours discussing with his sympathetic hostess the virtues of classical architecture, republican government, and a flourishing garden.

Two years older than Jefferson, Madame de Tessé was not without flaws. Her beauty was disfigured by a nervous twitch about the mouth, and her enthusiastic invocations of the rights of man must have echoed strangely in drawing rooms piled high with the spoils and insolence of the ancien régime. She was, too, something of a précieuse, and her salon possessed at times the pedantic air of a bluestocking assembly. But much could be forgiven a woman who seems from the first to have discerned in her Virginia visitor the qualities of a great man. She had known Voltaire and many of the other celebrated figures of the age, but Jefferson, she sensed, was different from these. She was one of the few people—perhaps the only person—in Europe at that time to possess a copy of the original draft of the Declaration of Independence (before it had been altered or—as Jefferson would have it—defaced by Congress), and she saw in its author a kind of classical lawgiver, as eloquent, she believed, as Cicero himself.

A civilization, illiberal and corrupt, had produced beautiful things, and out of manure, flowers had sprung. "Here it seems that a man might pass a life without encountering a single rudeness," Jefferson wrote. "The roughnesses of the human mind," he said, had been "thoroughly rubbed off" with the French. "Here we have singing, dauncing, laugh, and merriment," he told Abigail Adams. The people were always kissing one another. And this is the truest wisdom. They have as much happiness in one year as an Englishman in ten.

The civilization of the salon, the faces in a festival crowd, might deceive. But Jefferson judged French arts equally happy. "Were I to proceed to tell you how much I enjoy their architecture, sculpture, painting, music," he told a friend, "I should want words." His fetish for folios took him to the bookstalls beside the Seine; he subscribed to the *Encyclopédie,* the massive masterwork of the French philosophes; he visited the art openings and the music halls. He went so often to the Comédie Française, the Théâtre des Italiens, and the Opéra that he was obliged to apply for diplomatic privileges for his waiting carriage.

Still the foreboding remained. To come to France was for Jefferson the realization of a dream; but realized dreams exact penalties quite as substantial as broken ones do. For there was another strangeness in the soft enervating air of Paris, the strangeness of a weirdly encountered familiarity. The world Jefferson knew—the Virginia world in which he was at home—was only in part a Whig world. The life of the southern planters was in some respects more feudal than that of the French noblesse. The tidewater plantations were more Gothic than the castles of Mrs. Radcliffe. The same curiosities of character flourished there. The Virginia scions were as morbid as the heroes of Byron and Chateaubriand, their wives and relicts viragoish beyond anything in the imagination of Sir Walter Scott. At Monticello the spheres were as closely bound as at Fontainebleau. The overlord's word was as absolute there as at Marly. There was, in Jefferson's demesne, no Whig freedom of contract, no free exchange of goods and ideas: everything depended upon the whim of the master.

In France an impoverished peasantry supported a charming and even brilliant aristocracy; in Virginia all the hands ministered to the needs of men like Jefferson, that they might have leisure to cultivate their own bright talents. French peasants, with their "singing, dauncing, laugh, and merriment," had learned to smile through their tears, and so, too, had American slaves, who sang out even as they suffered under the slave driver's lash. (Singing was one of the few arts in which Jefferson acknowledged the superior excellence of his slaves; in music, he wrote in his *Notes on the State of Virginia,* "they are more generally gifted than the whites with accurate ears for tune and time.") He criticized French aristocrats for losing themselves in a decadent sensuality, but he knew that American slave owners had succumbed to the temptations of an even more deplorable sexual commerce. France possessed all the vices of what Jefferson called an unnatural aristocracy, a "tinsel" nobility founded not on the "virtue and talent" that made "natural" aristocracy possible but on feudal pride and dynastic hauteur. Yet Jefferson knew that Virginia, too, was dominated by what he called a "pseudo-aristocracy" of "founding" families, grandees who had formed themselves "into a Patrician order, distinguished by the splendor and luxury of their establishments."

Jefferson might have been, in his public work, a good Whig, but he was also, in his private life, a Virginia gentleman, which is to say he was a decayed knight. He was fastidious about things in which knights are bound to be particular, such as horses (the stock-in-trade of all equestrian orders). All his life Jefferson plumed himself on his strength and gracefulness in the saddle and on his ability to stable superior horseflesh. He was "very exacting of his groom," his great granddaughter remembered, and anxious to have "his horses always beautifully kept." When his "riding-horse was brought up for him to mount," she said, he would take out a "white cambric handkerchief" and brush it "across the animal's shoulders." The mount would be sent back "to the stable if any dust was left" on the cloth.

We shall not get far in understanding Jefferson and other high Virginians of his day if we do not grasp that they aimed always to be cavaliers; knights, that is, *sans peur et sans reproche.* (Hence the special sting, for Jefferson, of the inquiry into his conduct as war governor.) This desire lay at the heart of the Virginians' weaknesses; but it was also one of their strengths; and there is reason to believe that the Virginia knighthood, in the last half of the eighteenth century, was not nearly so decrepit as the French. Out of the Virginia squierearchy came Washington, and who among the *douzepers*— the paladins of the ancient French chivalry—would have cared to joust and tourney with such a champion as that? Jefferson looked down on Lafayette precisely because the younger man, in spite of his high breeding, his perfect honesty, his military traditions and knightly comradery, did not quite measure up to the Virginia standard of a gentleman. Lafayette's ambition—was it not, after all, a little coarse, a trifle vulgar? Jefferson found a harsher adjective: *canine* was the word he used in a letter to James Madison.

No wonder he was uneasy in the salons and withdrawing rooms of the Faubourg Saint-Germain, among the great dukes and the tubs of oleanders. He saw there too many grotesque but still recognizable versions of himself.

3

Passion

For a dream cometh through the multitude of business.

—ECCLESIASTES

In his discomfort he bought things. "I will beg the favor of you at the same time," Jefferson wrote a friend, William Stephens Smith, in 1786, "to inform me what a pair of chariot harness will cost in London, not foppish but genteel." "I must pray your taylor," he wrote Smith a little later, "to send me a buff Casimir waistcoat and breeches with those of cotton, and my shoemaker to send me two pr. of thin waxed leather slippers."

His debts were growing, and he was living beyond his means. He was master of more than ten thousand acres of land in Virginia, but although he was land rich, he was, like many planters, cash poor. His ministerial stipend was not nearly enough to cover his expenditures, and he asked James Madison to see whether his congressional overlords might be persuaded to give him, out of their frugal purse, a larger allowance. It was around this time, too, that Jefferson became aware of an even graver difficulty in his financial situation. The interest on certain debts which his father-in-law had contracted, and which Jefferson and his wife had inherited at the old man's death, was now compounding at a terrific rate, one that must eventually reduce the family, Jefferson foresaw, to "beggary."

Still he could not bring himself to stoop to mean economies. His eye delighted in beautiful things, and so did his ear and his palate. A quantity of fine prose, of elegant music, of wine of superior vintage, was almost a necessity for him; and although he professed the political creed of a rough and ready farmer—a stoical republican of old Cato's school—the truth was that he could not live without luxury. The voluptuary in him spent even to extravagance on damask draperies, sofas in gold leaf, chairs upholstered in pressed velvet, in blue silk, in red morocco, and he was by this time a confirmed victim of what he called the "malady of bibliomania." His library, he said, included some of the "choicest editions existing," an "abundance" of them "elegantly" bound in rich leather.

He apologized to his friends for asking them to act so often as his procurers. "Cannot you invent some commissions for me here," Jefferson asked young Smith, "by way of reprisal for the vexations I give you? Silk stockings, gillets, &c., for yourself, gewgaws and contrivances for Madame?" Smith was serving as John Adams's secretary in London when Jefferson wrote him these letters; "Madame" was Adams's daughter, Nabby, whom Smith married in 1786. In the spring of this year, Jefferson himself visited England, with a view to helping Adams negotiate commercial treaties.

Paris was strange, but London was stranger. The dark wet eaves-drip days made, Jefferson thought, for a suicidal climate, and in the land of Locke and Somers there was scarce an honest Whig to be found. The French had no liberty; the English, he decided, were busy dismantling theirs. The one case was merely sad; the other perverse. He found London a gloomy city, full of the moroseness of the north. It lay shrouded in fog and poisonous smoke, dark and gray like dead men's guts. The treaties came to nothing; the mission was a failure. England, Jefferson concluded, was a dismal place; but he conceded that its gardens were pretty, and "indeed went far beyond my ideas."

A few months after his excursion among the garden roses of England, Jefferson, having returned to Paris, paid a call on the firm of Legrand and Molinos, the architects who had designed the dome of the Parisian grain emporium, the Halle aux Blés et Farines. It was late summer, and the city was quiet. In August, Jefferson said, the great ones of Paris were gone, fled with the court or departed to their seats in the country. "We give and receive them you know," he said, "in exchange for the swallows." The architects took Jefferson to see the grain market; he hoped that it might serve as a model for a market to be built across the ocean in Richmond. Among those he met on this outing were two artists, Richard and Maria Cosway. He promptly fell in love with Mrs. Cosway.

She was Italian born, though of English, or possibly Irish, blood. Mr. Hadfield, her father, had opened an inn for English tourists at Leghorn (Livorno) in the 1740s; he had later moved to Florence, where Maria was born, probably in 1759. Her life possessed certain of the characteristics of a Gothic romance, one in which passionate devotion and passionate disgust are closely, even morbidly mingled; and her childhood itself was not free from a strain of Gothic horror. A mad nurse, it was said, murdered four of Maria's little brothers and sisters; she and two others, a sister and a brother, alone survived. At the convent school where she was sent to be educated, Maria was discovered to possess a talent for drawing—more than a talent: before she was twenty, she was elected a member of the Academia del Disegno at Florence and was there tutored by the painter Johann Zoffany. Later, at Rome, she worked with Pompeo Batoni, Anton Raphael Mengs, and Henry Fuseli, all of them leading painters of the age. When, in 1776, her father died, she is said to have expressed a desire to become a nun.

She went, not to a nunnery—not at first—but to London, and to the heart of a fashionable circle that included James Boswell, the biographer of Dr. Johnson, and Charles Towneley, a collector and antiquarian. Towneley was the scion of an old Roman Catholic family, the Towneleys of Towneley Hall in Lancashire; and he was one of the illustrious Dilettanti, a group of bibulous patricians who over flowing cups met to promote antiquarian scholarship. Although his uncle had fought for the house of Stuart in one of the Jacobite rebellions against Hanoverian Whiggery (the Whigs had stuck his head on a pike on Temple Bar), Charles Towneley's own pursuits were peaceful. He was educated at the English Catholic college at Douay (Douai), near Lille, in France (Roman Catholics were in those days debarred from study at Oxford and Cambridge); in 1765 he went to Italy to study art. He lived at Rome until 1772, and he there laid the foundation for an extraordinary collection of antiquities, much of which is now in the British Museum. Back in London, Towneley took up residence in a house in Park Street, Westminster, and filled it with art.

Maria, blond, beautiful, and talented, soon became one of Towneley's protégés. The collector's connoisseurship seems not to have been limited to antiquities; Towneley piqued himself on the possession of an unerring taste, and the same fastidious eye that appraised the merits of a piece of Roman sculpture, or the proportions of an Etruscan urn, enabled him to discover the superior qualities of his living acquisitions. He took pride in his discernment of Maria's virtues, and he was eager to show her off, much in the way his friend Sir William Hamilton—another dilettante, and the British minister at Naples—sought to display his own pièce de résistance, Emma Hart, afterward Lady Hamilton. Lady Hamilton would go on to win Admiral Nelson's heart, but Maria Cosway, with her superior delicacy of thought and manner, was perhaps the more splendid ornament.

Maria might have been expected to choose for a husband a man who could suitably share the pedestal she occupied in Towneley's Park Street pantheon. But although she had been born at the heart of the eighteenth century, Maria was not at all at home in it. Like the epicene trifler Horace Walpole, an English prime minister's son who affected to turn his back on the century his father had labored to build in order to indulge an eccentric passion for the Gothic style of the Middle Ages, Maria was oddly drawn to what the French call *moyenageux,* the medieval grotesque. She made concessions to the classical tastes of her age: she painted Georgiana, duchess of Devonshire, in the antique guise of the goddess Diana, and she always admired the work of her friend Jacques-Louis David, whose taste was severely classical. But when, in 1781, Maria came to marry, she chose not a well-proportioned eighteenth-century god but something closer to a satyr. Richard Cosway might have crept down from a gargoyle's perch.

He was an accomplished painter of miniatures; the pornographic snuff boxes he created for the Prince of Wales elicited wide admiration; and the success of his gaudy industry enabled him to make Maria what was called a good settlement. But he was also—it was undeniable—a figure of fun, a small man whom the wits likened to a monkey. They satirized him as the "macaroni painter," a foppish and absurd dandy who possessed a fatal tendency to overdress.* (Cosway once appeared at a Christie's auction wearing

---

*A *macaroni* was to the eighteenth century what an *exquisite* and a *fat* were to the nineteenth, a précieux, a fop, a dandy, one who wore long curls and was never without an opera glass. "There is a kind of animal," a contemporary observer wrote, "neither male nor female, a thing of the neuter gender, lately started up amongst us. It is called a Macaroni. It talks without meaning, it smiles without pleasantry, it eats without appetite, it rides without exercise, it wenches without passion."

a powdered toupee and a coat of mulberry silk embroidered with scarlet strawberries.) He had his admirers, it is true. The Prince of Wales became his patron and helped him make his fortune. But the king's words to his son have not redounded to Cosway's credit. "Among *my* painters," George III is supposed to have said, "there are no fops."

No sooner had Jefferson met Mrs. Cosway, on that late summer day in Paris, than he began to contrive "how to prevent a separation from" her. They both had other engagements to fulfill that afternoon, but "these were to be sacrificed," Jefferson said, that they "might dine together" at Saint-Cloud. "Lying messengers were to be dispatched into every quarter of the city with apologies" to stood-up friends. Jefferson himself sent word to the duchess d'Enville, the noblewoman to whom he was engaged to dine, that he had just then received a number of diplomatic dispatches "which required immediate attention" and prevented his coming to dinner.

Jefferson got his wish; he and Mr. and Mrs. Cosway dined together at Saint-Cloud that afternoon. (Dinner was a late-afternoon meal in eighteenth-century Paris, served at about four o'clock.) Later they watched one of the Ruggieri brothers' fireworks entertainments near the Faubourg Montmartre, and after Ruggieri's they heard music at Krumpholtz's. "How well I remember," Jefferson wrote, "the transactions of that day." When he came home that night, and fell into his bed at the Hôtel de Langeac, he "looked back to the morning," and felt as though a month had gone by.

4
Sentiment

Love as it exists in society is merely the mingling of two fantasies.

—CHAMFORT

SHE EMERGES IN many accounts as a shallow figure, a femme fatale, in one historian's words, a woman who might pass in a crowd, or make a figure in a country church, but who was not in the least a match for her sometime beau. To other historians Mrs. Cosway was less an empty woman than a cold one, an icicle rather than a trollop, tormented by cloistered passions, incapable, from nature or from an excess of religious scrupulosity, of satisfying Jefferson's manly needs. One scholar supposed that there was "some kind of crucial failure for Maria in the act of love."

The operative piece of evidence here is a diary—no longer extant—in which Maria's husband described his love affair with an artist called Mary Moser, a painter of flowers. The diary is said to have contained "many lascivious statements" about the mistress and "many invidious comparisons" between her and Mrs. Cosway. A cheap and facile jibe; there is no easier way to provoke a doubt, in the modern reader's mind, about the worthiness of a soul to be loved than to raise this question of sexual competency. But the intimations of sexual dysfunction are only the most obvious example of a failure of historiographical sympathy where Mrs. Cosway is concerned; few historians have been able to see in Jefferson's chantress anything more than a rotting tulip, outwardly pretty but inwardly decayed.

Jefferson saw her differently. He dwelled upon what he called her "music, modesty, beauty and that softness of disposition which is the ornament of her sex and the charm of ours." Theirs was a summer progress through the parks and across promenades of greater Paris, a month washed in the colors of a Fragonard. Statues modeled on those of pagan antiquity gazed down on the esplanades on which they strolled; sculptures of satyrs, naked in the stone, bore aloft flaming torches. There was even a temple to Pan, Arcadia's god, a place where the classicism of the French eighteenth century faded into the mannered follies of its decadence. There were visits to the Louvre and Versailles, evenings at the theater, a picnic at Marly, with its waterworks and royal château. The two rode out together to take a meal at an inn near Louveciennes; it stood in the shadow of Madame du Barry's pavilion there, the villa where that courtesan had once entertained her lascivious king, Louis XV. From Louveciennes the lovers went on to Saint-Germain and the Désert de Retz; here they found gardens and grottoes in the English style, as well as a Chinese orangery and a structure—evidently inhabitable—made to look like a broken column. It was as luxurious a romance as could be wished for, yet there was something not quite satisfying in the relationship. A crisis was reached, but somehow it was not passed. There were reasons for this.

In Paris, Stendhal said, "love is the child of the novels." In eighteenth-century Paris it was the child of sentimental novels.

Although later in life Jefferson would shake his head over the modern reader's excessive fondness for novels, when he was a young man, he was himself an enthusiastic reader of sentimental novels. He listed one of these, Rousseau's *Julie, ou la Nouvelle Héloïse,* in one of the catalogs of books he was always drawing up for friends who asked his advice on what to read. *La Nouvelle Héloïse* tells, in quantities of moist prose, the story of the apparently doomed love that a young tutor called Saint-Preux conceives for his better-born pupil, Julie. The neophytes in amour hope to rest in their "im-

petuous but chaste love," but in an "unguarded moment" they fall. Afterward they learn to content themselves with a virtuous, nonsexual attach-
ment to each other. In the letters he wrote to Mrs. Cosway, Jefferson cribbed
from the (moist and ecstatic) love poetry of Rousseau:

> How beautiful was every object! the Port de Neuilly, the hills along
> the Seine, the rainbows of the machine at Marly, the terras of St.
> Germains, the chateaux, the gardens, the statues of Marly, the pavil-
> lon of Lucienne [Louveciennes]. . . . How grand the idea excited by
> the remains of such a column [as that of the Désert de Retz]. . . . The
> wheels of time moved on with a rapidity of which those of our car-
> riage gave but a faint idea, and yet in the evening, when one took a
> retrospect of the day, what a mass of happiness we had travelled
> over! . . . On these days indeed the sun shone brightly!

All over England, Lytton Strachey observed, coarse and vigorous fathers
were succeeded, as the eighteenth century wore on, by refined and sentimental sons. The same process was at work in eighteenth-century America.
Big-boned Peter Jefferson had been too busy taming a wilderness to cultivate the softer qualities of his sensibility; and although his son, Thomas, admired his father intensely, he allowed that his education had been "quite
neglected." Where the father remained, to the end of his life, a rough-hewn
man of the colonial period, the Revolutionary son was a lover of delicacy. In
the letters he wrote to pretty women in Paris, Jefferson showed himself a
master of the most elegant forms of sentimental gallantry. He mixed, with a
charming extravagance, the most luxurious society gossip and the tenderest
confessions of the heart.

It is a thing quite new in his writing; Jefferson's Paris letters are polished
up to a brightness not found in the earlier correspondence. The newfound
suppleness may have been the by-product of his ongoing literary lucubra-
tions, his attention to epistolary models like those in Richardson's *Clarissa*, a
sentimental novel he admired. Or it may be that, unwifed as he now was, he
felt freer to unpack his heart in the letters he wrote to interesting women.
Whatever its inspiration, there is a quality of inevitability in the new manner. It would have been strange if Jefferson had not dabbled in the sentimental sauces. Even the most independent-minded man must make use of
the possibilities with which his age supplies him, if only because the errors
and fallacies he finds there will force him to seek out more durable things.

When he was a young man in Virginia, eagerly awaiting the latest vol-

umes from London or Paris, the books that were talked about were sentimental books. The men who wrote them enjoyed the kind of fame we asso-
ciate with movie stars today. After Rousseau died, at Ermenonville outside
Paris in 1778, overwhelmed by manias and delusions that had grown
steadily more morbid during the course of his life, his tomb rapidly became
a place of sentimental pilgrimage; the faithful shed copious tears before the
final resting place of their demented hero on the Isle of Poplars. "Mothers,
old men, children, true hearts and feeling souls," the epitaph read, "your
friend sleeps in this tomb." Women of fashion, among them Jefferson's
friend Madame de Tessé, sponsored readings of sentimental works like
Richardson's *Clarissa;* Marie-Antoinette's bookshelves were stocked with
Richardson and Rousseau. The young Goethe first came to the attention of
the world with his tale of Werther's unrequited love for "Lotte," a book
which ends when the hero, in his blue coat and yellow waistcoat, takes up a
pistol and blows his brains out in an agony of lovesickness. A wave of copy-
cat suicides followed the book's publication in 1774.

Jefferson, caught up among the sentimental flowers, dutifully made the
journey to Sannois, north of Paris, where Rousseau's old paramour, Sophie,
comtesse d'Houdetot, presided like an aged priestess over the still splendid
remains of her literary salon. Thirty years before, on a rainy day in 1757,
Sophie had ridden across the fog-shrouded fields, "on horseback and in
men's clothes," to Rousseau's hermitage at Montmorency. The model for
Julie in *La Nouvelle Héloïse* went mud-spattered and smiling into the great
man's cottage—and into his heart. Rousseau, who ordinarily did not care for
such masquerades—mere painted passion—confessed that he was "capti-
vated by the romantic air of this one." By the time Jefferson arrived in Sannois, the affair had long since passed into literary legend; the ancient
seductress was reduced to taking tourists to see the acacia tree under which
she had sat with Rousseau while he read to her from the freshly written
drafts of his book. Jefferson told Abigail Adams that he received "much
pleasure" from his visit to the faded sentimental violet.

It was not magnolias and moody passion alone that brought the men
and women of an enlightened age to sob over the pages of *La Nouvelle
Héloïse* or to contemplate taking their own lives after putting down *Werther.*
Had the sentimental poets offered nothing more than melodrama, they
could never have bewitched so many. The sentimentalists were read, not because they sang of love and seduction—their readers had enough of these in
their own drawing rooms—but because their song was blended with something that was stranger, and more exotic, to the eighteenth-century mind

than sex. To a polite and skeptical age the sentimental writers offered the deviant pleasures of mysticism.

These poets had at their fingertips a European mystical tradition as strangely exalted as anything in the spiritual annals of the Orient. Like the medieval love poets from whom they borrowed, the sentimentalists were preoccupied by an unseen force that moves the universe, and makes possible the harmonious revolution of its spheres. So elusive, however, is this force, so mysterious, that its nature can be grasped (or so the adepts maintain) only by those who have undergone a special initiation in love. This idea of a cosmos divinely ordered by love was still near enough, in the eighteenth century, to be persuasive, at least to some. Jefferson himself was not proof against the visionary chanting. The love poets revived, in the age of Louis XV, the erotic ideal of the thirteenth century. They played upon the European fascination with the tenderness of the unviolated rose, which they made the sign and seal of a modern philosophy of self-knowledge. The truest loves, they held, were unconsummated, or were consummated only after the lover underwent an arduous education in self-knowledge. This tuition was known as the road of love, and if it had once been traveled by the medieval chevalier, chastely adoring his lady, it was now trod by eighteenth-century Werther, destined never to possess his Lotte. Cheated out of the enjoyment of a carnal embrace, the most sensitive lovers were led by their passion to an appreciation of a higher form of love—to the divine love that moves the universe, or to the sublime compassion at the core of the human heart.

Curiously enough the sentimental dispensation was as influential in the study as it was in the salon. Sentimentalism was, if not the opium of the luminaries, then their spiritual claret. Jefferson spoke of a "moral sense" that was as "much a part of man as his leg or arm." Man, he said, was "destined for society," and his "moral sense" enabled him to act decently in it—made him a sociable, even benevolent creature. Jefferson attributed to the moral sense man's "dispositions to be grateful, to be generous, to be charitable, to be humane, to be true, just, firm, orderly, courageous &c." But this moral sense was only a manifestation of the more powerful energy of a *coeur sensible,* a feeling heart, the guarantor, Jefferson told Mrs. Cosway, of those "feelings of sympathy, of benevolence, of gratitude, of justice, of love, of friendship" without which men would lapse into a narrow and savage solipsism.

The temples of Enlightenment were built with stones taken directly from the dismantled medieval chantries; Jefferson's idea of an innate "sympathy" in man is a fatigued form of the *amor divino* of the medieval masters. Jefferson himself had no love for the Middle Ages, cared nothing for the roses and apses of the Nôtre-Dames; but he was, for a time, devoted to the sentimental cult whose priests carried on, in a faded form, one of the great mystical traditions of the West.

Her dress and toilet must have been impeccable; Jefferson tolerated little less in women. He had a horror of ladies who were "loose and negligent" of their appearance at the breakfast table. He instructed his daughter Patsy to be "as cleanly and properly dressed" at the beginning of the day "as at the hours of dinner or tea." "A lady who has been seen as a slut or a sloven in the morning," he warned, "will never efface the impression she then made with all the dress or pageantry she can afterwards involve herself in." "Nothing," he said, "is so disgusting to our sex as a want of cleanliness and delicacy in yours."

Mrs. Cosway's presentability at the breakfast table does not transpire; but she must have looked suitably lovely by the time Jefferson handed her into his carriage to escort her to the theater. Jefferson was determined to play the part of the sentimental lover with skill: he took Maria to the Théâtre des Italiens. There they saw the old Italian comedy in its decadence, by this time acted mainly by French players. After they watched the play— Florian's *Two Tickets*—Jefferson promised to read Maria's own letters to him "with the dispositions with which Arlequin in *Les Deux Billets,* spelt the words 'je t'aime' and wished that the whole alphabet had entered into their composition."

Had the Julie of *La Nouvelle Héloïse* been the object of his affections, the American minister would doubtless have carried the day. Yet carrying the day was precisely what the sentimental swain was *not* supposed to do—at least not yet. Such a lover might hint at the deepest intimacies, but he did so in a way that imposed spiritual rather than sexual obligations on the beloved, a duty to care for the surrendered soul. To a friend who was going to see Maria, Jefferson wrote, "Kneel to Mrs. Cosway for me, and lay my soul in her lap." One might lay one's soul in one's lady's lap, but nothing else—not, at least, at first.

How far the romance begun by Jefferson and Mrs. Cosway during a fête galante at Saint-Cloud in the summer of 1786 progressed in the purely carnal sense we do not—probably can never—know, but an agitated letter Jefferson wrote to Maria in the aftermath of her departure from Paris suggests a passion still unappeased, sexually unexpressed:

> I am indeed the most wretched of all earthly beings. Overwhelmed with grief, every fibre of my frame distended beyond it's natural powers to bear, I would willingly meet whatever catastrophe should leave me no more to feel or to fear. . . . I am rent into fragments by the force of my grief!

It is unlikely that their relationship was ever sexual; and the letters they exchanged when they were old are not those of people embarrassed by a shared but secret guilt. Maria's place is rather in the tradition of spiritual hetaerae (companions) than those of the flesh. In his letter to her, Jefferson's language is that of Rousseau's Saint-Preux *before* his fall into a carnal "abyss of shame." They are not the words of a man who has taken possession of the yearned-for thing.

The difficulty for Jefferson was that, although he adored Maria as the incarnation of all the sentimental virtues he had read about in books, her own character was more nearly Gothic, in its moral and spiritual configuration, than it was a work of modern sensibility. She preferred the medieval vision of love to its eighteenth-century update. She might promise Jefferson, in one of her letters, that she would "divert" his "pain" with an evening of "good Musik" and food. "I wont tell you what I shall have," she told him. "Temptations now are too Cruel for your Situation." But for all the glossy tenderness of her outward manner, she could not conceal a stubborn sadness at her core. In her artless way she said, "I hope you feel my distress." This was yet another instance of her teasing; but beneath the levity lay a genuine discomfort. Her letters to Jefferson, so apparently playful, are shot through with a darker coloring; her confessions of spiritual anguish come once too often to have been merely an attempt to strike a pose.

She was not, with her strange renunciations and fugitive fears, the frivolous coquette, the "spoiled" airhead with a "limited emotional capacity" whom the historians have given us; but the depth and complication of Mrs. Cosway's character have been obscured by studies that misread her quarrel with Jefferson. These accounts dwell on her sulking "pouts"—if that is what they were—and fail to see why she resisted certain features of her lover's vision, found them incomprehensible and perhaps even repellent.

The two lovers looked at each other across a gulf. He was, on the surface at least, a common-sense Whig who belonged to no established church. She was a Roman Catholic, named for the Virgin, and devoted to the memory of her patron saints, Louisa, Catherine of Genoa, and Cecilia. It is not, of course, unusual for two people divided by faith or politics to fall in love. Romeo and Juliet do so; a closer parallel to Jefferson's romance with Mrs. Cosway might be found in the Whig-Tory unions that are the consummation of so many of Sir Walter Scott's novels. In love, as in music, discord may for an interval give a sweetness to the tone; but only if the jarring strings can be made to serve a higher harmony.

5

Wound

My grief lies onward, and my joy behind.

—SHAKESPEARE

Mrs. Cosway LEFT Paris in the middle of October 1786 to return to
London with her husband. A few hours after she had gone, Jefferson sat,
"solitary and sad," beside his fire in the Hôtel de Langeac, and in the
watches of that night he composed a letter. He composed it painfully, with
his left hand, for he had fallen and broken the wrist of his right hand not
long before.

The letter was to Maria, and in it Jefferson recalled the scene, a few
hours earlier, when he had seen her off at the gatehouse of Paris. "Having
performed the last sad office of handing you into your carriage at the Pavil-
lon de St. Denis," he wrote, "and seen the wheels get actually into motion, I
turned on my heel and walked, more dead than alive, to the opposite door,
where my own was waiting for me."

If he was more dead than alive, so, too, was the romance itself. Differences that, in the freshest dawn of intimacy, rather intrigue than irritate

two awakened lovers become in time more vexing. He was a master of the English language; she was at home only in Italian. His letters are models of literary elegance; hers display a colloquial dishabille. She apologized, in Italian, for writing so often to him in English, a language, she said, "which does not belong to me." But the language barrier was the least substantial obstacle to their understanding each other. The question of religion was more formidable. Jefferson did not, it is true, possess the visceral antipathy to Roman Catholics that many Protestants in the eighteenth century felt. He believed the Roman dogmas to be, indeed, erroneous, and he held strong beliefs about the supposed evils of priestcraft; but he did not find those who professed the faith to be personally offensive. Quite the contrary: he valued the conversation and learning of the French abbés, and he admired at least one of Bishop Bossuet's books. In Paris he sent his daughter Patsy—and later her younger sister, Maria—to be educated by the nuns of Saint Bernard, although, according to the family tradition, he withdrew the girls after he learned that Patsy had thought of becoming a nun. He was a notably tolerant man, in his personal relationships if not in his rhetoric; still it is difficult to conceive of him carrying a Catholic bride to Monticello. It is no easier to conceive of Mrs. Cosway divorcing her husband in order to marry another man.

It was not, however, merely a difference of outward devotional practice that separated them or prevented their affection from finding expression in some more durable form. He might, after all, have learned to live with the savor of popery in her, her fidelity to the mass rite, her Aves, her Glorias, her Paternosters. She, in turn, might have come to tolerate his nullifidian cast of mind and cherish secretly the hope that his soul, unconfessed and unabsolved, might one day be reclaimed. But the futility of the thing went deeper than this. She promised him that she would be always his *"vera Amica,"* his true friend, but she could never wholly comprehend the sentimental persona he chose to assume with her. Nor was he any more able to penetrate the Gothic cast of her mind, what she called her "Night Thoughts."

"Why do you say so Many kind things?" she asked him in a letter she wrote not long after she received one of his sentimental missives. Maria could never have taken seriously the sentimental conception of a fenced and softened passion, made gentle through literary art. She had seen, at Schomberg House, where she lived, in London, with Mr. Cosway, ugly things, as ugly, in their way, as anything in Jefferson's own experience. Schomberg House, according to a contemporary, was a place where "from the very mixed Companies which frequent it, dangerous connections may be formed." About Maria herself there was cruel gossip. Some supposed that

Charles Towneley had taken advantage of her when she first arrived from Italy (though Towneley seems to have been more the bachelor aesthete than the *homme à femmes*). Others linked her to Pasquale Paoli, the Corsican patriot; to the Italian castrato Luigi Marchesi; to the Prince of Wales.

Still, too much has been made of the supposed strumpetry. Mrs. Cosway was never a demimondaine, and she was always received in the most respectable society. But we are, as a rule, happiest when we can reduce a spiritual crisis to a question of sexual hygiene; we want language supple enough to describe the more highly developed forms of yearning. The historians who have busied themselves with the rumor of Mrs. Cosway's sluttery have overlooked the suffering that seems to have been connected to it; they have failed to diagnose in her a form of acedia, arising from the "unsuccessful struggle towards the spiritual life."

In one of her letters to Jefferson, Maria described herself, in English, as being "full or ready to burst with all the variety of Sentiments" that a "very feeling one is Capable of." But she quickly broke off this exercise in sentimentality. *"Ma cosa fo!"* (What am I doing!) she exclaimed in the Italian in which her thoughts were truly housed. Sentimentality was Jefferson's specialty, not hers. "You seem to be Such a Master on this subject," she wrote in English, "that whatever I may say will appear trifelling." She must have preferred the medieval story of Héloïse—in which the carnal desire of Héloïse and her lover, Abelard, is a first step in the discovery of a more sacred form of passion—to *La Nouvelle Héloïse,* Rousseau's revision of the tale. Indeed, Maria once dressed up as the medieval Héloïse; a print commemorating the little masquerade survives and is in the possession of the queen of England.

She called out to him for help, but he was deaf to many of the notes that sounded in her cries. Her mood grew darker, and she complained to him, from the rooms that she shared with Mr. Cosway in London, of the oppressive atmosphere of the northern lands, "the rigor of the Melancholy" (*rigore della Malinconia*) that was "inspired by this unpleasant climate" (*ingrato Clima*). She was devoted to her church, and in England she lamented the abbey ruins, the deraignment of the monks, the impiety of Henry VIII. "There are no Monasteries," she told Jefferson, "which contain men of God who at all hours pray for us and for all those who do not pray, all who are lost."

These are not the ravings of an hysterical woman. Maria seems here to tremble not only for herself but also for her correspondent. For Jefferson, she believes, is among those "who are lost," those who do not pray or who, if they do pray, do not pray effectively, and whose salvation may therefore depend upon the intercession of others. Like Laodamia, Maria is concerned with the safety of a man in peril; her letter belongs not in the case histories of the modern psychologists but in the tradition of the *heroidum epistulae,* the letters of the heroines, the women who have loved heroes.

Years later Jefferson said of her that all "her gayety was gone" and that her mind was "entirely placed on the world to come." This would never be the case with him. It is unlikely that he ever sank to those depths of despair to which she confessed descending in one of her letters to him. Amid the "fog and smoke" of London, she said, "sadness (*la tristezza*) seemed to reign in every heart," if she judged aright from the faces she encountered in the street. In the dark land, with its heavy air, there were no bells, as there were in the south of Europe,

> ringing to announce to us some festival, service, or celebration; and even when [in the south] they call for a *Deprofundis* [a prayer for a departed soul] it is accompanied by the hope that that soul has passed to a Better Life, is enjoying the blessed quiet which the world never grants in full: [whereas in London] in the night you hear a voice at every hour which announces to us the fact that [the hour] has passed, which reminds us that it will never more return, and leaves us with the mortifying sense that we have *lost* it.

The mortifying sense that we have lost *it.* In the self-portrait Maria painted not long after her Indian-summer intimacy with Jefferson, cross and rood ribbon lie prominently on her bosom. When, in 1793, Jefferson, serving as secretary of state in President Washington's cabinet, learned that Maria had finally retired to a convent, he was saddened. "And Madame Cosway in a convent!" he exclaimed. He told his friend Angelica Church that he thought that her "very enthusiasm would have prevented her from shutting up her adoration of the God of the universe within the walls of a cloister."

6

Wine

We never keep to the present. . . . The fact is that the present usually hurts.

—PASCAL

JEFFERSON HAD FOR some time meditated a little tour in the south of France. "The climate and exercise," he said, "would, I think, restore my health." Now that Mrs. Cosway had left Paris, he was more determined than ever to make the trip. He intended to set out, he said, as soon as the "state of our business"—the diplomatic round at Paris—permitted.

Business was the professed object of the trip: his travels would give him, Jefferson said, "an opportunity of examining the canal of Languedoc," an engineering marvel, and of making a "tour of the ports concerned in commerce with us," such as Marseilles. These were the ostensible reasons for the journey, the reasons to list on a congressional expense report. But the trip was also an attempt by Jefferson to restore his spirits, which a combination of circumstances had left partially broken.

His health, in the months after Mrs. Cosway left Paris, had become more precarious; the wrist he had broken in September had not healed. "I have great anxieties," he wrote to James Madison, "lest I should never recover any considerable use of it." He had, he told Abigail Adams, been "strongly advised to go to some mineral waters at Aix in Provence"—Aix lay on the road to Marseilles—and take the cure.

Patsy Jefferson, perceptive schoolgirl, doubted that it was the wrist alone—"obstinately" swollen though it was—that drove her father to Provence. "I am inclined to think your voyage is rather for your pleasure than for your health," she wrote to him from her convent school. She was right; the voyage *was* a matter of pleasure. That winter her father was—or so he told a friend—"burning the candle of life *without present pleasure,* or future object." He was seeking pleasure—the pleasure that comes with the knowledge that one is improving the time, not wasting it, burning it up to no purpose.

"In the middle of my days," the prophet says, "I shall go to the gates of Hell," evidence that the phenomenon of the midlife crisis is older than Dante, is at least as old as Isaiah. Mrs. Cosway's "mortifying sense" that she had "lost" the passing hour found its answer in Jefferson's image of the burning taper. He had, he believed, passed the "meridian" of his life; he told Mrs. Adams that he doubted he would live a dozen more years.

Just as depressing as this sensation of time drunk up (and to no purpose!) was the disintegration of his affair with Maria. As he remembered their happiness together, it seemed to him now that not even at its height had it ever been quite free from ennui; even when the present moment was most beguiling, it had been touched by dread. "Heaven has submitted our being," he told Maria,

> to some unkind laws. When those charming moments were present which I passed with you, they were clouded with the prospect that I was soon to lose you: and now, when I pass the same moments in review, I recollect nothing but the agreeable passages, and they fill me with regret. Thus, present joys are damped by a consciousness that they are passing from us; and past ones are only the subject of sorrow and regret.

Imperfect though it might have been, the interval of dream sweetness had lifted his spirits. Now the moment had passed, but the brilliant vision had not entirely faded from his mind, and for a time he was torn, in his divided imaginations, between the belief that his love affair was certainly hopeless and the conviction that it could again be revived and would absolutely endure. It was inevitable, he told Maria, that he must lose her, yet he was unable to resign himself to the idea of a permanent separation. His confusion is apparent in a letter in which the parting valedictions are mingled with the hope of another meeting and a continued exchange of letters. "I am determined," he told her,

> when you come next not to admit the idea that we are ever to part again. But are you to come again? I dread the answer to this question, and that my poor heart has been duped by the fondness of its wishes. What a triumph for the head! God bless you! May your days be many and filled with sunshine! May your heart glow with warm affections, and all of them be gratified! Write to me often. Write affectionately, and freely, as I do to you. Say many kind things, and say them without reserve. They will be food for my soul. Adieu my dear friend!

He was grateful, he said, to have received a few lines from her—"they prove you think of me." But already there was, in his letters, a note of reticence, and slowly but steadily the waking reality overtook the recollected dream. He reproved himself for having displayed too much forwardness in love. He had been too bold, too giddy, too self-revealing. What on earth had persuaded him to send Maria the anguished letter he had composed on the day of her departure from Paris—that "history," he called it, "of the evening I parted with you"? He apologized to her for having transcribed these "effusions of the heart." His tone is light, but his embarrassment is obvious. He was, he said, "sensible" of his "transgression" and "promised to offend no more."

The onset of winter brought him fully awake. The last gleam vanished, and he was miserable. His letters of this period are a catalog of fatigue. He was living, he told Mrs. Trist, "from day to day, without a plan for four and twenty hours to come." "Laid up in port, for life, as I thought myself at one time, I am thrown out to sea, and an unknown one to me." "The good things of this life," he told Abigail Adams, "are scattered so sparingly in our way that we must glean them up as we go."

A reunion with Mrs. Cosway was, he began to think, unlikely—one more item in what he called his inventory of "impossible events." His relations with her, he concluded, must be at a distance. Their conversations, for the most part, would be in the mind. For if he could not, he said, be with her "in reality," why could he not be with her "in imagination" instead? He confessed to her that he was "never happier than when" he committed himself "into dialogue with you, tho' it be but in imagination." "Tell Mrs. Cosway she is an inconstant," he wrote to John Trumbull. "She was to have been in Paris long ago, but she has deceived us." No matter: he would, he said, catch up with her on the road to Provence. "The first evening that I find myself seated in a comfortable inn, warm, solitary, and pensive, I invite her to sup," he wrote to Trumbull, "and will commit our conversation to writing. It will be a very scolding one on my part."

His letters to her grew more improbable and fantastic; it was as though he was trying to keep a simulacrum of the dream alive by sundering the last threads that connected it to reality. He wished, he told her, that they had been formed "like the birds of the air," that they might fly to each other at once. He sighed, he said, for such a cap as Fortunatus had possessed, one that would enable him to go anywhere in the world in an instant. Or perhaps *she* would acquire such a cap and come to America. He would accompany her in a progress through Virginia, where she could sketch the natural bridge and the peaks of the Blue Ridge. A delusion, of course, but "I had rather be deceived," he said, "than live without hope."

Fantasy becomes active when life grows dull, and in insipid circumstances we are often capable of inspired reading. Jefferson found consolation, in the months that preceded his trip to the Mediterranean, not only in his make-believe conversations with Mrs. Cosway, but also in the work of a classic poet. At the end of 1786, he began to read Homer again. Not, this time, with Mr. Wythe, his old teacher in Virginia, but with Madame de Tott, one of Madame de Tessé's protégés. She had been born in Greece and spoke with fluency a demotic form of Homer's language. To assist them in their studies, Jefferson obtained the "best edition extant" of Madame de Tott's "divine countryman." The volume, he said, was distinguished by the "beauty of the type" and had the additional recommendation of "being without a single typographical error." (The publishers in Glasgow, Jefferson observed, had "offered 1000 guineas for the discovery of any error in it, even of accent," but the "reward was never claimed.") A letter from Jefferson to Crèvecoeur suggests that by January 1787 the two Grecians had got at least as far as the fourth book of the *Iliad*.

The following month, not long after the blazes of Candlemas were extinguished, Jefferson set out for Provence.

The wine helped. He had kept a cellar since 1767, when, not yet twenty-five, he had acquired his first bottles of Madeira. One of his first objects, after his arrival in Paris, was the acquisition of eighteen dozen bottles of Bordeaux, together with a few bottles of frontignac and muscat. Now, on his trip to the south, he would go at the vineyards himself.

He traveled, in his private carriage, southeast to Dijon, in Burgundy, attentive to the culture of grapes, "mixing and conversing" with the vignerons (grape growers) as often as he could. He rejoiced in the Burgundy wines of the Côte d'Or, the narrow strip of soil that stretches from Dijon south to Cheilly les Maranges, a "red mountainous" land that he thought resembled "extremely" the Virginia backcountry. For centuries the monks of the monastery of Cîteaux had labored in these vineyards, bringing to the cultivation of the soil the same zeal with which they sang their silver litanies. These were the monks of Saint Bernard's order, Cistercians whose white habits contrasted with those of the black stoles and black hoods of the Benedictines at Cluny. From their vaulted choirs and quiet cloisters the white monks had gone forth to work the sloping gardens of Meursault, Volnay, Pommard, and Chambolle-Musigny; Jefferson, in his commonplace book, recorded that Vougeot—a *clos* (enclosed vineyard) named for the stream from which the monastery drew its water—remained the "property of the monks of Cîteaux."

The shallow soil of the northern portion of the Côte, though only of what Jefferson called a "midling quality," was one in which the black grape, the pinot noir, flourished with a graceful vigor; it was from the fruit of this vine that the red wines of Burgundy had long been made. In the Middle Ages philosophers of the grape were already extolling the anxiety-purging virtues of Côte wines. The wines were *"nourrissant, théologique, et morbifuge,"* one wine sage exclaimed—a death-chasing beverage that nourished the bibber and opened him to the word of God.

It is another of his paradoxes that Jefferson, the unchurched celebrator of progress and Enlightenment, the romancer of the frugal life of the common farmer, should have been absorbed in the poetry of the Burgundies, with their fragrance of elegy, of aristocratic lament, of prophetic devotion, wines that exuded the soft vapors of half a thousand years of patient viticulture. The grapes themselves had pedigrees; the dukes of Burgundy were almost as jealous of these vegetable genealogies as they were of their own carnal ones. For years these princes sought to outlaw the coarse-bred gamay, a grape of plebeian provenance, even as they exalted the blacker blood of the pinot noirs, begetters of the majestic reds. Jefferson, who despised genealogical pretensions in men, was partial to the thoroughbred qualities of grapes. He pronounced Chambertin, a wine that had long beguiled the wine poets, the finest of the Côte d'Or reds. It was the favorite wine, too, of a young Corsican officer who in 1787 held an obscure commission in the French artillery, Second Lieutenant Napoléon Bonaparte.

As a man descended from a family with a history of mental instability, Jefferson had taken pains to develop rules and maxims designed to protect his own sanity. He had devised a variety of strategies to lift himself out of ennui. He liked to draw up architectural plans, read obscure books, speculate in curious lines of thought; he took more pleasure than most men do in shopping. Like Mr. Tilney in Jane Austen's novel, he understood muslins. There are, in the letters he exchanged with Abigail Adams in the months before he set out for Provence, references to muslin and chintz, to black lace and Irish linen, to damask tablecloths, ladies' underwear, and "shoes for Miss Adams." In one of his letters, Jefferson related how he had obtained, for this last-mentioned personage, the "two pair of Corsets she desired." "Should they be too small however," Jefferson wrote, he hoped that Miss Adams (by this time Mrs. Smith) would "be so good as to lay them by a while. There are ebbs as well as flows in this world. When the mountain refused to come to Mahomet, he went to the mountain."

A number of the rules by which Jefferson attempted to regulate the ebb and flow of his own life he communicated to his daughter Patsy. During his trip he wrote Patsy long letters in which he attempted to distill the "true secret, the grand recipe for felicity." "You know what have been my fears for some time," he told Patsy, "that you do not employ yourself so closely as I could wish. You have promised me a more assiduous attention, and I have great confidence in what you promise. It is your future happiness which interests me, and nothing can contribute more to it (moral rectitude always excepted) than the contracting a habit of industry and activity."

He warned her that indolence would lead to ennui, ennui to hypochondria, and hypochondria to hysteria. "It is while we are young," he said, that the "habit of industry is formed. If not then, it never is afterwards. The fortune of our lives therefore depends on employing well the short period of youth. If at any moment, my dear, you catch yourself in idleness, start from it as you would from the precipice of a gulph."

Patsy assured him, as a good daughter will, that his paternal anxiety was misplaced. "As for the hysterics," she said, "you may be quiet on that head, as I am not lazy enough to fear them." But she let slip that Latin was a chore. *"Titus Livius,"* she confessed, "puts me out of my wits." A mistake, on Patsy's part. "I do not like your saying that you are unable to read the antient print of your Livy," her father replied. "We are always equal to what we undertake with resolution."

And so on. It is good eighteenth-century stuff, of a piece with the Robert Adam moldings and the Chippendale cabinets in the period rooms of the museums. Jefferson's rules for the maintenance of proper moral hygiene resemble the advice that Lord Chesterfield gave his son in the once famous letters by which that nobleman tried to direct the thoughts and fix the principles of his boy. Both men placed a greater emphasis on perfection of manner—good form—than we would likely do today, were we in the habit of writing long letters to our children. But it was not only glossy manners that Jefferson hoped to see his daughter perfect. "The object most interesting to me for the residue of my life," he told her, "will be to see you [and your sister Polly] both developing daily those principles of goodness and virtue which will make you valuable to others and happy in yourselves, and acquiring those talents and that degree of science [i.e., knowledge] which will guard you at all times against *ennui.*"

The wisdom Jefferson imparted to Patsy was sound as far as it went, but it did not go far, and it seldom reached down to the deeper dreads. The rules needed to be reexamined.

He continued south through Burgundy, traveling in the lower sections of the Côte d'Or, putting more and more distance between his carriage and the grayness of Paris. He wandered through the vineyards of the Côte de Beaune, which begin just below the village of Nuits-Saint-Georges, and drank the wine. These vineyards, less fastidiously cultivated than those to the north, did not enjoy the prestige of the upper regions of the Côte d'Or; the wines produced here were not so powerful, nor were they (in the opinion of the wine sages) so poetical. But one Côte de Beaune wine, the Volnay, was, Jefferson believed, equal to the Chambertin in flavor, though "being lighter" than the wines of the northern *côte,* they did "not keep" as well. Because of its delicacy, the Volnay—a *vin de paille,* made from grapes that were pressed between layers of straw—did not "bear transportation" in the way the Chambertin did. As a result, the Volnay was cheaper than the Chambertin, and it was perhaps for this reason that Jefferson, who struggled to be a thrifty economist even though he was not naturally one, served it often at his table in Paris.

He was a connoisseur of wine and a student of ennui. It "is our own fault," Jefferson told Patsy, "if we ever know what *ennui* is." And yet he *did* know what ennui was; the little philosophy he preached down his daughter's throat—"Be not solitary, be not idle"—had not, after all, been enough to save *him*. In the aftermath of a Paris winter, in the ember days of his own middle age, Jefferson was looking for new ways to distribute the load of life's dread.

7

Liberation

It was her misfortune to have more intelligence than her friends. She could imagine everything that they would say to her about the beautiful sky in Provence, poetry, the south, etc., etc.

—STENDHAL

WE MUST FOLLOW him closely in his descent to the south.

Jefferson's was an age in which studious men grew up with the classical books of Greece and Rome. Horace and Virgil were equally the tyrants of their boyhood, the correctors and admonishers of their youth, and the friends and counselors of their maturity. Having lived for so long and on such intimate terms with the classical masters, it was only natural that the erudite votary should long to see with his own eyes lands that bore mute witness to the labors of art and the creation of beauty. For Jefferson, who was always to struggle with the puzzle of his own creative impulses, a visit to the shores of the Mediterranean would under any circumstances have been a decisive phase in his education. That his tour came now, at a time when he was seeking out new sources of inspiration, made its revelations all the more momentous. Let us, then, attend him diligently as he plucked his boughs, and daily and hourly made provision for his future art.

In the middle of March, he reached Lyons. He had no complaints to make, he wrote to his confidential secretary, William Short, "except against the weather-maker, who has pelted me with rain, hail, and snow, almost from the moment of my departure." Near the city of Orange, he crossed the olive line. The weather changed; the sun shone; he saw the parasol pines and the cypress trees. A little later in the month, just before the Ave was pronounced in the churches in honor of Lady Day, Jefferson arrived at Nîmes.

The traveler who comes unexpectedly upon an enacted fantasy is likely in the first moments of his arrival to exaggerate its strangeness, to mistake the remoteness of the provincial city, to misjudge the power of the alien sun that shines in shuttered streets. Jefferson paid the customary tributes to the perfection of the climate. It was ideal, he said, for one who loved "a warm sun, and a clear sky" as he did. He was, he confessed to Maria Cosway, "an animal of a warm climate, a mere Oran-ootan," and he was dazzled by the splendor of the Provençal sun. "It is wonderful to me," he wrote to Short, "that every free being who possesses cent ecus de rente, does not remove Southward of the Loire. It is true that money will carry to Paris most of the good things of this canton. But it cannot carry thither it's sunshine, nor procure any equivalent for it." And yet even as he took rooms in Nîmes, in the Petit Louvre, called for the barber to be shaved, and had his clothes washed, Jefferson was unnerved by his new environment.

"Here I am, Madam," he wrote to Madame de Tessé on March 20, 1787, from Nîmes, "gazing whole hours on the Maison quarée, like a lover at his mistress." To stand before the Roman temple known as the Maison Carrée (a corruption of Maison Carrée Longue, the House of the Long Square, or Rectangle) was as exhilarating an experience as an epiphany tends to be. But although it was only now consummated, Jefferson's love affair with the temple was already old; and the fulfillment of a long and deeply meditated desire, because it upsets all one's accustomed mental arrangements and notions of possibility, always leaves one a little drained.

A year before his visit to Provence, Jefferson observed that there is at Nismes in the South of France a building, called the Maison quarrée, erected in the time of the Caesars, and which is allowed without contradiction to be the most perfect and precious remain of antiquity in existence. It's superiority over any thing at Rome, in Greece, at Balbec or Palmyra is allowed on all hands; and this single object has placed Nismes in the general tour of travellers. Having not yet had leisure to visit it, I could only judge it from drawings, and from the relation of numbers who had been to see it.

Now, in Nîmes, he was able at last to "judge it" himself, and he devoted "whole hours" to gazing upon the Corinthian splendor of the Roman temple, its *frise trouvée* of swirling rosettes, its Egyptian lion gargoyles. But he hesitated to confess, even to Madame de Tessé, the extent of his enthusiasm; he instead disguised the depth of his feelings with a show of gallantry, and he made believe that the temple was his mistress.

In Nîmes, Jefferson bought two dozen white silk stockings and a dozen black ones; he drew on his bills of exchange; he bought medals and (of course) books. He also paid homage to the eternal gallantry of Provence, to the medieval traditions of courtly love from which his own sentimental ideas were remotely descended. The Provençal troubadours were, he observed, the "delight of the several courts of Europe." It was "from thence," he noted, "that the novels of the English are called Romances." The old gallantry still existed in Provence; the old Provençal dialect—a sweet bastard Latin that Jefferson thought quite startlingly beautiful—was still used to describe it. (Provence, like Aquitania, was a land of the langue d'oc, where the Occitan tongues were spoken. Here *oc,* from the Latin *hoc,* was used for "yes," not, as in the Frankish north, *oïl* or *oui,* from the Latin *hoc illud.*)

But at Nîmes, Jefferson's homage to the chivalric forms was performed in a spirit of mockery. True to the ideals of the knights and jongleurs of old Provence, he confessed to Madame de Tessé that he was playing the macho part of a *druz,* a Provençal lover. But by saying that he was in love with a building, not with a woman, he made the whole thing into a joke. He was gazing gallantly upon columns and pediments, not upon the flesh. "This is the second time I have been in love since I left Paris," he informed the countess. The first time, he said, "was with a Diana at the Chateau de Laye Epinaye in Beaujolois, a delicious morsel of sculpture, by Michael Angelo Slodtz. This, you will say, was in rule, to fall in love with a fine woman: but, with a house! It is out of all precedent!"

In the sentimental adventure in which he had dallied with Mrs. Cosway, Jefferson had been a *druz* in the full Italian sense of the word. He had been then what the Italians called a *drudo,* the lover of a married woman. Six months later, in the sunshine of Nîmes, Jefferson professed himself the lover of a Roman temple. Relaxing over a glass of the *vin ordinaire* (he pronounced it excellent, with "a strong body"), he seemed almost to breathe a sigh of relief.

Mrs. Cosway was in England when Jefferson arrived in Provence. But although she was remote in body, she was present in his mind. Theirs had been the perfection of a sentimental affair: all the ingredients of sentimental success—beauty, passion, even insuperable obstacles to love—had been present. The liaison was the culmination of Jefferson's sentimental education; but it had not, after all, been wholly satisfying. A sentimental affair was not *supposed* to be wholly satisfying; that was the point. Jefferson, however, was a practical man; he judged by results. He had gone to school with the sentimentalists, and he had developed a fondness for their favorite doctrines. Now he discovered the limitations of those dogmas, and it was only natural that there should be a reaction. It came in Nîmes, and it came as an explosion.

Jefferson's letter to Madame de Tessé from Nîmes is mild and amusing, but he could not resist building into it a little romance tinged with a darker coloring. He told Madame de Tessé how, as he gazed upon the columns of the Maison Carrée, the startled tradesmen of Nîmes—the stocking weavers and silk spinners—raised their eyebrows as they passed him by. The greasy aprons "consider me," Jefferson said, "as an hypochondriac Englishman, about to write with a pistol, the last chapter of his history."

In a stroke Jefferson conceived, in miniature, a sentimental romance of his own. As a young man who suffered from insomnia, he would construct a "love and murder novel" in his head whenever he could not fall asleep. Now, in Nîmes, he fashioned another conceit for himself, a "hypochondriac

Englishman." The central figure of his daydream is the eternal hero of all the sentimental fables, the sensitive damoiseau—the aspirant to knighthood and every form of gallantry—who is yet unable to act, is prone to ennui, unlucky in love, doomed to despair. Jefferson left Madame de Tessé to imagine his morbid troubadour pulling the trigger in front of the old Roman temple, blowing his brains out in the pillared shade. He then dispatched the letter and returned to his feasts of the sun.

8
Searchings

But still the heart doth need a language, still
Doth the old instinct bring back the old names.

—COLERIDGE, AFTER SCHILLER

I WAS ALONE thro the whole," Jefferson said of his journey, "and think one travels more usefully when they travel alone, because they reflect more." He was not entirely alone. While in Dijon he hired a manservant named Petit-jean who attended him during much of his trip. Jefferson had not wanted to take one of his regular household servants with him; such company would have been burdensome to him—an obstacle to reverie. The "plan of having servants who know nothing of me," he told William Short, "places me perfectly at my ease."

Few public men can have so delighted in being unobserved. Cut off, in Nîmes, from all whom he knew, Jefferson experienced the melancholy but not unpleasant sensation that the traveler feels when he is alone in a foreign city. He had slipped the silken leashes of Parisian society, and the softer harness of the diplomatic corps; he was happy, at last, to have his mind to himself. The tourist, he wrote, "retired at night to his chamber in an Inn, all his effects contained in a single trunk, all his cares circumscribed by the walls of his apartment, unknown to all, unheeded, and undisturbed, writes, reads, thinks, sleeps, just in the moments when nature and the movements of his mind and body require."

Solitude stimulated his mind, but so, too, did the ancient architecture he encountered. He was, he said, continually "nourished" by the "remains of Roman grandeur." These were "more in number, and less injured by time than I expected." There were "beautiful, fluted, Corinthian columns" at Vienne, a "sublime triumphal arch" at Orange (he beheld it, he said, "with rapture"), the massive stonework of the Pont du Gard northeast of Nîmes (part of the old Roman aqueduct), and a dozen other examples of "Roman taste, genius, and magnificence."

Jefferson was a searcher. The fanatical book buyer often is. He approaches each volume as though it contained a revelation. "While residing in Paris," Jefferson said, "I devoted every afternoon I was disengaged, for a summer or two, in examining all the principal bookstores, turning over every book with my own hand, and putting by . . . whatever was rare and valuable in every science."

A gentleman of sense and taste who happened also to be a searcher after truth must inevitably, in those days, have turned, in his quest for illumination, to the philosophical founts of antiquity. Such a man looked to the designs of the ancient architects for a model for his house, and he no less readily looked to the philosophy of the ancient moralists for a model for his conduct. Jefferson was no exception in this, even if in his heart he was not always able to accept the judgment of the oracles he consulted. He knew well enough what Pythagoras, Epicurus, Epictetus, and Socrates (these were his favorites among the ancient philosophers) would have said about his dalliance with Mrs. Cosway. The most valuable precepts of these thinkers, Jefferson said, relate to the "government of those passions which, unrestrained, would disturb our tranquillity of mind." In "this branch of philosophy," he said, the ancient sages "were really great." The wise men would have taken one look at the slender, blond figure of Mrs. Cosway and raised their philosophical eyebrows. What a train of misery and heartache, they would have said, must have followed his effort to keep the dream of making love to her alive. "Do not bite at the bait of pleasure," they would have told him, "till you know there is no hook beneath it." Jefferson's moral imagination was full of such "grave saws and maxims." For if his heart, not easily governable, still longed for Mrs. Cosway, his head, which had more readily submitted to the tuition of the magi, warned him against acquiescing in "follies" that would end by costing him a "great deal of pain."

It was the ideal of the enlightened Roman squire, retired to the quiet order of his villa, there to eat figs off cool marble and cultivate his olive trees, philosophically indifferent to the "bustle and tumult" of the world. "The art of life," Jefferson liked to say, "is the art of avoiding pain: and he is the best pilot who steers clearest of the rocks and shoals with which it is beset." "The most effectual means of being secure against pain," he believed,

is to retire within ourselves, and to suffice for our own happiness. Those, which depend on ourselves, are the only pleasures a wise man will count on: for nothing is ours which another may deprive us of. Hence the inestimable value of intellectual pleasures. Ever in our power, always leading us to something new, never cloying, we ride, serene and sublime, above the concerns of the mortal world, contemplating truth and nature, matter and motion, the laws which bind up their existence, and that eternal being who made and bound them up by these laws.

The words could almost have been spoken by Epicurus himself. "I too am an Epicurean," Jefferson told William Short. "I consider the genuine (not the imputed) doctrines of Epicurus as containing everything rational in moral philosophy which Greece and Rome have left us."

How delightful, then, it must have been for Jefferson to find in France that this art of avoiding pain had been wrought up into new forms of perfection. The French will always surpass other peoples in the splendor and opulence of their Epicureanism. The philosophy of the rational voluptuary has there been raised to the level of a science, even an art. Jefferson marveled at the music, the painting, and the architecture of the French; he was hardly less astonished by the exquisiteness of the French table. So gratifying were the dinner parties, Jefferson observed, that Frenchmen did not feel obliged to get drunk, during their course, to obtain their proper dose of pleasure. "They do not terminate the most sociable meals," he said, "by transforming themselves into brutes," as Anglo-Saxon gentlemen were wont to do. "I fancy it must be the quantity of animal food eaten by the English," he spec-

ulated in a letter to Mrs. Adams, "which renders their character insuscepti-
ble of civilization."

Jefferson taught himself to be as supercilious a connoisseur of rational
gratification as the haughtiest of the French masters. Some of the letters in
which he exposes the gaudier forms of pleasure-seeking in Paris recall the wit
of the moralist epicures of the French classical tradition—the black baubles
of La Bruyère, La Rochfoucauld, the chevalier de Méré—and were perhaps
composed in imitation of them. But there was always an element of affectation and conceit in these exercises. However much Jefferson profited from
his initiation in the standards of Paris, he could never have been satisfied
with a life of luxury and epicurism alone. The man who feels, as Jefferson
did, that he must act in the world, boldly and, if possible, nobly—such a
man is, from the Epicurean point of view, lost; he is a fool; he is beyond
reclamation. Jefferson, for all his love of pleasure and tranquillity, could
never have been content with so soft, so tepid, so unstrenuous a conception
of life as the epicures proposed. His destiny was more complex; he was not
meant for a looker-on and a critic, a flaneur with a diplomatic passport.

It was Jefferson's good fortune to have encountered, in Paris, fellow searchers
after truth who saw something more in Greece and Rome than the justification of a life of good dinners and genteel dissipation. These searchers were
intrigued by the art and mysticism of the classical peoples; these they took
to embody the secret of the ancients' virility or virtue—that active power to
beget works of order and works of art which belongs properly (so the ancients believed) to a man (in Latin, *vir*).

One of these searchers was Jefferson's friend Charles-Louis Clérisseau, an
artist who as a young man had gone to Italy on the Prix de Rome and had
there fallen in love with the ancient architecture. By the time Jefferson knew
him, Clérisseau was deeply versed in the history of Roman building and the
most elegant draftsman in Paris. Jefferson bought Clérisseau's book, *Antiquités de la France: Monuments de Nismes,* a volume filled with engravings of
the Roman architecture of Provence. Clérisseau, in turn, helped Jefferson to
prepare a plan of a capitol building for Richmond. Both men adored the
Maison Carrée at Nîmes, and their design for the Virginia capitol was ac-
cordingly based on it.

Another searcher whom Jefferson came to know well in Paris was Pierre-

François Hugues, the self-styled Baron d'Hancarville. He was a friend of
Mrs. Cosway's and a protégé of her patron, Charles Towneley. He had accompanied Jefferson and Mrs. Cosway to the gatehouse on the dreadful day
of Maria's departure from Paris. The eccentric "baron" had afterward ridden
back into town with the distraught American minister. "Mr. Danquerville,"
as Jefferson insisted on calling him, belonged to the tradition of the eighteenth-century charlatan, a lesser cousin of Casanova, Cagliostro, and Mes-
mer. He had something in common, too, with an older type of Mediterranean
swindler, those philosopher-conjurors from the north who liked to loll in
the southern waters.

Mr. Danquerville's experience of life was varied; he had been accused of
purloining the duke of Württemberg's silver, and he had been banished
from Naples for publishing pornography. He was learned in the sunken passageways and disreputable crypts of Greco-Roman culture; knew intimately
the private lives of the Twelve Caesars; had produced books, like his history
of the erotic cults of the Roman ladies, that betrayed both a massive erudition and a licentious taste. He amused the connoisseurs whose collections he
catalogued with a constant stream of fascinating talk, monologues in which
tales of fantastic exploits, and lubricious anecdotes of southern cities, were
interspersed with impressive disquisitions on the history of art.

Mr. Danquerville was—it is not to be denied—a parasite and sycophant;
his moral character will not bear scrutiny. But in his essays he illuminated
the primitive Mediterranean fertility rituals, the cults of gods such as Attys,
Adonis, Osiris, Thammuz, and Dionysus, who were believed to embody the
mysterious processes of life, death, and rebirth. Mr. Danquerville was a pur-
veyor of pompous naughtiness; but useful preaching may be done in lewd
houses, and in spite of his prurience he was one of the authors of an intellectual revolution that influenced the course of Jefferson's own thought.

M. Clérisseau was an architect, Mr. Danquerville was an antiquarian;
but, like the other spirits whom Jefferson sought out in Paris—the brilliant
Count Potocki, a Polish nobleman and student of the younger Pliny, and
the amiable Madame de Tessé, the devotee of Homer and Cicero—the
searchers were not looking merely for ways to build better buildings or for
more ingenious methods of interpreting classical texts. Whether they were
architects or painters, scholars or dilettantes, the searchers to whom Jefferson turned for inspiration and comradery were involved in a more complex
pursuit: they were trying to puzzle out the character of the ancient peoples
who had once dominated the Mediterranean. What enabled the Greeks and
the Romans to perform their extraordinary acts? What was the secret of

their astonishing creative power, the glowing efficient health that underlay their spectacular deeds?

The Mediterranean fertility mysticism that bewitched Jefferson's friends intrigued Jefferson himself. He drew on it to fashion his most notorious sentence: "The tree of liberty," he wrote to William Stephens Smith (a few months after he returned from Provence), "must be refreshed from time to time with the blood of patriots and tyrants. It is its natural manure."

Jefferson's words were provoked by Shays's Rebellion in Massachusetts and by the question of whether the United States should adopt a new constitution, but the language is as old as the fertility rituals of the Mediterranean. It is the language of the cult of Attys, transcribed in an eighteenth-century hand. Attys, a Phrygian king-god,* was said at his death to have been transformed into a pine tree; and each year his death was ritually replicated in a ceremony of counterfeited slaughter. The blood of such a being was a potent fertilizer—or so the ancient mythographers suggested. From the blood of Attys's brother god Dionysus sprung the pomegranate tree, and out of the precious liquid of Adonis's veins grew the anemone, although some say it was really the rosebush.

The tender vegetation god was thought to die with the first blasts of winter; the advent of the cold season marked the bloody expiration of a fertility deity. But in spite of his annual wound, Thammuz was reconstituted in the spring, when he caused the ground to be again fruitful. The revivified god made love to the earth. Dionysus found Ariadne sleeping at Naxos; he waked and married her. The aroused virgin was transformed into an earth mother; her marriage to the god was annually reenacted, at Athens, in the springtime feast of Anthesteria, "when the flowers (*anthe*) begin to appear." Jefferson possessed a marble sculpture that recalled the incident, copied from the original representation of a fatigued but still seductive Ariadne. In his catalog Jefferson identified the piece as "Ariadne reclined on the rocks at Naxos." The queen of spring is still to be seen at Monticello, drowsily awaiting the touch of her lord.

---

* The Phrygians were a Thracian people who settled in Anatolia, where they overthrew the Hittite state.

Garry Wills, who, like Jefferson, was trained as a classicist, understood Jefferson's invocation of the blood-smeared liberty tree to be "a voice from the Georgian manor talking a kind of remote and georgic poetry about the right 'seasons' for madness and bloodshed." But what did Jefferson think of the "remote poetry" that he incorporated into this letter to Smith, this famous—or infamous—reflection on the nature of politics and freedom? That it was charming and suggestive? Or that it was *true*?

Certainly Jefferson did not believe the bloody mythology of his liberty tree to be in any exact or literal sense true. He never urged his fellow citizens to fill up watering jugs with blood and sprinkle it on the liberty trees that once adorned every patriotic American town. He did not, as far as we know, go out of doors each December and burn Adonis in effigy before the pillars of Monticello. Nor is there any record of him ordering a bull to be slaughtered when the lilacs bloomed, that he might drink its blood in honor of Dionysus and propitiate the fecund power of the spring. Metaphors are by definition not literally true. But if they are any good, they are not wholly false. They are inspired approximations of truth, approximations to which we resort when the truths we have to express are so extraordinary that our ordinary language fails us.

Jefferson's friend Joel Barlow labored to demonstrate the precise sequence of events by which the fertility myths of antiquity were transformed into the modern "tree of liberty" that Jefferson cherished. Barlow was the son of a Yankee farmer, and during the long dull New England winter he had developed a thirst for the exotic atmosphere of the Mediterranean. He placed much emphasis on the story of Osiris. That unfortunate hero had been murdered, in Egypt, by his brother, Set, or Qeb; and like his cousin gods he had sprouted a tree—an erica, by some acounts; others say it was a tamarisk. The body of Osiris had, moreover, been dismembered by Set, and his privates flung into the Nile, where, in Barlow's retelling of the myth, they "communicated a fecundating power to that river which from that time became the source of life and vegetation to all Egypt."

Barlow grew warm in thesis. He became flushed with the intoxicating power of the archaic texts. Obscure documents were diligently scrutinized; remote scenes of blood and ecstasy were brought voluptuously alive; astonishing revelations followed. Did not the word *libertas* derive from the Latin fertility god, Liber? And was not Liber—a god of fresh starts and new beginnings, with his feast day on the threshold of the spring—sometimes identified with Dionysus? During Liber's festival—the Liberalia, in middle March—Italians dragged images of a great phallus into their towns on wagons, just as, in old Egypt, a replica of Osiris's severed member had been carried in lofty procession. The conclusion to be drawn was obvious: the tree of liberty, Barlow determined, was nothing other than the "amputated penis of Osiris."

Barlow's conjectures are no longer taken seriously by scholars. Philologists today believe that their eighteenth- and nineteenth-century predecessors exaggerated the importance of fertility magic in ancient religious rites. But like his fellow searchers, like Mr. Danquerville himself, Barlow helped to prepare the way for more sophisticated investigations of the influence of myth and ritual on the development of civilization. The searchers prepared the ground for the contributions of the succeeding century, for works like Nietzsche's *Birth of Tragedy* (1872) and Sir James George Frazer's *Golden Bough* (1890–1915). The searchers anticipated the achievements of later scholarship, but they were nevertheless not modern. It was not simply that their theories were more primitive, their data more limited, their methods more amateurish than those of subsequent generations of scholars. Their purposes were different. The eighteenth-century searchers expected their findings to change their lives. They wanted not simply to discover things but to learn from the things they discovered—indeed to imitate them. "The only way for us to become great," one of these searchers, Johann Joachim Winckelmann, said, "is to imitate the Greeks." Winckelmann sought greatness; other searchers merely sought sanity. The "classical" models of the Greeks and Romans deserved to be imitated, Goethe said, precisely because they were "healthy." They were an antidote to the modern malady that Goethe called the "romantic" disease and his friend Schiller called the "sentimental" sickness.

To seek the secret springs of action, to comprehend the processes by which chaos is transmuted into order, are laudable aims, but we must not think the searchers' quest without blemish. They liked to surround themselves with objects of virtù, as they called their antique statues, medals, coins, *bassi-relievi*. Jefferson could not compete with the European collectors who acquired such costly antiquities for their own cabinets and galleries; he had to satisfy himself with reproductions. He commissioned an *askos*—a kind of ancient wine pouch—to be made in silver by a Philadelphia smith; beneath the fireplace mantel in the dining room at Monticello, he installed figures of the Muses; he made a list of copies of famous statues that he hoped one day to acquire for Monticello.

But in what did all the rough antique magic of Jefferson and his little coterie of seekers issue, other than some pretty buildings, some (now) unread plays, and some (mostly bad) paintings? It is not always easy to judge rightly of the good and the evil that a particular mysticism produces. The metaphors, the images, the conceits of such a mysticism—its curious approximations of truths that are beyond ordinary comprehension—might, indeed, give some men the moral courage to do or to make noble things. But to take the case of Jefferson, would he really have done any less greatly if he had never learned to con his Virgil? It is impossible to say. We have only his own testimony to go by. Jefferson said that the antiquarian incense he was always happy to breathe contained an antidote to the terrors of the life cycle. Those smoking thuribles helped him to mitigate two things, his ennui (his despair of the present moment) and his dread of the future (his fears concerning the disposition and manner of his death). In turning the "classic pages" of the "Latin & Greek authors," Jefferson said, he enjoyed more than a "sublime luxury." The "classic pages," he wrote, were "sweet composers to that rest of the grave into which we are all sooner or later to descend." So hard did he squeeze the pulp of those words that he forced them, at last, to yield their residue of balm. The golden pages enabled him, he said, to "slumber without fear," and to "fill up" the "vacuum of *ennui*"—the "most dangerous poison of life"—in a way few other things did.

"I am immersed in antiquities from morning to night," Jefferson reported to Madame de Tessé from Nîmes. He inspected what was called the temple of Diana, which may once have been connected to a nymphaeum, a shrine sacred to the nymphs. Before the nymphs came, it belonged to Nemausus, a Celtic fountain god, whose rainwater spring it is. The temple is a ruin now, with pretty pedimented niches. Nearby, the Romans built their baths, and a French sapper, in the eighteenth century, built a park. His cream-colored balustrades sit atop the Roman porticos, with a rise of limestone behind them, covered in cedars and pines. But the nymphs are departed, and the fountain god, too, and Jefferson continued on his journey.

9

Cure

*Plato had an imagination; that all knowledge was but
remembrance.*

—BACON

FROM NÎMES he traveled to Aix, taking the ancient road that passes close
by the sepulchres of Arles. Along the sharp-cobbled Roman avenue, on the
eastern marches of the town, lies the great mass of the sarcophagi, sequestered from the wind in a vale of poplar trees. In the language of old
Provence, this place of sleeping stones is called Les Alyscamps. Jefferson, trying to decipher the ghostly syntax of the name, observed that in the French
of the Frankish north, it would have been called Champs-Élysées, Elysian
Fields—the place, that is, where the blessed dead of the city repose.

He went on through a country rich with clover, mulberries, and willow;
in the distance he saw the "high hills of Languedoc" in snow. He headed
north for a time, following the winding road through Tarascon up into the
Alpilles—the Little Alps—where the villages of Saint-Rémy-de-Provence and
Orgon squat amid "broken hills of massive rock." Then he turned south, tra-

versing a land "waving in vines," and found the sedge grounds surging with
unripened lavender. Approaching the valley in which Aix lies, he glimpsed
the sea, "rich and beautiful," together with a "perfect grove of olive trees."

He arrived in Aix on March 25 and took rooms at the Hôtel Saint-
Jacques. "I am now in the land of corn, wine, oil, and sunshine," he reported to William Short two days later. "What more can man ask of
heaven?" "If I should happen to die at Paris," he said, "I will beg of you to
send me here, and have me exposed to the sun. I am sure it will bring me to
life again." Successive days of Mediterranean sunshine had quite driven
away the hypochondriacal vision of suicide that had haunted him in the
shadow of the Maison Carrée. "The man who shoots himself in the climate
of Aix," he told Short, "must be a bloody minded fellow indeed." Jefferson
had especially good weather on his trip, or he exaggerated, for the purity of
the Mediterranean summer is not secure in Provence, even as late as May;
and the valley of the Rhone remains vulnerable to brown air and gray-
bellied clouds.

Aix is a dusty city today, but once it was celebrated for its sunshine and
its waters. Here the good king René, a poet-prince, presided over a brilliant
court in the days when Provence was still an independent kingdom. Here
Marius came and defeated a tribe of German savages who had invaded Gaul.
The Romans called the place Aquae Sextiae in honor of its springs and constructed around them a vast edifice of public baths. The waters were warm;
Jefferson recorded a temperature of "90.° of Farenheit's thermometer at the
spout." But they proved ineffectual, and they did his damaged wrist little
good. Still the sun ("my almighty physician," he called it) was splendid, and
the town itself seemed to him charming. To a friend he described the "delicious walks" he took in the spacious streets. The boulevards, he said, were
wide, and shaded from the southern sun by elms; along them stood, in their
withered gentility, the mansions of the old aristocracy of Aix, the seats of
families who for centuries had given a tone to the city's civilization, presided
in its *parlement,* administered the laws, maintained the standards.

At Aix he caught up with his correspondence. Besides dispatching two letters to Short, he finally got around to writing one to Patsy. He had failed to
send his daughter the weekly letter he had promised her, and she was naturally disappointed. Her father was, after all, a prodigious writer of letters—

his epistolary record, in which he maintained a catalog of his correspondence from 1783 to 1826, lists many thousands of letters in its 656 pages. Jefferson told his daughter that he had not written to her sooner "because I have been almost constantly on the road." This was disingenuous; Jefferson had managed to get off letters to Short, Madame de Tessé, and the ever-faithful Petit, his majordomo in Paris. Patsy was justifiably skeptical. "Until now," she wrote to her father upon receiving his letter from Aix, "you have not kept your word the least in the world."

But after all he *had* been busy; an eighteenth-century grand tour was a strenuous business. Put to one side any notions of aristocratic young men roaring over bowls of wine or hard-drinking milords carelessly disporting themselves in southern taverns. For the profane palmer the tour might indeed have been little more than a grand debauch, but for a devoted pilgrim like Jefferson it was something more. Although the idea of the grand tour has become debased—cheapened by the impiety of the patrician hordes from the north—the tour, properly understood, was a form of art, not a frolic, to be undertaken only after a period of intense preparation. A lazy acquaintance with a few books of Virgil and some scraps of Ovid would not do; the tourist, Edward Gibbon insisted, needed to possess a "copious stock of classical and historical learning," together with an "indefatigable vigor of mind." Gibbon, the author of *The History of the Decline and Fall of the Roman Empire*, would have approved the thoroughness of Jefferson's own preparations. The American minister not only knew his classics (and his Gibbon); he was, he confessed, "passionately fond" of works of travel, and in the records of other pilgrims he discovered the precepts that guided his own journey in the south.

Different tourists got different things out of their tours. Some went in youth, eager to experience an epiphany that would inspire their creative powers and possibly shape their careers. The twenty-six-year-old Gibbon discovered his life's work when, sitting near the Church of Santa Maria in the Aracoeli at Rome, he surveyed the site of what had once been the Roman Capitol. Jefferson had been a law student in Virginia when, half a world away, his English fellow searcher experienced a transfiguration of purpose. "It was at Rome," Gibbon said, "on the fifteenth of October 1764, as I sat musing amidst the ruins of the Capitol, while the barefooted friars were singing vespers in the temple of Jupiter, that the idea of writing the decline and fall of the city first started to my mind." Other travelers, like Goethe and Jefferson himself, went in middle age. Having exhausted the creative energies of youth, they went in search of renewal and rebirth, a fresh accession of imaginative power. The thirty-seven-year-old Goethe, dissatisfied, in the late summer of 1786, with his work, his friends, the whole tenor of his life in Germany, disappeared from Weimar one day and "almost by secret flight" crossed the Alps into Italy. Making his epochal visit to the south at the same time Jefferson made his, Goethe dated the beginning of his "second life" from the moment he entered the seat of Rome's empire.

Jefferson, too, needed to restring his lyre. His country had, with his assistance, declared its independence in 1776; now, about a decade later, the United States was involved in a different enterprise, the most daring act of republican constitution making in twenty centuries. This exercise that would eventually bear fruit in an empire more powerful than that of Rome, and grander than that of Venice—it was as though history, not content with her handiwork, were unwilling to rest until she had witnessed the rise of a third great imperial republic. With his powers of expression and his knowledge of constitutional history, Jefferson might have contributed much to this effort. But he was experiencing, in the altered world of the 1780s, a paralysis of political will, and in the fatigue of his middle forties he found himself able to accomplish relatively little in the public sphere.

His country, he knew, was in a state of crisis. Trade languished; money was scarce; the vital ports of the British West Indies continued to be closed to American shipping. Rumors of mutiny and discontent were abroad in the land; what began as faint murmurings of sedition grew louder when, in the fall of 1786, Daniel Shays led a crowd of debtors to harass the judges of western Massachusetts and shut down the courts of law. Many of the problems were rooted in the defects of the Republic's government. Under the Articles of Confederation, the nation was governed by a weak and factious legislature. Congress had the power neither to regulate commerce nor to levy taxes. Such powers as it did possess were ineffectively exercised by a caballing, quarreling, haranguing mob of politicians. There was no executive authority to enforce those laws that Congress was entitled to make and no executive machinery to implement the legislature's will. The national government was reduced to a specter, and the sword of state was wielded not by Congress but by the governments of thirteen sovereign states.

So imperfect a constitutional engine might not have mattered in a republic of virtue, but contrary to the expectations or, rather the hopes, of the patriots of the 1770s, the republic of virtue had not emerged with the defeat of the British. Statesmen skilled in anatomizing the body politic began now to understand that it never would emerge. Spartan patriotism was the product of historical circumstances that had prevailed in certain precincts of the

Aegean several thousand years before; those conditions did not exist in eighteenth-century America. It was therefore necessary, the foremost architects of state believed, to new-model the government. James Madison and Alexander Hamilton sought to mold and frame the Republic's constitution to fit the needs and capacities not of a tribe of civic warriors but of a polite and commercial people.

In the 1770s Jefferson had been in the vanguard: he had helped to do the hard thinking that had enabled America to make a successful revolution against its colonial masters. Now, in the 1780s, when hard thinking was again required, when America was trying to figure out how to make a modern (Whig) republic work, Jefferson fell victim to strange languors, dull states of mind, intellectual flaccidity. He was, it is true, an ocean away from the fast-moving currents of American politics, and he could not have participated directly in the constitutional debates even if he had wished to. But his Paris posting cannot entirely explain his indolence in the middle years of the 1780s. His strength had never been the strength of action, the commanding energy that demands to be displayed on the spot, in the press of business, in a crowd of public men—in the Revolutionary conclaves of Philadelphia, the Jefferson of the 1770s had been, for the most part, a mute. He had worked his magic rather with his mind, and with his pen, crafting sentences bright with startling imagery, and fashioned with a classic grace. The work of creating a modern commercial republic might have been different from that of declaring the nation independent, but essential to the success of both projects was that species of benign wizardry that reduces a complicated tangle of fact and theory to a few readily comprehensible truths.

His mind and his pen were equally available to Jefferson now; but he produced nothing comparable to the brief sententious essays that had clarified the chaos of the 1770s. Besides his *Notes on the State of Virginia,* which he published on the eve of his departure for Provence, the most involved piece of expository prose Jefferson had so far composed in the 1780s was a literary essay, "Thoughts on English Prosody." An interesting work, to be sure, but far from getting at the deepest problems of what scholars call the critical period in American history. Historians praise Jefferson's diplomatic efforts in the 1780s, but the negotiation of more favorable terms for the export of whale oil surely ranks among the least compelling achievements of his career.

As Jefferson pressed deeper into the European south, preparations were being made, in America, for a convention to assemble, in May at Philadelphia. The purpose of the convention was to draft a constitution for the United States.

Jefferson called the convention "an assembly of demigods." But he had contributed almost nothing to the previsionary labors that went into the momentous act of constitution making. He had not pushed himself to think through the problems. He had not formulated a program of constitutional reform. Jefferson knew the Articles of Confederation to be too weak, but a number of the proposed remedies were, he believed, too strong. He could not reconcile the two ideas. A Whig republic could not tolerate aggrandizing central powers: a workable republic required an executive strong enough to enforce the laws. But Jefferson, whose nature could be dreamy even though he insisted that it was always matter-of-fact, was unable to fashion a compromise between liberty and authority. He left his friend Madison to do what he himself could not.

He was always busy, even now; but there was no creative rising above. While the details of the Philadelphia assembly were being worked out—the preliminary proposals floated, the various factions formed—Jefferson was walking the bowered streets of Aix. They struck him as the "cleanest and neatest" he had "ever seen," as spotless, he said, as a "parlour floor." On his walks he dwelled on the "long chain of causes and effects" that had produced, not constitutional crisis in the United States, but the absence of dung in a southern city. The "preciousness" of the soil in the surrounding country, Jefferson reasoned, prevented its "being employed in grass." Where there was no grass, there could be few cows and little cow shit. What dung there was, he observed, had great value, and the "dung-gatherers (a numerous calling here) hunt it" as "eagerly in the streets as they would diamonds. Every one therefore can walk cleanly and commodiously. Hence few carriages. Hence few assemblies, routs [gatherings of fashionable people], and other occasions for the display of dress." He could not resist spinning webs of moral and political theory; the want of dung, he concluded, not only stimulated the exertions of jakes farmers, it also prevented the "progress of luxury at Aix." But he was vaporing away his ingenuity in trifles. In the spring of 1787, Jefferson appeared more interested in explaining the voluptuous bareness of Aix than in mastering the problem of constitutional breakdown in the United States.

He was that unusual politician whose genius was neither legislative nor administrative, but essentially poetic. His poetic nature delighted in order and simplicity, and he gloried in the Mediterranean plainness of Aix. At an earlier period in his life, however, he had been able to rise above mere aesthetic luxury and deal creatively—poetically—with politics as well. Now, in 1787, he seemed to have lost that gift.

Rejuvenation was the object, and a grand tour offered many paths to salvation. To the eighteenth-century tourist the idea of Rome itself was one source of regenerative power. Jefferson, in Provence, imagined the imperial city still unfallen, in the unstained glory of its prime. "For me the city of Rome is still existing in the splendor of it's empire," he wrote to Madame de Tessé, and walking the streets of Provençal towns, he tried to imagine what it must have been like to have lived in the ancient *provincia* under the early emperors.

The letters he wrote in Provence show him to have been in touch with all the critical epochs of the history of this corner of the Mediterranean. By the time he reached Aix, his imagination had become stratigraphic, and like an archaeologist who peels away layer upon layer of accumulated soil, he cleared away the historical dust—the sediment of centuries—under which the objects he sought lay buried. He alluded to the Greek colonists who established little trading towns in Provence centuries before the coming of the Romans, and longer still before the birth of Christ. He pondered the rise of Rome, and to Madame de Tessé speculated about the tribulations of a provincial existence under the Roman imperium. "Were I to give you news," he wrote the countess,

> I should tell you stories a thousand years old. I should detail to you the intrigues of the courts of the Caesars, how they affect us here, the oppressions of their Praetors, &c. . . . I am filled with alarms for the event of the irruptions dayly making on us by the Goths, Ostrogoths, Visigoths and Vandals, lest they should reconquer us to our original barbarism.

Jefferson lived now in one era, now in another, and submitted willingly to the dispensations of each. Surveying the monuments of the Caesars, he felt trepidation before the Gothic barbarians. In the conversation of eighteenth-century Provençals—their elegant demotic Latin—he caught the accents of a first-century Roman street.

The question was one of efficacy. How fecund were the fertile periods of history, its great creative ages, its choicer gardens? Could their potency—imprisoned now in ruined monuments and faded papyrus—seed the future, and be a cause of growth in modern men? This was the question with which the travelers and searchers of the eighteenth century struggled. For whether they went in youth or in middle age, whether they reached Rome or stopped short at the banks of the Po or the Arno, the truest pilgrims set out on their pilgrimages with an overriding object in mind: to be born again, made over in the Mediterranean air. In its highest forms the grand tour not only enlarged the traveler's imagination; it also sharpened his perception of order, his grasp of "mistress form."

Walking through the ordered gardens and dungless streets of Provençal towns, Jefferson contemplated the overripe cycles of history; teeming, like nature itself; the overmanured flowerings of civilization—renaissances, golden ages, the rise of splendid courts and high-souled strains of manners. And he contemplated the inevitable periods of decline and degeneration: the collapse of temples, the smashing of idols, the derogation of codes, the composition of melancholy poetry, and the cultivation of the elegiac modes. While reading in his copy of the *Decline and Fall of the Roman Empire,* Jefferson had come to understand what it must have been like to see a golden time pass, and in the margin of Gibbon's book he copied out a fragment of charred poetry. "I have seen the walls of Balclutha, but they were desolate," Jefferson wrote. The "stream of Clutha was removed from it's place by the fall of the walls," and the "thistle shook there its lonely head." Why the sight of empty cisterns and exhausted wells should stimulate all our vital powers is not easy to say; but certainly the most life-enhancing vacations are those that are spent among the dead.

The imponderables of place assisted the traveler like Jefferson in his effort at regeneration. The bare southern spaces, the cup of strong coffee, curiously brewed, drunk in the drowsy town at noon, the going up through thick-pleached vineyards to the foothills where the ruins themselves lie: each had its effect on his imagination. Startled goats leap from concupiscent bowers. A gecko scampers across the warm stones into the shade of star thistles. Broken walls loom up against the sky—azure, to be sure, for in a Mediterranean spring those depths of air may be as blue as the lapis lazuli. And then it is there: scattered marble and fallen stone, scrag and stubbled rosemary bushes—and the slightest feeling of disappointment. For amid the wind and serenity the mystery remains; the questions go unanswered; the search goes on.

10

Dreams

*Were my memory [in sleep] as faithful as my reason is then
fruitful, I would never study but in my dreams; and this time
also would I chuse for my devotions; but our grosser memories
have then so little hold of our abstracted understandings, that
they forget the story, and can only relate to our awaked souls,
a confused and broken tale of that that hath passed. . . . We
term sleep a death, and yet it is waking that kills us, and destroys those spirits that are the house of life.*

—SIR THOMAS BROWNE

IT WOULD HELP if we could see his dreams. We can't, of course. That music is fled; but Jefferson did leave us clues. What did he mean when he said,
late in life, that "I slumber without fear, and review in my dreams the visions
of antiquity"? In an 1819 letter to Nathaniel Macon of North Carolina, Jefferson suggested that his dreams were inspired, in part, by the poets and historians of antiquity. "I feel a much greater interest in knowing what has
passed two or three thousand years ago," he told Macon, "than in what is

now passing. I read nothing, therefore, but of the heroes of Troy, of the wars of Lacedæmon [Sparta] and Athens, of Pompey and Cæsar." To John Adams, Jefferson was blunter. "I have given up newspapers," he wrote to Adams in 1812, "in exchange for Tacitus and Thucydides."

The eighteenth-century searchers who looked to Mediterranean antiquity for moral courage are sometimes criticized for sentimentalizing ancient history, for finding in the Greek and Roman past so much smooth, sunlit marble and clean-fashioned civic art—"sweetness and light," as Jonathan Swift had it. And yet Jefferson, in his letter to Macon, confessed that he was drawn not to the serene qualities of ancient life but to its violence.

The Trojan War—Homer's theme, and Virgil's—was always marvelous to him, and he found the subsequent civil wars of antiquity at least as enthralling. The Peloponnesian War, between Athens and Sparta (Jefferson's "Lacedæmon") in the fifth century B.C. was as ugly a cousin-bred conflict as any—the self-murder of Greece, its ruins forever preserved in the blackened marble of Thucydides' war history. Yet Jefferson delighted in the smoking devastation. Nor were his tastes unusual: his generation was as drawn to the dark-directed dreams of antiquity as it was to the sweetness and the light. Like his fellow traveler Goethe—beguiled by the story of Iphigenia, the virgin laid out for sacrifice on Artemis's altar—Jefferson knew that there was blood on the ancient marble.

At the beginning of April 1787, he reached the port of Marseilles. This was the old Greek town of Massilia, now the second city of France. His mood was one of exultation. "My journey from Paris to this place," Jefferson wrote his philosopher friend Chastellux from Marseilles on April 4, "has been a continued feast of new objects, and new ideas."

He found lodgings in the Hôtel des Princes, on the Place Royale. It was, he said, a "tolerably good" inn. There were well-kept rooms, an excellent table, a service *avec goût et promptitude,* tasteful and quick. Then he set out to explore the city, in its great amphitheater of hills—the soft distances; the light floating feel of the public spaces; the buffo clowning of the people, the vocal caress of their street music. He made his way to the marketplace, where he discovered hundreds of "market-women," all "brawling, squabbling, and jabbering Patois." Like the souks of North Africa today, the eighteenth-century marketplace was a chaos of odor and activity. There were rope makers and soap boilers, tallow chandlers and Smyrna-cotton dyers, sewers of sailcloth and tanners of Spanish leather. Ships arrived laden with goods. Feluccas from Nice and Leghorn brought apples, chestnuts, oranges, and sardines; barks from Genoa came laden with flowers, onions, and flax. Jefferson, scouring about the market stalls, noted the prices of "cacao" (cocoa), coffee, and cotton; after making inquiries, he learned that thirty-two American ships had put in at the port since the end of the Revolutionary struggle.

A warm beaker of the south, to be sure; but for the northerner there is always a tincture of the sinister in the carnival; he feels the force of its Petronian punch.* The *carne vale* is, literally, a farewell to flesh, a remnant of the pagan idolatry. The Church tolerated—uneasily—the fertility magic of the carnival on condition that the lascivious mirth be expiated during the Lenten fast. It may be that such ecstasy can only be redeemed by a suffering god, or washed with tragical mops. So potent was the frenzy of the Dionysian cult that the Athenians were obliged to develop the tragic drama to mitigate its ferocity. The Greeks beseeched orderly Apollo to preserve them from "that horrible mixture of sensuality and cruelty" that is the "real witches' brew," and the secret imagination of the Mediterranean city. In 186 B.C. the Roman Senate passed a decree banning the Italian version of the Dionysian revels, the Bacchanalia. Never was legislative act more futile; not even the Senate can abolish sex, or the seasons.

Twenty centuries elapsed before Jefferson set foot in the old Roman fleshpots. The Romantic poets were about to pronounce the "mad pursuit" of the pagan cults an energy indestructible. Those poets went to the Mediterranean to involve themselves directly in the residue, in "Dance, and Provençal song, and sunburnt mirth." As a rule they beached their funeral pyres there. Jefferson, who visited the Mediterranean three decades before the corpse of Shelley was burnt upon the beach near Leghorn, and Keats expired of a consumptive fever in Rome, was more careful. He might amuse himself with a dreamy recantation of the shrieks and timbrelled anthems of the old rites, but he had no desire to be himself the oblation that the pale-eyed priest offered up in his temple.

Still he was always a good tourist, and he dutifully tasted what remained of the witches' brew, the dregs of the vintage. A quasi-erotic violence

---

*There is a tradition that Petronius, the voluptuary author of the *Satyricon* and the *elegantiae arbiter*—arbiter of elegance—in the court of Nero, was a native of Provence. He was an erudite student of all the forms of Mediterranean dissipation. See Tacitus, *Annals*, 16.18.

(*crudelis Amor,* cruel love) was always part of the old Italian comedy. Jefferson saw the comedy performed at Paris, of course, and possibly in Marseilles itself. He was much taken, he said, with the beauty of an actress, "young and handsome," who appeared in "the Spectacles" at Aix and Marseilles. Hers was not, he observed, "a legitimate Graecian beauty," such a beauty as the Asiatic Greeks who originally settled this coast possessed. As with all "fabricated wares," Jefferson said, the actress's good looks were "sophisticated with foreign mixture." The Italian comedies were themselves "fabricated wares." The hero of the comedies, Arlequin—Arlecchino—descends from a pagan demon spirit who, with his retinue of ribald horsemen, rode through the nightmares of the Middle Ages. The modern comic troupes—the Gelosi, the Desiosi, the Uniti—preserved a faint memory of the medieval pageants, and an older flavor of the masked Atellan farces that amused the theatergoers of Roman Italy. Such was the lineage of the players; but their material came directly from the music of Mediterranean life. The escapades of Pantalone and Dottore Graziano, of Scaramouche and Punchinello (Punch), were, Goethe saw, only comic forgeries of the everyday violence of a southern city. It was the music that Jefferson heard now, in the streets of Marseilles, in the cries of the flower women who hawked their narcissuses and hyacinths in the rue de Rome; in the airs of the organ-grinders who led their leashed marmoset monkeys about the Place Royale; in the stinking cries of the fishwives, or *poissardes,* who washed the tuna from Saint-Tropez.

The man who listened now, in a southern port, to Mediterranean madrigals was not himself in any abnormal degree a violent man. The *threat* of violence, Jefferson knew, was usually enough. The Count de Volney, visiting Monticello, was startled to find that his host, when he went to inspect the fields, carried with him a *fouet,* a small whip: Jefferson brandished the device at indolent slaves. Once when he and Patsy were being ferried across a river, the boatmen fell to quarreling, and the barge drifted toward the rapids. Patsy recalled how her father, his "face like a lion," told the ferrymen "in tones of thunder" to row "for their lives or he would pitch them into the stream." But even these threats of violence were exceptional behavior for him; more often he shrank from physical confrontation. He once exploded in wrath when his valet, Jupiter, failed to carry out an order with sufficient alacrity; Jefferson rebuked the slave "in tones which neither he nor the terrified bystanders ever forgot." But although he did not hesitate to deal violently with his slaves, he preferred to do so from a distance. He ordered *others* to see to it that a runaway slave was "severely flogged in the presence of his old companions," then kept in irons in a "jail."

Peaceful as his conduct (generally) was, Jefferson never deceived himself about the place of violence in the world. The processes of nature itself were violent. When in the famous passage in the Declaration of Independence he bowed reverently before "the laws of nature and of nature's God," he was not celebrating a purely benign force, the rational clockmaker of so many eighteenth-century deist daydreams. Nature, he knew, smiled upon slaughter: it used disease as a means of population control: it sanctioned the most insupportable kinds of cruelty. Nature in action was brutal—often fruitfully, sometimes beautifully so—but brutal all the same.

The livid claw that tore through the biological world had, Jefferson believed, sunk as deeply into political life. Political violence, he said, was as natural as the weather. "I hold it," he told James Madison a few weeks before he set out for Provence, "that a little rebellion now and then is a good thing, and as necessary in the political world as storms in the physical." He had himself lived through the violence of war and revolution. In the struggle to vindicate American liberty, blood had been spilled, men had died, corpses had piled up. Jefferson had, in his own person, been hunted like an animal by British dragoons. He had run for his life when Benedict Arnold sacked Richmond; some people said that during his flight he spent a night hiding in terror in a barn. (Jefferson himself was always silent on the matter.) Later, Lord Cornwallis tried to hunt him down, and organized a little raid on Monticello.

Jefferson outwitted his predators. But a man who has once been hunted does not easily forget the experience, and the rebel whom the British had chased later developed theories to explain the place of violence in the world. "A war between Russia and Turkey," Jefferson wrote, "is like the battle of the kite and the snake. Whichever destroys the other, leaves a destroyer less for the world." This "pugnacious humor of mankind," he said, "seems to be the law of his nature, one of the obstacles to too great multiplication provided in the mechanism of the Universe." Jefferson connected this propensity to slaughter to the erotic competition for life, with lust hard by hate in the struggle to survive and reproduce. "The cocks of the henyard," he said, "kill one another up. Boars, bulls, rams do the same. And the horse, in his wild state, kills all the young males, until worn down with age and war, some vigorous youth kills him, and takes to himself the Haram of females."

But Jefferson's theory of a "mechanism" designed to prevent "too great multiplication" in the universe is too neat, too clean, too reasonable to do justice to the savagery he himself had seen and felt. His clockwork explanations, so calm, so reasonable, so detached, do not touch the great shadowed questions of existence: why we are born, and how we grow; why we are compelled to make things, and through reproduction to perpetuate life; why we strive with one another; why we suffer and decay, and eventually die. Neither the rationalist nor the materialist theories of the Enlightenment reached the heart of these mysteries, nor could they explain why men should feel such sadness when they behold the violent processes at work in the universe, even in those cases where the violence is connected, as it sometimes is, to life's creative flowerings. We remember the confession of anguish that underlay his question to John Adams: "I have often wondered for what good end the sensations of Grief could be intended." He would, during the course of his life, watch five of his six children precede him to the grave. He had, half a decade before he arrived in Marseilles, watched an illness connected with childbirth torture and at last destroy his young wife. His enlightened theories were unable to account for the feelings which these losses provoked in him. They did not even give him an adequate means of acknowledging the incomprehensibility of the horror.

It is sometimes said that savants like Jefferson turned to the art of the Greeks and Romans because they found in the classical civilizations an aesthetic vocabulary commensurate with the severe and rational geometry of their enlightened ideals. In fact, Jefferson turned to the classical peoples precisely when his enlightened oracles failed him, and left him unreconciled to the terrors of life. He found, in the archaic poetry of the Mediterranean, conceits that could touch aspects of his existence beyond the reach of reason and common sense.

The primitive rituals and blood-soaked poetry of the ancients intrigued the man who now toured the streets of Marseilles, and images of the ferocious piety of antiquity crept into Jefferson's architecture. At the beginning of the eighteenth century, Palladio was still the reigning architectural presence. This architect who worked his art in the Italian Veneto had, in the sixteenth century, developed a new style of architecture, more faithful to the Roman precedents than the work of earlier Renaissance architects. As a young man

Jefferson turned to Palladio's work for a model; he originally intended Monticello to be a Palladian villa. During his residence in Paris, however, Jefferson discovered a fresher approach to classical architecture, an approach to building that was in some ways closer to the ancient models than Palladio's. Historians of art call it neoclassical architecture, a style whose practitioners could not be content with secondhand catalogs of engravings. They went directly to the ruins themselves.

The new generation of architects visited Roman sites at Herculaneum and Pompeii, which were just beginning to be excavated. They went to the Roman emperor Hadrian's villa at Tivoli (the ancient Tibur) in the Roman *compagna*. (Jefferson may have modeled the subterranean passageways of Monticello on the cryptoporticus of this villa.) They traveled to Tarquinia (Cornetu) and Chiusi, in the old country of Etruria, a strange and visionary land of tombs and necropolises (cities of the dead), where mysterious cults of the afterlife had once been tended by a morbid priesthood. Here Etruscan antiquities were coming to be unearthed; blackened bronze and carved sarcophagi; terra-cotta urns, rooted, like yew trees, in the graves and dreamless heads of the dead; shoveled up now into the bright air of an enlightened age, relics that proclaimed the Tuscan fascination with death and all that lies beyond it.

It was not easy work. In the hot sun, and during moonlit nights, the architects sketched the ruined temples of the confiscated gods. They slept in squalid inns, or among the ruins themselves, and in the broken splendor revised their drawings by the light of little campfires. Many of the sites were infested with mosquitoes and malaria. Grave robbers lurked among the tombs. Still they continued to draw, in spite of the dangers, and must have trusted in the rigor and fidelity of their artistic sacrifices to propitiate whatever unsavory spirits still lingered amid the dust and the cypress trees. For the most part these excursions were limited to Italy and southern France; but some of the neoclassical architects went farther afield, to Greece and even to the Syrian desert. James "Athenian" Stuart and Nicholas Revett went to Athens, where their research resulted in the publication of *The Antiquities of Athens,* volumes that introduced modern Europe to the architecture of ancient Greece. An Englishman named Robert Wood journeyed to the sun temples of Palmyra, in Syria, and to Baalbek (Heliopolis), in present-day Lebanon. Jefferson kept up with accounts of these expeditions; he acquired, for his library, Revett and Stuart's book on Athens, as well as Wood's *Ruins of Balbec, otherwise Heliopolis in Coelosyria.*

His friend Clérisseau was able to give him more information about the new techniques. The French artist was one of those complicated characters who seem to be at home only in the south. After emigrating, as a young man, to Rome, Clérisseau had there experienced a crisis of faith. As a pensionnaire of the French Academy, he had got into trouble when he refused to sign the certificate stating that he had received the Eucharist at Easter, as required by the academical statutes. A few months later, in December 1753, Clérisseau was taken ill with a fever; for a time he lay close to death. Eventually he recovered; and, rising from his sickbed, he discovered a new sense of vocation. He would be a psalmist of the southern temples, and devote the rest of his life to drawing ancient ruins.

Robert Adam, then a young architect from Scotland, always remembered his first encounter with Clérisseau. Adam was touring Italy when one day an acquaintance took him to see the transplanted Frenchman. Like many votaries of beauty, Clérisseau was himself physically ugly. His lips were misshapen, like Socrates'. Adam described him as a curious "creature" and treated him as an eccentric pet. "Mr. Wilton," Adam wrote, "introduced me to a most valuable and ingenious creature called Clérisseau, who draws ruins in Architecture to perfection." In the summer of 1757, Clérisseau and Adam made the long journey through Venice to Dalmatia, in what is now Croatia. At Spalato (the modern Split), on the Adriatic coast, the two men spent five hot weeks excavating the ruins of the Roman emperor Diocletian's palace.

Clérisseau and Adam's record of their fieldwork—published by Adam (who unfairly took most of the credit for it) in 1764—helped to complete the aesthetic education of the eighteenth-century searchers. Gibbon praised their "magnificent work" in the pages of the *Decline and Fall;* for the ambitious Adam, who wished, he said, to "make a great puff conducive to raising all at once one's name and character," the project yielded not only a piece of revolutionary scholarship but the beginnings of a reputation as well. In coming up with his designs for private villas, the great Palladio had looked to Roman temples for models; he knew very little about Roman houses. Clérisseau and Adam made good the defect in intelligence; their work revealed that the ancient peoples, in the construction of their villas, had routinely broken rules laid down by such authorities as Vitruvius. The lesson to be drawn was clear: if the ancients could break the rules in their houses, so could the moderns.

His firsthand experience, in Provence, of real Roman architecture proved even more liberating for Jefferson than had the emancipating labors of Clérisseau and Adam. His firsthand knowledge of ancient architecture enabled him to go beyond the apprenticeship of imitation, a servile devotion to manuals like Palladio's *Four Books of Architecture*. No longer dependent on merely bookish stimulants, Jefferson, in his post-Provence designs, showed a new self-possession in his art, and a new assurance in his handling of the classic forms. He was prepared to do things that no teacher could teach him; Monticello conforms neither to strict Palladian nor strict Roman (Vitruvian) canons. Like the University of Virginia, with which it shares an identity of style, Monticello makes its own laws.

But willing though the mature Jefferson was to discard precedent whenever it suited his purposes, he did not always do so; and in one area he adhered to the ancient precedents with a nearly absolute fidelity. When, nearly a decade after his visit to Marseilles, Jefferson was again able to devote time, and passion, to Monticello, he incorporated, in the soapy-smooth plasterwork of its friezes and moldings, an astonishing collection of Mediterranean dream creatures, the bestiary of nightmare. The entrance hall at Monticello is guarded by griffins; erotic demons preside in the master's bedroom; in the north piazza apotropaic Apollo's faces, forever luminous, give the evil eye to the disordered darkness of the north. In books of engravings, Jefferson found images, too, of the ancient blood sacrifice, copied directly from the ruined Roman temples. He faithfully reproduced this imagery in the decoration of the parlor—the principal room—of Monticello.

It is all there, in the band of neoclassical vanilla ice cream that runs along the upper wall of the chamber (as well as beneath the fireplace mantel and above the doors and French windows). The tools of ritual slaughter look just as they do in the temple of the emperors Vespasian and Titus in the Roman Forum, a monument not unlike those we Americans have raised to Jefferson himself and the other deified presidents in Washington. (An engraving, by Piranesi, of three columns and a fragment of entablature from this temple appears above the epigraph of this chapter.) There is the skull of the slaughtered bull, entwined with ribbons of white or scarlet wool; before it was led to its death, its horns would have been gilded with gold. There is the knife, and the ax; as the bull or the pig, the goat or the sheep, was led in procession to the altar, a young virgin would have gone before, perhaps concealing the knife in the basket of barley or cakes that she carried on her head. There is the urceus, or pitcher of water, depicted, in the Monticello frieze, in a tipping position, as though being emptied; for the water it contained would have been poured over the hands of each of the participants in the sacrifice, to cleanse them for the sanguinary meal. There is the aspergillum, the device used to sprinkle consecrated water on the altar and over the heads of those offering up the bleeding flesh. There is the bowl, or patera; it would have been filled with water, and set before the victim. The animal would then have bent its head to drink; by so bowing, the beast was understood to consent to its slaughter. With arms raised, the mysterious priest—in his white cap, or *albogalerus*—would have recited the invocation, the prayer, the wish, and the vow; with the knife he would have cut hairs from the animal's head and cast them into the fire.

The slaughter would then have followed, undertaken by a butcher known as the *victimarius*. The knife would have been used to dispatch a fatling; when an ox was sacrificed, the ax was necessary. Any women present would have been obliged to shriek—a high, shrill, sacrificial cry—as the ax fell. The animal's blood would have been collected in the bowl and used to stain the altar; the entrails would have been roasted, then eaten by the participants. Whereupon a great feast would have begun, with much boiling and roasting of flesh.

Jefferson—the man who believed that the tree of liberty could be kept fertile only through the shedding of blood—decorated his living room with the utensils of primitive slaughter. Like the blood-and-vegetation poetry of Virgil's *Georgics,* the primitive relics spoke to him, knives and all. When the axes fell, and the blood flowed, the drippings nourished all those places in the master's soul that reason and Enlightenment could not refresh.

Voices

*An evil-looking Ethiopian with a horribly eager look on him
came up to me in a dream and said, "You are mine."*

—THE CONFESSION OF PETRONAS, C. 863 A.D.

IN MARSEILLES he changed his plans. He had intended to head west out of
Marseilles, toward Montpellier and Béziers. But after poking around the rice
market in Marseilles, he decided to go east, toward Italy, instead. He had a
sound business reason for doing so: he had heard tales of a marvelous rice-
cleaning machine in use in the Piedmont. Perhaps the machine could be
replicated in America; he would have to investigate. Later he would confess
a different motivation: He wanted, he told Maria Cosway, "a peep . . . into
Elysium."

Five years before, when his wife died, Jefferson had no thought of Elysium, those blessed isles, which, though they are said to lie beyond the baths
of Western stars, two peninsulas, the Italian and the Balkan (or Greek), seem
in places to touch. He had thought then of another Mediterranean afterlife,
the underworld of Hades. Before he laid Martha in her grave, Jefferson had

turned to Homer, and he had copied out, in Greek, Achilles' words in the *Iliad:* "Nay if even in the house of Hades the dead forget their dead, yet will I even there be mindful of my dear comrade."

"Heu! quanto minus est cum reliquis versari quam tui memmenisse!" (Oh—to live with them is far less sweet than to remember thee!) Jefferson, while still a young man, came across these words in the course of his reading. An English poet he admired had engraved them on a funerary urn erected, in his Shropshire garden, in memory of a departed niece. Jefferson turned to the words in composing his own *éloge* for a lamented relation, his sister Jane, who died in 1765. The words became, in time, a family touchstone, an emblem of the Jeffersons' efforts to preserve the memory of their dead. After her father's death, Patsy inscribed the words on the first page of his commonplace book. It is true that two years after he returned from his journey to the Mediterranean, Jefferson, in Paris, told James Madison that the "earth belongs in usufruct to the living." The dead, he said, "have neither powers nor rights over it." The earth might belong to the living, but not the soul, at least not all of it. Portions of it, Jefferson knew, were consecrated to the memory of the dead, those departed devisees who retain a psychic property in our minds. They hold their ghostly estates, not as the usufructary does, in mere transcient squattage, but in fee simple absolute.

Jefferson would later liken his own dead to "seraphs," spirits who, though long "shrouded," he could never begin to forget. In the secret drawer in which he preserved his souvenirs of his wife, he kept, too, remembrances of "each of his living and lost children." There were words of "endearment, written in his own hand, upon the envelopes of the little mementos." The keepsakes were "arranged in perfect order, and the envelopes indicated their frequent handling."

If you have ever dreamed of a dead friend, you will understand something of the spirit culture of the ancient Mediterranean. In *La cité antique,* Fustel de Coulanges wrote:

> The dead were held [in the ancient Mediterranean] to be sacred beings. . . . [A] deceased person, on being neglected, became a malignant spirit; one who was honored became, on the other hand, a tutelary deity. . . . These human souls deified by death were what the Greeks called *demons,* or *heroes.* The Latins gave them the name *Lares, Manes, Genii.* "Our ancestors believed," says Apuleius, "that the Manes, when they were malignant, were to be called *larvæ;* they called them *Lares* when they were benevolent and propitious." Else-

where we read, "Genius and Lar is the same being; so our ancestors believed." And in Cicero, "Those that the Greeks called demons we call Lares."

Many of the ancient Greeks and Romans whose literature Jefferson read so attentively conceived of their mental life as an elaborate ghost story, one in which demons, spirits, genii (or *manes*), acted as tutelary forces that could either cripple a man's productive power or enable him to channel it more effectively. A demon, or "genius," according to some of these Mediterranean schemes (there were many), was a spirit allotted to a man at birth, a sprite or ghost that helped to determine the man's character and fortune. Among the Romans the genius was associated, too, with a power of creating or begetting, in particular the power that enables a man to beget children on the *lectus genialis,* the marriage bed. There were good demons (the *eudaimon*) and bad ones (the *kakodaimon* or *dysdaimon*). Such spirits might be cunning, discontented beings (the "evil genii" who Plutarch said disturbed men "with fears, and distressed their virtue") or beneficent, auspicious ones, better angels from whom men might derive inspiration and prudent counsel. A man, too, might be attended by more than one spirit; he might be allotted, for example, both a good spirit and a bad one (his "better" and his "worser"—or "evil"—genius).

Among the most celebrated of these demons was that of the fifth-century B.C. Athenian philosopher Socrates, who described his *daimonion* (literally, "divine oracle" or "sign") as a signal "I have had ever since I was a child," "a voice which comes to me and always forbids me to do something which I am going to do, but never commands me to do anything." Socrates' demon fascinated Jefferson. "What did Socrates mean by his Dæmon?" he asked John Adams in a letter. He rejected supernatural interpretations of Socrates' inner voice; such interpretations were "nonsense" or *"charlatanerie."* But he allowed that a man of great intellectual power "might readily mistake the coruscations of his own fine genius for inspiration of an higher order." Such a belief, he said, carried "no more personal imputation, than the belief of Socrates that he was under the care and admonitions of a guardian Dæmon." Socrates "was too wise to believe," Jefferson maintained, "and too honest to pretend that he had real and familiar converse with a superior and invisible being." The promptings of Socrates' demon, he concluded, were the "suggestions of his conscience," soul-whisperings that the philosopher interpreted as "revelations, or inspirations" bestowed, "on important occasions," by a "special superintending providence."

As with Socrates, so with Christ. In a letter to Dr. Joseph Priestley, Jefferson outlined an essay he hoped one day to write; in it he would take "a general view of the moral doctrines of the most remarkable of the antient philosophers." He intended, he said, to cover "Pythagoras, Epicurus, Epictetus, Socrates, Cicero, Seneca, Antoninus [Marcus Aurelius]." He would then "proceed to a view of the life, character, & doctrines of Jesus," but would "purposely omit the question of his divinity, & even his inspiration." What others took for divinity or divine inspiration in Christ, Jefferson attributed to his *"human* excellence." Like Socrates' demon, Jesus' inspiration could be explained in secular terms.

The brilliant or prophetic "forebodings" of the most inspired philosophers and poets were, Jefferson believed, not the supernatural inspirations of men working *syn daimoni,* in fruitful partnership with their demons; their high thoughts were rather the product of their own minds, consciences, and imaginations. Those credulous souls who insisted on attributing to divine or supernatural causes what was in reality a purely human genius were guilty of what Jefferson called "Dæmonism." Such misguided enthusiasts transformed the finer conceits of the human imagination into idols, false gods before which they fell in prostrate worship. Calvinism, Jefferson maintained, was a form of "Dæmonism," and so even was the Federalism of political opponents like Alexander Hamilton. "When General Washington was withdrawn," Jefferson wrote, "the energumeni of royalism . . . mounted on the car of State." A curious choice of words—in Greek the word *energumen* refers to a person possessed by a demon. Yet even as he disparaged the idea of supernatural inspiration, Jefferson continued to believe that the wisest men—and even many ordinary souls—*did* hear inner voices. These voices comprehended both what he called the "suggestions" of "conscience" or "reason" and the "coruscations" (flashes) of individual "genius." The Latin word *genius,* with all its faded mystic implications, was for Jefferson a shorthand way of describing the more exalted of these inner voices. The classical idea of the genius spirit became for him a metaphor for the complicated processes of human inspiration; beneath the fireplace mantel in his bedroom study at Monticello, in between the swags of vegetation, he placed the cherubic figure of a little demon boy, one who watched over his own creative efforts.

Scratch the surface of a modern idea, and you often find a tissue of decaying mysticism. Long before Jefferson designed his bedroom fireplace at Monticello, Renaissance thinkers began a makeover of the old Mediterranean notion of the demon or genius spirit; they worked to turn the supernatural concept into a secular one. The master of Monticello drew on the improvisations of Renaissance sages, thinkers who were themselves immersed in the *mystères littéraires,* the esoteric lore that derived from the spirit culture and mystery cults of Mediterranean antiquity. These philosophers no longer thought of the "genius" that incites men to creative achievement as an actual demigod or ghost of a dead soul. They instead turned the concept into a metaphor for the way men tap the mysterious powers lodged within the ragged entrails of their own brains. (A number of the ancient thinkers had been moving in a similar direction; the Greek philosopher Heracleitus, for example, taught that "character is for man his daimon.")

America's prime example of a Renaissance man—*l'uomo universale*—Jefferson carefully studied Renaissance methods. Those masters showed him to nurture the psychic growths that the ancients knew as spirits or demons. The universal man of the Renaissance was a manipulator, not only of various skills and talents but of various personas as well. The man of genius learned to carry on a conversation—a dialogue—with the different voices he found within himself. Thus Machiavelli, who made fun of the notion of literal demonic possession, undertook a series of imaginary nocturnal conversations with the dead. Montaigne, in his introspective essays (Jefferson read them in French) conceived of his dialogues with himself as an extended conversation with a departed soul, and he freely acknowledged the demonic element in his own mind. "The daemon of Socrates," Montaigne wrote,

> was perhaps a certain impulse of the will that came to him without awaiting the advice of his reason. In a well-purified soul such as his, prepared by a continual exercise of wisdom and virtue, it is likely that these inclinations, although instinctive and undigested, were always important and worth following. *Everyone feels within himself some likeness of such stirrings of a prompt, vehement, and accidental opinion.* It is my business to give them some authority, since I give so little to our wisdom. And I have had some as weak in reason as violent in persuasiveness—or in dissuasiveness, as was more ordinary in Socrates—by which I let myself be carried away so usefully and fortunately that they might be judged to have in them something of divine inspiration.

Shakespeare, too, drew on the idea of the demonic ghost (Brutus "in council" with his "genius"; the ghost of Hamlet's father; the bloody cherub who appears before Macbeth; the demon of Mark Antony, "noble, courageous, high, unmatchable," whose spirit yet droops before the genius of Octavian; the rival poet in the sonnets, "by spirits taught to write / Above a mortal pitch"). More crucially, Shakespeare took the conversation with the demon spirit and secularized it in the soliloquy, a form that enabled the audience actually to hear a soul discoursing with itself.

The nineteenth-century moralist John Ruskin might have exaggerated when he claimed that the Renaissance masters were victims of "demoniacal possession," perverse characters who developed a "science of the sepulcher." But Ruskin rightly realized that the Renaissance masters had creatively revised an older concept. If they did not actually converse with dead spirits, they *pretended* to converse with them and, in doing so, found a way to talk to themselves. By the eighteenth century, language had caught up with the new way of thinking. *Genius* took on its modern meaning: intellectual or spiritual power of an exalted type, coupled with a high imaginative creativity. Jefferson, for example, spoke of those qualities of "lively imagination, usually called genius." But the *methods* of genius had been understood long before this verbal adjustment took place.

Jefferson, with his involutions of character, his dark privacies, his idiosyncrasies of style, his geometric joys—the whole masquing subterfuge of his guises and personas—owed much to these Renaissance refinements of a classical idea. Scholars have long been aware of Jefferson's voices and personas; the historian Joseph Ellis, in his book on Jefferson, described the "mysterious mechanisms inside" the man that enabled his "different voices" to coexist. What scholars have failed to appreciate is the way Jefferson's efforts to marshal his different voices drew on the older techniques.

A careful student of the literature of both antiquity and the Renaissance, Jefferson learned how to attend to his *eudaimonia,* the good voices he encountered within himself. He learned how to talk to himself or, rather, to his various selves. The "voice of conscience" to which he sometimes referred was one of these voices. "If ever you are about to say any thing amiss or to do any thing wrong," he advised his daughter Patsy, consider before hand. You will feel something within you which will tell you it is wrong and ought not to be said or done: this is your conscience, and be sure to obey it. Our maker has given us all, this faithful internal Monitor, and if you always obey it, you will always be prepared for the end of the world: or for a much more certain event which is death.

But there were other voices, other personas, as well, like the "hypochondriac Englishman" he fashioned in Nîmes, the sentimental mask he wore before Mrs. Cosway, the good Roman he pretended to be in his letters to Madame de Tessé. Later in his life the guises would grow more elaborate, the music of his voices more complex. Jefferson's willingness, in late middle age, to give expression to new voices helps to explain the successes of the autumn and winter periods of his life. One of the most powerful of his voices, as we shall see, would emerge only in the 1790s—the decade in which he turned fifty—in the course of his conflict with Alexander Hamilton and the Federalist Party. The emergence of this voice and the assumption by Jefferson of the role of persecuted prophet of democracy would change the course of American history.

"The Spot at Which *I* Turned *My* Back"

All forms that perish other forms supply,
(By turns we catch the vital breath, and die).

—Pope

LIFE IS SO arranged that we have only so much time, and so much energy, to give even to the truest oracles, and Jefferson's peep into Elysium must be brief. He left Marseilles, saw the *bastides*—the country houses—of the well-to-do; and went up, through the pine valleys and limestone clefts, to the mountain villages. Here was a landscape of dilapidated southern farms—sheep and soiled chickens, a sow full to farrowing, a billygoat tied to the stob. The hill peasants who worked the terraced vineyards of Cuges-les-Pins and le Beausset were rough people with a "wild blaze" in their eyes. They were a remnant of what the Romans called Gallia Comata (the Gaul of the Longhairs), the fierce and warlike Gauls who refused to acquiesce in the gentle life of Gallia Togata (the Gaul of the togas, the Romanized Gaul of the Maison Carrée). "Es un Arabe," the city dwellers of the coast would say of one of these wind-bitten mountain characters. The hill peasants would shoot a handful of small shot at you if you took a single fig from one of their trees, but "for a friendly word" they would "give you a handful."

He went on in the sunlight, passing through villages bleached by the sun, washed in the colors of the Mediterranean palette: white, pink, peach, robin's-egg blue, villages in which the classical geometry of the south was everywhere evident, in the forms of triangle, rectangle, and square, in the love of line, and of order. Wherever he looked, he saw "hedges of pomegranates, sweetbrier and broom," and there was a "great deal of thyme growing wild" against a background of "barren" mountains. The vegetation changed as he came down from the hills: the pines yielded to stands of palms and masses of Arabian jasmine. The appearance, in Ollioules, of his first oranges confirmed in him a feeling of "rapture." This fruit—the "golden apples" of the Romans, nurslings of the Hesperian garden—was here cultivated only in walled gardens and in the most protected valleys, where it was sheltered from the master wind from the north, the mistral.

In Provence he was never tired, he said, of "rambling through fields and farms, examining the culture and cultivators." This "curiosity," he said, "makes some take me to be a fool, and others to be much wiser than I am." Hyères surprised him, with its groves of oranges, olives, and mulberries stretching to the sea. This was the oldest of the Mediterranean resorts for ailing northerners, and though its plains were open, on the south, to the Mediterranean, they were bounded by mountains to the northeast and west. Far removed from *cette fatigue du nord*, Jefferson studied the southern vegetation—the pomegranate, the almond, the aloe, the caper. There were poplars in pale spring green, and the palm trees, he said, stood "20. or 30.f. high." He saw the château of Giens a way off in the sea; farther out lay the visionary islands of Hyères, nurseries of prophecy, overgrown with lavender and strawberries.

He went north for a time, through Cuers, le Luc, and le Muy, and at last he reached Fréjus. This was the old Roman Forum Julii, where Julius Caesar's heir Octavian, afterward Augustus, had settled veterans of his legions. Today the amphitheater that diverted the emperor's graying thugs is used for bullfights, those entertainments which, in a later age, filled the void that opened up when the old gladiatorial contests ceased. But if truth be told, the ruins here are dull, and were long ago stripped of ornament and crafted decoration. Yet what remains is set in a lush vegetation, with curiosities of wall and lane, and cats' lairs, and intricate gardens.

Nice, or Nizza, was something new in his experience. It was a city of baroque, its facades gorgeously wrought in yellow, rose, and Sardinian red, the shutters in lime green and salt-stained blue. The old language of the place, the Nissart, a dialect cousin-german to those of Provence, can even now, it is said, be heard in the streets. Strange flowers, fruit of Africa, climb the walls; and negligent musk roses overspill the balconies.

Sheltered by the Alps, Nice was already, in the eighteenth century, a destination for the northern beau monde. The climate, Jefferson said, was "quite as superb as it has been represented," and he was amused by the city's "gay and dissipated society." The city had much to offer the idle rich of that day. There was a theater, a reading room, and a circulating library. And gambling, too; Nice, a free city, was celebrated for what Casanova called its "high play." For a time the French consul there, M. Jullien, operated a casino in his own house and acted as the banker. Whether Jefferson laid bets in a casino does not appear.

Then he ascended the heights of Cimiez (Cemenelum), the site, successively, of a Ligurian town, a Roman city, and a Christian bishopric. From the high places of this hill, the Bay of Angels is visible to the south and, to the north and east, the massive foothills of the Alps. The roses here, cultivated by Franciscan monks, grow so large, and so fragrant, that Anacreon, in his ode, seems only to tell the truth when he says that the sky spirits themselves are in love with them. The roses love the Sun, and eat his rays for food; perhaps the Greek poet was right, and the star loves the roses, and likes to be eaten by them.

Only from the voluptuous Anacreon, one of his favorite poets, would Jefferson have tolerated so unscientific a thought. One might almost believe, when one encounters the master of Monticello in his most matter-of-fact moods, that he had succeeded in liberating himself from all the forms of superstitious faith, and that he had no feeling for the unseen grace that mysteriously moves, and changes, the world, and everything in it. One might believe this, had one not been inside his house, and seen those grim idols smeared with an imaginary blood.

The ancient poets liked to tell stories of nymphs that became trees and gods that converted themselves into swans—stories not literally true, perhaps, but true to the spirit of life and faithful to all its vegetable, chemical,

2. *Patsy Randolph as a young lady, by Joseph Boze.* After her mother's death, she was her father's "constant companion," and the "solitary witness to many a violent burst of grief." (Photograph by Will Brown; courtesy of the United States Department of State)

3. *Abigail Adams, by Benjamin Blyth.* "The good things of this life," Jefferson told her, "are scattered so sparingly in our way that we must glean them up as we go." (Courtesy of the Massachusetts Historical Society)

1. *Jefferson as President, by Gilbert Stuart, 1805.* He could submit to the grim regimes of business for a time, but eventually he must have leisure to be again an artist and a farmer.

4. *Maria Cosway, by Richard Cosway.* Jefferson's dalliance with Mrs. Cosway was the perfection of a sentimental affair; all the ingredients of success—beauty, passion, even insuperable obstacles to love—were present. (Courtesy of the Cincinnati Art Museum)

5. *Jefferson in 1786, by Mather Brown.* Through his mother he was a Randolph, and no scion of such a house could be undisturbed by the mental wreckage associated with it. (COURTESY OF CHARLES FRANCIS ADAMS)

6. *The Maison Carrée at Nîmes, by Hubert Robert.* On a journey to southern Europe in 1787, Jefferson rehearsed a tragedy of hypochondria and suicide in the shadow of the Roman temple. (PHOTOGRAPH BY GÉRARD BLOT, COPYRIGHT © RMN; COURTESY MUSÉE DU LOUVRE)

7. *View of the unexcavated temple of Jupiter in the Roman Forum, now identified as the temple of Vespasian and Titus, by Piranesi.* The frieze displays the utensils of the ancient blood-sacrifice. "The tree of liberty," Jefferson wrote, "must be refreshed from time to time with the blood of patriots and tyrants. It is its natural manure." (Courtesy of Istituto Nazionale per la Grafica)

8. Top: *Detail of the frieze of the temple of Vespasian and Titus, by Desgodets.* The jug, the knife, the bowl, the ax, the cap. (Courtesy of Gibson Design Associates)

Middle: *Detail of the parlor frieze at Monticello.* Like the poetry of Virgil's *Georgics*, the primitive relics spoke to him, knives and all. (Courtesy of Monticello)

Bottom: *Detail of the frieze in Jefferson's bedroom of Monticello.* A demon or "genius" was a spirit allotted to a man at birth, and was often depicted as a cherub. (Courtesy of Monticello)

9. *An early design by Jefferson of Monticello.* Not long before he composed the Declaration of Independence, Jefferson lay in idleness and ill-health at Monticello, suffering from a mysterious malady. (COURTESY OF THE MASSACHUSETTS HISTORICAL SOCIETY, THOMAS JEFFERSON ARCHITECTURAL DRAWINGS, MHS IMAGE # 1252)

10. *Monticello.* He turned the house into a temple in which every entablature, every column, every cornice—every demon-creature and dream-beast—every knife and every ax, nourished some part of his imagination. (PHOTOGRAPH BY THE AUTHOR)

11. *Alexander Hamilton, by John Trumbull, 1806.* At a dinner party in April 1791, Hamilton shocked Jefferson by declaring that Julius Caesar was the greatest man who ever lived. (COURTESY OF THE NATIONAL PORTRAIT GALLERY, SMITHSONIAN INSTITUTION)

12. *Aaron Burr, by Gilbert Stuart, circa 1794.* By some instinct of vengeance, or insight into the complicated physics of fate, Jefferson set in motion a chain of catastrophes that would humiliate and, at length, destroy the most potent of his enemies. (COURTESY OF THE NEW JERSEY HISTORICAL SOCIETY)

13. *Jefferson, by Thomas Sully, 1822.* Not merely a Whig, he was partly a Tory; not merely a philosophe, he was partly a mystic: he aimed to be a poet-educator in the Greek sense, and forged a new democratic culture for his country. (Courtesy of the West Point Museum Collections, United States Military Academy, West Point, New York)

and biological transfluxions. Jefferson probed to the root stock the savage creativity of Eros, but the rosariums of the Mediterranean bid a man go up higher. Jefferson had already an intimation of the truth that his civilization whispers to those who listen. He had already been tempted, in his *Notes on the State of Virginia,* into a little disquisition on the ladder of Eros, the soul's progress from lust to love. Love, Jefferson said, differed from lust, because love was "the peculiar *œstrum* of the poet." A subtle and curious metaphor: what Jefferson meant is that lust is transformed by the *oestrum* of poetry—its frenzied sting, what the Greeks called its "divine madness"—into the higher passion known as love. Love did not originally exist in the mind; it was an overcoming (or mending) of mind through art. Art made possible the higher form of order known as love. It supplied the techniques that enabled men to turn what Jefferson called "eager desire" into something that "kindles" not the "senses only" but the "imagination" as well. These processes changed lust into love, passion into noble architecture, bloody revolution into ordered liberty, and so on.

He abandoned his carriage in Nice and, going up into the Alps on the back of a mule, passed from flowers to frost in an instant. With thoughts of Hannibal in his head, he crossed the mountains and descended to the plains of the Po, where he found another baroque city, Turin, and a strange new wine, the Nebiule (Nebbiolo). It was, he said, "about as silky as Madeira, as astringent on the palate as Bordeaux, and as brisk as champagne." He spent a day in a dairy trying to learn how to make Parmesan cheese, but the fabled rice-husking machine, the ostensible object of his quest, proved to be a mirage.

He went south to Genoa, and at Genoa—he stopped. The deeper south beckoned; but he had gone far enough. "I turned my back," he said, "on Rome and Naples." It is one of the unanswered questions of his life why, when he had the power to do it, he did not do the thing he most wanted to do. "It was," he said, "a moment of conflict between duty which urged me to return, and inclination urging me forward." Duty prevailed.

But fate sometimes bids us go slowly, when we ourselves would hurry. He took shipping at Genoa; but the wind changed, and the felucca drifted in the sunlight. In the stinking heat he became, he said, "mortally sick." At last the boat reached the shore; it put in at Noli, on the Ligurian coast of

Italy. He rode up the cliffs on the back of a mule and collapsed in a little *al-bergo* on the precipice.

Destiny, unpersuaded that the novice had been sufficiently instructed in all her shaping arts, wreathed for him another garland of vines, and arranged for him to prolong a little his novitiate in her forms. Not willing to risk another sea voyage, Jefferson went by land instead, and followed the coast as it loped, in rock, and jutty, and gullet-depth of bay, toward France. "Sometimes on foot, sometimes on a mule," he followed the westward curve of the Gulf of Genoa. He cut through plantations of palms and lemon groves, and rested in little fishing villages cut into the sheer rock of the Apennines. Towns that later became Riviera resorts—Albenga, Alassio, Saint Remo, Bordighera—were as yet unknown to fashion. Caïques and fishing boats floated in quiet aquamarine harbors. The villagers—a farmer with his donkey, a market woman selling figs—moved slowly in the languid air, with the fainéant grace of those who have made their peace with the power of the sun.

He ate well. There were "pheasants, partridges, quails" in abundance, he said, as well as beccaficos and ortolans. "I also like to dine on Becaficas," Byron would later write, and Jefferson, too, enjoyed the taste of this bird, which, when fattened with figs and grapes, is esteemed a delicacy in the Mediterranean. The ortolan, a songbird, was served as the stuffing of a quail and renowned for the subtle flavor of its flesh. Of course there was wine as well, together with "oil, figs, oranges, and every production of the garden in every season," Jefferson said. As for the sea, he wrote, it "yields lobsters, crabs, oysters, thunny [the Latin *thunnus,* or tuna fish], sardines, anchovies, &c."

The memory of the feverish voyage from Genoa faded, and he pondered the color of the Mediterranean. He did "not remember to have seen," he said, any account of the "cause of the apparent colour of the sea." The water was "clear and colourless if taken up and viewed in a glass"—quite "remarkably so." "Yet in the mass," he said, "it assumes *by reflection* the colour of the sky or atmosphere, black, green, blue, according to the state of the weather." Among the sun-bleached walls, in the baking brilliance, the idea that works its way into the minds of many who come to this coast—the idea of imitating the rose, and perfecting one's existence on some exquisite terrace, within spray of sea—worked its way into his. "If any person wished to retire from their acquaintance," Jefferson wrote in his notebook, "to live absolutely unknown, and yet in the midst of physical enjoyments, it should be in some one of the little villages of this coast, where air, earth and water concur to offer what each has most precious." Offer, in charity, what each has most precious, for he has begun to perceive a new order in things.

PART THREE

FALL

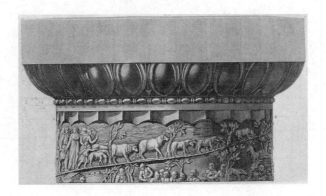

I

Fire and Hate

Before learning to love, we must learn to hate.

—John Henry Newman

He went back, by way of Bordeaux, to Paris, and by the middle of June 1787 he was again in the Hôtel de Langeac. Two years later he left France to return to America; he reached Monticello just before Christmas 1789. The days of sojourn and deliberate holiday were over; he was about to return to the forum.

He came home to America to find a letter from George Washington on his table. While he was in France, a new Constitution had been proclaimed, elections had been held, and General Washington had been installed as president of the reconstituted Republic. The president now wrote to Jefferson asking him to be his secretary of state. Jefferson hesitated to accept the invitation. He had, he said, "gloomy forebodings" about the prospect of service in the cabinet. He would prefer, he said, to return to his Paris post. But the president was not a man to be spurned. In March 1790, two weeks after his daughter Patsy married Thomas Mann Randolph in a ceremony at Monticello, Jefferson set out for New York, at that time the capital of the Republic.

He traveled north through a strange country. "We return," he said, "like foreigners, and, like them, require a considerable residence here to become Americanized." In New York itself he seems never to have breathed easily. The late-winter weather was worse than that of Paris. The society was limited. The New York merchant princes possessed something of the pride of the French aristocracy, but nothing of its charm, and Jefferson was never one to love the manners of a bourgeoisie.

Unamused in those drawing rooms, he devoted himself to business. As secretary of state Jefferson was entrusted with matters of domestic administration as well as of foreign policy, and his first task was to prepare a report on weights and measures. The philosophe in him hoped to persuade Congress to adopt a measuring system founded on the decimal. He was at work on the report when, as the spring thaw–weather set in, his head began to ache. The pain, he said, "came on every day at Sunrise," and in a "very severe" form. It "never left me till sunset." He continued, however, to labor on the report. What had "been ruminated in the day under a paroxysm of the most excruciating pain" was, he said, "committed to paper by candlelight." Only in the semidarkness were the necessary calculations made. A few days before the onset of the headache, Jefferson had his first news of Mrs. Cosway in many months. From a friend in London, he learned that Maria was "with child for the first time" and had been "extremely ill" with morning sickness.

Genuine action is always in some way a revelation of one's self, or of a part of one's self. But it was not until Jefferson entered President Washington's cabinet and began to quarrel with his colleague Alexander Hamilton that he discovered objects around which he could coil his untethered passions.

The two men soon to be enemies were most unlike each other. Both were, indeed, Whigs. But Jefferson was, in his innermost vocation, an artist; Hamilton, a warrior. Jefferson, by nature reflective, and in all his habits retiring, was still learning how to act, though he was now in the second half of his forties. Hamilton was in the deepest fibers of his being a man of action, and already he yielded the white staff of a treasury lord with supreme confidence, though he was not more than five and thirty. Jefferson, the cadet of the Randolphs, had grown up assured of place and position in the world.

Hamilton, who was born, probably out of wedlock, on a West Indian island, had had to work for all that he was, with no pillow of property on which to fall back in making his career. His wits and his charm were all that he could count on when, as a boy, he vowed to escape a sullen Caribbean destiny. That he succeeded in carrying out this vow is one proof of the master reach of his will. He came to New York and got an education—at King's College (now Columbia University). He joined the Revolutionary army and was made aide-de-camp to General Washington. He showed valor in battle, married the daughter of a Hudson River patroon, and opened a law office. More recently he had written a sheaf of *Federalist* papers, and helped in other ways to get the Constitution ratified, even though it was not the Constitution he wanted.

For all their differences, there was, in the early days, some sympathy between the two men. One day in June 1790 Jefferson, while walking to President Washington's house on Broadway, came upon Hamilton in the street. The treasury secretary, Jefferson later remembered, was "in despair" and wanted to talk. Jefferson recalled how his companion walked him "backwards & forwards before the President's door for half an hour" as he "painted pathetically" the problem the Republic confronted. The country's finances were in disarray. In his report on public credit, issued a few months before, Hamilton had argued that there was only one way to end the crisis. The government, he believed, had not only to discharge the debts it had itself incurred to pay for the Revolution, but it had, too, to assume the debts of the several states. (The state governments, Hamilton seemed to believe, could not be trusted to act responsibly in fiscal matters). Once the federal government had consolidated the state and national debts, it could then "fund" the aggregated debt—pay it off, that is, over time.

The problem with the proposal was that a number of states, among them Virginia, had already paid off part of their war debt. Jefferson's friend James Madison, a member of the Virginia delegation and the most influential man in the Congress, saw little good in a proposal that would require his state to contribute to the easing of other people's burdens, and much evil in a policy that would give extraordinary powers to the national government. Hamilton did not disparage this opposition. He hoped, rather, to soften its fierceness by coming to an understanding with its leading figures. Might not some of the Virginia congressmen, he asked himself, be persuaded to vote for the bill if in return the capital of the Republic were transferred to the banks of the Potomac?

When Hamilton broached the possibility of a compromise with the secretary of state, Jefferson was cautious. He was, he said, "really a stranger to the whole subject." But he was, he admitted, concerned that the quarrel over finances might lead to "a dissolution" of the union. And so he invited Hamilton and Madison to dine with him the next day in his house in Maiden Lane. The details of the negotiations are dim to the historian, and Jefferson, writing at a later date, probably exaggerated his role as a disinterested arbiter. But a compromise was eventually reached; the assumption bill passed; and provision was made for fixing the seat of government in the sogland of the Potomac.

Jefferson, by his own admission, had not yet mastered the financial question when Madison and Hamilton came to dine with him on that summer day in 1790. But within a few months he felt himself sufficiently informed to pass judgment on Hamilton's program. In December the treasury secretary submitted to Congress his plan for a national bank. Jefferson put himself on guard. In February he warned friends in Virginia about the ascendancy of "stock-jobbers" in the national councils. There "are certainly persons" here, he wrote, "who are driving too fast."

Before the submission of the bank plan, Jefferson had been prepared, in spite of a lingering uneasiness about his colleague's intentions, to give the treasury secretary the benefit of the doubt. After the submission of the plan, however, there could no longer be, for Jefferson, any question of a charitable indulgence of Hamilton's program. For there could no longer be, in Jefferson's mind, any doubt about the direction in which the treasury secretary intended to take the Republic. A hundred years before, the Whigs who made the Revolution of 1688 had laid the foundation for a new financial order in England, one intended to secure their political and social revolution. A young man in his thirties, poor, brilliant, and ambitious, had taken charge of the exhausted finances of the kingdom: Charles Montague had proceeded to restore the public credit of England. Now, in the aftermath of another revolution, another young man, poor, brilliant, and ambitious, thought he saw a way to do what Montague had done before him. Hamilton believed that the English boy wonder's miracle—his funded debt, his Bank of England, his "Dutch" system of government borrowing—could be replicated by him, the West Indian boy wonder, in the post-Revolutionary United States. The benefits of such a system, Hamilton was convinced, would be great: a restoration of public credit would bring lower interest rates, a rapid expansion of commerce, new sources of financial nourishment for the gosling government.

Whatever uneasiness he might have felt in the past about Hamilton's plans, Jefferson was certain that his colleague had this time gone too far. In proposing a national bank, the treasury secretary had trespassed on a sacred principle of the American Revolution. The patriots who made the Revolution belonged to the class of English Whigs known as "country" Whigs, so-called because they believed themselves to represent the sentiments of the whole body of honest Englishmen. Their minds had been formed, for the most part, on remote farms, amid plowshares, pigs and cows, and rural scenery. The country Whigs drew their inspiration from the soil, and although they approved of the political settlement of the Revolution of 1688, they disliked the way in which the financial questions had been handled. They distrusted the new methods of dispersing risk through speculative investment. They found repellent the government's efforts to raise cash by borrowing money at interest. They feared the corrupting effect of new institutions (like the Bank of England) that had been created to superintend the complicated government bond issues. They despised the court Whigs—oily, city-bred men with a limited experience of cows—who had put the new machinery in place.

Jefferson followed closely the old patriotic line. Hamilton, he believed, had begun to implement the most hideous features of court Whiggery. The executive officers of the new government would, he feared, soon be beholden to the bankers and jobbers who floated its loans. The funded debt would, he predicted, become a "machine for the corruption of the legislature." The president's men would use the borrowed money to bribe legislators, thereby laying the foundation for tyranny. Where enough lawmakers could be converted into trucklers, Jefferson reasoned, the head of state would be as powerful as a French king at Versailles, or a Roman emperor in the Golden Palace. Americans had not struggled in their revolution to unbind the yoke of the English "bank-mongers" only to see the harness refitted, in their own republic, by a clever young adventurer from the islands.

In its slow progress toward the Potomac, the federal government had, by the end of 1790, gotten as far south as Philadelphia. Jefferson took a house on Market Street. Here he unpacked his crates, finally come from Paris, got his rooms into a state of tolerable elegance, dined (often) with Mr. Madison, and made investigations into a crop pest called the Hessian fly. Here, too, the secretary of state began to work out a rhetoric of opposition—a rhetoric, rather than a theory of opposition, for Jefferson's antipathy to Hamilton's program was a matter of instinct, not analysis. He never attempted to distinguish those parts of the Hamiltonian system that were undeniably useful from those parts that might fairly be objected to as misguided or vicious. He was content instead to rehearse the "country" clichés of the gentlemen farmers of Virginia, their belief that land was the principal source of wealth, that stockbrokers were "gambling scoundrels," that the practices of bankers were little changed from the darkest days of medieval usury.

There is an explanation for this failure of intelligence. Had Jefferson attempted, patiently and methodically, to separate the good from the bad elements in Hamilton's policy, he would have been forced to confess openly what had begun to trouble him privately: that there were good and bad elements in the Whig theory of political economy itself. He shrank, however, from candidly acknowledging that the "perfect liberty" of trade that he extolled was helping to bring into being many of the things he deplored—and would have done so whether or not Hamilton ever funded a debt or erected a bank. Jefferson held the Whig faiths in free markets, political, commercial, and spiritual. But he hesitated to own that these faiths contributed to the growth of the cities he feared, to the displacement of the traditional modes of husbandry he loved, to the large-scale systems of industrial enterprise he disliked, to the sophisticated forms of speculation he abhorred.

He was convinced that the progress of Whig liberty would lead, gradually but surely, to the enlargement of man's capacity to pursue to happiness; but he at the same time vaguely sensed, what he could never easily admit, that the story would be one of loss as well as gain. "Let our work-shops remain in Europe," he had declared in his *Notes on the State of Virginia*. He knew that the vast industrial enterprises growing up in the more economically advanced countries had already begun to overshadow the traditional husbandry of the land and to diminish the importance of those small-scale crafts that are inseparable from husbandry. (Jefferson named three of these crafts: carpentry, masonry, and smithery.) Devoted though he was to the progress of commerce, and delighting in many of its effects, he could not look upon certain of its tendencies without a shudder.

Men, Jefferson believed, are good and strong ("virtuous," he said in his *Notes*) only where they are able to husband gardens, or are engaged in crafts akin to husbandry. Husbandry, Jefferson wrote, "is the focus" (in Latin, the "altar hearth") in which man "keeps alive that sacred fire, which might otherwise escape from the face of the earth." The farmer husbands, the craftsman stokes, the "sacred fire" of his passion and with that active flame transforms the world—transforms the land in the farmer's case, metal in the smith's, wood in the carpenter's, stone in the mason's.

Jefferson's "sacred fire" is a husbanding passion, the generative, begetting, procreative power. The progress of civilization had, Jefferson knew, made possible other forms of husbandry besides farming and farm craft: poetry, for example, which is the husbandry of words; physic (or medicine), which is the husbandry of the body; philosophy, which is the husbandry of the soul. But the same progress that produced these fruitful garden labors had also multiplied what Jefferson believed to be corrupt and sterile professions, such as banking, stockbroking, and securities speculation. These occupations, Jefferson argued, did not lead their professors to transform their own passion into the virtuous flame of action or to mold the plastic materials of life into a fire-kissed perfection of order. On the contrary, they were "barren & useless" activities that led to the putrification of passion, not to its virtuous combustion; they nourished "vice and idleness" in people, not habits of useful and effective labor; they were productive of weeds and factories, not beautiful things, like a vineyard, or a poem.

Jefferson here touched the rawest place in the modern system of political economy; but he was as yet unable to do the work he needed to do, the searching out of ways to preserve traditional habits of craft and husbandry in the altered conditions of modernity. He did not see how the patient husbandry that creates the small farm, and the loving craftsmanship that genders the little village, could find fresh pasturages in the richer, freer, but in some ways darker world that the progress of commerce had brought into being. His labors later in life show how well he understood that the blackest qualities of Whig liberty are subtly connected to its brightest ones; but he had as yet no idea how to separate the evil in it from the good. He chose instead to blame everything he disliked about the progress of trade and the dispersion of risk through speculative investment on Hamilton and his system.

2
*H*arlots and *H*eretics

The burden of the valley of vision.
What aileth thee now, that thou art wholly gone up
to the housetops?

—Isaiah

JEFFERSON TRIED TO scuttle Hamilton's banking balloon by telling President Washington, in February 1791, that the bank would violate the Constitution. Hamilton refuted the argument with ease, and the president accepted the treasury secretary's refutation. At the end of February, the president signed the act incorporating the bank into law.

It was during this winter that Jefferson's head began, for the first time, to ache constantly. The first months of 1791 were the lowest period of his public service since he had occupied the governor's chair in Virginia ten years before. Hamilton, with an ambitious magic that carried all before him, got the better of Jefferson in almost every scrape. He outmaneuvered his rival in the cabinet, where, Jefferson said, they were daily pitted against each other like two prize cocks. The secretary of the treasury secured the confidence of the president; he mastered a querulous Congress; he saw his financial policies prevail in the teeth of the opposition of the secretary of state; he helped to shape the Republic's foreign policy, though this formed no part of his portfolio. Jefferson, thrown on the defensive, began to despair.

What is surprising is that this time he was able to rouse himself from his despair and fight. When he was governor of Virginia, surrounded by enemics, foreign and domestic, he had failed to act decisively. When the question of replacing the Articles of Confederation arose in the 1780s, he was unable to produce a plan. But now, when his fortunes were at their lowest ebb, his bitterness stirred up all his active powers. He took strength, he said, from the sacredness of his cause. He declared that even in the very camp of the "energumeni of royalism" he would not betray the true faith. (John Adams, he said, might do a thing like that, but not Thomas Jefferson.) "An apostate," Jefferson wrote, "I could not be; nor yet a hypocrite: and I found myself, for the most part, the only advocate of the republican side of the question."

To President Washington he bewailed the wickedness of his enemies. He told the president of his "excessive repugnance to public life," and the "particular uneasiness of my situation" in Philadelphia, where the "laws of society oblige me always to move exactly in the circle which I know to bear me peculiar hatred, that is to say the wealthy aristocrats, the merchants closely connected with England, the new created paper fortunes." "Thus surrounded," Jefferson said, "my words [are] caught, multiplied, misconstrued, & even fabricated & spread abroad to my injury."

There was self-pity in this, but there was also anger. Rage is a potent stimulant, though often an ineffective one. Jefferson, as governor of Virginia, had been wrought up to fury by the treachery of the Loyalists; but in drawing a bill of attainder against one of them, he had vented his anger in a way that betrayed his own principles. Now, however, he found a useful way to hate.

"It cannot be denied," Jefferson wrote to George Mason in February 1791, "that we have among us a sect" that believes that the English constitution, with its "king, lords & commons," contains "whatever is perfect in human institutions." The "ultimate object" of this sect, Jefferson said, was "to prepare the way for a change, from the present republican form of government,

to that of a monarchy, of which the English constitution is to be the model."
Although Jefferson told Mason that he believed "that the great mass of our
community is untainted with these heresies," the enactment of Hamilton's
bank bill made him tremble for his country. "It would give you a fever," he
told his friend Philip Mazzei, "were I to name to you the apostates who have
gone over to these heresies, men who were Samsons in the field & Solomons
in the council, but who have had their head shorn by the harlot England."
He was grateful when Thomas Paine's *Rights of Man* came into his hands in
the spring of 1791. He hoped that the pamphlet would cauterize the "political heresies which have sprung up among us." He had in mind especially
John Adams's *Discourses on Davila,* serialized by the vice president in one of
the Philadelphia papers. Jefferson told President Washington that Adams,
who had "originally been a republican," had ceased to be one "since his
apostacy to hereditary monarchy & nobility."

This language of harlots and heretics was not merely for effect. Using
words with which the Jewish prophets had condemned the betrayors of Israel, Jefferson pronounced his anathemas against Hamilton and the other
Federalist heresiarchs. It was an inspired choice. Who has ever hated so
beautifully, or loved so ecstatically, as Isaiah? Jefferson's Old Testament poetry was effective in a way that the fertility mythology of his "tree of liberty"
never could have been. Every American, in Jefferson's day, knew his Bible.
Comparatively few had received a classical education. Nearly every adult in
the country knew who Ezekiel was. Not one in a hundred could have identified Osiris.

Jefferson had established himself as a prophet in Jerusalem, and in the
midst of his despair he spoke comfortably: he predicted that the Federalist
money changers would be turned out of the Temple. The schismatical
speeches, the vain oblations, of the party of Hamilton might for a time deceive, but eventually the imposters would be found out. Their "Pharisaical
homage" to banks and lords and kings would be repudiated. In a letter to
Lafayette, Jefferson said that the heretical "preachers" of the alien dogmas remained "without followers." "Our people," he said, remained "firm & constant in their republican purity."

Still it was not enough that the mass of the people was yet faithful. The
republican church, Jefferson believed, had somehow to be transformed from
a pacific one into a church militant. The communion of republican saints
had to be persuaded to rise up and cast out the "apostates." Only when they
had smote the oppressor could the primal faith of the republic be restored.
Already Jefferson envisioned the country's return, after the debauched

prodigality of Hamilton's ministry, to the aboriginal purity of its creed. But although he had begun to dream of ransoming a captive Israel, his vision of republican atonement, and republican regeneration, must have seemed at times quixotic.

Certainly the redemption could not take place until Hamilton's own bright star had been shot out of the horizon. But in the spring of 1791 the likelihood of such a happy disaster appeared remote, for never had Hamilton's sun shone more brightly. He had all but kissed hands and been installed as President Washington's prime minister. He was, moreover, diabolically resourceful—or so Jefferson believed. The enchanters and wizards of old Israel had, with their false juggling arts, deceived the children of alienated Judah. Now Hamilton and the other "high priests of federalism" were, Jefferson said, endeavoring to enslave the American people in similar chains of magic.

In April 1791 President Washington set out on a tour of the southern states. The cabinet was left in charge of affairs at Philadelphia. Some now forgotten matter of business arose, and in order that they might collectively address it, Jefferson gave a dinner to the principal officers of the government at his house on Market Street.

It must have been one of the more impressive residences in Philadelphia. There was a stable, a garden, and a garden house. Jefferson had taken a great deal of pains to create an elegant library, and he had his bed put into a kind of alcove, or recess, as he would later do at Monticello. The rooms themselves were filled with furnishings from Paris, and although his majordomo, Petit, would not arrive until midsummer, the secretary of state no doubt saw to it that his guests ate well, with dinner served in the "half Virginian, half French" manner he had begun to perfect during his Paris years.

One did not drink bad wine in Jefferson's house. The vintage would have been French—a Bordeaux, probably, or a good, bloody Burgundy—and on this night must have been especially bewitching, for the guests talked freely, and they talked memorably. Jefferson remembered how, after the "cloth was removed" and the bottle produced, the business at hand was brought up. Whatever it was, the question was quickly resolved. Conversation turned to other subjects, and soon a ripple of grander talk went round the table.

The subject of the little symposium was the British constitution. "Purge that constitution of its corruption," the vice president, John Adams, allowed, "and it would be the most perfect constitution ever devised by the wit of man." Jefferson looked to Hamilton. What reply would *he* make? The treasury secretary was for some time silent. At length he spoke. "Purge it of its corruption," Hamilton said, and "it would become an *impracticable* government." As "it stands at present, with all its supposed defects, it is the most perfect government which ever existed."

This was nothing new. Hamilton had said as much at the Constitutional Convention. But to Jefferson the comments possessed a deep significance. They confirmed his belief that Hamilton now aimed at nothing less than to "undermine and demolish the republic." The Constitution was to be "warped in practice into all the principles and pollutions" of his "favorite English model." The free state was to be replaced by a "monarchy bottomed on corruption"—bottomed, that is, on the ability of the executive officers of the government to buy votes in the legislature.

The wine went round the table. Were more bottles brought up? Probably. Jefferson was not a deep drinker, but he knew how to keep his guests talking. He recalled how, as they sat over their wine, Hamilton took notice of the elegant dining chamber. The treasury secretary wondered about the paintings on the wall, for the room, Jefferson said, was "hung around with a collection of the portraits of remarkable men," among them Bacon, Newton, and Locke. Hamilton asked his host who they were. "I told him," Jefferson said, that "they were my trinity of the three greatest men the world had ever produced, naming them." There was another pregnant pause. The "greatest man," Hamilton said, "that ever lived, was Julius Cæsar."

How is the faithful city become an harlot! Thy princes are indeed rebellious, with their idols of gold and their talk of the things which are Caesar's! And yet—is the episode not as revealing of Jefferson as it is of Hamilton? Horrified, as he was, by the uncircumcised desires of Hamilton's heart—his heretical Caesarism—could he not see, in the light of those dim candles, the strangeness of his own? Jefferson's piety, his devotion to a holy "trinity" of protective saints, his certainty that it was Hamilton, not he, who was worshiping false gods, mere idols, reveal in the Enlightened sage a cast of mind, a moral tone and style, that would not have been out of place on the shores of Massachusetts Bay a century before. Jefferson's dogmas were, to be sure, republican dogmas, not Christian ones. But he was as confident as any New England parson that men shall know the truth, and that the truth shall make them free.

3
Forebodings

Be strong, and do it.

—CHRONICLES

IN MAY 1791 Jefferson and his friend James Madison took a trip together. They went north, by way of Albany, to Lake George and Lake Champlain, then headed south through Vermont and the western reaches of Massachusetts to Connecticut and Long Island. They fished for speckled trout and studied strawberries; being politicians, they probably talked about politics as well as pretty flowers. Jefferson's headache had by this time vanished, and he returned to the forum refreshed for the fight.

He did not fight alone. He had added a poet to his State Department staff: Philip Freneau, a friend of Madison's from their days at the College of New Jersey (now Princeton), came to Jefferson's office ostensibly as a "translating clerk." His real business was to edit *The National Gazette*, Jefferson's answer to *The Gazette of the United States*, the court circular of Hamilton and the Federalists. How else to call attention to the treasury secretary's corruptions? What better way to point out his efforts to fill the government with flunkies? "I have never enquired," Jefferson told President Washington, "what number of sons, relations & friends of Senators, representatives, printers or other useful partisans Colonel Hamilton has provided for among the hundred clerks of his department, the thousand excisemen, custom-house officers, loan officers &c. &c. &c." He had never asked Hamilton, he told the president, to justify his "dealing out of Treasury-secrets among his friends." But really it was too disgraceful, reminiscent of the excesses of imperial Rome or Hanoverian Britain. So intolerable, indeed, that Jefferson promptly made a place in the government for his own pamphleteering protégé, Mr. Freneau.

The portage to prophecy is never smooth, and Jefferson, who was just beginning to be comfortable in his role of prophet, discovered how painful it is to have one's prophetic words flung back in one's face. When in the past he had discovered within himself an inspired voice, and had given it a free scope, he had seen his words overmaster all others. It was *his* language that defined, as it still defines, the spirit of 1776, and it was *his* rhetoric that re-made Virginia's feudal state, when, in his words, he had "laid the axe" to the root of the old aristocracy. Now, in the 1790s, he found his words caught, crushed, and hurled back at him by a man, a younger man, one who, though he was not so inspired a political poet, was an even greater master of the controversial arts.

The lampoons were cruel and effective. Hamilton, writing under the name Catullus, the amorous Roman poet, invited Americans to unmask Jefferson. "When the vizor of stoicism is plucked from the brow of the Epicurean," he wrote, "when the plain garb of Quaker simplicity is stripped from the concealed voluptuary," the secretary of state would be seen for what he was. Another Federalist ridiculed *"Generalissimo"* Jefferson for his cowardly "exploits at *Montecelli*" during the Revolutionary War and made fun of the "Philosopher" who had proved the "inferiority of Blacks to Whites, because they are more unsavory and secrete more by the kidnies." Like Hamilton, this Federalist, too, dwelled upon the "flimsy veil"—the "modest garb of pure Republicanism"—with which "plain Thomas" attempted to conceal his "aristocratic splendor, sensuality, and Epicureanism." Fortunately for Jefferson the Federalist press knew nothing of his friend Mr. Danquerville and his researches into the Roman erotic cults.

The treasury secretary scored some palpable hits in the newspaper war, but Jefferson and his partisans found mire enough of their own to sling. In December 1792 Jefferson's friend James Monroe, now a senator, and two other lawmakers questioned Hamilton about rumors of impropriety in his conduct. More than a year before, a young woman had called on Hamilton at his house in Philadelphia. The treasury secretary was alone at the time; Mrs. Hamilton had taken the family to New York to escape the heat of the Philadelphia summer. The pretty young woman, to all appearances a lady, who presented herself to the cabinet officer was Mrs. James Reynolds. She told Hamilton that she had been badly treated by her husband and was desperately in need of money. Hamilton thought her a "pretty woman in distress" and agreed to give her a banknote. He later remembered how Maria Reynolds had intimated her desire for something more than merely pecuniary tenderness. Their affair went on for several months before Mrs. Reynolds and her husband demanded money from Hamilton. The treasury secretary acquiesced in the blackmail. When confronted by Monroe and his colleagues, he explained that he was guilty not of official misconduct but of an error in judgment in his private life. He then confessed to his love affair with Mrs. Reynolds.

Monroe accepted Hamilton's explanation, but rumors of the treasury secretary's vulnerability were by this time abroad, and they emboldened the opposition in Congress. An inquiry was opened. Although Jefferson told President Washington that he had never "intrigued among the members" of Congress "to defeat the plans of the Secretary of the Treasury," he seems to have done so now. He quietly drafted resolutions asking Hamilton to account for himself. Early in the new year one of Jefferson's allies, William Branch Giles, one of the least savory members of the Virginia school, brought the interrogatories before the House of Representatives. But if Jefferson hoped, through this subterfuge, to bring Hamilton down, he was disappointed. The treasury secretary moved quickly to quash the challenge to his leadership. He answered the questions put to him with characteristic perspicacity, and a call for his censure was easily voted down.

Jefferson was far from having triumphed in his struggle with Hamilton, but he had at least managed to act. He had begun to transform his Virginia "country" doctrines into the foundation stones of a national opposition party—the Republican Party, the ancestor of the modern Democratic Party—and he had established himself as its chief rhetorician and preeminent prophet. With perception and decision he fingered the vulnerable places in Hamilton's authority, and through Madison and Giles he was able to build, in the House of Representatives, a new machinery of partisan resistance. But the close-fought battles taxed his spirit, and he was soon looking for a way out. His "propensities to retirement," he wrote to President Washington, grew "every day more and more irresistible." "The motion of my blood," he told Madison,

> no longer keeps time with the tumult of the world. It leads me to seek for happiness in the lap and love of my family, in the society of my neighbors & my books, in the wholesome occupations of my farm & my affairs, in an interest or affection in every bud that opens, in every breath that blows around me, in an entire freedom of rest or motion, of thought or incogitancy, owing account to myself alone of my hours & actions.

Why did he retire just when he had begun to persuade the public mind to accept the print of his thoughts? Partly because he believed he could be more effective advising the opposition to Hamilton from a distance. It is a tricky business to be at once a leading member of a presidential administration and a leading critic. A less nervous man than Jefferson might well have found the strain intolerable. As a "private man," unbound by obligations of loyalty, he would, he said, be freer to express his political beliefs. But undoubtedly, too, he was eager to get back to Monticello and set the place to rights. He had been an absentee landlord too long, and his estates, in the care of a steward, had fallen into disrepair. He had, besides, for many years meditated the renovation of his house. He could submit patiently to the grim regimes of business for a time, but eventually he must have leisure to be again a farmer and an artist.

At the end of December, he resigned as secretary of state, and early in January he reached Monticello. "I have returned," Jefferson wrote to a friend, "with infinite appetite, to the enjoyment of my farm, my family & my books." He was, he said, done with politics, and perhaps at some level he thought that he was. He cherished "tranquillity too much," he told President Washington, "to suffer political things to enter my mind." Politics were, he said, "entirely banished" from his imagination. "I have never seen a Philadelphia paper since I left," he wrote to Madison three months after quitting office. He added that in the interval he had "never had a wish to see one, and believe that I shall never take another newspaper of any sort." "I think it is Montaigne who has said, that ignorance is the softest pillow on which a man can rest his head," Jefferson told Edmund Randolph, who succeeded him as secretary of state. "I am sure it is true as to everything political, and shall endeavor to estrange myself to everything of that character."

His claim that he was now "totally absorbed" in "rural preoccupations" was exaggerated. His letters from Monticello show that he was actively advising Madison almost from the moment of his retirement. He was not so "completely withdrawn" from "spectacles of usurpation and misrule" as he liked to pretend. Politics continued to agitate him, and he worried that Madison was not up to the task of countering the influence of Hamilton. "For God's sake take up your pen," he exhorted his friend, "and give a fundamental reply" to the Federalists.

But he was a politician only part of the time. The rest of the time he was a squire. In a letter to Mrs. Cosway, he painted a fanciful picture of himself in Roman retirement, "eating the peaches, grapes and figs of my own garden." He only wished, he said, that he "could eat them in your native country, gathered on the spot and in your good company." He had become, he said, a "real farmer," busy in "measuring fields, following my ploughs, helping the haymakers." He followed the plows, indeed, with a whip in his hand, and the sight of the haymaking at Monticello was perhaps not as picturesque as he made it seem. (The Count de Volney, on a visit to Monticello, was startled to find his friend's slaves living a ragged life, "demi-nudité misérable et hideuse.") But no doubt Jefferson was only being honest when he told Mrs. Cosway, "How better this, than to be shut up in the four walls of an office, the sun ever excluded."

The crystal mornings of the winter months, when the sky was clear and the chimneys smoked in the sun thaw, were succeeded by the classical noontimes of April and May, when on bright days the very air of his porticos was *Antony and Cleopatra;* high Roman; with touches almost tropical, the violent daubery of spring bloom. Jefferson thought of himself as "living like an antediluvian patriarch among my children and grandchildren, & tilling my soil." It may be that he reverted, in his manners, to the days when a man might freely till many soils. One of his slaves, Sally Hemings, bore two children around this time: a daughter, Harriet, was born in the fall of 1795 (and died in infancy), and another daughter, Beverly, was born sometime thereafter. Jefferson may have fathered both girls, although even after the DNA tests there is still no definite proof of this. Sally Hemings would bear four more children in the coming years: a daughter, unnamed, who died in infancy; a fourth daughter, who, like the first, was called Harriet; and two sons, Madison and Eston. Some historians believe that all of these children were fathered by Jefferson. Yet even if the fact of his paternity could be established beyond all doubt, we would still know almost nothing about the nature of the master's relationship with his slave. The quality of those intimacies, their tenderness or their brutality, is lost to history. Jefferson's love of Mrs. Cosway is eternally preserved in the words he wrote to her and she to him, but unless lost documents come to light, his unlanguaged transactions with Sally Hemings must forever remain dumb to the curious inquirer.

He would not, he said, exchange a "retirement I doat on" for the "empire of the universe." But this slackening of ambition's sinews was not so satisfactory as Jefferson made it seem. The initial euphoria of freedom—the dream wonder of "philosophical evenings in the winter, and rural days in the summer"—gave way to another shadowed time. "My health," he wrote to Madison in April 1795, "is entirely broken down within the last eight months." Solitude was part of the problem. Jefferson was forever seeking a quiet refuge of privacy; but now he was continually by himself, often for long periods of time. In his private apartments, aloof from his hundred slaves (or most of them, at any rate), he lived like a Chinese scholar retired to his brushes, weaving for himself a net of books and dreams. His daughters, involved in their own lives, were often away, and during the winter months especially, when visitors were rare, Jefferson fell more deeply into the studious chinoiserie of the scholar dreamer. "From 1793 to 1797," he told his daughter Maria, "I remained closely at home, saw none but those who came there, and at length became very sensible of the ill effect it had upon my own mind, and of it's direct and irresistible tendency to render me unfit for society, and uneasy when necessarily engaged in it."

He had perfected the art of interior conversation, but like others who have carried soliloquy to its limits, he found it difficult to put aside the screens with which he had hidden himself. "I felt enough of the effect of withdrawing from the world then," he said, "to see that it led to an antisocial and misanthropic state of mind, which severely punishes him who gives into it." "I am convinced," he concluded, that "our own happiness requires that we should continue to mix with the world, and keep pace with it as it goes; and that every person who retires from free communication with it is severely punished afterwards by the state of mind into which they get."

It was the thunder gloom that precedes the storm. As much as anything, his motive in retirement was Monticello itself. The cherry trees blossomed in the spring of 1796, and the peach trees, and all was "noise, confusion, and discomfort" as the brickmasons went about their work. New walls rose, and the black liquid palaces that presided in his imagination began to become real. He had his reasons, and motives deeper than reason. His own instinct for architecture, long denied, reasserted itself. It was not a temple of reason that he constructed on that mountain top—at least not entirely. He labored to make the house a temple in which every entablature, every column, and every cornice—every demon creature and dream beast, every knife and every ax—respresented, and fed, some part of his imagination, the dark spots as well as the light.

4

The Garden of Vision

*the prophetic soul
Of the wide world dreaming on things to come*

—Shakespeare

As Monticello began to ripen into its final perfection of form, so, too, did the prophetic voice he had first learned to heed in the depths of his Philadelphia despair. James Madison managed the mechanical aspects of Jefferson's 1796 campaign for the presidency; but Jefferson himself arranged its music.

That he ran for president at all is at first sight startling. He professed to despise politics as a vocation. He had resolved, at his retirement in 1793, to pursue public life in the leisurely spirit of a great Whig lord, one who chases his opponents for the same reason he chases his foxes: to escape boredom, and to be sociable with his friends. He would never again, he vowed, make the mistake of besmearing the whole of his life with the ordure of officialdom.

To hear him tell it, he was dragged back into the forum against his will. His name "was brought forward," he said, "without concert or expectation on my part; (on my salvation I declare it)." The claim may be dismissed. Madison and others might have initiated the campaign, but Jefferson himself was always free to stop it. At the merest shake of his head, his subalterns would have bid the legions halt. But Jefferson never did shake his head. He hated the burdens of public life, yet he loved the pleasures. However little given he might have been to admitting it, power was his natural element. He was, it is true, baffled by the problem of action, for he wanted to act nobly, and this is never easy to do and is sometimes impossible. But action must always be distinguished from power. Merely to exercise authority, to drone in a senate, or ride through Persepolis in a golden chariot—this is not action; it is power. The man who would act must have power, but the man who has power does not always, or even usually, act. Jefferson had possessed power of some kind or another ever since he was a young man. In President Washington's cabinet he had had still more of it. And he found, as many people do, that when he gave it up, he missed it.

But to do him justice, he did not seek power only for himself. He sought it in order to act. He was, he believed, contending for great principles. He was at the head of a large party of men, the leader of all those who opposed the policies of the present government. He not unreasonably supposed that he was uniquely suited to the task of bringing order to this opposition, and forming it into a unit capable of obtaining and exercising power. Mr. Madison was doubtless a capable and even brilliant man, but he did not have on him, as Jefferson did, the stamp of importunate destiny, the mark with which the fates set some men apart as specially their own.

The nature of his personal authority is a little mysterious to us, but the gift was doubtless great. From his first appearance in Philadelphia, while still quite youthful, other men looked upon him as out of the ordinary run. His fellow lawmakers in Virginia made him their governor almost at the first opportunity. President Washington summoned him to his first cabinet and asked him to sit in one of the tallest chairs.

Yet even when conjoined to his appetite for power, this conviction of his political attractiveness cannot entirely explain Jefferson's decision to seek the president's house in 1796. Something else was at work. He seems really to have believed that he possessed the visionary entitlement of a prophet. He once proposed, for the Great Seal of the United States, a picture of the "children of Israel, led by a cloud by day and a pillar of fire by night." His high breeding would never have permitted him to admit as much, even to himself, but there can be little doubt that the impudent parallel had suggested itself. He felt the similarity of his own destiny and that of the prince who led his people out of Egypt.

Hamilton had by this time retired from government and resumed his law practice. Although he was not a candidate for office in 1796, his principles continued to animate the Federalist policy. Jefferson was incredulous that his old friend John Adams, the leading Federalist candidate for president in 1796, could see any good in the man, and he seems still to have had hopes that Adams might be converted from the Hamiltonian heresies in which he had acquiesced. In an effort to bring his brother of '76 back to the fold of republican orthodoxy, Jefferson wrote sarcastically to Adams of the "subtlety of your arch-friend of New York." Hamilton, Jefferson informed the vice president, had been secretly working to defeat Adams's presidential bid. Adams's "arch-friend" had "been able to make of your real friends tools to defeat their and your just wishes."

Arch-friend—it is a pun, or rather a series of puns, for *arch* means "consciously or affectedly playful" (Hamilton, Jefferson tells Adams, is playing with you), and *arch,* too, means "chief; superior; principal" and is meant here ironically (*I know that this man is not your "arch" friend, your best friend; by calling him your best friend I am rebuking you for having betrayed me—and the Revolution itself—by entering into a kind of partisan alliance with him*). But the real pun, the strong pun—the pun that harmonized most deeply with Jefferson's sentiments and followed most closely the direction and tendency of his thoughts—is the Miltonic one. In writing of the subtlety of Adams's arch-friend, Jefferson had in mind the subtlety of the arch-*fiend,* the subtlety of the serpent, which "was more subtle than any beast in the field."

The election of 1796 brought Adams the presidency. Jefferson, who finished in second place, became vice president. He was, he said, not unhappy with the result, and he claimed to "rejoice at escaping." For a time the two freshly elected magistrates entertained a hope that they might be able to work together in office. But Madison reminded his old friend of his duty to his supporters, and Jefferson, not without a pang, spurned Adams's offer of conciliation. Even if Jefferson had made an effort at cooperation, it is not obvious that Adams could have persuaded his cabinet to work constructively with a man the Federalists regarded as their enemy. Adams had inherited from Washington a set of courtiers who owed him no personal loyalty: the leading figures of the new administration regarded Hamilton as their true chief. Adams did not love Hamilton or even trust him, and he disliked many of his ideas. He not unnaturally resented the way many in his party frankly adored the genius of the younger man. But the new president did not have the stomach for a purge, and his policy, in Jefferson's view, was merely an extension of the old Hamiltonian one. President Adams was surrounded, Jefferson said, by a multitude of Hamiltons. It was these fiends, he supposed, who really directed the administration. Jefferson later said that Adams, as president, refused to consult him "as to any measures of the government." He neglected to add that he did not *want* to be consulted: he had his own reasons for staying away from the consistory.

The relationship between the president and the vice president might in other circumstances have been repaired; but the country was all agog over the revolution in France, and the possibility of reconciliation vanished in the vituperative smoke. Those who, like President Adams, hated the revolution, hated it deeply. Jefferson supported it, passionately and without reservation. While he was in Paris, he had personally advised a number of the revolutionaries. He had written briefs for Lafayette. He had given a dinner to the leaders of one of the moderate factions in the Hôtel de Langeac, at which he had talked out possible courses of action with the enlightened noblemen. His imagination had been touched by a "contest" on which, he said, the "liberty of the whole earth" depended. He continued to sympathize with the revolution even after it degenerated into terror and bloodshed. One of his old Paris friends, a liberal French duke, was stoned to death by the mob. Jefferson professed to deplore the spilling of innocent blood, but he said that there was no other way. He likened the dead to those who had "fallen in battle."

Certainly the bloody altars did not diminish his faith in the revolutionary cause. With rhetoric as beautifully garlanded as the ox skulls he was designing for his house, Jefferson made apologies for the human sacrifices. He drew on the language of the saints to describe his zeal for the revolutionaries' success. Rather than see the revolution fail, he told William Short, "I would have seen half the earth desolated." "Were there but an Adam & an Eve left in every country, & left free," he said, "it would be better than as it now is." The sanguinary violence that accompanied the revolutionary démarches was not only necessary; it was in many instances desirable. It would inspire other peoples to rise up and butcher their own tyrants. The French example, Jefferson said, would "kindle the wrath of the people of Europe against those who have dared to embroil them in" futile efforts to crush the revolution and trample on the tricolor. It would inspire them "to bring, at length, [their own] kings, nobles, and priests to the scaffolds which they have been so long deluging with human blood." More manure, indeed—although Jefferson conceded that it was less pleasant to study the growth of these European liberty trees than it was to consider the progress of his Virginia gardens. "I am still warm whenever I think of these scoundrels," he said, referring to his favorite trilogy of villains, "kings, nobles, and priests," but "I do it as seldom as I can, preferring infinitely to contemplate the tranquil growth of my lucerne and potatoes."

If Jefferson, as vice president, still believed in the benign character of France's revolution, many others did not. Orthodox Federalists wondered whether the French were not preparing to export their Jacobinical cockades to the United States. The Gallic Brutuses seemed not to be content with the reformation of France alone. Hot words issued from the revolutionary synods of Paris. Had not the Americans, the French patriots asked, recently concluded a treaty with the British that threatened French interests? (This was Jay's Treaty of 1795, which Jefferson had condemned as a Federalist sop to England.) When the new American emissary, Charles Cotesworth Pinckney, arrived in Paris to present his credentials, the French government refused to accept them.

In America unease over France's intentions grew. President Adams dispatched envoys to seek explanations. At the instigation of Talleyrand, the foreign minister, a cash bribe was demanded of the American diplomats. Word of this attempt to extort tribute from a sovereign nation and sister republic provoked fury in the United States. Was it a prelude to invasion? The country was daily in apprehension of a French descent. With apparent zeal and misgivings, President Adams put the country on a war footing. Congress authorized the building of a fleet. A great army was to be raised. George Washington, in retirement at Mount Vernon, was made generalissimo, and Hamilton himself appeared in the uniform of a major-general, ready to assist his old chief. Jefferson, a critic of the war hawks, made excuses for the tawdriness of the French and insisted that Britain posed a greater danger to American interests than France. He was reviled in the newspapers as a traitor and a Jacobin.

President Adams and his party were on the verge of a great triumph, but in a few fatal weeks they grew stupid with success. In the summer of 1798, important bills were carried by Federalist majorities in Congress and signed into law by the Federalist president. One of these, the Alien Act, gave the president the power to deport dangerous foreign nationals. Another, the Sedition Act, made it a crime to say bad things about the government. The passage of this legislation commenced the ruin of the Federalists. The man whom they most abhorred, Vice President Jefferson, could now claim, with some justice, to be that most politically appealing thing, a persecuted prophet.

Jefferson began at once to rally his party. He condemned the evildoers who had laid waste to Jerusalem. The Republic had been as a garden enclosed, an orchard of pleasant fruits, but into the garden the serpents had stolen. Under President Adams, Jefferson said, the same "cunning" and "artifice" that had enabled Hamilton to turn the "government over to antirepublican hands" was being employed to manipulate public opinion and oppress private liberty. The orthodox body of the citizenry, though true in their hearts to the "spirit of 1776," were the "dupes" of these "artful manœuvers" and had been persuaded by their "seducers" to be "willing instruments in forging chains for themselves."

In epistolary fury Jefferson shot off letters to men whose support he would need to fight the battles that must come. In Philadelphia hotels he plotted strategy with sympathic lawmakers. He put a reprobate writer called James Callender on the rolls. Callender earned his keep: he denounced President Adams as a "hideous, hermaphroditical" monster, and he penned the first public account of Hamilton's transactions with Mr. and Mrs. Reynolds. The uncharacteristic ferociousness of Jefferson's activity was strangely coupled, however, with a serenity of temper. He had not sinned against the light; he had a great work to do; his hour was finally come. Even as he and his people were, he said, "suffering deeply in spirit," all his presentiments of action grew more intense; it could only mean one thing; the moment of redemption was at hand. "A little patience," Jefferson wrote to John Taylor of Caroline in the spring of 1798, "and we shall see the reign of witches pass over, their spells dissolve, and the people, recovering their true sight, restore their government to it's true principles."

The audacity of his prophetic mission is remarkable, all the more so when one examines the materials out of which he fashioned it. Jefferson had, as a young man, made a careful study of the classic texts of seventeenth-century English Protestantism. The young squire had read himself out of the casual, careless Anglicanism for which his Cavalier roots would seem to have predestined him; he had read Locke, Milton, and copious quantities of lesser Roundhead prose and poetry. These works were full of the poetry of the Old Testament, and Jefferson took from them something of the fervent and prophetic spirit they breathed. But although he seems to have been deeply affected by this reading, he for a long time suppressed its possibilities. He was busy with the law and the Revolution, with Paris and the Mediterranean; he taught himself to be contemptuous of anything that smacked of Calvinist "Dæmonism."

Now the long suppressed poetry of Protestant salvation came rushing back to the surface of his consciousness, metastasized into the language of republican prophecy. The new voice enabled Jefferson to salvage his own political fortunes; it gave him the moral credibility he needed to pose as the savior of a republic fallen into the clutches of the Federalists. And it allowed him, too, to reshape the mythology of the emerging American democracy. Americans, in the new vision, were a chosen race, a "peculiar" people, in the language of the Puritan saints. Their revolution was the "first chapter," Jefferson said, in the "irresistible" spread of the rights of man. Their government was "the world's best hope." There had, it was true, been a backsliding, a moment of muddy merrymaking round the golden calves and funded debts of Federalism; but if they heeded the prophet's voice—if they turned out the apostates and made their way back to the "touchstone" of civic faith—Americans could yet avoid the fate of the heathen, the pagan, and the Hamiltonian.

His deepening sense of prophetic vocation inaugurated a period of astonishing creativity in the political sphere. Jefferson told Madison that he felt like a gladiator "daily going into the arena," doomed "to suffer martyrdom in every conflict." But the martyr took this hurt and interpreted it as the pain that the unhonored prophet must inevitably endure in his own country, and in his own house. He became startlingly—one had almost said demonically—productive; in the wilderness of Monticello—a more comfortable wilderness, it is true, than that which the Hebrew holy men knew—the inspired seer refined the first principles of his creed. As always Jefferson was an original; elegant wines and French cuisine did duty, in his case, for locusts and wild honey. How convenient, too, to have a mountaintop from which to thunder forth one's broadsides! What might Moses on Mount Sinai have given for the comfortable apartments of a neoclassical villa! But true to the spirit of an earlier prophetic type, Jefferson dutifully crafted words designed to bring the sheep back to the sheep-cote.

Jefferson's 1798 draft of the Kentucky Resolutions was the most politically potent document he had penned since the Declaration of Independence, though its authorship was for many years kept secret. In his draft Jefferson declared the Alien and Sedition acts unconstitutional, and he sketched a state's right to nullify acts in which the federal government had arrogated to itself undelegated powers. The Kentucky legislature adopted the resolutions in November, dropping only Jefferson's nullification language.

The prophetic voice was altogether effective in its work. Jefferson created what was to become the world's most durable democratic party, and he laid the groundwork for the campaign in which he captured the president's house from his Federalist adversaries. There would be nothing like it in American politics until Abraham Lincoln, in the heat of a prairie summer, looked into the Gospels and told the Republicans of Illinois that "a house divided against itself cannot stand."

Lincoln was the superior political poet. No less an authority than Walt Whitman acknowledged the sixteenth president's mastery. The author of the *Leaves of Grass* bowed to his captain in the street.* But if Lincoln is America's greatest political poet, Jefferson has the honor of second place.

---

*Whitman, while living in Washington during the Civil War, often saw the president and his wife out for their afternoon rides in a phaeton. "We have got so that we exchange bows, and very cordial ones," the poet said of his relations with the president.

5

Temptations

Dare to be great, without a guilty crown;
View it, and lay the bright temptation down.

—DRYDEN

Iᴛ ᴡᴀs ᴘᴇʀʜᴀᴘs inevitable that this trick of listening—carefully!—to his soul gabble should have led, in so diligent a man as Jefferson, to a certain flamboyance of personality, imperfectly concealed beneath a mask of reserve and a pose of porticoed detachment. The music had, by the year 1800, grown quite orchestral. The contradictions multiplied. The old paradoxes bred new ones. Here was a man whom President Washington, before his death, had come to think capable of shabby tricks. And President Washington was right: Jefferson *had* grown capable of "dirty and shabby" tricks. He had a bad habit of condemning opponents in colorful language that he knew was likely to find its way into a newspaper. When the criticisms did indeed make it into the public prints, he would piously disavow any intention of publicity. But the philosopher-jongleur was also an idealist, the enthusiast of enskyed heights, the builder of a mystic mountain palace. He was a poet of liberty—and the whipper and humiliator of slaves. He was an unpious philosophe in the Enlightenment tradition, and a prophet passionately engaged in a struggle to preserve the orthodox dogma of his party. He was a champion of visionary Jacobinism who was yet an honest Whig, a strict and cheeseparing cherisher of legal forms, private property, gentleman-like manners, and all the other modes of eighteenth-century civility.

The personality of his rival, Hamilton, was at least as flamboyant as Jefferson's and seemed hardly less outrageous in its mixture of good and evil. But in neither man's case did the lurid flambeaux of his imaginations betray him into an extravagance or viciousness of policy. Hamilton's enemies feared that he would overthrow the republic in a Caesarean or Napoléonic coup d'état. Jefferson's opponents worried that he would pursue a program of violence and revolutionary confiscation. But each man suppressed whatever inclinations to an apocalyptic politics he possessed, and each used his power to promulgate policies that were, for the most part, beautifully dull.

The renunciations, by both men, of a politics of thrasonical swagger is one reason why the American Revolution succeeded where so many others have failed. Nowhere was this willingness to sacrifice personal ambition, and to suppress all pretensions to the glorious activity of empire, more evident than in the *un*revolutionary election which Jefferson would later call the "revolution of 1800," an election in which, after vicissitudes, an attempt at a revolutionary coup d'état was foiled, and one political party peacefully surrendered power to its rival.

Jefferson was careful of his letters now, and rather than trust the post he often sent them, as he had in Paris, by private courier. The real rhetorical work of the campaign had been done. The party line had been laid down; Jefferson could rely on his lieutenants to make the case for his elevation. This, indeed, he insisted that they do. He enjoined the faithful both to write their own squibs and to support the squibbery of others. "Every man," he said, "must lay his purse and his pen under contribution." He had quietly opened his own purse to his old comrade James Thomson Callender, who had obliged by writing a tract called *The Prospect before Us.* For this work the journalist was brought before Mr. Justice Chase, a rabid Federalist, on a charge of violating the Sedition Act. Callender was tried, convicted, and flung into prison. There he languished, for a time, in miserable obscurity. But the country had not heard the last from him.

The strategy for the campaign was laid out by Jefferson himself. War councils were convened, in Philadelphia, in Francis's Hotel. Much depended on the outcome of the vote in New York. That state's leading politicians had long looked to New England for allies, and they had helped to deliver the presidency to John Adams in 1796; but they were now willing to listen to the overtures of Virginia. To win the New Yorkers to his cause, Jefferson needed to secure the services of a reliable agent, one who, through a dexterous personal diplomacy, could organize the tribal energies of the state, which were divided between the rival factions of the Clintons and the Livingstons.

Jefferson learned that Aaron Burr was on the market. Colonel Burr's manners were supple, and his morals suppler; his services were known to be on sale to the highest bidder. An alliance between Burr and the Virginia dynasts was hastily concluded; and having received the assurances he needed, Burr skillfully managed the Republican effort to win seats in the New York legislature. Smooth and plausible, with his Lord Chesterfield manners and graceful ways, he assembled a popular slate, and on election day the Republicans were victorious. The result was gratifying to Jefferson, for these lawmakers would choose the state's presidential electors in the fall. As a reward for what Jefferson called Burr's "extraordinary exertions and successes," the colonel was designated the Republican candidate for vice president.

Hopeful of victory, Jefferson left Philadelphia in the middle of May to return to Virginia. He spent the next months closely sequestered at Monticello, where he followed reports of the collapse of the Federalist batallions. The turmoil in those ranks was evident for all to see when, in October, Hamilton came out publicly against the reelection of his party's president in his *Letter Concerning the Public Conduct and Character of John Adams.*

By the middle of December, he was in the new capital at Washington City. It was confidently given out that he had won the election. Lifted up by the electoral energies of a nation, and brought once more into continual contact with public men, Jefferson was naturally a little stiffer, in thought and manner, than he had been while stoking the altar fires of Monticello. He had become a name, and the labor of maintaining a public face will always diminish a little one's inward liberty, the free elastic play of the mind. On the other hand he was more decisive now, brusquer in dealing with men and directing their energies.

Then, as Christmas week approached, he heard rumors of a difficulty in the election results. By December 19 it appeared that, through a failure of the Republicans to manage their electors properly, Jefferson and Burr would tie each other in the electoral college. Had the Republicans been more astute, they would have made arrangements for Burr to go a few votes short of Jefferson. Burr would have received enough ballots to guarantee his victory over Adams; he would have been assured of the vice presidency. But he would not have been in a position to upset the triumph of his chief. The necessary arrangements, however, had not been made, or were never carried out, and two days before Christmas the outcome was beyond all doubt. There were seventy-three electoral votes for Jefferson and the same number for Burr.

The deadlocked election would be decided in the House of Representatives. The Federalist congressmen, many of them lame ducks who had been voted out in the recent balloting, held the balance of power in that assembly. Some of them now threw their support to Burr, a few out of spite to Jefferson, others because they really feared him. Jefferson's serenity, however, was as yet undisturbed. The Federalist plans to push Burr forward were, he believed, unlikely to succeed. He still trusted in the good faith of his colleague, and he said that Burr had been "honorable and decisive" in rejecting the Federalist efforts to "debauch" him.

He was soon undeceived. Jefferson had, from the beginning of their courtship, preferred to overlook the real character of his ally. It was not pleasant, for a man of his pretensions, to enter into partisan engagements with a man like Burr. For the evidence as to what Burr was was unmistakable. George Washington, that knowing judge of men, was, almost as soon as he knew Burr, unable to trust him. According to one story, the general had come upon Burr, then a staff officer, reading a confidential paper on his desk. The descendant of heaven knows how many Puritan divines, the grandson of the pious Jonathan Edwards—the inheritor of all the New England traditions of godliness and virtue—had, through a biological trick, a perversion of the stock, become one of the devil's disciples. Hamilton, who shared Washington's contempt for Burr, said that he was as "unprincipled and dangerous a man as any country can boast—as true a Catiline as ever met in midnight conclave." Burr was "voluptuary by system," Hamilton said, and "in every sense a profligate." His ultimate ambition was to "reform the government *à la* Bonaparte."

Jefferson, who had for some time closed his eyes to the true nature of Burr, now found that he had no choice but to open them. For in the midst of the constitutional chaos of a deadlocked election, Burr, though he was by this time in all his professions and alliances a Republican, let it be known that he was "willing to consider the Federalists as his friends." He was prepared to "accept the office of president as their gift." "Why," Burr is supposed to have said, "our friends must join the Federalists, and give the president." A group of Federalists was inclined to make Burr the present he desired, if only to keep their old enemy Jefferson out of the president's chair.

Apologists for Jefferson criticize the Federalists for having dallied with the candidacy of a mountebank in the winter of 1800–1801. They prefer to overlook the extent and fidelity of Jefferson's own romance. Long before that fatal February, Jefferson had consorted with Burr. It was he who had set the charlatan to work for the Republicans in the New York wards, and he who had given him the role of crown prince in the struggle against Federalism. Neither party could lay claim to an absolute purity of conduct where Burr was concerned. But as preparations were made in the House of Representatives for a final referendum on the ambitions of Burr, Jefferson—the most brilliant Republican of the age—and Hamilton—the most farsighted Federalist—each had the chance to wash out the scarlet of those earlier sins.

The problem the country confronted in the election of 1800 was different from the problems with which it had struggled in the past. Reasonable Americans no longer aspired, as many of the patriots of 1776 had, to construct a republic of virtue. They were, for the most part, content with the commercial (Whig) republic that their new Constitution had created. The old heroic forms of virtue, they now saw, were not the only foundation upon which a free state could be built. On the contrary, the new Constitution frankly acknowledged the reality, indeed the primacy, of private interest, even as its structure worked to mitigate whatever ill effects a multitude of interests privately pursued must produce in the body politic.

The roots of the crisis of 1800 are to be found not in the extinction of the idea of popular virtue; they are rather to be found in the superabundance of heroic virtue that the nation's leaders possessed. For even as they discarded the idea of mass virtue, Americans continued to believe in the necessity of virtuous leadership. They continued to believe, as Hamilton said, that it was necessary to entrust to a "few choice spirits" the direction of affairs.

Americans got what they wanted—in spades. The upper pavilions of the Republic in the decade before 1800 were bright with talent, energy, and ambition. The light of those luminaries still shines across the centuries. In addition to President Washington, there were John Adams, James Madison, Alexander Hamilton, and Jefferson himself. New men, too, were beginning to appear on the balconies, with enough oil to keep the lamps burning brightly in the future. There were John Marshall, James Monroe, and Albert Gallatin.

But here, a skeptic might say, lay the problem. Heroic virtue, so necessary an ingredient of inspired leadership, is a quality as dangerous as it is desirable. Like genius, to which it is very nearly allied, such virtue reveals itself in brilliant and audacious acts. But although it is always a magnificent quality, heroic virtue is often an unpredictable one. It is easily led astray. The man of intense virtue yearns for glory: he abhors the prosaic: he despises the mundane. That desire for fame that brings him to do great things does not always lead him to do good ones, and although he always undertakes to do beautiful deeds, he does not always care whether they are decent ones. The Roman historian Sallust said that in his time two men at Rome possessed "prodigious virtue" (*ingenti virtute*): one of these was the younger Cato; the other was Julius Caesar. The precedent could not inspire confidence. Caesar's virtue led him on to dictatorship; Cato's virtue was powerless to stop him.

Each of the men who aspired to direct the course of American affairs after the retirement of President Washington suspected the quality of his rivals' virtue. Of the three most influential men in the Republic after Washington—Adams, Jefferson, and Hamilton—no one trusted any other. Their fears were not, at the time, as unreasonable as they now seem. By all rational calculation the Revolution ought to have ended—as almost every other revolution in history has—in the despotism of a strong man, in the autocracy of Caesar or Augustus, Cromwell or Bonaparte. That the United States had not, by 1800, succumbed to such a fate was due largely to the person and character of General Washington. But the miracle of Washington, Byron observed, was unique.* He stood alone. The brightness of his virtue had once shone down all the lesser lights, but as the 1790s wore on, his genial star began to droop. In 1797 he retired from office. Two years later he was dead. Many Americans supposed that now that he was gone, a war of the *diadochoi,* as the successors of Alexander the Great were called, would begin in earnest.

If history were any guide, the man who emerged victorious from this contest would move rapidly to secure his power. For the survivor of such a struggle is rarely able to look with equanimity upon his vanquished opponents. Their continued existence is both a threat and a reproach. The jealous eye of a Roman emperor could not look with complacency even upon those who, though they had never contended for the palm, were judged *capax imperii*—capable of empire, "presidential timber," men whose merit intimated that they might, in time, be plausible candidates for the first place. The psychology of triumphant tyranny would dictate the stages by which the American Revolution was closed.

Would John Adams emerge as a dicator? Would Hamilton? Would Jefferson himself? The ghastly spectacle of emergent despotism was ever before the eyes of the prime contenders for power. It was a vision overlaid, to their eighteenth-century sight, with the gory phantasma of the Roman revolution—images of imperial butchery in the Forum, of republican marble stained with civil blood, of lusty citizens bathing their hands in the mush of human offal. So real, at that time, did the possibility of a Caesarean coup d'état seem that men who had long shown a scrupulous respect for their country's laws and ideals were tempted to ignore, destroy, or make a mockery of them. John Adams signed the Sedition Act. Jefferson, after the Sedition Act went into effect, flirted with the idea of persuading Virginia and

---

*Where may the wearied eye repose
    When gazing on the Great;
Where neither guilty glory grows,
    Nor despicable state?
Yes—One—the first—the last—the best—
The Cincinnatus of the West,
    Whom Envy dared not hate,
Bequeath the name of Washington,
    To make man blush there was but one!
        —Byron, *Ode to Napoleon Buonaparte*

Kentucky to threaten secession from the Union—a course that, once embarked on, might have destroyed the Republic. (Madison talked his old friend out of the idea.) Hamilton, in a moment of anger, wondered whether a sneaky way could not be found to undo the damage of the recent New York voting, the election that had resulted in the triumph of Burr and the Republicans. (Hamilton's old friend John Jay ensured that the idea was quickly buried.) Such were the pressures upon them in a palled period that even decent men toyed with the possibility of wreckage. Now, in February 1801, a man infinitely flabbier in all the exertions of character stood on the threshold of the president's house.

The balloting began on February 11. For five days it continued. Always the result was the same. Eight states, it appeared, were for Jefferson; six were for Burr; while in two, Maryland and Vermont, the delegations were evenly divided.* It was during this heavy interim that the two great rivals, Hamilton and Jefferson, acted their heroic parts—acted them, indeed, by refusing to behave gloriously, as glory was in those days understood.

The conventionally glorious act for Hamilton to have undertaken would have been to work for Burr's election. If glory were defined as what Julius Caesar would have done in similar circumstances, the answer was clear: Caesar, had he been in Hamilton's place, would have set himself to the election of Burr. The effect of Burr's elevation would have been republican chaos, and Caesarean ambition requires precisely such chaos if it is to thrive. Hamilton knew that he could never hope to attain the first place under the constitutional system of 1789. His Caribbean birth, the exposure of his affair with Mrs. Reynolds, his inability to disguise his contempt for stupidity—would all tell against him in a free election. But the Republic, he knew, was not likely to last long under the strong but degraded mind of Burr; that violent personality had already intimated to Hamilton a dissatisfaction with the "miserable paper machine" of the Constitution. Why, Burr asked Hamilton, had he not, as a major general during the crisis over France, overthrown the pathetic government? After all, Burr said (in French), "great souls don't bother about small things." But although Hamilton, even now, might privately have entertained Caesarean fantasies, he threw all his influence to Jefferson.

---

*The Constitution provides that when the House of Representatives chooses the president, "the Votes shall be taken by States," "and a Majority of all the States shall be necessary to a Choice." Jefferson needed the vote of at least one more state delegation. U.S. Constitution, 2.1.3.

Jefferson labored under temptations of his own. He always said that nothing, even in the most suspenseful moments of the deadlocked voting, could have induced him to bargain for the presidency. He later described how, when Gouverneur Morris approached him at the door of the Senate, he told Morris that he believed it was his "duty to be passive & silent during the present scene," and that he "should certainly make no terms, should never go into the office of President by capitulation, nor with my hands tied by any conditions which should hinder me from pursuing the measures which I should deem for the public good." But assurances of some kind were given to the Federalists by at least one of Jefferson's supporters, General Samuel Smith of Maryland. If there is not enough evidence to prove that a bargain was struck, Jefferson seems nevertheless to have conveyed a message to those who controlled his political fate. This was done discreetly, of course; the candidate could not be seen to sue for his office. But somehow he intimated to his old enemies that he would not act unreasonably if they saw fit to give him the president's house. Jefferson's willingness to come to such an understanding—if that is what it was—has been criticized as grasping and indelicate. But politics is the art of compromise, and he may have done nothing more than intimate that he would not be fanatic—that he would not be *uncompromising*—in the conduct of his office.

Jefferson's assurances, together with the force of Hamilton's arguments, were enough to break the deadlock. On February 17, Federalist congressmen from Vermont and Maryland abstained from the voting, thereby delivering those states to Jefferson. On the thirty-sixth ballot he was elected president of the United States.

The thing to do, had Jefferson been less scrupulous, would have been to break these unprovable pledges of moderation once he was in possession of the president's house. He could then have acted on his dreams. What *happiness* it would have been for him so to act. He had risen from his little furrows of malaise in order to show himself capable of mastery. Now the power was his, and how delightful it must have been for him to act in obedience to his visions. But he never did. The obligations entailed by Hamilton's bank and Hamilton's debt were faithfully honored; a strict neutrality in foreign affairs was observed. He had learned the hardest lesson that the science of action teaches—when *not* to undertake an act that is within one's power.

Each man for a long time misunderstood the other; and each man in the end came round to a juster assessment of the rival. Jefferson accused Hamilton of crypto-Caesarism; but although he no doubt accurately divined his rival's private dream, he failed to see how effectively Hamilton had blocked the avenues down which the adventurer in him might have marched his Caesarean parade. Fancy an aspiring Caesar sticking the black cockade of the Hanovers in his hat and trying to fund a debt! The Caesarean politician excels at spending money, not at paying it back. Such a politician would never have modeled his program, as Hamilton did his, on the policies of the British court Whigs of the eighteenth century, so much inglorious bourgeoiserie.

Hamilton was no less blind to the strengths of Jefferson's character—at first. Ten years before, he said that Jefferson was enchanted by the delicious prospect of popular power, a vision of a perpetual ascendancy obtained through demagogic arts and ratified by the suffrages of the ignorant masses. Although the Virginia sage had, like Caesar himself, "*coyley refus*[ed] the proffered diadem," he nevertheless grasped tenaciously at what Hamilton called the "substance of imperial domination." If Hamilton ever believed this, he did not believe it in the winter of 1800–1801, when he resolutely supported his old enemy for president.

Each of the two coursers struggled fiercely to outdistance the other. But by the close of the election of 1800, each man had come to believe that the other's virtue was less dangerous than that of the remaining aspirant. Each saw in the other a man who, in spite of his loftier inclinations, had learned to obey a drab civic genius. This explains why Hamilton labored so strenuously to ensure that Jefferson, not Burr, became president in 1801 and why Jefferson, to the end of his life, said that Hamilton was in his personal character an honest man, something that could never, even remotely, be maintained of Burr.

PART FOUR

WINTER

I

Authority

Do you triumph, Roman? do you triumph?

—SHAKESPEARE

ON MARCH 4, 1801, he became the third man to take the oath and assume the office of president of the United States. He walked from his boarding house to the Capitol that morning alive to the Roman significance of the moment. To the "auspices of this day," he declared when he stood before his fellow citizens in the Senate chamber, were committed the "honor, the happiness, and the hopes of this beloved country."

The auspices of the day—its good omens, in other words. In ancient Rome the omens would have been interpreted by augurs, scrutinant of the habits and activities of birds. Before the Romans gave battle or installed (in-*augur*ated) a man in a place of public trust, there was augural work to do, to determine whether the gods smiled on the contemplated deed. At his own investiture Jefferson performed all the augurous duties himself. His mind, he said, was in a properly prophetic state; it was filled, he said, with "anxious and awful presentiments" of the future.

What did he see? He saw, he said, a nation "advancing rapidly to destinies beyond the reach of *mortal* eye." Beyond reach of *mortal* eye, but visible always to the developed eye of the seer. Jefferson here paraphrased Milton and rehearsed the text of *Areopagitica,* sacred to all good Whigs and unfallen liberals:

> Methinks I see in my mind a noble and puissant nation rousing herself like a strong man after sleep, and shaking her invincible locks; methinks I see her as an eagle mewing her mighty youth, and kindling her undazzled eyes at the full midday beam, purging and unscaling her long-abused sight at the fountain itself of heavenly radiance, while the whole noise of timorous and flocking birds, with those also that love the twilight, flutter about, amazed at what she means, and in their envious gabble would prognosticate a year of sects and schisms.

Eagles fly alone, as must all true prophets. Like Milton, Jefferson disdained the crowd of timorous spirits that flocked together in the dusk, afraid of progress. He resolved to follow not those courtly peacocks but Milton's mantic bird. He had, like her, built his nest upon a solitary height, one from which he could contemplate "transcendent objects." It was from this perch, presumably, that he first beheld the vision of the republican rapture enounced in the inaugural address—his picture of a "*rising* nation, spread over a wide and fruitful land, traversing all the seas with the rich productions of their industry."

Unlike many of the other Virginia statesmen, Jefferson was not an orator. The Senate chamber was a good room in which to speak; in that hall a strong voice carried well. But on inauguration day 1801 the audience in the farther rows strained to hear what the new president said next. He began to speak of the "contest of opinion through which" the country had just passed. In a voice too soft to travel, Jefferson observed that the election had been the occasion of much rough usage. It had given rise to an "animation of discussions," he said, that must have startled people "unused to think freely and to speak and write what they think." The allusion here was not to Milton but to Tacitus, the "first writer in the world," Jefferson once said, "without a single exception." In his *Historiae,* Tacitus describes the privilege of Roman citizens, in a happy time, to "think as we please, and speak as we think."

The address was studiously and even laboriously composed; it went through three drafts. Its allusions are sometimes obscure, but they are never merely literary. By stirring up the spirit of Tacitus, Jefferson purchased rights to the Roman historian's theme, the death agony of Roman liberty, or what the president called the "throes and convulsions of the ancient world." The European peoples, the president observed, had never recovered the freedom they lost when the Roman republic fell. Now, however, the Europeans were seeking anew their "long-lost liberty"—seeking it "through blood and slaughter," the "agonizing spasms of infuriated man."

But on this day the president refused to concern himself with the rights and wrongs of the French Revolution. He cared only about the revolution's effect on the American garden that lay before him. The "agitation" of those "billows" had, he said, reached "even this distant and peaceful shore." The evil wind had wrought a division of opinion in the United States. No matter. Every "difference of opinion," the president declared, "is not a difference of principle." "We have," he said, "called by different names brethren of the same principle. We are all Republicans, we are all Federalists."

Some historians have read the apparently conciliatory words as disingenuous, a merry threnody preached over the defunct carcase of Federalism. In the American garden there was no place, the president seemed to imply, for the stunted apples of the New England river valleys, where the Federalist soil was richest and deepest. But if the orchards of New England were tainted with apple blight, Jefferson was not above making use of New England's rhetorical apple juice. The president had always been a stalker of words, and though he cheerfully consigned the Federalist ideals to historical oblivion, he did so only after taking their choicest figures for himself. Nearly two centuries before, John Winthrop, on the *Arbella,* had declared that Massachusetts Bay must be "as a Citty upon a Hill, the eyes of all people" would be upon it. Jefferson, ready now to squeeze the pulp of his own prophecies, preached a similar destiny for the secular republic. The United States, he declared, must be a light to the nations. America, he said in his inaugural address, was a "*chosen* country." It was a second Israel, only more spacious, "with room enough for our descendants to the thousandth and thousandth generation." The president had seized from the Ephraimites their own high poetry, and had annexed it to the cause of the emergent American nation-state.

He had all the instincts of a verbal predator, but Jefferson's object here was to pacify, not to frighten. He knew that the struggle between Federalist and Republican merely perpetuated, in a new era, the ancient opposition of Yankee and southerner, Puritan and planter, Roundhead and Cavalier. But the president was determined to end this war by giving both sides a new idea to cherish, to be shared jointly between them—the idea of the American nation-state, clothed in the poetic forms of old New England. He spoke well—even many Federalists admitted as much. But how, they wondered, would he act?

As always with him, the adjustment to a new climate took time. He was a mountain squire, and he was now compelled to pass many months in the lowlands, where the new capital, Washington City, lay. The Potomac soil, washed by tidewater, was malmy and slack; the water was strange; the meat spoiled rapidly. The languor left even the bowels lax, and the new president was continually troubled by diarrhea. Some unfinished attempts at classical temples, it is true, shimmered in the heavy light, a proof of will successfully exerted, but even so the idea that the capital of a great republic could flourish here must have seemed at times improbable. It was difficult to obtain fresh vegetables in Washington, so great was the torpor. How much more difficult must it have been to procure the effective government of a republican empire.

The summer came. Miasmic mornings were succeeded by hot afternoons, and the president plotted his escape. Under no circumstances, Jefferson said, would he pass the sultry season at Washington. It was dangerous, he said, for a person "from the mountains" to pass the "bilious months on the tidewater." At the end of July, he left the capital for Monticello, and in a cooler zone he reflected on the ordeals through which he had just passed— the campaign for office, the election struggle, the early months of the presidency. He was a trifle sulky: it was, he concluded, "a year of my life lost to myself." But in time he adjusted to his new life. He went out regularly on horseback, and he ceased to be troubled in his bowels. His days were full. He rose at sunrise, breakfasted, and worked till one o'clock, busy either at his writing table or in talking to visitors. He sometimes pretended to spend more hours at his desk than he really did. The president, John Quincy Adams observed, liked to tell large tales. "You can never be an hour in this man's company," Adams said, "without something of the marvellous."

By one o'clock he was done with office work and would set out on horseback to explore the countryside. At half past three he received his dinner guests. The ease of the president's manners dispelled the dull anxiety that usually hangs over a state table, and even many Federalists were charmed. Jefferson entertained in the manner of an eighteenth-century Whig gentleman, with a tincture of the "Virginia carelessness" inlaid. The president was expansive in his talk, though he tried to avoid political topics. The food was good, the drink superfine. "The wine was the best I ever drank," Senator William Plumer of New Hampshire said, "particularly the champagne, which was indeed delicious." The Federalist senator wished only that the president's "French politics were as good as his French wines."

The democratic manners of the house were, it is true, exaggerated. Much has been made of the president's apparel, the threadbare coats, the corduroy smallclothes, the partiality to woolen hose in an age when gentlemen wore silk. An English diplomat, Anthony Merry, was appalled by the reception the president gave him. Jefferson greeted him, Merry said, "not merely in undress" but "actually standing in slippers down at the heels." The president's "pantaloons, coat, and under-clothes," he said, were all "indicative of utter slovenliness." Merry concluded that the president's dress implied a "state of negligence actually studied." Merry was right: there was affectation in Jefferson's simplicity, and pride in his humility. The president set to work preparing a memorandum, "Rules of Etiquette," in which he laid out the principles of "pêle mêle" that were to govern his democratic court. The "Rules" were meant to show up the falseness of European manners, but the laborious effort at simplicity was not altogether successful. If the contrived carelessness of the "Rules" lessened some forms of pain, they aggravated others, and they opened Jefferson to the charge of hypocrisy.

The president reveled in his radicalism; he would show diplomatists schooled in the egregious hierarchies of Europe how things were done in an egalitarian republic. Yet the reality is that Jefferson himself was never able quite to overlook the inferiority of another man's breeding. The president subscribed in theory to the idea that every Jack might be a gentleman; but in practice he was always conscious, when dealing with people of European descent, of the subtle gradations of rank. The baseness or obscurity of a man's birth did not escape his notice; in one of his letters, he touched obliquely on Hamilton's dubious beginnings. The inheritor of patrimonial lands despised the "new created paper fortunes." The scion of the gentry was contemptuous of the chandling arts of burghers. As for people of African heritage, Jefferson insisted on their inferiority to whites in every civilized activity other than singing.

He ostentatiously did away with levees, those receptions at which the first two presidents had presented themselves to the formal inspection of society. But his predecessor, John Adams, exaggerated only a little when he said that "Jefferson's whole eight years was a levee." They were a triumph of style over substance. The president might have acted like a radical at the dinner table, but in his policy he was content merely to rearrange the flowers. President Adams's great-grandson Henry observed that Jefferson in office governed like a moderate Federalist. The president's own ally George Clinton of New York thought him an "accommodating trimmer." His moderation confirmed Hamilton's prediction that the prophet would grow prosaic in power and preside over a "temporizing rather than a violent system."

It is true that Jefferson succeeded in abolishing Hamilton's internal (excise) taxes. And he labored to reduce the size of the federal establishment. But the Bank of the United States remained open throughout his presidency; its operations were indeed expanded at the direction of his treasury secretary, Mr. Gallatin. The obligations of the national debt—the president called them "sacred"—were faithfully discharged, and the government continued to borrow money. Jefferson had always disliked the navy, but he did not dismantle it; and not long after taking office, he dispatched a squadron of frigates to cow the pasha of Tripoli.

The objects of his policy were those of a modest Whig. He would consider his government a success, he said, if he could somewhat "reform the waste of public money" and "thus drive away the vultures who prey upon it." "If we can prevent the government," he said, "from wasting the labors of the people under the pretense of taking care of them, they must become happy"—and his own administration a success. In a candid moment the president admitted that he dreamed of doing more. He conceded how far short he fell "of effecting all the reformation which reason could suggest and experience approve, were I free to do whatever I thought best." But a deeper wisdom bade him move slowly. When he reflected "how difficult it is to move or inflect the great machine of society" and "how impossible to advance the notions of a whole people suddenly to ideal right," he became convinced, he said, of "the wisdom of Solon's remark,—that no more good must be attempted than the nation can bear."

2
Disorder

There's a plumber laying pipes in my guts, it scalds.

—JOHN WEBSTER

FISHER AMES MUST have pulled his muffler a little tighter round him whenever he thought of Mr. Jefferson in the president's house. The withered Ames was the most frigid of Federalists, and he expected that under their new president Americans would soon know the "loathsome steam of human victims offered in sacrifice." Ames's own flesh was slowly rotting. A morbid voluptuary, "half in love with easeful death," he had learned to savor his descent to the tomb. The old bird derived a kind of pleasure from his own wasting. Could he have seen the knives and axes with which President Jefferson was arranging to decorate his living room at Monticello, the longed-for rendezvous with the grave might have come sooner.

Federalists like Ames were continually accusing Jefferson of fanaticism. But the president, so far from being a zealot, did not even possess a program. No wonder he was proud of his "Rules of Etiquette." The rearrangement of the chairs in the presidential dining room was among the most radical acts of his administration. When it came to matters outside the presidential staterooms, he was less bold. In the realm of political economy, Jefferson was, during most of his presidency, cautious even to timidity; not until the end of his presidency did he abandon his policy of studied moderation. He hardly touched Hamilton's handiwork. "We can pay off his debt in 15 years," the president told Dupont de Nemours, "but we can never get rid of his financial system." It "mortifies me," he said, "to be strengthening principles which I deem radically vicious, but this vice is entailed on us by the first error."

A sad denouement, indeed, for a prophet. But sound statesmanship, an English politician observed in the aftermath of the Revolution of 1688, is "not what is commonly believed, the forming of schemes with remote views; but the making use of such incidents that happen." So, at least, Jefferson discovered, not without some bitterness. That the incidental happenings of his own administration included the reappearance on the scene of James Callender only added to the burden of regret.

Callender was now out of prison, angrier, if that were possible, than he had been before Mr. Justice Chase's assizes, when he had been convicted of violating the Sedition Act. A Scot by birth, full of pride and jealousy, Callender was one of those men who never in his life beheld with equanimity a greater than himself. The itch to malign was always present in him, and no variety of lèse-majesté was beyond the fantastic insolence of his imagination. In Britain he libeled Lord Gardenstone, who was his patron, Dr. Johnson, the king himself. He then sailed to America, where he was welcomed by Jefferson, who persuaded himself that Callender was a "man of genius suffering under persecution." But although Callender found, in the Republican prints, the kind of fishpond into which he could safely pour the burden of his venom, his personal affairs were perplexed. His wife became sick, and in 1798 she died—died miserably, it was said, in a dirty bed. After her death, Callender went south, to Virginia, where, before Mr. Justice Chase imposed his interdiction, he wrote for the Republican press in Richmond. He had some idea, he said, of traveling up the James and settling in the vicinity of Monticello. In a letter to Jefferson, he described a pretty ambition, one inspired, perhaps, by the brandy to which he was now thoroughly addicted. He hoped, he said, to go upriver and find fifty acres of "clear land" and a "hearty Virginia female," one who knew how to "fatten pigs, and boil hommony, and hold her tongue."

Jefferson discouraged Callender from "coming into my neighborhood." But he gave his protégé small sums of money, advances that Callender repaid by crafting those loose libels that no politician, however pure his intentions, can entirely do without. For Jefferson it was a satisfactory arrangement. The work of disparaging rivals was, he knew, as necessary in politics as the application of manure in farming. Defamation had, he said, become a "necessary of life." One's "dish of tea in the morning" was hardly digestible "without this stimulant." Still it was a sordid activity, uncongenial to a gentleman. Besides, the slanders took time and effort to contrive. It was in every way more convenient to set a man like Callender to the task, a man who was poor, perversely brilliant, without character to preserve or reputation to lose.

It was not until Callender got out of jail that he understood just how little his patron cared for him. Jefferson, safely installed in the whitewashed mansion on the Potomac, received the journalist's entreaties with what Callender called an "ostentatious coolness and indifference." The president seemed eager to forget the unseemly traffic in words and money that had helped to make his elevation possible. He had little interest now in recalling the crooked and indirect ways by which he had come to his prize, and even less desire to pamper the grub whose pen had helped him negotiate those greasy labyrinths. Jefferson unceremoniously dropped the unuseful equerry.

Callender was soon trembling with rage. His idol—his comrade in the struggle for liberty, the man whose writings he had ranked with those of Xenophon and Polybius—had coldly spurned all his efforts to advance their friendship. The insults stimulated an imagination of revenge, and it was in a vengeful state of mind that Callender set out for Charlottesville in 1801. He longed to handle the relics, to meditate in the groves, to pray in the shrines sacred to the sainted prophet of the Republicans. But he would do so with the passion that destroys sanctity rather than exalts it, and in a fit of hagioclastic zeal he determined to show up his old protector's stigmata for a fraud.

Returned from this curious pilgrimage, Callender again appealed to the president. He wrote a letter. The letter went unanswered. He came to Washington, and was told to see Mr. Madison. He wished, he said, to be made postmaster at Richmond. The position was not forthcoming. He complained that he had not gotten back the amount of the fine he had paid under the Sedition Act. (He had been pardoned by the new president and was entitled to a remittance.) Jefferson, informed of these grievances, instructed his secretary to give him fifty dollars.

Callender, unsatisfied with these requitals, hinted at his knowledge of scandalous facts. But he did not, just now, publish all that he had learned in Charlottesville. He was content to refute publicly the president's assertion that their transactions had been to no purpose. Jefferson admitted that he had been Callender's benefactor, but he protested that he had never been his patron or given him any reason to suppose that he approved of his writings. Callender gave the lie to these protestations of presidential ingenuousness when he quoted from one of Jefferson's own letters to him. In the letter Jefferson thanked him "for the proof sheets you enclosed me. Such papers cannot fail to produce the best effect. They inform the thinking part of the nation. . . . You will know from whom this comes without a signature; the omission of which has [been] rendered almost habitual with me by the curiosity of the post offices." But Callender was merely putting the president on notice, and it was not until another year of neglect had passed that he came forward with his tawdriest revelations.

During those twelve months Callender seems gradually to have realized that he had nothing further to hope for from the president. At last in the summer of 1802, he told the world what he had discovered during his sojourn at Charlottesville. The president, he wrote in the *Richmond Recorder,* lived at Monticello in open concubinage with one of his slaves. "Her name is Sally," Callender wrote. "By this wench," he said, "our president has had several children."

The "sluices of calumny," Jefferson said, had been opened, and he was again unwell, this time with rheumatic complaints. Callender himself would soon be dead, his corpse floating in a shallow stretch of the James. But the story of Sally Hemings survived the annihilation of the scribe. How could it be otherwise? How could Americans be expected *not* to delight in this picture of their philosopher-president lolling, on a lewd bed, with his envassaled courtesan? The tale was rapidly disseminated to the farthest corners of the Republic.

The rheumatic pains only hinted at the deeper dissatisfactions of the president. An artist delights above all else in purity of form. This he loves to contrive, not only for its own sake, but that he might impose it on the chaos and disorder around him. Jefferson's most successful political acts nearly always involved the imposition of literary form on the messiness of public life. The *Summary View* and the Declaration of Independence brought order to the muddy sty of revolutionary politics. In the 1790s he used his Old Testament rhetoric to lick into shape the amorphous, unformed opposition to Federalism. These successes were in contrast to his dismal record as an ad-

ministrator. For all his attention to detail—his copious lists and statements
of account—Jefferson was a miserable manager. He had not the tenth part
of Hamilton's executive mastery. Now, as president, he was again a ministering man; he had little time to be either a prophet or a poet. He did not fail
this time, but the work could never satisfy his urge to shape and create. This
was true even of his greatest act as president, the purchase of the Louisiana
Territory. A glorious work, to be sure, but costly to a man who abhorred
messiness. In order to extend his country's frontiers, the president was
forced to sacrifice his own cherished principles of constitutional order.

Jefferson had for many years dreamed of extending the American "empire of liberty" into the vast territory of the West. But for a long time this vision of continental felicity remained quixotic. The United States had no title
to the great mass of western lands, and a foreign power at New Orleans controlled the Mississippi Delta and its vital outlet to the sea. Louisiana, the
great obstacle to American expansion, was a contrivance of Louis XIV of
France, who in the seventeenth century had carved the territory out of the
plain of the Mississippi. The Sun King's plaything was ceded to Spain in
1763 in connection with the settlement of the Seven Years' War, and for several decades afterward it remained a possession of the Spanish crown. Reasons of state, too tedious to describe, dictated the retrocession of the
province by Spain to France, where it fell into the hands of the young Bonaparte, who for a time was ambitious of dominion in the New World.

To Americans in the West, whose livelihoods depended on the naviga-
tion of the Mississippi, the prospect of a French adventurer at the mouth of
the river was not in the least agreeable. The Spanish regime, hated though it
was, had the merit of being ineffective; Bonaparte was likely to administer
Louisiana energetically. But soon enough the great man's interest in the New
World began to wane, and by 1803 it had all but vanished. He was too
much the European to penetrate the mysteries of an alien hemisphere, and
at all events his head was filled with plans for an invasion of England. This
would require money, and Louisiana, he saw, might fetch a handsome price.
In April 1803 he authorized his ministers to sell the territory to the Americans for fifteen million dollars. Later in the year the treaty was ratified by the
American Senate.

The Louisiana Purchase ranks among the greatest conquests in history.
It was certainly one of the drabbest. Seldom has a ruler gratified so vast a territorial ambition without brandishing a single saber or shedding a single
drop of blood. The purchase was not, however, without an unruliness of its
own. For the text of the Constitution nowhere authorizes the government to

go about acquiring land from foreign powers. A fidelity to the letter of that document was, Jefferson believed, a mark of the true Republican, a point of honor that distinguished him from the fast and loose play of the Hamiltonians. "To take a single step beyond the boundaries" fixed in the Constitution, Jefferson had once written, "is to take possession of a boundless field of power, no longer susceptible of any definition."

For a moment Jefferson agonized over the lawlessness of his act. Fisher Ames, in his transit to the dust, must have relished the irony. President Jefferson had been more Federalist than the Federalists themselves. The president cast about for a means of assuaging his feelings of shame. Perhaps, he thought, the Constitution could be amended, to ratify his recklessness. But the moment passed; and the Constitution went unamended.

3

Death and Charity

See what a scourge is laid upon your hate,
That heaven finds means to kill your joys with love.

—Shakespeare

The averrals of Callender, whether true or false—and even today we cannot be sure which they were—were widely reported in the newspapers. They could only add to the burden of Jefferson's anxiousness. So, too, though in a different way, did the other uneasinesses of his domestic existence, which was constructed around the lives of his daughters, Patsy and Maria, and their husbands.

Patsy's husband, Thomas Mann Randolph, bore, at this time, little resemblance to the young horseman who had captured the girl's heart a dozen years before. The promising youth had grown into a "bashful timid man," a bookish, burrowing creature whose eyes blinked hard in the daylight. Afflictions, possibly of a nervous character, had troubled Randolph in the middle years of the 1790s and seem to have worked a permanent change in the constitution of his mind. After visits to doctors and spas, he recovered his health, but he was unable to pursue vigorously any single course of action. Books, farming, politics—they all interested to him, but he could not piece together a successful life out of any of them. He decided, at one point, to stand for a seat in the Virginia legislature, but he failed to show himself on the hustings. His father-in-law, who had promoted the candidacy, was mortified by this bashfulness. Randolph, for his part, crept back into his hole, and submitted to the fumes of another pipe dream. He resolved to take his family to the Mississippi Territory and set up as a cotton farmer.

The narcotic power of this vision, too, faded, and Randolph was persuaded to drop the idea of a Mississippi destiny. He instead secured a seat in Congress. But still he continued obscurely miserable. His temperament did not fit him for success in a legislature. He was no orator, and he was ineffective in committee work. Living, with his father-in-law, in the president's house, he had no gift for political friendship, and as he retreated deeper into his books, he developed an exaggerated sensitivity to slights. His wife, while remaining outwardly dutiful, could not conceal the greater esteem she felt for her father. The president's well-being was always, she said, "the *first* and most important object with me." Randolph must early in their marriage have learned that, where Miranda's affections were concerned, Prospero would always engage their tenderest part.

Patsy's sister, Maria, had married a happier man, Jack Eppes, one who was always laughing and cracking jokes. But some of the smiles faded when their firstborn child died, while still a baby, in 1800. Jefferson wrote at once to his daughter. He had, he said, no smoothing words for her, nor would he "attempt consolation where I know time and silence are the only medicines." But the pity of it moved him deeply, and he could not, he said, "find expressions for my love." Maria gave birth again, in 1804, to a baby girl. But although the baby was healthy, the mother fell sick with fever and bellyache. She was carried, on a litter, from the Edgehill plantation to Monticello, where her father found her so weak "as barely to be able to stand." Her stomach was "so disordered as to reject almost every thing she took into it." She had, too, a "constant small fever," and an abscess was "rising in her breast." Jefferson pressed sweet wines on her. "The sherry at Monticello is old and genuine," he assured her husband, "and the Pedro Ximenes much older still and stomachic." She died on April 17 at the age of twenty-five. As he followed the untimely bier, Jefferson thought life a "field of slaughter." He had, he told his old friend Page, "lost even the half of all I had." His "evening prospects," he said, now hung "on the slender thread of a single life," that of his daughter Patsy.

A "north west wind has been blowing three days," Jefferson wrote from Monticello. The spring was "remarkably uncheary." In a "blighted" season he received a letter from Abigail Adams, who wrote to console him after she learned of his daughter's death. She had cared for Maria when, many years before, the little girl stopped in England on her way to her father in Paris. A correspondence between Mrs. Adams and the president ensued, but the letters degenerated into acrimony over politics, and they soon ceased altogether. The two mourners drew away from each other, to ponder their frosts austerely.

The president turned for relief to an unexpected quarter. The previous spring, as he was preparing to leave Monticello to return to Washington, a little book came into his hands, *Socrates and Jesus Compared*. The author was one of his English friends, Dr. Priestley, and the volume provided the president with a "subject of reflection" as he rode back to the capital. It inspired in him, too, thoughts of making a book of his own. The essay he envisioned would demonstrate the special excellence of Jesus' teachings when compared with those of other sages.

To his friend Dr. Benjamin Rush, Jefferson sent an outline of the proposed essay. Jesus' "moral doctrines," the president argued, were "more pure & perfect than those of the most correct philosophers." Jesus "went far beyond" them in "inculcating universal philanthropy, not only to kindred and friends, to neighbors and countrymen, but to all mankind, gathering all into one family, under the bonds of love, charity, peace, common wants and common aids." The book, when completed, would "evince the peculiar superiority of the system of Jesus over all others." Those teachings, Jefferson said, "show a master workman" whose "system of morality was the most benevolent & sublime probably that has been ever taught, and consequently more perfect than those of any other antient philosopher."

Now, in the winter of 1804, the president set out to distill the essence of this teaching. He had, he told Dr. Priestley, "sent to Philadelphia to get two [New] [T]estaments Greek of the same edition, & two English." Early in February Jefferson received the Gospels and began to prepare his "digest." "It was the work of 2 or 3 nights only at Washington," he later remembered, "after getting thro' the evening task of reading the letters and papers of the day." By the middle of March, the book was back from the bookbinder's.

Jefferson called it the *Philosophy of Jesus* and referred to it as his "wee-little book." "A more beautiful or precious morsel of ethics," he said, "I have never seen."

Benevolence, philanthropy, love—the tradition of charity (*caritas, agapē*) that Jefferson found at the heart of Christ's ministry has been restated many times, and in many forms, since it was first taught. But the president was no longer content, as he had been when he was younger, with the revised editions. In February 1804 he went back to the originator of the tradition, the "master workman" who believed what at first sight seems improbable, that men can be "transformed wholly into love."

Jefferson had discovered the charity of Christ, but even the *Philosophy of Jesus* could not prevent him, as 1804 wore on, from indulging an impulse at least as firmly planted in his nature as love of his fellow man.

Jefferson had for some time nursed the idea of drumming Vice President Burr out of his party. Burr had betrayed his trust in the presidential contest; once installed as vice president, he had frustrated the progress of Republican legislation in Congress, where he sat as president of the Senate. Nor could Jefferson have been pleased to learn that his vice president had gone, on one of the anniversaries of President Washington's birth, to a Federalist banquet, where he had toasted the "union of all honest men."

The president no longer needed the vice president. Jefferson had initially entered into alliance with Burr in order to build up the New York wing of his party. That service, however, was done, and paid for. The vice president, who affected a stout chivalry in public, remained a hero in the eyes of many New Yorkers, but this popularity proved to be his undoing. For the Clintons now controlled New York, and conscious of Burr's threat to their preeminence, they moved quickly to destroy the competitor prince. George Clinton was the governor of the state, and he rapidly stripped his rival of all practical influence there. Jefferson happily consented to the work of destruction. The president put his patronage powers at the disposal of the Clinton and the Livingston interests, and he looked on with philosophical indifference as the vice president's protégés went hungry.

The president was all the while meditating a more decisive humiliation for Burr. Early in 1804 Republican congressmen caucused to choose their candidates for the presidential election in the fall. Jefferson was of course chosen to lead the Republican ticket. Burr, however, did not emerge from those conclaves as his running mate—the president saw to *that*. Governor Clinton was instead given the deputy honor. Even before the caucus vote made his excommunication official, Burr had despaired of his future with the Republicans, and had set himself to the work of political improvisation. From these desperate studies he now emerged a candidate for governor of New York, and a traitor.

Jefferson could not possibly have foreseen all of the consequences of his decision to emasculate Burr. But by some instinct of vengeance, or insight into the complicated physics of fate, he had set in motion a chain of catastrophes that would humiliate and, at length, destroy the most potent of his remaining enemies.

Burr's first task, as a gubernatorial aspirant, was to counter the influence of the Clintons in New York. The Clinton interest was naturally putting up its own man for governor. Burr therefore entered into negotiations with the Federalists. He was prepared to do more now than salute their honesty at banquets. His heart, he let it be known, had never been with the Republicans. He longed to be a Federalist—their champion, in fact, a *preux chevalier* who could rally the North against the tyranny of Virginia. Federalists like Timothy Pickering of Massachusetts and Roger Griswold of Connecticut were sympathetic to these professions. Did not the times require boldness? And who better for boldness than Burr? Certainly not Alexander Hamilton, the old Federalist chief. General Hamilton could only counsel his party to be patient. Clearly he was not the man of destiny whom the Federalist brokers sought.

In February 1804, about the time Jefferson was preparing his *Philosophy of Jesus,* Federalists gathered in Albany to consider the candidacy of Burr. Hamilton, in town on law business, came in to denounce Burr's ambitions as a threat to the Republic. Much, he said, would be lost, little gained, if the Union were destroyed as a result of Burr's provocations. But Hamilton had by this time lost the confidence of his party. The Federalists rejected his advice and backed the vice president. They were prepared to gamble that Burr, whose viciousness, disguised under an exterior of Chesterfieldian smoothness, had been proved, and whose capacity for mischief was known, was the best man to protect them from Jefferson, whom they insisted on regarding as dangerous, even though in three years he had done little to injure them beyond sacking a customs officer or two in the New England port towns.

The motives of the Federalists in striking their bargain with Burr are difficult to comprehend unless the peculiar mentality of that party in its last and most decayed phases is understood. The leading Federalists were, like Pickering and Griswold, New Englanders, and their black prognostic sensibilities convinced them that a crisis was fast approaching. The writings of the Federalist prophets are a catalog of apocalyptic presentiment, the work of men who, like Fisher Ames, felt themselves to be exiles in their own country, and saw already their dug graves before them. Upon every act they placed the least charitable construction. Every virtue, however bright, was in their eyes freaked with vice. Jefferson might so far have acted the part of an accommodating trimmer in office, but, although apparently a mild man, the president was, the Federalists believed, slowly eating away at the vitals of public order. Infidelity was spreading in the land; the hideous dogmas of democracy were everywhere preached; property itself was not secure. It was the constant burden of old Boston, the howl of New Haven. The lights, one by one, were going out; the temple of New England's soul was under assault.

In many places in New England, these hysterical anxieties had already, by 1804, begun to go out of fashion. Unitarianism was in the air; liberalism had invaded the colleges. William Ellery Channing, a founder of the American Unitarian church, had begun to catechize the youth of New England in the new dispensations. With these reforming tendencies, however, the highest and driest of the Federalists would have nothing to do. Living amid the crumbling masonry of the old order, the high priests of Federalism, in their icy shrouds, lived in perpetual fear of the onslaught, at once democratic and atheistic, that would wreck their churches, destroy their clergy, and bring low their bench and their bar.

Burr, of course, could not save them. He could not save himself. He lost his race for governor of New York in spite of the machinations of the Federalists. He blamed Alexander Hamilton for the defeat. Hamilton had, in after-dinner talk, spoken of the "despicable" nature of Burr's character, and the talk had got into a newspaper. For Burr the report of these maledictions was enough; he had already begun to think of Hamilton as a shadow on all his lucid ambitions. If ever he were to go up higher, he would have first to reckon with this man.

The vice president flung down his gauntlet. Hamilton took it up. To decline the challenge would have looked like cowardice, and a coward, Hamilton knew, could never hope to keep his place as a leader of men. The duel took place on a bank of the Hudson, Jersey-side, on the morning of July 11, 1804. The bluffs of Weehawken rose above the two men, and a dazzling summer sun. Within hours Hamilton was dead, and Burr under indictment for having murdered him.

Jefferson was in Washington when the duel took place, looking forward to his summer holiday at Monticello. "I presume Mr. Randolph's newspapers," he wrote to Patsy, "will inform him of the death of Colo. Hamilton, which took place on the 12th." The president was otherwise silent. John Adams candidly admitted that Hamilton's "most determined Ennemies, did not like to get rid of him, in that Way." But what Jefferson felt when he learned of the episode—the double felo-de-se that destroyed the lives of his two greatest enemies and condemned the mutilated corpse of Federalism to perpetual irrelevance—must remain a dark shadow of conjecture.

Tricks

But man, proud man,
Dres'd in a little brief authority,
Most ignorant of what he's most assur'd—
His glassy essence—like an angry ape
Plays such fantastic tricks before high heaven
As make the angels weep; who, with our spleens,
Would all themselves laugh mortal.

—SHAKESPEARE

AT THE END of 1804, Jefferson was reelected president by a wide margin. In March of the following year, he went again to the Capitol and gave another inaugural address, duller, indeed, than his first, but with the Old Testament poetry even more deeply trenched. "I shall need, too," the president said—as though he were old John Cotton, or old John Eliot, or some other New England worthy—"the favor of that Being in whose hands we are, who led our forefathers, as Israel of old, from their native land, and planted them in a country flowing with all the necessaries and comforts of life." Having

offered up these "supplications," as he called them, to Jehovah, the president
turned from the crowd and went back to his mansion on the Potomac.

The constant exercise of executive power, even by a man of lofty mind,
will always work a kind of coarsening in his feelings and perceptions. This is
true especially if the magistrate has little opportunity for constructive political work. Jefferson had for some time entertained doubts about the uses to
which Americans were putting their "antient Whig liberty." He worried that
they would "forget themselves, but in the sole faculty of making money." Yet
by what constructive act could he, their president, alter their habits or upraise their souls? Impose, from above, some nobler ideal, as the French revolutionaries tried to do?

No, he could not do that. He would not betray his Whig belief that men
must choose for themselves, even if, in the eyes of a philosopher, they sometimes chose foolishly. The beautiful republic could never be built by coercion, or through the aesthetic ministrations of a demiurge. Still the limits of
his office must have been frustrating to a man who liked to mold the putty
himself, and his unexercised mind inevitably grew less supple. Fortunately,
however, there were distractions.

The Federalist conspiracy to outfit a champion who could rescue them from
Jefferson had melted away. But the president was alive to a continuing danger, and he remained troubled by his political opposition. He urged his partisans in the state governments to intimidate the Federalist presses through
prosecutions for defamation. A "few prosecutions," he had written to Governor Thomas McKean of Pennsylvania in 1803, "of the most prominent of-
fenders would have a wholesome effect in restoring the integrity of the
presses." But the president warned McKean to take care. "Not a *general* pros-
ecution," Jefferson said, "for that would look like persecution; but a *selected*
one. The paper I now enclose appears to me to offer as good an instance in
every respect to make an example of, as can be selected." The state of Pennsylvania subsequently indicted Joseph Dennie, the editor of a Philadelphia
paper with a Federalist line, on a charge of seditious libel.

At the same time Jefferson launched an assault on the Federalists' last remaining stronghold in the judiciary. The federal bench, the president believed, had become a tool of faction. Had not the Federalist chief justice,
John Marshall, claimed for his judges the right to nullify those acts of the

president and the Congress that (in their eyes) violated the Constitution? (So the chief justice held in *Marbury* v. *Madison*.) What was that decision, the president wondered, if not the effort of a party man to thwart the will of the people, as embodied in the actions of their elected president and the votes of their elected lawmakers?

Jefferson moved to disbench the most obnoxious judges. Judge John Pickering of New Hampshire was impeached by Republican congressmen in the House and convicted after trial in the Senate. The House next impeached Mr. Justice Chase, James Callender's old foe—target practice, some believed, for the impeachment of the chief justice himself. A trial was held in the Senate in 1805, with Burr, the outgoing vice president—still under indictment for the murder of Hamilton—presiding. But the House managers, led by John Randolph of Roanoke, proved inept marksmen, and Mr. Justice Chase was acquitted.

It was not only the newspaper men and the judges, but the British, too, who now helped to relieve the president of the uncreative dullness of his office. Britain was at war with Napoléon, in the last of its epochal struggles with French absolutism. America professed to be neutral in this contest; but many Britons thought the Republic's neutrality a sham. They accused the Americans of running enemy goods in their ships. Chatham's boy, William Pitt the Younger, had again kissed hands and formed a ministry; the new cabinet determined to deal harshly with American shipping. Boats and cargo were seized; sailors were impressed into the service of the British navy; the port of New York was blockaded by British warships. Jefferson denounced these acts of violence, but he was more cautious here than when harrying editors and jurists. The president's private language in the diplomatic circles of Washington was temperate and even conciliatory, and his known aversion to military violence undermined all his public threats of menace. He had got the reputation, in the diplomatic corps, of a soft, mammering man, a carpet knight who would neither joust nor tilt. Jefferson resented this: he was not, he protested, a Quaker. Nevertheless, the secretary of state, Mr. Madison, was instructed to draw up plans not for war but for trade retaliation.

The most colorful jester in this diverting minstrelsy was undoubtedly Aaron Burr. The former vice president's comedy had now entered its final act. Fortune's finger was on him. He owed more money than he could pay, and he was still under indictment for the murder of Hamilton. But Burr's mind, always fertile, was, in its desperate phases, a hatch and brood of dark ingenuity. While still vice president he had offered his services to the British government. The British minister at Washington, Mr. Merry, informed his superiors in Westminster that the vice president proposed to "lend his assistance to his Majesty's government in any manner in which they may think fit to employ him." Burr had particularly in mind, the diplomat wrote, a project "to effect a separation of the western part of the United States from that which lies between the Atlantic and the mountains, in its whole extent."

Not long after surrendering the seals of office, Burr headed west, to Pittsburgh, to see how the land lay. From Pittsburgh he drifted down the Ohio River to Cincinnati, where he met Senator Samuel Smith and Senator Jonathan Dayton and acquainted them with his projects. He went next to Nashville, where he talked grandly of liberating the Americas from the yoke of the Spanish. His manners, both in his dealings with men and with women, are reputed to have been beautiful; and with his careless buccaneer courage he soon found followers. Andrew Jackson, at this time a major general in the Tennessee militia, was impressed by his declamations, and he readily helped Burr build boats. Having secured the good graces of Nashville, the former vice president followed the Cumberland River to the Ohio, where, at Fort Massac, he met General James Wilkinson, the governor of the Louisiana territory. Wilkinson was an old friend of Burr's, and deep in all his hopes and counsels. After their meeting Wilkinson went north, to Saint Louis, and Burr headed south, toward the Gulf of Mexico. By early June 1805 the former vice president was at New Orleans, the future seat, or so he fancied, of his empire.

In recruiting his disciples, Burr did not hesitate to claim as an accomplished fact what in reality was only a hope. That the British government, he said, had agreed to back him and stood ready to supply him with money and ships. This was a lie: Burr had applied to the British ministry for help, but the ministers had not as yet given him an answer. The distinction was to Burr an insignificant one, and for his proselytes he painted a beguiling picture of the confederacy he would found. The borders of this dominion were, to be sure, fluid. To some he spoke of a federation of the western states that had grown up around the Ohio and Cumberland rivers. To others he sketched a conquest of Mexico, where he would monopolize the mines and reign, in remote splendor, in the place of the Aztec priest-kings.

The final contest between Jefferson and Burr furnishes an instructive chapter in the history of the artist in politics. Jefferson was himself a great artist, and he had consecrated his life to an ideal of noble and beautiful action. But how far ought the artist to dictate terms to the politician? Many eminent authorities, Virgil and Machiavelli among them, believed that the same creative descents that are necessary to art have a place in politics as well. Jefferson had, in his rhetoric, toyed with the idea that creative violence is a driver of political progress—is like a storm in the atmosphere, such as washes out the dirty air. We have seen how, in the 1780s, he intimated that the true politician is nature's priest and must possess a deep insight into all the processes by which empress biology takes life in order to make it.

As he matured, however, Jefferson drew away from the idea that the politician ought, like the artist, to try to imitate the creative work of nature. The French revolutionaries might have believed that they could remake the human soul and shape it to their own conceit; but like the other heroes of the American Revolution, Jefferson discarded the specious but seductive notion that the character of men can be modified by chiseling statesmen. Yet no sooner had the president rejected the idea that the state can be a work of art than he confronted a man—a plotter against his own government—who continued to look upon politics as a vehicle for all his shaping aspirations. Burr, like Nero, believed that the ideal prince must be an artist. Burr's gorgeous ambitions, his hallucinatory visions, his thirst for a beautiful imperium, were the conceptions of a frustrated aesthete; and the songs with which he seduced his minions, soft, insidious, enchanting, were the airs of a poet manqué.

After remaining two weeks at New Orleans, Burr resumed his travels. He was variously at Natchez, Nashville, and Saint Louis. In November 1805 he returned to Washington in order to make his final arrangements with the British government. The British minister, Mr. Merry, regretfully informed him that no offers of money or ships had been forthcoming from Westminster. This was a great blow, but Burr so far recovered his spirit as to express the hope that His Majesty's government would not foolishly throw away the chance to underwrite so splendid an endeavor. He proceeded to describe, to the minister, the revolution that was to take place the following year at New Orleans. This enterprise, however, though glorious, was yet full of hazard. Burr would require, at a minimum, the assistance of two British ships of the line and the same number of frigates. He would also need a bank draft in the amount of £110,000. Mr. Merry assured the former vice president that he would forward the requests to Whitehall.

Burr next called upon his old chief in the president's house. He asked Jefferson for employment. The president, though cordial, refused to promise him a place. It was a curious interview, for around this time another plot was forming in the high fantastic mind of Burr. In the default of British assistance, he thought he saw another way to procure money and ships. He would quietly sneak a number of armed men into Washington, seize the president, plunder the treasury, and take the vessels in the naval yard. He would then hoist the sails and turn the rudder for New Orleans.

So compelling, to the desperado, did these lunacies seem that he devoted several months to trying to turn them to account. The capital, however, remained unseized, and the president unmolested when, in August 1806, Burr again went west. This time he took his daughter, Theodosia, with him. On an island in the Ohio River, just below Parkersburg, the father and the daughter regaled their followers with talk—of fictitious bullion and imaginary legions—quite as insubstantial as the river mists. At the same time Burr persuaded one of these naïfs to advance him a substantial sum of money on the credit of his future empire in the Southwest. His despairs must have been great whenever he allowed himself to measure the real strength of his conspiracy against the glorious démarches he communicated to his followers, but so insinuating was his talk that even many sober men were taken in, and perhaps he had come to believe in his own confections. Great powers, Burr said, were working steadily to advance his ends: British sterling and British warships were at his disposal; divinity itself had smiled upon his ambition. The "gods," he wrote to General Wilkinson in the summer of 1806, "invite us to glory and fortune; it remains to be seen whether we deserve the boon."

For some time Jefferson had heard reports of strange agitations in the West. But it was not until late in October 1806 that he moved to suppress his former vice president's conspiracy. He assembled the cabinet and informed them that acts of a "Catilinarian character" had been undertaken by Burr as part of a "scheme of separating the Western from the Atlantic States, and erecting the former into an independent confederacy." Communications from various officials attesting to the existence of a conspiracy were laid before the cabinet, and possible courses of action were debated. As a result of the deliberations, letters were sent out to the Republic's western magistrates, warning them of the plot, and gunboats were ordered to Fort Adams, on the Mississippi, to "stop by force the passage of suspicious persons going down." A month later, on November 27, a presidential proclamation was issued, ordering the arrest of the conspirators.

In spite of the proclamation, Burr remained at liberty, and with a little fleet of thirteen boats floated down the Mississippi toward New Orleans. A free people, soberly engaged in commercial and agricultural pursuits, is not easily persuaded to abandon these endeavors in order to chase a delusionary Caesar. They find it difficult to believe that, lurking among them, breathing their pure innocent air, are men who have taken the speeches of Milton's Satan too closely to heart and have mistaken Sallust's *War Against Catiline* for an essay in contemporary political possibility. Grand juries had, indeed, been convened at Frankfort, Kentucky, but no indictments had been handed down. Not until the end of December did the former vice president feel compelled to leave Nashville to put the machinery of his revolution in motion. With two boats he set out on the Cumberland. He was joined, near Fort Massac, by another party of conspirators, who had floated down the Ohio. The little fleet of thirteen boats, with perhaps sixty men aboard them, made for New Orleans.

Burr was, Jefferson said, like a "crooked gun, or other perverted machine." Such a weapon could not be expected to shoot straight. But who would have guessed that the bullet could go quite so wide of the mark? Jefferson's imagination had long been haunted by cryptomonarchists, would-be kings, aspiring Caesars, enemies of the Republic. The whole fabric of his prophetic office had been woven out of his conviction that his special destiny was to protect the tree of liberty from the imperial marauders who threatened to cut it down. Now, at last, a pretender to the throne had declared himself—and the Republic yawned. Burr's assertion of *la gloire* was so foreign to most Americans that he might have uttered it in Chinese.

If Jefferson still harbored any fears for the future of democracy in America, they ought to have been put to rest by the sight of Colonel Burr on the run for his life in the Mississippi Territory. The former vice president had come down the great river only to find that his conspiracy had collapsed. He had, perhaps, as much to fear now from his own band of brigands as from the government that sought his arrest. All his promises to his followers had proved false, and all his plans had been revealed as either the fabrications of ambition or the delusions of mania. Only with difficulty had Burr succeeded in maintaining his authority until now. He could hardly expect these bandits, each of whom was hardly less desperate than he himself was, to continue to dance attendance on his will. In his despair Burr abandoned his disciples and dressed himself in the rough clothes of a riverboat pilot. He put a white felt hat on his head and went into the woods. For some time nothing was heard of him.

At length he was found skulking near the frontier of Spanish Florida, some miles north of Mobile. He was arrested and brought to Fort Stoddert, where he was held, for a time, in close confinement. The prisoner was then taken through the Carolinas to Virginia. In the little town of Chester, South Carolina, Burr's spirit failed him. He threw himself from his horse and cried in the dust. But the officer commanding the expedition was without pity for him. He flung the former vice president "back like a child into the saddle, and marched on." At the end of March 1807, the cavalcade reached Richmond.

5

Failure

You would play upon me; you would seem to know my
stops; you would pluck out the heart of my mystery.

—SHAKESPEARE

I N A CROWD Jefferson often seemed "cautious and shy," "wrapped up in impenetrable silence and mystery." In a private setting, however, the president made a different impression. Margaret Bayard Smith, whose husband, Samuel Harrison Smith, was a Washington newspaperman, recalled a visit Jefferson made to their house in the capital. The conversation was at first limited to the "commonplace topics of the day." But "before I was conscious of it," Mrs. Smith wrote, Jefferson had drawn her "into observation of a more personal and interesting nature." "I know not how it was," she said, "but there was something in his manner, his countenance and voice that at once unlocked my heart." Mrs. Smith wondered whether the possessor of this "benignant and intelligent" face and "almost femininely soft and gentle" voice could really be the "vulgar demagogue," the "bold atheist," the "profligate man" she had so often heard denounced.

He grew more whimsical as he aged. He had a favorite mockingbird, which he kept in his study in the president's house. The bird's cage was suspended in a mass of roses and geraniums; Jefferson would frequently open it and let the creature fly about the room. The bird liked to perch on his shoulder, and it sang to him when he took his siesta. The president believed that his pet possessed not only an "affectionate disposition" but also "uncommon intelligence."

He delighted, too, in his grandchildren. At the age of ten, his granddaughter Ellen Wayles Randolph entered into a "contest with her grandfather to see who could write the other the most letters." Jefferson confessed that he was the loser in this epistolary race. "I believe it is true," he wrote to her, "that you have written me 2. letters to my one to you." "Whether this proceeds from your having more industry or less to do than myself," the president wrote, "I will not say." "Our birds and flowers are well," he assured her, "and send their love to yours."

All these soft spots of character were soon devoted to the task of preserving that most valuable of possessions, domestic peace. Doubtless it grieved him to watch the sad progress of Patsy's marriage. The more fragile the vessel, the greater the ballast of conceit needed to steady it, and Thomas Mann Randolph's pride now involved him in a number of difficulties. He traded sharp words with his cousin John Randolph of Roanoke; preparations were made for a duel. He quarreled next with Jefferson's other son-in-law, smiling Jack Eppes, who was now a widower and also a congressman. They were both living with Jefferson in the president's house, but after the argument with Eppes, Randolph moved out. He told Jefferson in a letter that he was sure the president loved him less than he did the jollier son-in-law.

Jefferson wrote at once to Randolph in his lodging house. "I had for some days," he said, "perceived in you a gloom which gave me uneasiness. I knew there was a difference between Mr. Eppes and yourself, but had no idea it was as deep seated as your letter shews it to be." He assured Randolph that his "affections" for both him and Eppes "were warm." "What acts of mine can have induced you to suppose that I felt or manifested a preference for him, I cannot conceive."

The son-in-law must have been touched by the letter, for when a friend, William Burwell, went to him, he found Randolph—or so Burwell informed the president—"inspired with shame for having left you." Randolph professed "the same love and respect for you he always did." With "some difficulty," Burwell wrote, he "succeeded in quieting Mr. R.'s mind." But the sadness was deep-rooted, and Randolph told Burwell that he was "indiffer-

ent to live." What was more ominous, he had got a brace of pistols and a
sword.

Jefferson wrote another letter. He was, he assured Randolph, his father,
not only in law but also in love. "I have been guilty of an error for which I
take just blame to myself," he said, "really loving you as I would a son (for I
protest I know no difference). I took it too much for granted you were as
sensible of it as myself." He begged him to come back to the president's
house.

The fates had woven for the president another net of troubles, and in the
midst of these perplexities his headache returned, though for the last time.
His son-in-law retired to Virginia, but his breakdown renewed all Jefferson's
anxieties for his daughter and her children. The dull routines of administer-
ing a presidency were becoming intolerable. Creative activity was his hedge
against gloom; but the business of office left him little time for the nourishment of those networks of hawthorn and privet, and by 1807 his mental
fences were full of gaps and meuses.

The conclusion of Burr's plot was a bitter revelation to him. During the
course of the conspiracy, the disgraced vice president had been gradually reduced to playing a buffo. His trial for treason was equally a harlequinade.
Chief Justice Marshall presided over a spectacle that was called a trial, and
after an interval of foolishness, Burr was acquitted. Yet if Burr was a comic
Catiline, what sort of Cicero was Jefferson, who had saved the Republic
from him? The idea that the camps of his enemies were crowded with
would-be Catilines and Caesars had for many years been the justification of
his public career. These undetected apostates, Jefferson maintained, were
trying to subvert the Republic, and only he could save it. It now appeared,
however, that he had been chasing phantoms. There was no comprehensive
conspiracy to destroy the free state. There never had been. There were only
the puerile treasons of Burr.

Years before, President Washington had tried to convince Jefferson that
there were not ten influential men in the country who wanted a king. Jefferson did not believe him. "I told him," Jefferson said, "there were many more
than he imagined." Washington replied that if Jefferson was right, if a large
body of influential men *did* scheme to bring in a king, "he thought it a proof
of their insanity." History vindicated Washington's judgment: America pos-

sessed no cavern dark enough to nourish the kind of comprehensive conspiracy Jefferson fretted about. Hamilton, whatever might have been his theory of politics, never made any practical attempt to establish a monarchy. He ended up supporting Jefferson for president, and after the death of his oldest son, Philip, he embraced an ideal of Christian resignation. He busied himself with the fattening of his fowls and the cultivation of his garden—the "usual refuge," he said, "of a disappointed politician." Jefferson had been certain that John Adams was an apostate, that the "glare of royalty and nobility, during his mission to England," had converted him from republican principles. Wrong again. Burr, indeed, *did* want to be an emperor, but only with great difficulty could he find ten influential men to support him.

Jefferson had not been wrong to be anxious about the fate of the Republic in the 1790s. His vigilance had been justified by the whole previous history of man's efforts to establish and maintain republican governments. Jefferson could not, at that time, have been certain that men like Adams and Hamilton were as honest—as noble—as they in fact were and as subsequent history showed them to be. But the historical record was now fixed beyond dispute, and Jefferson ought in conscience to have revised his theories. When Aaron Burr was permitted to leave federal court in Richmond a free man, the conclusion to be drawn was obvious: the Republic was safe—had never been anything but. So safe that it could dispense with the traditional prerogative of the state to hang traitors and slice out their insides. Why bother? No one had any desire to emulate Burr. His doom annulled, he wandered, for a time, in Europe; in Paris he left a card upon Talleyrand. Even Talleyrand had scruples about receiving him: he instructed his major-domo to inform "Monsieur Burr," when he called again, that over the mantel of his fireplace there hung the portrait of Alexander Hamilton. Plots Burr would still lay, and inductions dangerous; but, although the old suavity remained, it had lost its suasive power, and no one would listen to his schemes. After lingering in the European capitals, the decrepit roué returned to New York, married an heiress, stole her money, and died at eighty, in 1836.

Jefferson never did revise his theories. Such a revision would have required him to admit that he had been wrong, and confessions of error were not quite in his way. But he had some private sense of squandered opportunity, a regret of all those years of hewing and slashing at ghosts, years he might have devoted to more constructive work. If Jefferson was inclined to be angry in his last years in office, if he rushed unwisely into bad policies, if his administration was tinctured with the fanaticism he had for so long avoided, it might have been because he was trying to rewrite those chronicles of wasted time.

While he had been busy fighting the insubstantial shades of Caesar and Octavian, graver problems had been neglected. The Whig system was certainly the most desirable form of political order ever devised by the wit of man; but it was not perfect; for people who lived under a Whig regime too often failed to do justice to the high possibility of their freedom. No modern (Whig) republic will long remain what Jefferson wanted America to continue to be, a sanctuary for farmers and rural craftsmen, a haven for the husbanding passions. A free state will inevitably grow large and prosperous. It will breed cities, build banks, trade stocks, raise up factories, speculate in debt securities. How can such a state preserve, amid these commercial splendors, those qualities of character, of craftsmanship, of order, that do not flourish in trade, that tend, rather, to wither under its chaotic force? Jefferson touched on the question many times during the course of his career, but he never answered it. Now, in rage and regret, he found an easier way to arrest the free energies that were undermining his visions of republican simplicity.

Jefferson's actions, in the last years of his presidency, make a more compelling case for presidential term limits than anything in his own writings in support of that proposition. Even a conscientious man who wields supreme executive power for too long is likely to fall into a careless impatience to have his way. He may not say, as the Sun King was supposed to have said, *"L'État, c'est moi,"* but he is a figure as remote. For even as his mastery of the state becomes more complete, he grows daily stranger to it; he has been for so long set so far above his fellows that he has ceased to understand them as he once did.

Jefferson's great mistake, in the twilight of his presidency, grew out of difficulties with his oldest nemesis, George III. The poor king, it is true, was now, in his brutish dotage, a confined lunatic at Windsor; but His Majesty's navy continued to prey upon American shipping. The depredations were by any standard acts of war, but Jefferson was convinced that war was an out-moded solution to the problems of nations. He preferred the soft phrases of peace to the violent rhetoric of military action. Even the warmest advocate of trade measures, however, is unlikely to find an inspiration in Jefferson's example.

The president responded to British aggression by curtailing American trade. The retaliatory measures culminated in the passage, at the end of 1807, of the Embargo Act. By this law the ports of the United States were closed to foreign maritime trade. Successive laws closed any remaining loop-holes in the legislative brickwork. The people of the United States could no longer lawfully engage in commerce with the nations of the earth.

A large part of the American economy was swiftly destroyed. Flourishing trades perished under the malediction of the government. Jefferson called it coercion by "peaceable means." But the policy failed—utterly. The em-bargo, a historian sympathetic to Jefferson wrote, wrought "discords, casual-ties, and sufferings." The "nation plunged from unparalleled prosperity into an economic decline from which it would not fully recover for a quarter century." The New England states were brought to the edge of rebellion, and Jefferson's own luster was visibly impaired.

The president, however, persisted in his experiment in pacific coercion. Everyone agreed that the policy was a failure; it produced no discernible change in the conduct of England; Jefferson's own treasury secretary, Mr. Gallatin, did not believe in it. But the president continued to insist that the policy failed only because it was evaded, and he gave orders for its stricter enforcement. Blood was spilled in Vermont: on the shore of Lake Cham-plain, smugglers shot dead three militiamen acting as federal agents; a night runner called Dean was hanged for the crime. For the first time in his presi-dency, Jefferson strayed from the principles of drab virtue; he zealously pur-sued his visionary scheme even though it was, by his own admission, more costly than war.

The policy of forced economic primitivism arrested, for a time, the com-mercial energies that were altering the landscape of America in ways that Jef-ferson could not abide. There was some private motive of pique in this, but of course the president could not permanently prevent the progress of American commerce. Nor would he have wished to do so, even if he could. He remained committed to the Whig ideal of a "perfect liberty of trade." Yet still he felt compelled to strike this spastic ludditical blow against it, as much as if to say that, although he dearly loved Whig liberty, there was something in the uses to which it was put that he hated deeply.

On March 1, 1809, the Embargo Act was repealed, and trading was again permitted between the United States and the nations of the earth, with the exception of Britain and France, whose commerce was still proscribed. A few days later Jefferson relinquished his office. His friend and secretary of state, James Madison, succeeded him as president.

6

Flowers

*These, however, were assuredly within the knot of my unfold-
ing brain—as the saffron of the crocus, yet beneath the earth.*

—Ruskin

I have now the gloomy prospect," Jefferson said, "of retiring from office
loaded with serious debts, which will materially affect the tranquillity of my
retirement." Some of these liabilities were especially embarrassing to the defunct president. He owed more than ten thousand dollars to Washington
tradesmen, a sum he could not possibly pay out of his own accounts. He
wrote to his banker imploring him to arrange a loan. He was, he said, "under an agony of mortification," for "nothing could be more distressing to me
than to leave debts here unpaid, if indeed I should be permitted to depart
with them unpaid, of which I am by no means certain."

Loans were made, creditors were satisfied, and Jefferson rode off to
Monticello. He retired, he said, "from scenes of difficulty, anxiety, and of
contending passions, to the elysium of domestic affections and the irresponsible direction of my own affairs." The humiliation of unpaid debts was

soon forgotten amid the liberal magic of a life lived rustically at home. "The whole of my life," he told visitors to his house, "has been a war with my natural taste, feelings and wishes." "Domestic life and literary pursuits," he said, "were my first and my latest inclinations." Returned to his mountain, he was "like a bow" that, though "long bent," when "unstrung flies back to its natural state." He resumed, he said, "with delight the character and pursuits for which nature designed me."

This was oversimple. God had made him a lover of art and a lover of power. Both passions were genuine, but they were not always or even usually compatible with each other. Still he did become grumpy and sick when he could not make things, and in the last years of his presidency he had made very little.

The hedges were now carefully fertilized, and soon grew thick with leaves and a rich confusion of May-blossoms. In the country, Jefferson said, "man who has nothing to do" is the "prey of *ennui*." But he himself had plenty to do. He was busy with his farm, his garden, his family, and the unonerous obligations of provincial society. It was a little like the life preserved in Jane Austen's novels, only in a Virginia setting, and with the baronet determined to counteract provincial habits of dullness by vigorously exercising his mind. Jefferson's mental exertions, however, are partly hidden from us. As in the temple a veil covered the sanctuary, so the doors of his private apartments were locked, and shuttered porches were set up at the windows, that no profane eye might search his secret studies. Like an Asiatic Greek sage he withdrew deeper into his colonnades; for hours at a time he shunned the chatter of the Ephesians. Yet the former president, when he emerged from those privacies, humming one of his old psalm tunes or Scottish melodies, delighted no less in the cultivation of his outer gardens. The culture of his flower beds seemed to give him as much pleasure as the self-culture of the study and the library. People shared with the plants, Jefferson said, a "short reign of beauty and splendor" and then must retire. "The Hyacinths and Tulips are off the stage," he wrote to one of his granddaughters, "the Irises are giving place to the Balladonnas, as these will to the Tuberoses; as your mamma [Patsy] has done to you, my dear Anne, as you will do to [your own daughters], and as I shall soon and cheerfully do to you all in wishing you a long, long, good night." But although he was, Jefferson said, "an old man," he was "but a young gardener."

"My business," he wrote, "is to beguile the wearisomeness of declining life, as I endeavor to do, by the delights of classical reading, and of mathematical truths, and by the consolations of a sound philosophy, equally indifferent to hope and fear."

He made peace with John Adams, and they resumed a friendship that had been blown down in the political storms of the previous decades. Jefferson was pleased to have a correspondent on whose intelligence he could rely. With whom else could he discuss Socrates and Plato, Cicero and Demosthenes? "But why am I dosing you with these Ante-diluvian topics?" Jefferson wrote to Adams in 1814, after he had treated him to an elaborate analysis of the character and philosophy of Plato. "Because I am glad to have some one to whom they are familiar, and who will not receive them as if dropped from the moon."

Lifting a little those draperies and portieres, we see that Jefferson's "Antediluvian" researches were not always high and serious. He amused himself, in his scholarly sequestrations, with tales of the debaucheries of kings. These "documents of regal scandal," one visitor to Monticello noted, were "favorites with the philosopher." At the same time Jefferson's interest in obscure words, esoteric allusions, and learned puns grew. (Few writers of English have had recourse to words like *oestrum, energumeni,* and *hierophant.*) He insisted that language was a living organism: it must evolve and adapt itself to the requirements of the changing world. "Dictionaries," Jefferson said, "are but the depositories of words already legitimated by usage. Society is the work-shop in which new ones are elaborated." Yet he himself remained faithful, in his own writing, to the archaic splendor of English; and he must, like Horace lamenting the death of old Latin, have despaired of "words going off, and perishing like leaves." His library was full of ancient curiosities. There was a first edition of *Paradise Lost,* a Chaucer in the old black-letter type, a *Piers Plowman* from the sixteenth century. These proofs and records of the descent of the language—a cartulary of words— gave the poet a clearer title to his English. Where words were concerned, Jefferson parted company with the common man and followed Virgil and Horace instead. *"Procul, O procul este, profani"*—"Far off, O keep far off, you uninitiated ones." The democrat in politics had given himself up to the mandarin modes of style.

7

Love and Order

Haec sat erit, divae, vestrum cecinisse poetam,
dum sedet et gracili fiscellam texit hibisco.

To have sung of these things, goddesses,
While he sat and wove a frail of slim hibiscus
Will suffice your poet.

—Virgil, *Eclogues,* X

His debts grew, and his harvests were poor. But Jefferson continued to buy rare wines, to lay before his guests exquisite tables, to refine the splendor of Monticello, and to polish the elegance of Poplar Forest, his retreat, in the style of a pedimented octagon, in Bedford County. He stood ready to guarantee the loans of his friends. When one of these went bankrupt, Jefferson was forced to bear the burden of the entire twenty-thousand-dollar debt. All told he owed more than one hundred thousand dollars.

He had adhered too scrupulously to his Virginia doctrines. He had refused to invest in enterprises other than his own. He never understood the utility of those speculative investments that enable people to mitigate the risks of life by acquiring rights to the profits of others. Jefferson's wealth was almost entirely invested in land and slaves. In the boldest entrepreneurial effort of his career, he laid out, in the 1790s, capital for a nail-making operation at Monticello. He also built a flour mill on the Rivanna, though he seems never to have derived much profit from it. There were experiments, too, with spinning jennys and sheep farming. None of these was enough to save him from ruin. When the soil grew tired, and the labor of the harvest failed, when the merino lambs were mauled by dogs, and the neighbors preferred to buy their nails from British merchants, Jefferson had no investments on which to fall back, other than his library, his house, his land, and his slaves.

He was reduced to wringing his bread from the miscarriages of others. When, during the War of 1812, the British sacked Washington and destroyed the Library of Congress, Jefferson seized the opportunity to liquidate one of his most substantial investments. In 1815 he sold some six thousand volumes to the nation. In exchange for these books he received around twenty-four thousand dollars. But he could not, he said, "live without books," and he soon began to acquire more of them. His new library, in time, numbered about a thousand volumes, many of them precious editions of the Greek and Latin classics.

America was changing. Jefferson knew it, even if he never ventured, for the remainder of his life, very far from Monticello. He lamented the growth of American cities and deplored his countrymen's efforts at the "mimicry" of an "Amsterdam, a Hamburg, or a city of London." But still the cities grew.

Human nature, he knew, must change where it had to swim in such vast pools of indifference. Certain qualities of character that flourished in the small farm, in the little village, in the tiny city—all compact and polislike— would gradually disappear. Jefferson had long cherished a fantasy of ideal community, an intimate organization of friends and relations; he was always trying to persuade protégés and acolytes to buy land near him and settle close to him at Monticello. He yearned to re-create the intimacy of thought and endeavor that had characterized his relations with the teachers of his youth, Dr. Small and Mr. Wythe, a community of sympathetic scholarship that he was always to characterize in Greek terms. "They were truly Attic societies,"

Jefferson said of the erudite coteries that had given joy to his youth. Mr. Wythe especially he remembered as "my faithful and beloved Mentor," a man who counseled him as wisely and sympathetically as Homer's character guided the developing soul of the young Telemachus in the *Odyssey*. It was in communities of this kind, among close friends, that mens' highest and most charitable impulses could flourish as they could not in other places. "We are told you are becoming more recluse," Jefferson once wrote to a friend. "This is a proof the more of your taste." "A great deal of love given to a few," he said, "is better than a little to many."

Something of this instinct for community asserted itself in Jefferson's design for the University of Virginia, which he intended to be an "academical village." How rich must the resulting conversations be, where the citizen-scholars, in their little porches and Athenaeums, lived, worked, and dined together. As an old man Jefferson made yet another attempt to resurrect the Athenian ideal in America: he revived a proposal, one that had beguiled him in the past, to divide every county into units called hundreds or wards. Each ward, he said, would "be a small republic within itself, and every man in the State would thus become an acting member of the common government, transacting in person a great portion of its rights and duties." "As Cato, then, concluded every speech with the words, *Carthago delenda est*," Jefferson wrote, "so do I every opinion, with the injunction, 'divide the counties into wards.'"

The presidency had not tasked him to no purpose. He had learned, from observation and experience, that the defects of a Whig system could not be corrected through public acts or presidential proclamations or reform legislation. No, the qualities of soul that the Whig machine, for all its rich benefits, tended to degrade must find shelter elsewhere.

But where? If he had once made use of trade embargoes to advance his ends, Jefferson now turned to small groups and communities—to the family, the neighborhood, the school. The animating principles of these associations are different from those that govern a commercial firm or a political party. The principles of the *Philosophy of Jesus* have only a slender application to the work of a man who is engaged in business or politics. The advice Jefferson gave his grandchildren, to "pity and help *any thing* you see in distress," cannot be the rule of the statesman's conduct or the businessman's. It was not Jefferson's duty, as president, to pity and help Burr in the final distresses of his treason. It is not the duty of a banker to pity and forgive his defaulting debtors. But a motive of benevolence does, or ideally should, actuate a man in his work as a husband and a father, as a friend, a neighbor, a teacher, and, yes, a worshipper of God.

The modern state could not be such a beehive, a community of self-sacrificing creatures. The city, Jefferson saw, could no longer be a smithy of the virtues, as it had been for the Greeks: human character now reached its highest perfection not in the polis, but in the pack. The faithful steward with an ambition to upraise his fellow citizens' souls must therefore turn away from the state and look, as the aging Jefferson did, to the tribe.

Jefferson set himself, in retirement, to understand the elements that make associations grounded in benevolence—in love—possible. He became the explicator of the little community, the minor forms of moral and spiritual order. Jefferson disapproved of the "Rhetor Burke," but he was in retirement a close student of what Burke called the "little platoons" in which human beings invest their love. ("To be attached to the subdivision," Burke said, "to love the little platoon we belong to in society, is the first principle— the germ as it were—of public affections.") Jefferson investigated the little platoons less as a philosophe and statesman than as an artist and a poet, that is, as a maker of order. (All making of things, the Greeks used to say, is *poeisis*, or poetry.) He eschewed grandiosity in these efforts, and was content instead to weave the frails of slim hibiscus.

His old friend Mrs. Cosway was not so differently engaged. Her history, since her Indian-summer dalliance with Jefferson, had been full of perplexity, but at last she had known peace. The daughter she had borne Mr. Cosway, many years before, had died at the age of six. Her husband never recovered from the shock of the death. He kept the girl's embalmed body in his house, where it lay in a sarcophagus of his own design. Maria, who fled to the Continent, returned to England to nurse him in his last illness. He was by this time completely insane. He possessed, he said, a fragment of Noah's ark, a feather from the phoenix, the crucifix of Abelard, and he had been initiated into the mysteries of Orpheus. He was on speaking terms, he believed, with Dante and Praxiteles; and he had persuaded the Blessed Virgin to model for him in his studio.

Maria had never herself taken the veil; but she seemed to live most contentedly in the cloister. Convent bred in youth, she in middle age founded a convent school for young ladies. The school was set in a garden of orange trees at Lodi, on the plain of Lombardy, a gift of the duke of Lodi. In time the school became associated with an Austrian religious order and was known as the College of the Dame Inglesi. Maria herself was created Baroness Cosway by the Habsburg emperor Francis I in recognition of her services to religion and the education of youth. Her ambition, she told Jefferson, was "to see these children I have had the care of turn out good wives, excellent Mothers *et bonnes femmes de ménage* [good housewives] which was not understood in these countries and which is the primary object of Society and the only usefull."

Jefferson, replying to Maria's letter, told her of his own labors to build the University of Virginia. "The sympathies of our earlier days harmonize, it seems, in age also," he wrote. "You retire to your college at Lodi and nourish the natural benevolence of your excellent heart by communicating your own virtues to the young of your sex. . . . I am laying the foundation of an University in my native state. . . . I have preferred the plan of an academical village rather than that of a single massive structure." "It's within view, too, of Monticello, so it's a most splendid object, and a constant gratification to my sight."

Maria begged Jefferson to tell her what his school looked like. "I have had my saloon painted," she told him, "with the representation of the 4 parts of the World, & the most distinguished objects in them." But she was "at a loss for America." "Washington town," she said, "is mark'd and the Seminary." She hoped Jefferson would favor her "with some description" of it.

Historians have made fun of Jefferson's cloistress for calling the University of Virginia a seminary. Jefferson, more careful of his etymons, would not have. A seminary, he knew, was only a garden, what the Romans called a *seminarium,* a seed plot. In a letter to James Madison, he referred to UVA as "our seminary." If Baroness Cosway had created a garden for the growth and morphosis of young souls, so, in his own way, had Jefferson himself.

8

Degeneration

For he is superstitious grown of late,
Quite from the main opinion he held once
Of fantasy, of dreams, and ceremonies.

—SHAKESPEARE

H<small>E CAME NOW</small>, bundled in a blanket, to what he called the "hoary winter of age." In that icicle zone, he said, "we can think of nothing but how to keep ourselves warm." He shuddered at the approach of the cold weather, when the brain itself, under its fringe of white hairs, took on the quality of a winter landscape in storm.

Writing grew more difficult; the wrist he had broken years before was now arthritically stiff. Walking itself had ceased to be easy, and he limited himself to taking a turn or two in his garden. He found even this exercise, he said, immensely tiring. Yet he was still able to ride a horse, and as he approached his eightieth year, he rode "without fatigue 6. or 8. miles every day and sometimes 20." A visitor who knew him at this time found that he continued to enjoy life "highly, and very rationally." But Jefferson said that when he could "neither read nor ride," he would "very much desire to make" his bow. The "life of a cabbage," he said, was "surely not worth a wish."

His swollen prostate caused him much agony, and he took laudanum (opium) to ease the pain. By the end of 1825, he was well enough to ride five miles a day. But his estate remained overcharged with debt, and he wrote to his old friend James Madison of the probable loss of Monticello. His only hope, he said, was a lottery, to be administered by the state of Virginia, in which he would auction the bulk of his land and slaves. With the money raised from the sale, he could, he believed, preserve Monticello itself for his family. The scheme was destined to fail, but Jefferson did not live to know the full extent of the humiliation.

His public career had been dedicated to the high and brilliant, though sometimes overwrought, vindication of Whig liberty. The work of his private life and retirement was devoted to constructing little pavilions of order strong enough to withstand the gales of the Whig world he had helped to build. His contributions in these closed kingdoms, though less famous, were quite as valuable as his polished exercises in the forum and the curia. If his public work was made up of large, state-shaking endeavors, the private oeuvre was a concise little collection of gems, bright, sharp, and intricate.

Old as he was, he had entered another period of creative unleashing. Intervals of ennui and *tedium vitae* were in him always succeeded by periods of intense plastic power. This energy he now lavished on his exemplary temples. Monticello, and the life of the family it sheltered, would always be the foremost of these works of art. There, Jefferson said, he lived "in the midst of my grandchildren," and with Patsy, the "cherished companion of my early life, and nurse of my age." Monticello was, he said, an "essay in architecture." In more ways than one. It was the creation of an *architectus,* a chief builder. It was the work of a mister man, a master craftsman, and as such it was an essay in order, and also in love.

But he could be under no illusion about love's efficacy, even at Monticello. Even where it is closely sheltered, the order that love creates is always fragile, vulnerable to the pressures and temptations of the world, to the difficulties that failures of career or finances bring, to the different problems that success and wealth create. Jefferson's family was no more exempt from love's incompetencies than any other. Jefferson watched his granddaughter Anne grow up to marry a rake called Bankhead. The young man's character was thoroughly debauched, and he was a brutal drunk. When he was deep in his cups, his wife feared for her life, and she once hid from her husband in a potato hole. Anne's brother, young Thomas Jefferson Randolph, went up to Bankhead one day in Charlottesville to upbraid him for his treatment of his sister. Bankhead took out a knife and stabbed Randolph. The former president, learning of this, mounted his horse and rode into town. His grandson remembered how Jefferson, coming to the place where he lay, "knelt at my head and wept aloud." Bankhead continued to pursue his dissolute courses, and in a few years Anne herself was dead, her heart broken.

Anne's father, Thomas Mann Randolph, had, by the time of this explosion, recovered enough spirit to contemplate a return to politics. He stood for governor of Virginia on an antibanking platform, one that was dear to his father-in-law's heart. Randolph won the election, but Patsy chose not to accompany him to Richmond or to interest herself in the work of his governorship. For the greater part of his term of office, she remained at Monticello with her father. The passage of ten years had not discovered in Randolph any greater capacity for political business. He spent many hours drunk, and when he retired from the pilot's chair his spirit was again in cinders. His son took over the management of his affairs and, as part of an effort at economy, sold the estates at Edgehill and Varina. Randolph retired quietly to a little house, and for long periods of time he stayed away from Monticello.

The Randolphs' daughter Ellen recorded the story of her father's descent into those saturnal gloomings. He lived to know the bitterest touch of sorrow, the loss of his family's esteem. Ellen could not forbear to contrast her father's morose Saturn's-day disposition with the large-hearted Sunday amiability of Jefferson himself. "My own belief," she said, "is that nothing but the mingled dignity, forbearance and kindness of my grandfather prevented some outbreak which might forever have alienated two men bound by the strongest ties." Ellen believed that Jefferson, through his sunny magnanimity, spared her mother the "heaviest of misfortunes, a positive disunion between her father and her husband."

But there was also happiness in Jefferson's last years. The University of Virginia was the cause of some of it. In designing the university, Jefferson thought out carefully the elements that make for vitality in a little platoon. A naked open daylight was not, he knew, enough; there must be masques and mummeries as well. For the mystical touches he drew on his own idiosyncratic classicism. Ox skulls, fatally garlanded, and cherubic demon-spirits grace the porticoes of the pavilions; at the top of the lawn stands the rotunda, built in the style of the Emperor Hadrian's pantheon in Rome. Hadrian's temple was consecrated to the worship of the pagan gods; Jefferson's rotunda was a library and promoted the adoration of books. Yet the former president had no desire to force his talismanic tokens on the gentlemen-commoners of Virginia. On the contrary, the scholars would, through their exercises in his stoas, learn to master the antique forms, not merely mimic them. In their brighter emulations they would adapt the old visions, as Jefferson had done, to the demands of their own destinies, and to the requirements of their own demons.

The order of Monticello was made possible by the disorder Jefferson created in other places. The perfection of the house was subsidized by the unruliness of debt and slavery. Slavery violated Jefferson's own rules of conduct, both his public ideal of a free society and his private ideal of benevolence—of loving and doing justice to other human beings. Slavery was a lawless, disordered institution, yet Jefferson embraced it in order to bring, out of the nasty womb, Monticello.

The problem of disorder is rooted in the weakness of love. Jefferson, with all his grave faults, understood that love's empire is limited. Its sphere can be extended only so far. He would have rejected as specious the utopias sketched by the modern philosophers, who have argued that the Whig system of loveless labor can be replaced, in its entirety, by a pattern of community grounded not in the competition of men against one another but in their care for one another's souls. In their idea of the "communal" or "social" man, the high communitarians betrayed the deeper image of their heart, the idea of the loving man, the man who is not alienated either from himself or from the things and people who surround him. But Jefferson would have told these philosophers that they had cast their dreams in too large a scale. They did not understand, as he did, that such perfections of community flourish only where they have been wrought with a miniaturist's touch. Jefferson resisted the error into which so many progressive thinkers have fallen, the belief that love's efficacy can be extended beyond the bounds of the family and the tribe into larger groupings of men.

"There is a ripeness of time," he told John Adams, "for death." It was, he said, "reasonable we should drop off, and make room for another growth."

His health had, for some time, been poor. In February 1826 graver symptoms appeared. His bowels had begun again to bother him, a sure sign, in those days, that the end was near. An habitual diarrhea in a very old man was at that time death's herald. The griping pains undermined all the patient's vital strength, and he began to rot inwardly. In March, Jefferson made his last will. In it he provided for the freeing of several slaves, all of them connected to the Hemings family; but he said nothing of the liberation of Sally.

The snows dissolved, the spring came, and in May he made a final entry in his farm book. A month later he entered a last expense in his account book, for cheese, as it happened. Toward the end of June, as he began to go fast to decline, he composed a letter in anticipation of the fiftieth anniversary of the Declaration of Independence. The golden day was to be celebrated in less than a fortnight; he dearly wished to see it. The letter he wrote was a valediction, the last statement of his belief that "the mass of mankind has not been born with saddles on their backs, nor a favored few booted and spurred, ready to ride them legitimately, by the grace of God."

It is said that, during the last days, he "spent much time reading the Greek dramatists and the Bible." But he looked, too, to another source for inspiration. During his long life Jefferson had often dipped into the records of the Roundheads, the annals of seventeenth-century English Protestantism, for a model and a muse. In his last letter he turned again to the language of the Puritan saints. The boots and spurs were borrowed from an old soldier of Cromwell's army, Richard Rumbold, who, just before his execution by officers loyal to the house of Stuart, said that he was sure there was "no Man born marked of God above another; for none comes into the World with a Saddle on his Back, neither any Booted and Spurr'd to Ride him."

By early July, Jefferson was himself on the threshold of eternity. Intervals of lucidity were followed by long periods of stupor. The near approach of death was now evident to all, and his house was crowded with relations awaiting, in sad suspense, the inevitable hour. On the morning of the third, he took tea. Volumes of Aristotle and Seneca lay upon his reading table, as well as two French pamphlets. He dozed drowsily for much of the rest of the day. When he woke, in the evening, he thought that he had slept through the night. "This is the fourth of July," he said, though it was still the third. Later he was waked again and pressed to take laudanum. "No," he told Dr. Dunglison, "nothing more." Unsoothed by opium, his sleep became "disturbed and dreamy." He "sat up and went through all the forms of writing." Before midnight he spoke out. "Warn the Committee to be on the alert!" the old rebel said. At some point during his death vigil, he declared that he was, like Simeon, ready to sing the sweetest canticle, the Nunc Dimittis. "Lord," he said, "now lettest thy servant depart in peace, according to thy word."

Epilogue

———

The trouble is, we want to know more than we can see.

—FONTENELLE

JEFFERSON IS OFTEN said to have become a sage in the last years of his life. He is thought to have attained to some high wisdom, or learned an unnerving secret of creation. Certainly he did become a wise man, but it is not easy to say in precisely what his wisdom consisted.

Nor is there any use, where a man of such various genius as Jefferson is concerned, in trying to find a single solution to the riddle. The qualities that make a magus are always enigmatic, and Jefferson's soul is as difficult to elucidate as any other great man's. The techniques with which he plumbed the deep and original parts of his mind are perhaps a little easier to understand. Just as he learned to make the most of the seasons, the springtimes and the spare times, the wintertimes and the foison times, so he learned to make the most of his own cycles of fallowness and creativity. When the imaginative energy was building within him yet found no outlet, he felt only despair. But he learned that, given the right inducements, the dammed-up rivers would flow. He spent a great deal of time contriving the inspirations that liberate; some of them may be seen even now in the architecture of Monticello.

The uses to which he put his creative powers cannot be understood apart from his historical situation. The quarrel between the Whig and the Tory had, during his lifetime, entered a new and decisive phase. That quarrel is, to be sure, an eternal one, for though it has assumed many forms, it is essentially the antagonism between the realist and the mystic, between the matter-of-fact man and the artist, between the man of prose and the man of poetry. But in Jefferson's day unprecedented problems required men to address the ancient antipathies in fresh ways.

Jefferson was the architect of a Whig revolution, yet he was always happiest creating patterns of order that had about them a Tory enchantment of spirit. It was perhaps only to be expected that the matter-of-fact Whig in him should have had mixed feelings about the shaping power that made these Tory exercises possible. "You will see I am an enthusiast on the subject of the arts," he once told James Madison. "But it is an enthusiasm of which I am not ashamed." Yet he *was* a little ashamed of his enthusiasm. He told John Adams that he disliked the idea of plunging into the "fathomless abyss of dreams and phantasms." He affected to despise the visionary authority of Morpheus. He dismissed the "incoherences of our own nightly dreams." They did not admit of "explanation" and were perhaps not worthy of it.

The visitor who has wandered about the lucid chambers of Monticello knows better. Jefferson decorated his house with the mystic residue of primitive peoples' dreams. Inscribed in the frothy whipped cream of those friezes is a zoology of nightmare. A part of him disliked drawing on the depths, but he knew that genuine craftsmanship requires the maker to find out his most profound constructive instincts. One must sometimes go very far down to find a way to see the stars. Jefferson understood this perfectly. He consulted charts as old as Odysseus and as fresh as the Renaissance. He learned better than most people do how to talk to himself—how to cherish the stray pieces of consciousness he found within him. The Renaissance masters taught him to treat his various voices like bright playful children, little prodigies who must be given scope for the expression of their elegant (demonic) energies.

The result of these Jeffersonian plunges into himself and the European soul was the fishing out of an insight into how the quarrel between the Whig and the Tory might be, if not patched up, then brought to a satisfactory truce. The Whig believes in the primacy of the individual man, and he thinks that large bodies of men ought to be governed by contracts and bills of rights. The Tory dreams of communities united by a shared yearning for God and the Ideal. Jefferson believed the Tory's aspirations to be, indeed, impracticable, but he sympathized with the Tory's desire for order and coherence. The modern man fell in love, or read Montaigne, or smelled the cooking, and he saw no necessary connection between the disparate experiences: they formed no whole. But the man who found a place in a little platoon *could* find an order in things.

If we study with care Jefferson's idea of the nature and purpose of the sheltering pavilion in the modern world, we will be forced to revise our understanding of the institutions that make up what is called civil society. We will be brought to see that this phrase is too drab to do justice to the elements that make these sanctuaries vital, the work of faith and labor of love—the traditions, rites, and mysteries—that give an institution (a family, a school, a neighborhood, a church) a claim not only on our minds but also on our hearts.

We never shall succeed in realizing the dreams of the violent Tories of the old school. Nor, perhaps, would we wish to do so, even if we could. But Jefferson showed how certain qualities of soul that the Tory cherished might yet flourish in the little communities that make up the modern republic. These communities are, or rightly understood can be, the moral gymnasiums of the modern (Whig) civilization, places in which people learn to exercise their characters, and in which they are taught to develop certain qualities of soul that, though they have no instrinsic value in the marketplace, are necessary to the continuance of civilized life.

Jefferson sometimes invoked the "vestal flame" that burned on the city altar in old Rome and the similar fire that burned in the Prytaneum in ancient Athens. There was "nothing more sacred within the city than this altar, on which the sacred fire was always maintained." But Jefferson never proposed lighting such a fire in Washington. He placed his vestal flame in his house. He modeled the dome of Monticello on the temple of Vesta in Rome, and transferred the civic flame of the polis to the hearth of the private family. A visitor to Monticello remarked that it was a great pity that the room beneath the dome, a "noble and beautiful apartment," was not furnished and only rarely used. It "might be made the most beautiful room in the house." As if a man would clutter his temple!

Jefferson's insight into the nature and function of the little community in a modern world was full of moral intelligence. Unfortunately he buried it under a mountain of less perceptive rhetoric. He condemned the "hyperbolical extravagances" of the ancient mystical traditions. He described the metaphysical "whimsies" of these traditions as the product of deluded "Hierophants." (A hierophant was a priest charged with superintending the secret rituals performed by the ancient Greeks at Eleusis, near Athens.) He spoke slightingly of the *"ignes fatui"* (foolish fires) that burned in the "gloomy and hypochondriac" minds of those who carried on the old traditions, and he ridiculed the perverse *"deliria"* of their "crazy imaginations." Some of his words will always give pain to those who more candidly admit the importance of mystic faith.

He loved to play the child of light, the rational *illuminato,* yet he drew on the very traditions he censured in order to tread out his own prophetic wine. He unfigured the metaphors of others and disrobed their images, then used them himself to express truths that no other language could reach. He made fun of the idea of transubstantiation, but what was his own house if not a shrine to the faith by which joyful spirits are transshaped into flowers, mulberry trees, precious stones, and eminent stars? Say what he might, he *did* believe that anxiety can be converted into action, that chaos can be transformed into order, that lust can be wrought up into love. When he came to edit the Gospels, he was careful to preserve Jesus' parables of love.

He spoke of the progress to be made, "under our democratic stimulants, on a great scale, until every man is potentially an athlete in body and an Aristotle in mind." Jefferson did not here give the Greek term for this ideal, though of course he knew it, for it had found a rich pasturage in his heart. It is the ideal of *kalos kagathos,* "beauty and perfection of mind and body." It is the excellence of the great-souled man (the *megalopsychos*), the excellence that enables him, in the charming phrase of the Greek, to "take possession of the beautiful." The ideal had its origin in the aristocratic poetry of old Greece; the greatest of the Greek poet-statesmen sought to broaden its appeal and to bring its grace within the grasp of the common citizen, who could then use it in the ordering of his own life. In this way the Greek statesman became an educator. He was like Solon: he made the latent poetry of his people active. He gave them *paideia.* A word not easily translated, *paideia* means teaching, schooling, the nurturing of children—education. It also means tradition, literature, civilization, culture. A poetry that lingers only as a memory in the mind of a city or nation must be reckoned dead; the *paideia* statesman entrances precisely because he is able to lug the guts of the primeval vision into the present. Solon drew on the poetry of archaic Greece, which had been brought to perfection by the Asiatic Greeks of Ionia, and used it to mould the future of a new Greece with its spiritual innards at Athens. Jefferson, a no less creative personality, took up the mystic torches of the Old World, which had for many centuries given light to the European soul, and used the fire to forge a democratic *paideia* in the New World of America. He is a teacher of new ways of ordering life, and yet like those of Emerson, who is his pupil and ephebe, Jefferson's new ways are so entwisted in the old ways that one hesitates to call them novel. How far he succeeded in his formative work is a question; but his labors, like those of Lincoln—the other great teacher-statesman in our history—will always have a peculiar sweetness for the American.

What is too bad is that his ostensible contempt for all the unknowable and unsayable things has obscured his more tender feelings for the forms of civilized mysticism and their role in fostering desirable patterns of order. It is a continuing grief to me that he could never avow the significance of his imaginative life more openly. In studiously concealing the act and figure of his heart, he gave fresh impetus to the charge that is sometimes leveled against the liberalism that grew out of the enlightened ideals of the Whigs, the charge that it tended, in Lionel Trilling's words, to envisage the world in a "prosaic way," that in exalting the rational powers of the mind it tended to "constrict and make mechanical" our "conception of the nature of the mind," that it did violence to the imagination and stifled the life of the emotions.

Through his silence Jefferson contributed to the progress of these anemias. If the votaries of liberalism have been content to worship at the altar of progress, and have taken that dull fool for a god, the fault is partly Jefferson's. John Stuart Mill, among the greatest of the liberals, was not as sensitive or imaginative a man as Jefferson, but he was less dogmatic in his politics and infinitely more candid in admitting those mistakes that have darkened the face of liberalism. Even if all his progressive objects were realized, Mill confessed, still he would continue to be dejected. Even if we could achieve all the modern ends—even if we could extract sunbeams from cucumbers and fill all the urinals with rosewater—still we could not do without something more.

He built his house to face the west, the sunlit future that he hoped to shape and into which he longed to escape. The past threatened to prevent this marvelous flight, this exodus from the superstitious shadows, from the tyranny of unreasonable laws and customs. He was unable to restrain his outrage when he considered how the dead weight of the past pushed humanity down, kept men and women from reaching the kingdom of the future, the lucent empire where reason and common sense prevailed. "The earth," he said, "belongs to the living, not the dead." The rhetoric of the present and the future flowed copiously from his pen, but Jefferson was himself unable to live without the old things he affected to condemn.

He left this testament:

> [C]ould the dead feel any interest in Monuments or other remembrances of them . . . the following would be to my *Manes* the most gratifying. On the grave a plain die or cube of 3.f without any mouldings, surmounted by an Obelisk of 6.f height, each of a single stone: on the faces of the Obelisk the following inscription, & not a word more[:]

> *"Here was buried*
> *Thomas Jefferson*
> *Author of the Declaration of American Independence*
> *of the Statute of Virginia for religious freedom*
> *& Father of the University of Virginia."*

because by these, as testimonials that I have lived, I wish most to be remembered.

The Declaration of Independence is here, the most sublime of the Whig manifestos, and so is the Statute for Religious Freedom, hardly less important. It is the testament, surely, of a thorough Whig. So much common sense! Ah, but see where he hopes the epitaph will gratify his *"Manes"*—the residue, that is, of his soul. He died a little before one o'clock on the afternoon of July 4, 1826. But his *manes*—his demons—survive.

A Note on Designs

The designs in this book reproduce engravings of classical art and architecture by Giovanni Battista Piranesi (1720–1778). Piranesi's work helped to form the taste of the neo-classical school of the eighteenth century, one to which Jefferson looked for inspiration in his own art. Jefferson acquired a copy of one of Piranesi's books for his library, and he corresponded with Piranesi's son.

The decoration at the beginning of each chapter depicts the unexcavated Temple of Jupiter Tonans (Thunderer)—now identified as the Temple of the Deified Vespasian and Titus—in Rome; Jefferson turned to this temple for the model of the Corinthian motifs in the parlor at Monticello. The engraving at the beginning of Part I ("Spring") reproduces details from the Temple of Fortuna Virilis—now identified as the Temple of Portunus, the god of the harbor—at Rome; Jefferson drew on this temple for inspiration for the frieze in his bedroom-study at Monticello. The engraving at the beginning of Part IV ("Winter") reproduces details of the Theater of Marcellus at Rome; Jefferson looked to the theater for a model for Doric motifs used in the exterior entablature of Monticello. The other engravings in the book contain details and motifs similar to those used by Jefferson in the decoration of Monticello.

Notes and Sources

This book is, in part, a book about Jefferson traveling, and where possible I have preferred, in the notes, those editions that a traveler following in Jefferson's footsteps might conveniently carry with him on his journey. Particularly valuable, in this connection, are *Jefferson Abroad*, a volume of letters and memorandums written by Jefferson in Europe, edited by Douglas L. Wilson and Lucia Stanton, and the Library of America edition of Jefferson's *Writings*, edited by Merrill D. Peterson.

KEY TO BRIEF CITATIONS

DNB	*The Dictionary of National Biography* (London, New York: Oxford University).
Ford, *Writings*	Thomas Jefferson, *The Writings of Thomas Jefferson,* 10 vols., ed. Paul Leicester Ford (New York: Putnam's, 1892–99).
Jefferson Abroad	Thomas Jefferson, *Jefferson Abroad,* ed. Douglas L. Wilson and Lucia Stanton (New York: Modern Library, 1999).
Lipscomb and Bergh, *Writings*	Thomas Jefferson, *The Writings of Thomas Jefferson,* 20 vols., ed. Andrew A. Lipscomb and Albert Ellery Bergh (Washington, D.C.: Jefferson Memorial Association, 1903–5).
Papers	Thomas Jefferson, *The Papers of Thomas Jefferson,* 29 vols. to date, ed. Julian P. Boyd et al. (Princeton, N.J.: Princeton University, 1950–).
Writings	Thomas Jefferson, *Writings,* ed. Merrill D. Peterson (New York: Library of America, 1984).

PROLOGUE

xiii   *"burning the candle of life":* Jefferson to Elizabeth House Trist, Paris, December 15, 1786, in *Jefferson Abroad,* 113.

xiii   *the "empty bustle" of Paris:* Jefferson to Anne Willing Bingham, Paris, February 7, 1787, ibid., 125.

xiii   *He drew, in a letter:* ibid., 125–26.

xiv   *"My temperament," Jefferson said:* Jefferson to John Adams, Monticello, Va., April 8, 1816, in *Writings,* 1382.

xiv   *"being becomes a burthen"*: Jefferson to Martha ("Patsy") Jefferson, Aix-en-Provence, March 28, 1787, in *Jefferson Abroad*, 136.

xiv   *"No laborious person," Jefferson said:* ibid.

xiv   *"Not less than two hours"*: Jefferson to Thomas Mann Randolph, Paris, August 27, 1786, ibid., 92–93.

xv   *"I have known some great walkers"*: ibid., 92.

xv   *"shakes off sleep"*: Jefferson to Peter Carr, Paris, August 19, 1785, ibid., 19. The *"object of walking"*: ibid., 18.

xv   *"a fixed and an early hour"*: ibid., 19.

xv   *"without an hour"*: Jefferson to Dr. Vine Utley, Monticello, Va., March 21, 1818, in *Writings*, 1417.

xv   *a liberating (Whig) revolution:* The classic account of the first Whig revolution, the English Revolution of 1688, is Thomas Babington Macaulay's *History of England from the Accession of James II*, as exciting now as when it appeared a century and a half ago; available in many editions, but be wary of abridgments (5 vols., 1849–61). The most intelligent defense of Whig thought is Friedrich A. Hayek's *The Constitution of Liberty* (Chicago: University of Chicago Press, 1960). Among the most perceptive criticisms of Whiggery are to be found in John Ruskin's work; see especially Ruskin's memoir, *Præterita: Outlines of Scenes and Thoughts . . . (1886–89)*, one of the most perfectly written books in English.

xvi   *"sworn upon the altar of God"*: Jefferson to Dr. Benjamin Rush, Monticello, Va., September 23, 1800, in *Writings*, 1082.

xvi   *Ever since Garry Wills:* Garry Wills, *Inventing America: Jefferson's Declaration of Independence* (Garden City, N.Y.: Doubleday, 1978).

xvii *the superabundance of creeds and destinies:* But is this plenitude of possibility a uniquely modern (Whig) phenomenon? Other creeds were, to be sure, on sale in the medieval markets, but so strong was the animating vision of Christendom that it assimilated the challenges (such as that of Aristotle, delivered by way of Islamic philosophy) or suppressed them. Not until the appearance of Luther did a dissenter from the prevailing orthodoxy succeed in obtaining a significant share of the European spiritual markets.

xvii *"I am of a sect"*: Jefferson to Ezra Stiles, June 25, 1819. People say that Jefferson was a deist. How can they be so sure? "I never told my own religion," he once said to Mrs. Smith. See Jefferson to Mrs. Samuel H. (Margaret Bayard) Smith, Monticello, Va., August 6, 1816, in *Writings*, 1404. He at one point professed himself "a *real* Christian," but it is not clear what exactly Christianity meant to him. "*I* am a *real* Christian," he wrote, "that is to say, a disciple of the doctrines of Jesus, very different from the Platonists, who call *me* infidel and *themselves* Christians and preachers of the gospel, while they draw all their characteristic dogmas from what its author never said nor saw." Jefferson to Charles Thomson, Monticello, Va., January 9, 1816, ibid., 1373 (emphasis in original).

xvii *"All honor to Jefferson"*: Lincoln to Henry L. Pierce and others, April 6, 1859, in Lincoln, *Speeches and Writings: 1859–1865*, ed. Donald E. Fehrenbacher (New York: Library of America, 1989), 19.

xvii *"I have a breathless feeling"*: Quoted in Merrill D. Peterson, *The Jefferson Image in the American Mind* (1960, reprint, New York and Oxford: Oxford University Press, 1962, reissued 1985), 352.

xviii *F.D.R. laid the cornerstone:* ibid., 430–31.

xviii *Each April:* ibid., 360–61.

xviii *"the most extraordinary collection"*: John F. Kennedy, *"Let the Word Go Forth": The Speeches, Statements, and Writings of John F. Kennedy*, ed. Theodore C. Sorensen (New York: Delacorte Press, 1988), 360.

xviii *"his classical voyage"*: Quoted in Karl Lehmann, *Thomas Jefferson, American Humanist* (New York: Macmillan, 1947), 31.

xx   *odor of phrases"*: This was Frederick Scott Oliver's assessment of Jefferson's legacy in his strange and brilliant book, *Alexander Hamilton: An Essay on American Union* (New York: G.P. Putnam's Sons, and London: Archibald Constable & Co., 1907), 256. The book, with its picture of Hamilton as an American Superman, was a favorite of Theodore Roosevelt's.

xx   *the "most dangerous poison":* Jefferson to Martha Jefferson, Languedoc, May 21, 1787, in *Jefferson Abroad*, 147.

xx   *Ennui was what:* On Montaigne's notion of "soul error," see Roger Shattuck, *Proust's Way: A Field Guide to "In Search of Lost Time"* (London: Norton, 2000), 84. Pascal analyzed the problem in his *Pensées:*

> We never keep to the present. We recall the past; we anticipate the future. . . .
> We are so unwise that we wander about in times that do not belong to us, and
> do not think of the only one that does; so vain that we dream of times that are
> not and blindly flee the only one that is. . . . Let each of us examine his thoughts;
> he will find them wholly concerned with the past or the future. We almost never
> think of the present, and if we do think of it, it is only to see what light it throws
> on our plans for the future. . . . Thus we never actually live, but hope to live, and
> since we are always planning how to be happy, it is inevitable that we should
> never be so.

Blaise Pascal, *Pensées* (1670; reprint, trans. A. J. Krailsheimer [New York: Penguin, 1988]), 43. Swift observed that very "few men, properly speaking, *live* at present, but are providing to *live* another time." Jonathan Swift, "Thoughts on Various Subjects, Moral and Diverting" (1706; reprint in *The Portable Swift*, ed. Carl C. Van Doren [New York: Penguin, 1986]), 82. But the idea is as old as Lucretius and Ecclesiastes.

xx   *time becomes more precious:* See Jefferson to Peter Carr, Paris, August 18, 1785, in *Jefferson Abroad*, 16.

PART ONE: SPRING

1. DECAY

3   *His first memory:* Sarah Randolph, *The Domestic Life of Thomas Jefferson* (1871; reprint, Charlottesville: Thomas Jefferson Memorial Foundation, by University Press of Virginia, 1978), 23.

4   *a "hard student":* Jefferson to Dr. Vine Utley, Monticello, Va., March 21, 1819, in *Writings*, 1416.

4   *"horse racers, card players, fox hunters":* Jefferson, "Autobiography," in *Writings*, 4–5; Jefferson to L. H. Girardin, January 15, 1815, in Lipscomb and Bergh, *Writings*, 14:231.

4   *The racecourse beckoned:* Dumas Malone, *Jefferson and His Time*, 6 vols. (Boston: Little, Brown, 1948–1981), 1:64.

4   *In the mornings he would go:* See Jefferson's description—"enthusiastic moment of the death of the fox"—in Jefferson to L. H. Girardin, January 15, 1815, in Lipscomb and Bergh, *Writings*, 14:231.

4   *the music of their sisters' singing:* "I was vastly pleased with her playing on the spinette and singing." Jefferson to William Fleming, Richmond, Va., c. October 1763, in *Papers*, 1:12–13, a letter that contains Jefferson's youthful reflections on the "ups and downs of a country life."

5   *"all body and no mind":* "Now, take any race of animals, confine them in idleness and inaction, whether in a stye, a stable or a state-room, pamper them with high diet, gratify all their sexual appetites, immerse them in sensualities, nourish their passions, let everything bend before them, and banish whatever might lead them to think, and in a few generations they become all body and no mind." Jefferson to John Langdon, March 5, 1810, in Lipscomb and Bergh, *Writings*, 12:378.

5   *too much powder:* "And as for admiration I am sure the man who powders most, parfumes most, embroiders most, and talks most nonsense, is most admired." Jefferson to John Page, Fairfields, Va., December 25, 1762, in *Papers*, 1:5.

5   *"Devilsburgh":* Jefferson to John Page, Williamsburg, Va., January 23, 1764, and April 9, 1764, ibid., 1:14, 17. In spite of its evils, the presence of men like Mr. Wythe and Dr. Small made Williamsburg what Jefferson later called "the finest school of manners and morals that ever existed in America."

5   *mortified by his profligacy:* Jefferson's guardian was apparently less perturbed by the young man's conduct. "No, no; if you have sowed your wild oats in this manner, Tom," the benevolent gentleman wrote to Jefferson, "the estate can well afford to pay your expenses." Randolph, *Domestic Life* (Charlottesville: Thomas Jefferson Memorial Foundation, by University of Virginia, 1978), 37. See also Henry S. Randall, *The Life of Thomas Jefferson,* 3 vols. (1858), chap. 1; Malone, *Jefferson and His Time,* 1:57; and Claude G. Bowers, *The Young Jefferson: 1743–1789* (Boston: Houghton Mifflin, 1945), 22.

5   *There was an unhealthiness:* On the climate and diseases of the tidewater, see David Hackett Fischer, *Albion's Seed: Four British Folkways in America* (New York: Oxford University, 1989), 236. President Washington described the tidewater climate to Sir John Sinclair in 1796: "Towards the seaboard of the Southern States, and farther south more so, the lands are low, sandy, and unhealthy; for which reason I shall say little concerning them, for as I should not choose to be an inhabitant of them myself, I ought not to say anything that would induce others to be so." Quoted in Henry Adams, *History of the United States* (1889–91), reprinted as *History of the United States of America during the Administrations of Thomas Jefferson,* ed. Earl N. Harbert (New York: Library of America, 1986), 27.

6   *Jefferson's father, Peter Jefferson:* Peter Jefferson's father, Thomas Jefferson, was in rank a gentleman, but there is some reason to believe that Peter Jefferson's paternal grandfather, who was also called Thomas Jefferson, was in early manhood a yeoman farmer. See Malone, *Jefferson and His Time,* 1:8.

6   *"traced thro' many generations":* Rev. Jonathan Boucher, quoted in David Hackett Fischer, *Albion's Seed,* 275.

6   *"indolent," "impatient of reproof," and "irritable":* Martha Jefferson Randolph to Jefferson, Edgehill, Va., November 18, 1808, in Thomas Jefferson, *The Family Letters of Thomas Jefferson,* ed. Edwin Morris Betts and James Adam Bear, Jr. (Columbia: University of Missouri, 1966), 360. In this letter Martha Jefferson (by now Martha Jefferson Randolph) is describing to her father the character of her son, young Thomas Jefferson Randolph. "His judgment," she wrote, "when not under the influence of passion is as good as can be expected at his age but he is indolent impatient of reproof and *at times* irritable. He is however anxious to learn rigidly correct in his moral and affectionate in his temper. *I see enough of the Randolph character in him to give me some uneasiness as to the future"* (emphasis in last sentence added).

6   *The family traditions:* In the 1730s, a decade before Thomas Jefferson's birth, one of William Randolph's granddaughters, Mary Isham Randolph of Tuckahoe, eloped with a slave overseer, an Irishman called Enoch Arden. The lovers were married, and afterward Mary gave birth. Mad with rage at Arden's presumption in marrying into the gentry, Mary's kinsmen fell upon the young couple in their abode at Elk Island, on the James River. There, according to legend, they slew Arden and the child, then took Mary back to Tuckahoe, where she suffered from periodic bouts of insanity for the rest of her life. Mary went on to marry James Keith and by him had a daughter, also called Mary, afterward the mother of John Marshall, the great chief justice. Late in life Mary Keith is said to have received a letter from a man purporting to be Enoch Arden and to have gone permanently insane. The story is recounted in Jean Edward Smith, *John Marshall: Definer of a Nation* (1996; reprint New York: Owl Books, 1998), 24–25.

6   *young manhood dissipated in drink:* William Randolph of Turkey Island was the half nephew of Thomas Randolph, a poet who led a dissipated life in seventeenth-century London. He drank sack with Ben Jonson in the Devil Tavern, near Temple Bar, and was dead before he was thirty. *DNB,* 16:723–24. Even if one allows for the exaggerations of gossips and historians, the Randolphs were an eccentric family; their morbid qualities were carried on, into the nineteenth century, by John Randolph of Roanoke, a states'-rights congressman who in time turned against his cousin Thomas Jefferson and antagonized him with a malignant wit, the product of what the legislator called his "sublunary" Randolph genius.

6 *Jefferson took no satisfaction:* Jefferson, "Autobiography," in *Writings,* 3. Malone supposes that Jefferson was "not wholly indifferent to his ancestry" when a young man. *Jefferson and His Time,* 1:5.

6 *"aristocratical, pompous, clannish, indolent":* Jefferson to Marquis de Chastellux, Paris, September 2, 1785, in *Jefferson Abroad,* 30.

6 *"some good traits":* Jefferson to Elizabeth House Trist, Paris, December 15, 1786, ibid., 113.

7 *William Byrd II, living, it is true:* Quoted in David Hackett Fischer, *Albion's Seed,* 290–303.

7 *"The whole commerce":* Jefferson, *Notes on the State of Virginia,* query 18: Manners, in *Writings,* 288.

8 *The rapacious plant:* On the fall of tobacco prices and the growing extravagance of the planters, see Merrill D. Peterson, *Thomas Jefferson and the New Nation: A Biography* (1970; reprint, New York: Oxford University, 1975), 39.

2. ANXIETY

10 *the faithlessness of women:* See Thomas Jefferson, *Jefferson's Literary Commonplace Book,* ed. Douglas L. Wilson, The Papers of Thomas Jefferson, 2d ser. (Princeton, N.J.: University of Princeton, 1989), 70–71, sec. 117 (Euripides); 73, sec. 132 (Euripides); 76, sec. 146 (Euripides); 98–99, sec. 241 (Milton); 117–23, sec. 301–23 (Thomas Otway, Nicholas Rowe, David Mallet, Robert Dodsley).

10 *The son copied out Cicero's words:* For Jefferson's excerpts from Cicero, see Jefferson, *Literary Commonplace Book,* 56–61, sec. 59–79. "Perhaps the most persistent motif in the Literary Commonplace Book," Wilson wrote, "is death." Douglas L. Wilson, introduction to Jefferson, *Literary Commonplace Book,* 16.

10 *he toyed with the Stoic mask:* On Jefferson's experimentation with a Stoic attitude toward the world, see especially his letter to John Page, Shadwell, Va., July 15, 1763, in *Papers,* 1:10–11.

10 *an intense and undying love:* That Jefferson professed an *undying* love for Miss Burwell may be deduced from his statement to Page that "if Belinda [as he called her] will not accept of my service it shall never be offered to another." ibid., 1:10.

11 *"Was SHE there?":* Jefferson to John Page, Fairfields, Va., December 25, 1762, ibid., 1:5.

11 *"How does R.B. do":* Jefferson to John Page, Shadwell, Va., January 20, 1763, ibid., 1:7.

11 *"lay siege" to her:* Jefferson to John Page, Shadwell, Va., July 15, 1763, ibid., 1:9.

11 *"I was prepared":* Jefferson to John Page, Williamsburg, Va., October 7, 1763, ibid., 1:11.

11 *"With regard to the scheme":* Jefferson to William Fleming, Williamsburg, Va., March 20, 1764, ibid., 1:15–16.

11 *a "violent head ach":* ibid., 1:15–17.

12 *in "such exquisite pain":* Jefferson to John Page, Shadwell, Va., January 20, 1763, ibid., 1:7–8.

12 *"melancholy fit":* Jefferson to John Page, Williamsburg, Va., October 7, 1763, ibid., 1:11.

12 *"solemn notions":* Jefferson to John Page, Shadwell, Va., July 15, 1763, ibid., 1:11.

3. EXHILARATION

13 *Scotch-Irish newcomers:* See the excellent description in Willard Sterne Randall, *Thomas Jefferson: A Life* (1993; reprint, New York: HarperPerennial, 1994), 89–92.

14 *"Goths and Vandals of old":* Quoted in Willard Sterne Randall, *Thomas Jefferson,* 92.

14 *semi-barbarous":* "Then succeed our own semi-barbarous citizens, the pioneers of the advance of civilization . . ." Jefferson to William Ludlow, Monticello, Va., September 6, 1824, in *Writings,* 1496.

14 *"I enjoy Homer":* Jefferson to Dr. Joseph Priestley, Philadelphia, January 27, 1800, in *Writings,* 1072.

15 *"offered love to a handsome lady"*: Jefferson to Robert Smith, July 1, 1805.

15 *lieutenant of Albemarle:* Commission of lieutenant of Albemarle, June 8, 1770, in *Papers,* 1:42–43.

15 *the "emancipation of slaves"*: Jefferson, "Autobiography," in *Writings,* 5.

15 *"nothing liberal could expect success"*: ibid.

15 *a "mulatto slave called Sandy"*: Advertisement for a runaway slave, September 7, 1769, in *Papers,* 1:34.

15 *But her eyes, like his:* Later Jefferson's eyes are described as blue or light gray. They perhaps "changed color in the light." See Joseph J. Ellis, *American Sphinx: The Character of Thomas Jefferson* (1997; reprint, New York: Vintage, 1998), 29.

15 *"exquisitely formed"*: Randolph, *Domestic Life,* 43.

16 *"bright" mulattoes:* Fawn M. Brodie, *Thomas Jefferson: An Intimate History* (New York: Norton, 1988), 83.

16 *"He appeared to me to speak"*: Jefferson, "Autobiography," in *Writings,* 6.

16 *"I well remember the cry"*: Jefferson to William Wirt, Monticello, Va., August 14, 1814, in Lipscomb and Bergh, *Writings,* 14:169.

16 *successive British ministries:* Charles James Fox, *Memorials and Correspondence of Charles James Fox,* 4 vols., ed. Lord John Russell (London: Bentley, 1853), 1:106–27.

16 *a few hundred thousand pounds:* ibid., 1:106.

16 *impotent to beget revenue:* Thomas Babington Macaulay, "The Earl of Chatham," in *The Works of Lord Macaulay,* 8 vols., ed. Lady Trevelyan (1875; reprint, London: Longmans, 1879), 7:256.

17 *Some have questioned the closeness:* See, for example, Garry Wills, *Inventing America: Jefferson's Declaration of Independence* (Garden City, N.Y.: Doubleday, 1978), 15–18.

17 *"forwardness & zeal"*: Jefferson, "Autobiography," in *Writings,* 6.

17 *"cooked up" a resolution:* ibid., 8.

17 *"to avert us from the evils"*: ibid.

17 *Jefferson's paper was a petition:* ibid., 9–10. See also Jefferson to John W. Campbell, Monticello, Va., September 3, 1809, ibid., 1210: "The Summary View was not written for publication. It was a draught I had prepared for a petition to the king, which I meant to propose. . . . Being stopped on the road by sickness, I sent it on to the Speaker, who laid it on the table for the perusal of the members."

18 *he arrived in Philadelphia:* Henry S. Randall, *Life of Jefferson,* 1:111–12; Malone, *Jefferson and His Time,* 1:202–3.

18 *Jefferson's name was inserted:* "And I was informed afterwards by Peyton Randolph that it [the Summary View] had procured me the honor of having my name inserted in a long list of proscriptions enrolled in a bill of attainder commenced in one of the houses of parliament, but suppressed in embryo by the hasty step of events which warned them to be a little cautious." Jefferson, "Autobiography," in *Writings,* 10.

18 *a terrible significance:* See Macaulay, *History of England,* in his *Works,* 4:276.

18 *"attaint, attinctus, stained, or blackened"*: William Blackstone, *Commentaries on the Laws of England: A Facsimile of the First Edition of 1765–1769,* 4 vols. (Chicago: University of Chicago Press, 1979), 4:373–82; Philip B. Kurland and Ralph Lerner, eds., *The Founders' Constitution,* 5 vols. (Chicago: University of Chicago, 1987), 3:343–49.

4. ACTION

19 *their public-spirited toughness:* The Americans were at this time influenced by the Roman ideal of public virtue. When, after the expulsion of the kings, the Roman republic was established, "every man began to lift his head higher and to have his talents more in readiness. For kings hold the good in greater suspicion than the wicked, and to them the virtue of others (*virtus aliena*) is always fraught with danger. But after liberty was won the free state grew incredibly strong" because men competed with each other to display their virtue. Then it was that "each

man strove to be the first to strike down the foe, to scale a wall, to be seen by all while doing such a deed." Sallust, *Bellum Catilinae*, in *Selections*, trans. J. C. Rolfe, (1921; reprint, Cambridge, Mass.: Harvard University, 1998), sec. 7. See also Alexis de Tocqueville, *Democracy in America* (1835, 1840; reprint, ed. and trans. Harvey C. Mansfield and Delba Winthrop [Chicago: University of Chicago, 2000]), 593.

19   *"little spice of ambition"*: Jefferson to James Madison, Monticello, Va., April 27, 1795, in *Writings*, 1026.

19   the *"half-way house"*: Jefferson, "Autobiography," ibid., 9.

19   *"shock of electricity"*: Jefferson and the Virginia radicals had called for a day of fasting, humiliation, and prayer, which took place in the colony on June 1, 1774; the effect of this, Jefferson said, was like a "shock of electricity, arousing every man & placing him erect & solidly on his centre." ibid., 8–9.

21   the *Blue Ridge fringed with white:* Willard Sterne Randall, *Thomas Jefferson*, 248.

21   *his daughter Jane died:* Malone, *Jefferson and His Time*, 1:210.

21   *taken refuge on the man-of-war:* Christopher L. Ward, *The War of the Revolution*, 2 vols., ed. John Richard Alden (New York: Macmillan, 1952), 2:845–49.

21   *"slightly injured by a grapeshot"*: ibid., 2:848.

21   *"perfect phrensy"*: Jefferson to John Randolph, Philadelphia, November 29, 1775, in *Papers*, 1:269.

22   *"If anything has happened"*: Jefferson to Francis Eppes, Philadelphia, November 7, 1775, ibid., 1:252.

22   *unspecified "malady"*: Jefferson to Thomas Nelson, Philadelphia, May 16, 1776, ibid., 1:291.

22   *one of his violent headaches:* Edmund Pendleton to Jefferson, Williamsburg, Va., May 24, 1776, ibid., 1:296.

22   *for six weeks he lay:* Jefferson to Thomas Nelson, Philadelphia, May 16, 1776, ibid., 1:292.

22   *"order-loving, rigid" qualities:* Brodie, *Intimate History*, 115.

22   *"triggered"*: Willard Sterne Randall, *Thomas Jefferson*, 257.

22   *perfectionists"*: Al J. Mapp, Jr., *Thomas Jefferson: A Strange Case of Mistaken Identity* (Lanham, Md.: Madison Books, 1989), 106.

22   The *"successes of our arms"*: Jefferson to John Randolph, Philadelphia, November 29, 1775, in *Papers*, 1:268–69.

22   *"To undo his empire"*: ibid., 1:269.

22   *"Believe me Dear Sir"*: ibid. (emphasis added).

23   *he tended, in the hoarfrost mornings:* Malone, *Jefferson and His Time*, 1:214.

23   *"it is of all states"*: Jefferson to John Randolph, Monticello, Va., August 25, 1775, in *Papers*, 1:241.

23   *looked "with fondness"*: ibid.

24   *"almost a new man"*: Jefferson to John Page, Philadelphia, May 17, 1776, ibid., 1:293.

24   *in an "uneasy anxious state" about Mrs. Jefferson:* "I am here in the same uneasy anxious state in which I was the last fall without Mrs. Jefferson who could not come with me." Jefferson to Thomas Nelson, Philadelphia, May 16, 1776, ibid., 1:292.

24   *On Friday, June 7, 1776:* Jefferson, "Autobiography," in *Writings*, 13ff.

24   *"turned the vote of that colony"*: ibid., 18.

25   *"Yesterday," John Adams wrote:* John Adams to Abigail Adams, Philadelphia, July 3, 1776, in Abigail Adams, *The Book of Abigail and John: Selected Letters of the Adams Family, 1762–1784,* ed. L. H. Butterfield, Marc Friedlaender, and Mary-Jo Kline (Cambridge, Mass.: Harvard University Press, 1975), 139, 142.

25   *"captivating" innocent Africans:* Jefferson, "Autobiography," in *Writings*, 22.

25   *cockades of the Whig revolution:* On the "link between 1688 and 1776," the two greatest Whig revolutions, see David S. Lovejoy, "Two American Revolutions, 1689 and 1776," in *Three British Revolutions: 1641, 1688, 1776,* ed. J. G. A. Pocock (Princeton, N.J.: Princeton University, 1980), 244–62.

25   to *"place before mankind"*: Jefferson to Henry Lee, Monticello, Va., May 8, 1825, in *Writings*, 1501.

25 *The universe had changed:* Some readers will note that I have not connected Jefferson's invocation of "the laws of nature and of nature's God" to the philosophical tradition of natural law. Although the words certainly have a place in the natural-law tradition, their place has sometimes been misunderstood. The commentary of Carl Becker, in his study of the Declaration, is helpful:

> Thomas Aquinas, in the thirteenth century, noted three distinct meanings of the word "natural" as applied to man. The third of these meanings, which mediaeval writers had taken over from the classical world, Aquinas defines as "an inclination in man to the good, according to the *rational* nature which is proper to him; as, for example, man has a natural inclination to know the truth about God, and to live in society." Natural law was accordingly that part of law discoverable by right reason.

But, as Becker notes, "right reason" occupied a "strictly subordinate place in the medieval hierarchy of laws."

> According to Aquinas, the highest of all laws, comprehending all others, was the Eternal Law, which was nothing less than the full mind of God. Something, but not all, of the mind of God could be known to man: part of it had been revealed in the Bible or might be communicated through the Church (Positive Divine Law); and part of it could be discovered by human reason (Natural Law).

Natural law was "that part of the mind of God which man could discover by using his reason, but God had provided beforehand, through the Bible and the Church, a sure means of letting man know when his reason was not right reason but unreason." *The Declaration of Independence: A Study in the History of Political Ideas* (1922; reprint, New York: Vintage, 1958), 37–39. Contrast the Declaration of Independence. Only part of Aquinas's scheme of law—natural law—is to be found there. "Having deified Nature," Becker wrote, the eighteenth century could conveniently dismiss the Bible and drop the concept of Eternal Law altogether. . . . Nature was now the new God." ibid., 40, 51. In the scheme of Aquinas, man exercised his practical reason subject to the authority of divine law, as revealed in Scripture and through the teaching of the Church. This is very different from the Whig scheme set forth in the Declaration; in that document divine authority has receded into the mists; God appears there almost as a creature of Nature ("the laws of nature and of nature's God"). Pope Leo XIII had a point when he said that liberal theories of natural law (like those in the Declaration) were a travesty of Aquinas's teaching. Leo XIII, "Human Liberty" (1888; reprint, in *Saint Thomas Aquinas on Politics and Ethics,* ed. Paul E. Sigmund [New York: Norton, 1988]), 152–53.

26 *with a new set of tools:* There

> is no expression in any ancient or mediaeval language correctly translated by our expression "a right" until near the close of the middle ages: the concept lacks any means of expression in Hebrew, Greek, Latin or Arabic, classical or mediaeval, before about 1400. . . . From this it does not of course follow that there are no natural or human rights; it only follows that no one could have known what they were.

Alasdair C. MacIntyre, *After Virtue: A Study in Moral Theory* (Notre Dame, Ind.: University of Notre Dame, 1981), 67.
Only once in Jefferson's draft: Michael Novak has shown that there are other vestiges of the old Tory unity in the Declaration of Independence; he notes, among other things, the significance of Jefferson's invocation of the "Creator" in the document, a word that implies that the world "was created—was not an accident." Michael Novak, *God's Country: Taking the Declaration Seriously:* The 1999 Francis Boyer Lecture (Washington, D.C.: AEI Press, 2000), 15.

26 *Honor is a feudal idea:* See R. W. Southern, *Saint Anselm: A Portrait in a Landscape* (New York: Cambridge University, 1990), 225–26.

Part Two: Summer

1. Distress

29 *"extremely damp":* Jefferson to James Monroe, Paris, March 18, 1785, in *Jefferson Abroad,* 10.
29 *called the city "sunless":* Jefferson to William Hamilton, Washington, D.C., July 1806, in *Writings,* 1168. Jefferson was speaking particularly of England, but we know that he thought Paris no less destitute of sunshine.

> Our sky is always clear; that of Europe always cloudy. . . . It is our cloudless sky which has eradicated from our constitutions all disposition to hang ourselves, which we might otherwise have inherited from our English ancestors. During a residence of between six and seven years in Paris, I never, but once, saw the sun shine through a whole day, without being obscured by a cloud in any part of it.

Jefferson to Count de Volney, Washington, D.C., February 8, 1805, ibid., 1155.
30 *The British generals chose:* Ward, *War of the Revolution,* 2:868–69, 872–74.
30 *Tuckahoe, Fine Creek:* Malone, *Jefferson and His Time,* 1:339.
30 *Blenheim, Enniscorthy, and Poplar Forest:* ibid., 1:358.
30 *"inflicted a wound on my spirit":* Jefferson to James Monroe, Monticello, Va., May 20, 1782, in *Writings,* 778.
30 *He nursed her:* Henry S. Randall, *Life of Jefferson,* 1:384.
31 *"in the most secret drawer":* ibid.
31 *"really too burthensome to be borne":* "This miserable kind of existence is really too burthensome to be borne. . . . Were it not for the infidelity of deserting the sacred charge left me, I could not wish its continuance a moment." Jefferson to Elizabeth Wayles Eppes, [October 3, 1782], in *Papers,* 6:198.
31 *as "papa spoke very little French":* Martha Jefferson to Eliza House Trist, ibid., 8:437.
32 *They "were obliged to send immediately":* ibid.
32 *"I have had a very bad winter":* Jefferson to James Monroe, Paris, March 18, 1785, in *Jefferson Abroad,* 10.
32 *"Patsy," he told another correspondent:* Jefferson to Francis Eppes, Paris, February 5, 1785, in *Papers,* 7:636.
32 *"The departure of your family":* Jefferson to John Adams, Paris, May 25, 1785, in John Adams, *The Adams-Jefferson Letters: The Complete Correspondence between Thomas Jefferson and Abigail and John Adams,* ed. Lester J. Cappon (Chapel Hill: Institute of Early American History and Culture at Williamsburg, by University of North Carolina, 1959; reprint, 1988), 23.
32 *"It is in vain to endeavor":* Jefferson to Francis Eppes, Paris, February 5, 1785, in *Papers,* 7:635.

2. The Faubourg Saint-Germain

33 *a house called the Hôtel de Langeac:* See "Lease for the Hôtel de Langeac," c. September 5, 1785, in *Papers,* 8:485–92.
33 *"in every circumstance but the price":* Jefferson to Abigail Adams, Paris, September 4, 1785, in *Jefferson Abroad,* 33.
34 *"genteel" American ladies:* Jefferson to Martha Jefferson, Aix-en-Provence, March 28, 1787, ibid., 136–37.

34 *"voluptuary dress and arts":* Jefferson to John Banister, Jr., Paris, October 15, 1785, ibid., 51.

35 *"If any body thinks":* Jefferson to George Wythe, Paris, August 13, 1786, ibid., 86.

35 *"Of twenty millions of people":* Jefferson to Elizabeth House Trist, Paris, August 18, 1785, ibid., 15.

35 *However pronounced:* For Jefferson's reflections on the "real evils of aristocracy," see his "Observations on Démeunier's Manuscript," June 22, 1786, ibid., 76–80.

35 *The Marquis de Lafayette opened doors:* Malone, *Jefferson and His Time,* 2:15.

35 *great rich warrior families:* The Noailles family counted among its ancestors warriors who had taken part in the First Crusade. André Maurois, *Adrienne: The Life of the Marquise de La Fayette,* trans. Gerard Hopkins (New York: McGraw-Hill, 1961), 3.

36 *His friendship with Jefferson:* "Lafayette's enthusiastic admiration for Jefferson is abundantly recorded, but it is hard to make out anything closely equivalent on Jefferson's side. . . . Only once in the preserved correspondence between Jefferson and Lafayette is a personal note struck, and it is a disconcerting one." Conor Cruise O'Brien, *The Long Affair: Thomas Jefferson and the French Revolution, 1785–1800* (Chicago: University of Chicago, 1996), 32.

36 *Jefferson was made uneasy:* Jefferson to James Madison, Paris, March 18, 1785, in *Papers,* 8:39; Jefferson to James Madison, Paris, January 30, 1787, in *Jefferson Abroad,* 123.

36 *He "is a most valuable auxiliary":* Jefferson to James Madison, Paris, January 30, 1787, in *Jefferson Abroad,* 123; see also Jefferson to John Jay, Paris, October 23, 1786, in *Papers,* 10:485.

36 *Madame de Tessé was not without:* See *Papers,* 10:158–59; William Howard Adams, *The Paris Years of Thomas Jefferson* (New Haven, Conn.: Yale University, 1997), 227–30; and George Green Shackelford, *Thomas Jefferson's Travels in Europe, 1784–1789* (Baltimore: Johns Hopkins University, 1995), 106. On her republicanism, see Henry S. Randall, *Life of Jefferson,* 1:468.

37 *"Here it seems":* Jefferson to Charles Bellini, Paris, September 30, 1785, in *Jefferson Abroad,* 43.

37 *"The roughnesses of the human mind":* Jefferson to Elizabeth House Trist, Paris, August 18, 1785, ibid., 15.

37 *"Here we have singing":* Jefferson to Abigail Adams, Paris, August 9, 1786, ibid., 10:203.

37 *"Were I to proceed":* Jefferson to Charles Bellini, Paris, September 30, 1785, in *Jefferson Abroad,* 43.

37 *His fetish for folios:* Helen Duprey Bullock, *My Head and My Heart: A Little History of Thomas Jefferson and Maria Cosway* (New York: Putnam's Sons, 1945), 7.

37 *diplomatic privileges:* See *Papers,* 10:353.

38 *Singing was one of the few:* Jefferson, *Notes on the State of Virginia,* in *Writings,* 266.

38 *He criticized French aristocrats:* Jefferson's attitude toward the decadent sensuality of ancien régime France is reflected in his letters. The "chaste affections," he wrote, were despised in Paris. "Intrigues of love," he noted, occupied the young aristocrats: the men were caught up in the "spirit of female intrigue destructive" of their happiness or consumed by "a passion for whores destructive" of their health. Jefferson to Charles Bellini, Paris, September 30, 1785, in *Jefferson Abroad,* 42–44; and Jefferson to John Banister, Jr., Paris, October 15, 1785, ibid., 51. "Conjugal love" had "no existence among" the great ones of Paris, and the settled passions of "domestic happiness" were "utterly unknown" in well-to-do households. As for "fidelity to the marriage bed," Jefferson said, such fastidiousness was considered an "ungentlemanly practice" in Paris. Jefferson to John Banister, Jr., ibid.

38 *an unnatural aristocracy:* For Jefferson's thoughts on "natural" aristocracy versus "pseudo-aristocracy," see Jefferson to John Adams, Monticello, Va., October 28, 1813, in *Writings,* 1305–6.

38 *"into a Patrician order":* Jefferson, "Autobiography," ibid., 32.

38 *"very exacting of his groom":* Randolph, *Domestic Life* (Charlottesville: Thomas Jefferson Memorial Foundation, by the University of Virginia, 1978), 49.

39 *canine was the word:* Jefferson to James Madison, Paris, January 30, 1787, in *Jefferson Abroad,* 123.

39 *the tubs of oleanders:* For this staple of the aristocratic *hôtels* of Paris, see Stendhal, *The Red and the Black: A Chronicle of the Nineteenth Century* (1830; reprint, 2 vols., based on translation by C. S. Scott, ed. Ann Jefferson [New York: Everyman, 1991]), 2:76.

3. Passion

40 *"I will beg the favor of you"*: Jefferson to William Stephens Smith, Paris, July 9, 1786, in *Jefferson Abroad*, 84.

40 *"I must pray your taylor"*: Jefferson to William Stephens Smith, Paris, October 22, 1786, ibid., 108.

40 *an even graver difficulty*: On the complicated question of Jefferson's debts, see Malone, *Jefferson and His Time*, 1:443–44.

41 *chairs upholstered in pressed velvet*: William L. Beiswanger, Peter J. Hatch, Lucia Stanton, and Susan R. Stein, *Thomas Jefferson's Monticello* (Chapel Hill: Thomas Jefferson Memorial Foundation, by University of North Carolina, 2002), 88.

41 *the "choicest editions existing"*: Jefferson to Samuel Harrison Smith, Monticello, Va., September 21, 1814, in *Writings*, 1354.

41 *"Cannot you invent some commissions"*: Jefferson to William Stephens Smith, Paris, July 9, 1786, in *Jefferson Abroad*, 84.

41 *like dead men's guts*: See John Ruskin's description of English weather in Ruskin, *Fors Clavigera: Letters to the Workmen and Labourers of Great Britain*, ed. Dinah Birch, Whitehouse Edition of John Ruskin (1871–84; reprint, Edinburgh: University of Edinburgh, 2001), letter 8, 29,

41 *"went far beyond my ideas"*: Jefferson to John Page, Paris, May 4, 1786, in *Jefferson Abroad*, 73.

42 *"We give and receive them"*: Jefferson to David Humphreys, Paris, August 14, 1786, in *Papers*, 10:251.

42 *She was Italian born*: DNB, 4:1203. Maria's youth is shrouded in obscurity, and there are discrepancies in the information that has come down to us. These do not materially affect the story. Bullock, for example, says that Charles Hadfield, whom she describes as a wealthy Manchester merchant, had his hostelry in Florence, not Leghorn. According to her, he died in 1778, not 1776. Compare *DNB*, 4:1203; Stephen Lloyd, *Richard and Maria Cosway: Regency Artists of Taste and Fashion* (Edinburgh: Scottish National Portrait Gallery, 1995), 41–42.

42 *Maria as an artist*: Grove Dictionary of Art, 34 vols. (New York: Grove's Dictionaries, 1996), 8:20 and Bullock, *My Head and My Heart*, 16.

42 *Charles Towneley, a collector*: DNB, 19:1024–25.

44 *Towneley and his circle*: John Brewer, *The Pleasures of the Imagination: English Culture in the Eighteenth Century* (New York: Farrar, Straus, 1997), 267–68.

44 *The Prince of Wales became*: Bullock, *My Head and My Heart*, 14.

44 *"Among my painters"*: ibid., 145.

44 *"how to prevent a separation"*: Jefferson to Maria Cosway, Paris, October 12, 1786, in *Jefferson Abroad*, 97–98.

44 *the duchess d'Enville*: Also spelled *d'Anville*.

44 *"which required immediate attention"*: Jefferson to Maria Cosway, Paris, October 12, 1786, in *Jefferson Abroad*, 97–98.

44 *Later they watched*: Jefferson to Maria Cosway, Paris, October 12, 1786, *Jefferson Abroad*, 98; Bullock, *My Head and My Heart*, 21; Shackelford, *Jefferson's Travels*, 70–71.

44 *"How well I remember"*: Jefferson to Maria Cosway, Paris, October 12, 1786, in *Jefferson Abroad*, 98.

4. Sentiment

45 *"some kind of crucial failure"*: Brodie, *Intimate History*, 225.

45 *"many lascivious statements"*: Bullock, *My Head and My Heart*, 144–45.

45 *"music, modesty, beauty"*: Jefferson to Maria Cosway, Paris, October 12, 1786, in *Jefferson Abroad*, 99.

46 *excessive fondness for novels*: "A great obstacle to good education is the inordinate passion prevalent for novels, and the time lost in that reading which should be instructively employed." Jefferson to Nathaniel Burwell, Monticello, Va., March 14, 1818, in *Writings*, 1411.

46   *He listed one of these:* Jefferson to Robert Skipworth, with a list of books, Monticello, Va., August 3, 1771, ibid., 743.

46   *"impetuous but chaste love":* Jean-Jacques Rousseau, *Julie, ou la Nouvelle Héloïse* (1761), reprinted as *La Nouvelle Héloïse,* trans. Judith H. McDowell (University Park, Pa.: Penn State University, 1986), 78, letter 29.

47   *"How beautiful was every object!":* Jefferson to Maria Cosway, Paris, October 12, 1786, in *Jefferson Abroad,* 98, 102.

47   *coarse and vigorous fathers:* Lytton Strachey, "Horace Walpole," reprinted in *Biographical Essays* (New York: Harcourt, Brace, 1969), 190.

47   *had been "quite neglected":* Jefferson, "Autobiography," in *Writings,* 3.

47   *a sentimental novel he admired:* Jefferson to Robert Skipworth, with a list of books, Monticello, Va., August 3, 1771, ibid., 743.

48   *"Mothers, old men, children":* Simon Schama, *Citizens: A Chronicle of the French Revolution* (New York: Knopf, 1989), 157–59, 213.

48   *the hero, in his blue coat:* Johann Wolfgang von Goethe, *The Sorrows of Young Werther* (1774; reprint, trans. Meyer, Elizabeth, and Louise Bogan, in *Selected Works* [New York: Everyman, 2000]), 118.

48   *Sophie, comtesse d'Houdetot:* Bullock, *My Head and My Heart,* 8.

48   *"on horseback and in men's clothes":* Jean-Jacques Rousseau, *The Confessions* (1781, 1788; reprint, trans. J. M. Cohen [New York: Penguin, 1953]), 408.

48   *he received "much pleasure":* Jefferson to Abigail Adams, Paris, June 21, 1785, in *Jefferson Abroad,* 13.

49   *the unviolated rose:* Shakespeare has Duke Theseus contrast the blessedness of the unviolated rose with the carnal happiness of the "rose distill'd":

> *Thrice blessed they that master so their blood,*
> *To undergo such maiden pilgrimage;*
> *But earthlier happy is the rose distill'd,*
> *Than that which withering on the virgin thorn*
> *Grows, lives, and dies, in single blessedness.*

A Midsummer Night's Dream, 1.1.76ff. See also Dante, *Paradiso* (14th century reprint, trans. Allen Mendelbaum [New York: Bantam, 1986]) 23.73ff, 31.1ff.

49   *The truest loves:* In the sentimental conception of love, as in the medieval erotic tradition from which it descended, sensual pleasure was prolonged because sexual consummation was delayed or never occurred; such consummation was viewed by the sentimental lover as a *danger* to love, not as its fruition: love was altered in the fulfillment, and altered for the worse. "The slightest change in our present condition," Rousseau has Saint-Preux tell Julie in *La Nouvelle Héloïse,* "could only seem to me to be an evil one. No, even were we united forever by a sweeter bond, I wonder whether our happiness would not soon be destroyed by its excess. The moment of possession is a crisis in love." Jean-Jacques Rousseau, *Nouvelle Héloïse,* 44, letter 9. Or as Rousseau said in another place, "I loved her too well to wish to possess her." *Confessions,* 413.

49   *the road of love:* Dante, *La Vita Nuova* (c. 1293; reprint, trans. Barbara Reynolds [London: Penguin, 1969]), 7.35.

49   *the divine love:* Dante, *Inferno,* 1.39; *Paradiso,* 33.85ff, 145.

49   *The opium of the luminaries:* Garry Wills describes the influence of the Scottish moral philosophy on Jefferson's thought in *Inventing America.* Wills emphasizes the influence of Francis Hutcheson's ideas on Jefferson; more recent scholarship has pointed to Jefferson's debt to Lord Kames. It should be noted that in the foreword to a new edition of *Inventing America,* Wills observes that critics have misunderstood his emphasis on Hutcheson. "I was," Wills writes, "trying to make a more general case for [Jefferson's] reliance on the Scots, and Hutcheson I took as their typical voice, as what Arthur Herman calls 'the founding father of the Scottish Enlightenment.'" *Inventing America: Jefferson's Declaration of Independence* (Boston: Mariner Books, 2002), viii.

49 *a "moral sense":* Jefferson to Peter Carr, Paris, August 10, 1787, in *Jefferson Abroad,* 182–83.

49 *"feelings of sympathy":* Jefferson to Maria Cosway, Paris, October 12, 1787, ibid., 103.

50 *"loose and negligent":* Jefferson to Martha Jefferson, Annapolis, Md., December 22, 1783, in *Papers,* 6:417.

50 *be "as cleanly and properly dressed":* ibid.

50 *the Théâtre des Italiens:* Bullock, *My Head and My Heart,* 26; William Howard Adams, *Paris Years,* 223.

50 *"the dispositions with which Arlequin":* Jefferson to Maria Cosway, Paris, October 12, 1786, in *Jefferson Abroad,* 105.

50 *"Kneel to Mrs. Cosway":* Jefferson to John Trumbull, Paris, August 24, 1788, in *Papers,* 13:546.

51 *"I am indeed":* Jefferson to Maria Cosway, Paris, October 12, 1787, in *Jefferson Abroad,* 96.

51 *It is unlikely that their relationship was ever carnal:* See the relevant note to chap. 6, "Wine," below.

51 *Jefferson's language is that of Rousseau's:* Compare the tremulous anxiety in Jefferson's letter with the hysterical anguish of Rousseau's Saint-Preux, who at this point in *Nouvelle Héloïse* has merely kissed his Julie:

> "What have you done, ah! what have you done, my Julie? You wanted to reward me and you have destroyed me. I am drunk, or rather, I am insane. My senses are disordered; all my faculties are disturbed by that fatal kiss. You wished to ease my pain? Cruel one, you sharpened it. It was poison that I gathered from your lips. It is seething within me, it inflames my blood, it is killing me, and thus your compassion has caused my death."

Jean-Jacques Rousseau, *Nouvelle Héloïse,* letter 14, 52.

51 *"abyss of shame":* ibid., letters 26–29, 71–78.

51 *"divert" his "pain":* Maria Cosway to Jefferson, September 20, 1786, in *Papers,* 10:393–94.

51 *the "spoiled" airhead:* For the reference, see Brodie, *Intimate History,* 208.

52 *devoted to the memory:* Her full name was Maria Louisa Catherine Cecilia Cosway, née Hadfield.

52 *Sir Walter Scott's novels:* Particularly those in which the Whig hero finds a way to overcome both his own scruples and those of the Tory lady he loves—for example, Francis Osbaldistone in *Rob Roy* (1817), Henry Morton in *Old Mortality* (1816), and Alan Fairford in *Redgauntlet* (1824).

5. WOUND

53 *"solitary and sad":* Jefferson to Maria Cosway, Paris, October 12, 1787, in *Jefferson Abroad,* 96.

53 *"Having performed the last sad office":* ibid.

54 *"which does not belong to me":* Maria Cosway to Jefferson, September 20, 1786, in *Papers,* 10:393–94.

54 *Bishop Bossuet's books:* Jefferson to Robert Skipworth, with a list of books, Monticello, Va., August 3, 1771, in *Writings,* 745.

54 *Patsy had thought:* Henry S. Randall, *Life of Jefferson,* 1:538.

54 *"vera Amica":* Maria Cosway to Jefferson, [November 17, 1786], in *Papers,* 10:539.

54 *"Why do you say":* Maria Cosway to Jefferson, [London, October 30, 1786], ibid., 10:494–96.

55 *the "unsuccessful struggle":* T. S. Eliot, "Baudelaire," reprinted in *Selected Essays: New Edition* (New York: Harcourt, Brace, 1950), 375.

55 *"full or ready to burst":* Maria Cosway to Jefferson, [London, October 30, 1786], in *Papers,* 10:494–96.

55 *Maria once dressed up:* Lloyd, *Richard and Maria Cosway,* 47, 121.

55 *"the rigor of the Melancholy":* Maria Cosway to Jefferson, [London, October 30, 1786], in *Papers,* 10:494–96.

55 *"There are no Monasteries":* ibid.

56 *all "her gayety was gone":* Quoted in Bullock, *My Head and My Heart,* 148.

56 *"fog and smoke"*: Maria Cosway to Jefferson, [London, October 30, 1786], in *Papers*, 10:494–96.

56 *"Madame Cosway in a convent!"*: Jefferson to Angelica Church, Germantown, Pa., November 27, 1793, in *Writings*, 1013.

6. Wine

57 *"The climate and exercise"*: Jefferson to James Monroe, Paris, March 18, 1785, in *Jefferson Abroad*, 10. Jefferson had contemplated the trip for some time. In September 1786 he wrote that "[a]bout the first of the next month I shall accompany the court to Fontainbleau and after a short stay there, make a tour to Lyons, Toulon, Marseilles &c. the canal of Languedoc, Bordeaux &c. to Paris. This will be more agreeable and more useful than lounging six weeks at Fontainbleau." Jefferson to John Banister, Jr., Paris, September 7, 1786, in *Papers*, 10:332. Jefferson's dislocated wrist, however, prevented him from making the journey in the fall: "I intended to have visited the South of France this fall, but am prevented by this unlucky accident to my wrist which I cannot in the least use yet. We are now however satisfied that it is set, and that time alone is necessary for it's reestablishment." Jefferson to John Trumbull, Paris, October 13, 1786, ibid., 10:460.

57 the *"state of our business"*: Jefferson to James Monroe, Paris, March 18, 1785, in *Jefferson Abroad*, 10.

57 *"an opportunity of examining the canal"*: Jefferson to James Madison, Paris, January 30, 1787, ibid., 124.

58 *"I have great anxieties"*: ibid.

58 *"strongly advised"*: Jefferson to Abigail Adams, Paris, December 21, 1786, in John Adams, *Adams-Jefferson Letters*, 159.

58 *"obstinately" swollen*: ibid.

58 *"I am inclined to think"*: Martha Jefferson to Jefferson, Paris, March 8, 1787, in *Papers*, 11:203.

58 *"burning the candle of life"*: Jefferson to Elizabeth House Trist, Paris, December 15, 1786, in *Jefferson Abroad*, 113 (emphasis added).

58 the *"meridian" of his life*: Jefferson to Count van Hogendorp, Annapolis, Md., May 4, 1784, in *Papers*, 7:208–9.

58 *he told Mrs. Adams*: Abigail Adams to Cotton Tufts, September 8, 1784, in Adams family, *Adams Family Correspondence*, 6 vols., ed. Richard Alan Ryerson, Joanna Revelas, Celeste Walker, Gregg Lint, and Humphrey Costello (Cambridge, Mass.: Harvard University, 1963–92), 5:458.

58 *"Heaven has submitted our being"*: Jefferson to Maria Cosway, Paris, November 29, 1786, in *Jefferson Abroad*, 112.

59 *"I am determined"*: ibid.

59 *"they prove you think of me"*: Jefferson to Maria Cosway, Paris, October 13, 1786, ibid., 107.

59 that *"history," he called it*: ibid.

59 *"effusions of the heart"*: Jefferson to Maria Cosway, Paris, November 19, 1786, ibid., 110. The correspondence between Jefferson and Mrs. Cosway at this time is incidentally another evidence that their love never went very far beyond the pales of propriety. *He* was conscious of having been too much in earnest with her in the letter he wrote her on the night of her departure from Paris; but Mrs. Cosway, for her part, saw nothing untoward in the composition and was rather touched than offended by Jefferson's effusions. He thanked her for this largeheartedness, and— almost as though he were relieved that she had not thought the letter strange—grew mischievously bold. "Your goodness," he told her, "seems to have induced you to forgive, and even to flatter me" for having written at such intimate length. "That," he added, with some mirth, "was a great error." For when sins "are dear to us," he said, we are "but too prone to slide into them again." The "act of repentance itself" is often sweetened with the "thought that it clears our account for a repetition of the same sin. The friendly letter I have received from you might have been taken as a release from my promise"—the promise, that is, to write her no more effusive letters. Ibid. Now there were calluses, grave ones, on Jefferson's character, but gratuitous cal-

lousness, in a matter of delicacy, was not among his faults. It is almost inconceivable that Jefferson should have written so lightheartedly of the "sin" (venial at most) of effusive letter writing if he and his correspondent had, a few weeks before, been engaged in (what he knew Mrs. Cosway must have regarded as) the mortal sin of adultery—the violation of her marriage bed. To have written so lightly of seduction after he himself had seduced—he must have been blackguardish beyond anything even his enemies have alleged to have done *that*.

59   *"from day to day"*: Jefferson to Elizabeth House Trist, Paris, December 15, 1786, ibid., 113.

59   *"Laid up in port"*: ibid., 113–14.

59   *"The good things of this life"*: Jefferson to Abigail Adams, Paris, November 1786, in John Adams, *Adams-Jefferson Letters*, 157.

59   *"impossible events"*: Jefferson to Elizabeth House Trist, Paris, December 15, 1786, in *Jefferson Abroad*, 113.

59   be with her *"in reality"*: Jefferson to Maria Cosway, Paris, December 24, 1786, ibid., 114.

60   he was *"never happier"*: Jefferson to Maria Cosway, Paris, November 29, 1786, ibid., 112.

60   *"Tell Mrs. Cosway"*: Jefferson to John Trumbull, Paris, February 23, 1787, in *Papers*, 11:181.

60   *"The first evening"*: ibid. Jefferson's use of the word *conversation* admits of a bawdy construction; in his day the word meant, among other things, "sexual intercourse" or "intimacy." *Criminal conversation* is, or until recently was, a statutory definition of adultery in many American states.

60   *"like the birds of the air"*: Jefferson to Maria Cosway, Paris, December 24, 1786, in *Jefferson Abroad*, 114.

60   for such a cap: ibid.

60   Or perhaps she: ibid., 114–15.

60   *"I had rather be deceived"*: ibid., 115.

60   the *"best edition extant"*: Jefferson to Madame de Tott, Paris, November 28, 1786, ibid., 111.

60   had *"offered 1000 guineas"*: Jefferson to Wells and Lilly, Monticello, Va., April 1, 1818, in *Writings*, 1414.

61   the fourth book of the Iliad: Jefferson to Saint John de Crèvecoeur, Paris, January 15, 1787, in *Jefferson Abroad*, 116.

61   One of his first objects: William Howard Adams, *Paris Years*, 47.

61   to Dijon, in Burgundy: Jefferson to William Short, Lyons, March 15, 1787, in *Jefferson Abroad*, 130; Jefferson, "Notes of a Tour into the Southern Parts of France, &c.," ibid., 152.

61   *Jefferson in Burgundy*: Jefferson, "Notes of a Tour of France," ibid., 151.

61   half a thousand years: At least. There "is some reason to believe that the vineyards of Burgundy are as old as the age of the Antonines. . . . The Pagus Arebrignus is supposed by M. d'Anville to be the district of Beaune, celebrated, and even at present, for one of the first growths of Burgundy." Edward Gibbon, *The History of the Decline and Fall of the Roman Empire* (1776–88; reprint, 7 vols., ed. J. B. Bury [London: Methuen, 1920–25], 1:57 and n. 104.

62   he understood muslins: Jane Austen, *Northanger Abbey* (1817; reprint, New York: Everyman, 1992), 17.

62   muslin and chintz: Jefferson to Abigail Adams, Paris, August 9, 1786, in John Adams, *Adams-Jefferson Letters*, 148–50; Jefferson to Abigail Adams, Paris, February 22, 1787, ibid., 173; Jefferson to Abigail Adams Smith, Paris, January 15, 1787, in *Jefferson Abroad*, 117.

62   *"two pairs of Corsets"*: Jefferson to Abigail Adams Smith, Paris, January 15, 1787, in *Jefferson Abroad*, 117.

62   the *"true secret, the grand recipe"*: Jefferson to Martha Jefferson, Languedoc, May 21,1787, ibid., 147.

62   *"You know what have been"*: Jefferson to Martha Jefferson, Aix-en-Provence, March 28, 1787, ibid., 135–36.

62   *"It is while we are young"*: ibid., 136.

63   *"As for the hysterics"*: Martha Jefferson to Jefferson, Paris, April 9, 1787, in *Papers*, 11:282.

63   *"I do not like"*: Jefferson to Martha Jefferson, Aix-en-Provence, March 28, 1787, in *Jefferson Abroad*, 136.

63   perfection of manner—good form: Dr. Johnson was being unfair when he said that Chesterfield's letters taught only the "morals of a whore and the manners of a dancing-master." James Boswell, *Life of Samuel Johnson* (1791; reprint, New York: Everyman, 1992), 164. What bothered Dr.

Johnson was not so much Chesterfield's zeal for genteel forms of etiquette as his lack of zeal in supporting the doctor's own labors to produce his *Dictionary.* But even though his criticisms were exaggerated, Dr. Johnson had a point when he condemned the shallowness of Chesterfield's philosophy.

63   *"The object most interesting":* Jefferson to Martha Jefferson, Languedoc, May 21, 1787, in *Jefferson Abroad,* 147.

63   *south through Burgundy:* Jefferson, "Notes of a Tour of France," ibid., 152.

64   It *"is our own fault":* Jefferson to Martha Jefferson, Languedoc, May 21, 1787, ibid., 147.

7. LIBERATION

66   *"except against the weather-maker":* Jefferson to William Short, Lyons, March 15, 1787, in *Jefferson Abroad,* 129.

66   *Jefferson arrived at Nîmes:* Was the visit to Nîmes and its antiquities a pretext on Jefferson's part, artfully arranged to disguise sensitive diplomatic work? In the fall of 1786, Jefferson received at Paris a letter from a Brazilian medical student called José da Maia. The American minister not unnaturally thought that da Maia might have interesting things to say about the state of affairs in Brazil. In a letter from Marseilles, Jefferson explained to John Jay, the American secretary of foreign affairs, that he had informed da Maia that "I would go off my road as far as Nismes, under the pretext of seeing the antiquities of the place, if he would meet me there." Jefferson to John Jay, Marseilles, May 4, 1787, in *Papers,* 11:339. Jefferson did indeed meet da Maia at Nîmes, and he forwarded to Jay an account of their conversation; the two men talked, among other things, of the possibility of a revolution against the Portuguese in Brazil. Malone, *Jefferson and His Time,* 2:119. But it is difficult to accept Jefferson's assertion to Jay that his visit was merely a cover for intelligence gathering. Before he knew anything of da Maia, Jefferson had heard reports of a marvelous temple at Nîmes, "one of the most beautiful, if not the most beautiful and precious morsel of architecture left us by antiquity." Jefferson to James Madison, Paris, September 20, 1785, in *Jefferson Abroad,* 34. Da Maia or no, Jefferson would have "turned off" his road to see the Maison Carrée. But Jay was his superior in the diplomatic corps, and Jefferson wanted to assure him that he was hard at work during his trip to the south, and not drunk with aesthetic excess. Jefferson, at this time in his life, was always anxious, in his letters to men of affairs, to portray himself as a hardheaded master of business; it was in his letters to female correspondents that he spoke of the depth of his passion for art. In his letters to men, he was apt to be more guarded. "You see I am an enthusiast on the subject of the arts," he wrote to James Madison. "But it is an enthusiasm of which I am not ashamed." Ibid., 35.

66   *"a warm sun":* Jefferson to Madame de Tessé, Nîmes, March 20, 1787, ibid., 132.

66   *"an animal of a warm climate":* Jefferson to Maria Cosway, Paris, January 14, 1789, ibid., 275.

66   *"It is wonderful to me":* Jefferson to William Short, Aix-en-Provence, March 27, 1787, ibid., 134.

66   *"Here I am, Madam":* Jefferson to Madame de Tessé, Nîmes, March 20, 1787, in ibid., 131.

66   *Jefferson's love affair:* Jefferson had seen engravings of the Maison Carrée in Charles-Louis Clérisseau's *Antiquités de la France: Monumens de Nismes* (Paris: Pierres, 1778). See especially pl. 9. See also E. Millicent Sowerby, ed., *Catalogue of the Library of Thomas Jefferson,* 5 vols. (Washington, D.C.: Library of Congress, 1952–59), 4:376.

66   *there "is at Nismes":* Jefferson to James Buchanan and William Hay, Paris, January 26, 1786, in *Jefferson Abroad,* 58.

67   *"whole hours":* Jefferson to Madame de Tessé, Nîmes, March 20, 1787, ibid., 131.

67   *Egyptian lion gargoyles:* The inspiration for the lion gargoyles was probably Egyptian; Nîmes was settled by Roman veterans who had served in Egypt, and the city has long preserved the memory of its connection to the Nile. To this day the coat of arms of Nîmes contains the image of a crocodile fettered to a palm tree. Egyptians adorned many of their shrines—as well as their aqueducts, spouts, and cisterns—with gaping lions' heads, because, Plutarch explained, the Nile overflows its banks when for the first time each year "the sun comes into conjunction with Leo."

Plutarch, *Isis and Osiris* (1936; reprint, Cambridge: Loeb, 1987), sec. 366. See also Diodorus Siculus, *Library of History*, (Biblothēkē historikē), 1.89.

67	the *"delight of the several courts"*: Jefferson to William Short, Aix-en-Provence, March 29, 1787, in *Jefferson Abroad*, 138.

67	a sweet bastard Latin: Compare Byron, *Beppo*, st. 44. An eighteenth-century Provençal lover called his mistress *madelicado* (my pet) or, more extravagantly, *ma bergiero* (my shepherdess). Of a *homme à femmes*, the Provençals said, He would be enamored of a cat if it had a cap on (*L'amourraoharie d'uno gato corriffado*). See Frederick Augustus Fischer, *Travels to Hyères, in the South of France* (London: R. Phillips, 1806), 36–37.

67	*"This is the second time"*: Jefferson to Madame de Tessé, Nîmes, March 20, 1787, in *Jefferson Abroad*, 131.

68	druz *in the full Italian sense:* "Provençal gallantry was established in sharply separated grades through which one had to pass successively. At first one was *feignare*, hesitant, then *pregaire*, beseeching, then *entendaire*, a listener, and finally, *druz*, a lover. In Italian *drudo* means the lover of a married woman." Stendhal, *Memoirs of a Tourist* (1838; reprint, trans. Allan Seager [Evanston, Ill.: Northwestern University, 1962]), 194.

68	*"a strong body"*: Jefferson, Extracts from "Notes of a Tour of France," in *Jefferson Abroad*, 159–60.

68	The greasy aprons *"consider me"*: Jefferson to Madame de Tessé, Nîmes, March 20, 1787, ibid., 131.

68	*"love and murder novel"*: Henry S. Randall, *Life of Jefferson*, 1:28.

8. Searchings

70	*"I was alone"*: Jefferson to John Banister, Jr., Paris, June 19, 1787, in *Papers*, 11:477.

70	The *"plan of having servants"*: Jefferson to William Short, Lyons, March 15, 1787, in *Jefferson Abroad*, 131.

71	*"retired at night to his chamber"*: Jefferson to Madame de Tott, Marseilles, April 5, 1787, ibid., 141.

71	*"nourished" by the "remains"*: Jefferson to Madame de Tessé, Nîmes, March 20, 1787, ibid., 131–32; and Jefferson to William Short, Aix-en-Provence, March 29, 1787, ibid., 138.

71	*"While residing in Paris"*: Jefferson to Samuel Harrison Smith, Monticello, Va., September 21, 1814, in *Writings*, 1353.

71	Pythagoras, Epicurus, Epictetus, and Socrates: See Jefferson to Dr. Joseph Priestley, Washington, D.C., April 9, 1803, in *Writings*, 1121.

71	the *"government of those passions"*: Jefferson to Dr. Benjamin Rush, Washington, D.C., April 21, 1803, in *Writings*, 1124.

72	*"Do not bite"*: Jefferson to Maria Cosway, Paris, October 12, 1786, in *Jefferson Abroad*, 101.

72	*"grave saws and maxims"*: ibid.

72	*"follies" that would end:* ibid., 96.

72	the *"bustle and tumult"*: ibid., 101–2.

72	*"The art of life"*: ibid., 101.

72	*"The most effectual means"*: ibid.

72	*"I too am an Epicurean"*: Jefferson to William Short, Monticello, Va., October 31, 1819, in *Writings*, 1430. By this time Jefferson had largely abandoned the Stoic philosophy that had intrigued him in his youth. On his Epicurianism, and on his debt to Pierre Gassendi, the seventeeth-century interpreter of Epicurus, see Peterson, *Jefferson and the New Nation*, 53–54.

72	*"They do not terminate"*: Jefferson to Charles Bellini, Paris, September 30, 1785, in *Jefferson Abroad*, 43. The allusion is apparently to Shakespeare, *Othello*, 2.3.285ff.

72	*"I fancy it must be"*: Jefferson to Abigail Adams, Paris, September 25, 1785, in *Jefferson Abroad*, 36.

73	Jefferson taught himself: Jefferson's letter to Mrs. Bingham of February 7, 1787 (*Jefferson Abroad*, 125–27), was perhaps composed in imitation of La Bruyère. See Jean de Bruyère, *The Characters of Jean de la Bruyère*, ed. and trans. Henri van Laun (1885; reprint, New York: Brentano's, 1929), particularly chap. 8, "Of the Town," 164–82, and chap. 12, "Of Mankind," 271–327.

73 *in which he exposes the gaudier:* Mrs. Bingham was convinced that Jefferson exaggerated the irresponsible levity of the Parisians in his letter of February 7, 1787, as a writer will when he strives for literary effect. "I agree with you," she replied, "that many of the fashionable pursuits of the Parisian Ladies are rather frivolous, and become uninteresting to a reflective Mind; but the Picture you have exhibited, is rather overcharged. You have thrown a strong light upon all that is ridiculous in their Characters, and you have buried their good Qualities in the Shade." Anne Willing Bingham to Jefferson, Philadelphia, June 1, 1787, in *Papers,* 11:392.

74 *Mr. Danquerville's experience of life:* Brewer, *Pleasures of the Imagination,* 269–70; Francis Haskell, "The Baron d'Hancarville: An Adventurer and Art Historian in Eighteenth-Century Europe," in Haskell, *Past and Present in Art and Taste: Selected Essays* (New Haven, Conn.: Yale University Press, 1987).

74 *a massive erudition:* See d'Hancarville's preface to William Hamilton, *Collection of Etruscan, Greek, and Roman Antiquities from the Cabinet of the Honble. Wm. Hamilton . . . ,* 4 vols. (1766). D'Hancarville also published *Monuments de la vie privée des douze Césars . . .* and *Monuments du culte secret des dames romaines . . .* (1784). The two volumes are apparently pornographic; when I went to examine the last-mentioned volume in the New York Public Library, I was told that it had disappeared from the shelves.

74 *primitive Mediterranean fertility rituals:* The theme of life creation and life perpetuation played a part in the mystery cults, or *mysteria,* of Mediterranean antiquity, among them those of Demeter, the corn goddess, and her daughter, Persephone, which were celebrated each autumn at Eleusis, near Athens; the Orphic mysteries; and the Bacchic (Dionysian) *orgia.* The promise of eternal life guaranteed by the Dionysian mysteries constituted, Nietzsche believed, the largest part of their appeal and played a part in inspiring his own philosophy. "For it is only in the Dionysian mysteries," Nietzsche wrote,

> in the psychology of the Dionysian condition, that the *fundamental fact* of the Hellenic instinct expresses itself—its "will to life." *What* did the Hellene guarantee to himself with these mysteries? *Eternal* life, the eternal recurrence of life; the future promised and consecrated in the past; the triumphant Yes to life beyond death and change; *true* life as collective continuation of life through procreation, through the mysteries of sexuality.

Friedrich Nietzsche, *Twilight of the Idols; The Anti-Christ* (1888; reprint, trans. R. J. Hollingdale [New York: Penguin, 1990]), 119–20 (emphasis in original). See also Walter Burkert, *Greek Religion: Archaic and Classical* (1977; reprint, trans. John Raffan [Cambridge, Mass.: Harvard University, 1985]), 277ff.

74 *he was one of the authors of an intellectual revolution:* In his book *Recherches sur l'origine, l'espirit, et les progrès des arts de la Grèce . . .* (1785), d'Hancarville speculated that the "origin of all arts, in every culture," was to be found in a "common primitive religion" of sexuality. Like other eighteenth-century searchers, he supposed that the ancient fertility cults were "founded on the worship of a generative power," a "universal god of creation symbolized by the male organ of reproduction, the union of male and female sexual organs, or . . . other emblems of fertility." Alessandra Ponte, "Architecture and Phallocentrism in Richard Payne Knight's Theory," in *Sexuality and Space,* ed. Beatriz Colomina, Princeton Papers on Architecture (New York: Princeton Architectural Press, 1992), 274, 282. See also G. S. Rousseau, "The Sorrows of Priapus: Anticlericalism, Homosocial Desire, and Richard Payne Knight," in *Sexual Underworlds of the Enlightenment,* ed. G. S. Rousseau and Roy Porter (Chapel Hill: University of North Carolina, 1988), 101–53. D'Hancarville's friend Richard Payne Knight carried these speculations further in his notorious researches into Priapos Ithyphallos, a Mediterranean fertility god who "played a role in nearly all" the mystery cults. See Walter Burkert, *Ancient Mystery Cults,* Carl Newell Jackson Lectures (Cambridge, Mass.: Harvard University, 1987), 104–5; and Brewer, *Pleasures of the Imagination,* 268–69. As eccentric in his character as d'Hancarville himself, Knight was one of those patrician Whigs who dominated English life in the eighteenth century. He had passed a sickly childhood in the west of England; he had made a pilgrimage to Sicily; and he had been

elected to Parliament and to the Society of the Dilettanti, memberships that allowed him to indulge both his antiquarian and his senatorial inclinations. Though an ailment of a nervous, or
"hypochondriacal," nature forced Knight frequently to retire to his country seat, Castle Down-
ton in Herefordshire, for periods of rest, his abilities were in other directions unimpaired, and
he possessed a remarkable capacity for business and a remarkable nose for controversy. Drawing
on d'Hancarville's learning and on Sir William Hamilton's collections, Knight composed, in the
1780s, a small volume called *Treatise on the Worship of Priapus*. The book was duly printed by
the Dilettanti in 1786, and it promptly caused a scandal. The *Treatise* was at once a patrician
joke, a source of amusement to the more urbane spirits among the Dilettanti, and an attempt to
understand the significance of phallus worship in the ancient fertility cults.

75   *"The tree of liberty":* Jefferson to William Stephens Smith, Paris, November 13, 1787, in *Jeffer-*
son Abroad, 206.

75   *Attys, a Phrygian king-god:* James George Frazer, *The Golden Bough: A Study in Magic and Reli-*
gion, 12 vols. (1890–1915; reprint, New York: Avenel, 1981), 1:296–301.

75   *From the blood of Attys's brother god:* ibid., 1:280, 323.

75   *Dionysus found Ariadne:* Carl Kerényi, *Dionysos: Archetypal Image of Indestructible Life*, trans.
Ralph Manheim (Princeton, N.J.: Princeton University, 1996), 109; and Burkert, *Greek Reli-*
gion, 239–40. The mythology of Dionysus is extraordinarily intricate, and of course I do not
pretend to offer a comprehensive account of it here.

75   *"when the flowers":* M. C. Howatson, ed., *The Oxford Companion to Classical Literature*, 2nd ed.
(New York: Oxford University, 1989), 38.

75   *Jefferson possessed a marble sculpture:* Frazer, *Golden Bough*, 1:104–5; and William Howard
Adams, *Jefferson's Monticello* (New York: Abbeville Press, 1983), 119, 198, and pl. 190. *The*
Sleeping Ariadne was a gift to Jefferson from James Bowdoin, governor of Massachusetts.

76   *"a voice from the Georgian manor":* Wills, *Inventing America* (New York: Doubleday, 1978), 30.

76   *a bull to be slaughtered:* Dionysus was often represented as a bull. Frazer, *Golden Bough*, 1:325.

76   *Metaphors are by definition:* No more did T. S. Eliot—who drew on the same fertility mysticism in *The Waste Land* (1922)—believe in the literal truth of the ideas he worked into that
poem. In Eliot's "dead land" the tree has already died. The "dead tree," the poet declares near
the beginning of the poem, "gives no shelter." Jefferson's tree must be manured with blood if
it is to be kept strong. Eliot's tree requires only water. But in the "stony" country of *The Waste*
Land, there "is no water"—"only rock," "mountains of rock without water," a "dead mountain of carious [decayed, rotten] teeth that cannot spit," a "dry sterile thunder without rain."
Jefferson never embraced a hyacinth girl in order to bring about a good harvest at Monticello,
and Eliot, so far as we know, never went out naked to perform a rain dance. Eliot had no more
literal faith in the efficacy of a pilgrimage to the Chapel Perilous (see Part V of *The Waste*
Land and related notes) than Jefferson had in the bloody manure that he invoked in his letter
to Smith. Eliot called the fertility myths he used in his poem "symbols"—metaphors, that is.
See Notes on "The Waste Land," in T. S. Eliot, *Collected Poems: 1909–1962* (New York: Harcourt, Brace, 1963, 1971), 70: "Not only the title," he wrote, "but the plan and a good deal
of the incidental symbolism of the poem were suggested by Miss Jessie L. Weston's book on
the Grail legend, *From Ritual to Romance*." Weston, in the book cited by Eliot, argues that the
Grail legend preserves, in a Christian context, the essence of the ancient mystery cults, in
which candidates are initiated into the "mysteries of generation, i.e., of physical Life" and "the
Spiritual Divine Life." Weston, *From Ritual to Romance* (1920; reprint, New York: Dover,
1997), 172, 175–77. It is true that Eliot, a Christian poet, put Weston's pagan scholarship to
a Christian use in *The Waste Land*, but it would, I think, be misleading to suggest that the pagan ideas serve a purely decorative purpose there. I am inclined to believe that Eliot felt the
pagan conceits to be in some imaginative or metaphorical sense true, else he would not have
used them: they would have made his poetry false. Yet it is unlikely that he believed the conceits to be wholly true, or exactly true, or literally true, else he would indeed have gone out
and performed a rain dance.

76   *Jefferson's friend Joel Barlow:* I am here indebted to Simon Schama's fascinating exposition of Barlow and the liberty tree myth in *Landscape and Memory* (New York: Knopf, 1995), 245–63.

76 *in Barlow's retelling:* ibid., 252–55.

76 *During Liber's festival:* See Georges Dumézil, *Archaic Roman Religion, with an Appendix on the Religion of the Etruscans,* 2 vols., trans. Philip Krapp (Chicago: University of Chicago, 1966), 1:377–78; and John R. Clarke, *The Houses of Roman Italy, 100 B.C.–A.D. 250: Ritual, Space, and Decoration* (Berkeley: University of California, 1991), 212.

77 *Osiris:*

> The myth of Osiris, killed and dismembered by Seth, mourned, searched for, found and reassembled by Isis, who then conceives and gives birth to Horos, is well known, especially through Plutarch's book *On Isis and Osiris.* The mysteries of Isis are described in the most expansive mystery text we have from pagan antiquity, the last book of the *Golden Ass* of Apuleius.

Burkert, *Ancient Mystery Cults,* 6.

77 *Barlow helped to prepare the way:* Their fascination with ancient fertility cults led the eighteenth-century searchers to paint an in many ways distorted picture of ancient religion; and their errors of emphasis and interpretation misled subsequent generations of scholars. See, for example, Burkert's criticism of Frazer, whose *Golden Bough,* according to Burkert, gives the erroneous impression that "fertility magic was the centre and origin of ancient religion as such." *Greek Religion,* 266. See also Burkert, *Ancient Mystery Cults,* 75–76.

77 *"The only way":* Compare the advice of Horace: "You must give your days and nights to the study of the Greek models." Horace, *The Art of Poetry,* in *Classical Literary Criticism,* trans. T. S. Dorsch (New York: Penguin, 2001), 88.

77 *The "classical" models:* "The classical I call the healthy and the romantic the sick." Goethe, quoted in Walter Kaufmann, *Nietzsche: Philosopher, Psychologist, Antichrist* (1950; reprint, Princeton, N.J.: Princeton University, 1975), 380.

77 *the "sentimental" sickness:* Johann von Schiller, "Über naive und sentimentalische Dichtung ("On Naive and Sentimental Poetry," 1795–96.) The great canvases of Mrs. Cosway's friend Jacques-Louis David that hung in the salons during Jefferson's residence in Paris convey some idea of what the searchers sought in their neoclassical quests. Jefferson admired the paintings intensely; he later said that he did not "feel an interest in any pencil but that of David." One painting of the school of David had a special fascination for him. When Benedict Arnold sacked Richmond half a decade before, Jefferson, then the governor of Virginia, had been forced to flee his capital. Arnold had dispatched troops to find him out. It is not known where Jefferson spent the night of January 5, 1781; his enemies claimed that he lay wretchedly in a barn, cowering in fear. Jefferson himself never spoke of the matter, but it is not surprising that a painting by David's favorite pupil, Jean-Germain Drouais, should have startled him when he saw it, in Paris, on the eve of his departure for Provence. *Marius Imprisoned at Minturnae,* when Jefferson beheld it in the rue Sainte-Nicaise, "fixed me," he said, "like a statue." A "quarter of an hour" passed, or "half an hour, I do [not] know which, for I lost all ideas of time, 'even the consciousness of my existence.'" Like Jefferson, Marius, the hero of Drouais's painting, had been driven from his capital by a traitor to his country. Marius was a political leader at Rome when Sulla Felix—an ambitious general who had been deprived of a lucrative command in Asia—marched on the city at the head of six legions, the golden eagles glittering before them. Marius fled to the countryside, where, according to Plutarch, he hid himself in bogs, in remote copses, in ditches. Unlike Jefferson, however, Marius was captured by his enemies: he was dragged from the fens and brought naked into a provincial town. The town elders sent in a young barbarian to kill him; but Marius, draped only in a cloak, looked his assailant fiercely in the eye. Drouais chose for the subject of his painting the moment when the young man's resolution failed him in the face of the old man's fortitude. "I cannot kill Gaius Marius" the youth said and fled the room. Madame de Tott pointed out to Jefferson that the painting was inaccurate, that Marius had in reality been a far old man who had grown flabby and soft with the effeminate pleasures of his villa at Misenum. Jefferson acknowledged the justness of her criticisms, but they did not alter his opinion of the picture. It was, he said, "superb." The "strong expression given to the countenance of Marius," he told her, "absorbed all my atten-

tion." See Jefferson to Madame de Tott, Paris, February 28, 1787, in *Jefferson Abroad,* 129; Jefferson to Madame de Tott, Marseilles, April 5, 1787, ibid., 140; and Hugh Honour, *Neo-Classicism* (Harmondsworth, England: Penguin, 1968), 194–95. On his trip to the south of France, Jefferson noted the "sublime triumphal arch of Marius" at the entrance to the city of Orange. See Jefferson to Madame de Tessé, Nîmes, March 20, 1787, in *Writings,* 891.

78 *statues . . . for Monticello:* These included a *Diana as Huntress* and a *Venus Pudica* (modestly trying to cover up) after the Medici Venus in the Uffizi Gallery, Florence.

78 *In turning the "classic pages":* Jefferson to Dr. Joseph Priestley, Philadelphia, January 27, 1800, *Writings,* 1072.

78 *"sweet composers to that rest":* Jefferson to John Brazier, Poplar Forest, Va., August 24, 1819, *Writings,* 1423.

78 *the "vacuum of* ennui*":* ibid.

78 *the "most dangerous poison of life":* Jefferson to Martha Jefferson Languedoc, May 21, 1787, *Jefferson Abroad,* 147.

78 *"I am immersed in antiquities":* Jefferson to Madame de Tessé, Nîmes, March 20, 1787, *Jefferson Abroad,* 132–33.

78 *Nîmes:* See Clérisseau, *Antiquités de la France,* pl. 28; Thomas Pownall, *Notices and Descriptions of Antiquities of the Provincia Romana of Gaul, Now Provence, Languedoc, and Dauphine, . . .* (London: J. Nichols, 1788), ix; and Theodore Andrea Cook, *Old Provence* (1905; reprint, Oxford, England: Signal, 2001), 104–81. This last book is an excellent guide to the antiquities of Provence.

9. Cure

79 *the sepulchres of Arles:* Dante, *Inferno,* 9.112ff.

79 *this place of sleeping stones:* Jefferson, "Notes of a Tour of France," in *Jefferson Abroad,* 160; Cook, *Old Provence,* 185.

79 *the "high hills of Languedoc":* Jefferson, "Notes of a Tour of France," in *Jefferson Abroad,* 160.

79 *"broken hills of massive rock":* ibid., 161.

80 *"waving in vines":* ibid., 162.

80 *unripened lavender:* "The waste grounds throw out thyme and lavender." Ibid.

80 *"rich and beautiful":* ibid.

80 *"I am now in the land":* Jefferson to William Short, Aix-en-Provence, March 27, 1787, in *Jefferson Abroad,* 134.

80 *"The man who shoots himself":* Jefferson to William Short, Aix-en-Provence, March 27, 1787, in *Papers,* 11:247.

80 *"90. ° of Farenheit's thermometer":* Jefferson, "Notes of a Tour of France," in *Jefferson Abroad,* 162.

80 *But they proved ineffectual:* "Having taken 40. douches, without any sensible benefit, I thought it useless to continue them." Jefferson to William Short, Toulon, April 7, 1787, in *Papers,* 11:280.

80 *"my almighty physician":* Jefferson to James Monroe, Paris, March 18, 1785, in *Jefferson Abroad,* 10.

80 *the "delicious walks":* Jefferson to William Short, Aix-en-Provence, March 27, 1787, ibid., 134.

80 *shaded from the southern sun:* The elm trees of Aix have since been replaced by plane trees.

81 *"because I have been almost constantly":* Jefferson to Martha Jefferson, Aix-en-Provence, March 28, 1787, in *Jefferson Abroad,* 135.

81 *"Until now," she wrote:* Martha Jefferson to Jefferson, Paris, March 25, 1787, in *Papers,* 1:238.

81 *a "copious stock":* Edward Gibbon, *Memoirs of My Life and Writings* (1789; reprint, New York: Penguin, 1984), 143.

81 *"passionately fond":* "When I was young," Jefferson said, "I was passionately fond of reading books of history, and travels." Jefferson to the editor of the *Journal de Paris,* Paris, August 29, 1787, in *Jefferson Abroad,* 191.

81 *"It was at Rome":* Gibbon, *Memoirs,* 16.

82 *The thirty-seven-year-old Goethe:* Matthew Arnold, "A French Critic on Goethe," reprinted in Matthew Arnold, *Selections,* ed. Miriam Allott and Robert H. Super, Oxford Authors (New York: Oxford University, 1986), 418.

83 *he produced nothing comparable:* Even Dumas Malone, Jefferson's champion, conceded that Jefferson's "most important actual contribution to the constitutional thinking of this period was made indirectly, through the books he sent Madison from France. *Jefferson and His Time,* 2:162. In his chapter "Considering the American Constitution," Malone shows Jefferson reacting to developments rather than shaping them. Ibid., 2:153–79, especially 165. Jefferson's letters of this time bear Malone out; see, for example, *Writings,* 910–18.

83 Notes on the State of Virginia: Jefferson had distributed the work privately, to friends and people he admired, before he published it in the Stockdale edition of 1787. Jefferson's "Report on Government for the Western Territory" (1784) was an exercise in drafting legislation, not an expository essay.

84 *"an assembly of demigods":* Jefferson to John Adams, Paris, August 30, 1787, in *Jefferson Abroad,* 196–97.

84 *He had not formulated:* Jefferson's indecisiveness would continue even after the Philadelphia convention completed its work. There was a "great mass of good" in the proposed Constitution, Jefferson said, but also a "bitter pill or two." He approved of much in the draft document, but there were "some things" in it that "staggered" him, among them the omission of a Whig bill of rights and the absence of a limit on the number of terms a man could serve as president. See Jefferson to John Adams, Paris, November 13, 1787, ibid., 204; and Malone, *Jefferson and His Time,* 2:168.

84 *the "cleanest and neatest":* Jefferson to William Short, Aix-en-Provence, March 27, 1787, in *Jefferson Abroad,* 135.

84 *"long chain of causes and effects":* ibid.

85 *"For me the city of Rome":* Jefferson to Madame de Tessé, Nîmes, March 20, 1787, ibid., 133.

85 *"Were I to give you news":* ibid.

85 *he caught the accents:* The Provençal language, Jefferson observed, once "took precedence of the French under the name la langue Romans." He confessed that he had once thought the "Provençale only a dialectic of the French." In Provence he discovered that "French may rather be considered as a dialect of the Provençale. That is to say, the Latin is the original." No "nasal sounds disfigure" Provençal, Jefferson said, and

> on the whole it stands close to the Italian and Spanish in point of beauty. I think it a general misfortune that historical circumstances gave a final prevalence to the French instead of the Provençale language. It loses it's ground slowly, and will ultimately disappear because there are few books written in it, and because it is thought more polite to speak the language of the Capital.

Jefferson to William Short, Aix-en-Provence, March 29, 1787, ibid., 138.

86 *While reading in his copy:* Sowerby, *Catalogue Jefferson,* 1:47.

86 *The imponderables of place:* Author's impressions of the Mediterranean.

10. DREAMS

87 *slept "without fear" and reviewed:* Jefferson to Nathaniel Macon, Monticello, Va., January 12, 1819, in *Writings,* 1415.

88 *"I have given up newspapers":* Jefferson to John Adams, Monticello, Va., January 21, 1812, ibid., 1260.

88 *criticized for sentimentalizing ancient history:* "We are affected quite differently," Nietzsche wrote,

> when we probe the concept "Greek" which Winckelmann and Goethe constructed for themselves and find it incompatible with that element out of which Dionysian art evolved—the orgy. I have, in fact, no doubt that Goethe would have utterly excluded anything of this kind from the possibilities of the Greek soul. *Consequently Goethe did not understand the Greeks.*

Twilight of the Idols, 119.

88 *"sweetness and light"*: This was how Swift characterized the culture of antiquity in his *Full and True Account of the Battle Fought Last Friday between the Ancient and the Modern Books in Saint James's Library:*

> As for us Ancients, we are content with the bee to pretend to nothing of our own, beyond our wings and our voice, that is to say, our flights and our language. For the rest, whatever we have got has been by infinite labour and search, and ranging through every corner of nature; the difference is that instead of dirt and poison, we have rather chosen to fill our hives with honey and wax, thus furnishing mankind with the two noblest of things, which are sweetness and light.

The phrase was subsequently popularized by Matthew Arnold in *Culture and Anarchy* (1869).

88 *"My journey from Paris"*: Jefferson to Marquis de Chastellux, Marseilles, April 4, 1787, in *Jefferson Abroad,* 139.

88 *a "tolerably good" inn*: Jefferson to Madame de Tott, Marseilles, April 5, 1787, ibid., 142.

88 *well-kept rooms, an excellent table*: *Conducteur de l'étranger dans Marseille . . .* (Paris: Maison, 1839), 110–11.

88 *Marseilles*: Frederick Augustus Fischer, *Travels to Hyères,* 22–25.

88 *"brawling, squabbling, and jabbering"*: Jefferson to Madame de Tott, Marseilles, April 5, 1787, in *Jefferson Abroad,* 142.

89 *thirty-two American ships*: Jefferson to John Jay, Paris, June 21, 1787, in *Papers,* 11:487.

89 *a remnant of the pagan idolatry*: To "my mind," Richard Hurrell Froude wrote to John Henry Newman, "it is the Carnival that is the real practical idolatry, as it is written, 'the people sat down to eat and drink, and rose up to play.'" Quoted in John Henry Newman, *Apologia pro Vita Sua* (1864; reprint, New York: Penguin, 1995), 64–65. On pagan practices in the carnival, see Frazer, *Golden Bough,* 1:244, 252–57, 270, 272.

89 *The Church tolerated—uneasily*: Newman observed that the carnival was "one of those very excesses, to which, for at least three centuries, religious Catholics have ever opposed themselves, as we see in the life of Saint Philip [Neri], to say nothing of the present day." *Apologia,* 65.

89 *"real witches' brew"*: Friedrich Nietzsche, *The Birth of Tragedy* (1872), reprinted as *The Birth of Tragedy and The Case of Wagner,* trans. Walter Kaufmann (New York: Vintage, 1967), 39.

89 *the "mad pursuit"*: Keats, "Ode on a Grecian Urn" (1820).

89 *"Dance, and Provençal song"*: Keats, "Ode to a Nightingale" (1820).

90 crudelis Amor: See Virgil, *The Eclogues,* 10.

90 *an actress, "young and handsome"*: Jefferson to William Short, Aix-en-Provence, March 29, 1787, in *Jefferson Abroad,* 137.

90 *"a legitimate Graecian beauty"*: Jefferson to Madame de Tott, Marseilles, April 5, 1787, ibid., 142.

90 *their material came directly*: The Sun King himself, secure in the splendor of Versailles, did not fail to perceive the grotesqueries, the cruelties, the suppressed sensualities, that underlay the masked fetes of the commedia dell'arte. "I should very much like to know," Louis XIV asked the prince de Condé, "why people who are so greatly scandalized at Molière's comedy say nothing about Scaramouche?" M. (François) Guizot, *L'histoire de France depuis 1789 . . . ,* 5 vols. (Albany, N.Y.: Lyons, n.d.), 4:421. In 1697 the king expelled the Italian players from France (they were later permitted to return), but the players' music was only such as the king might have heard in his own Mediterranean cities.

90 *in the streets of Marseilles*: Frederick Augustus Fischer, *Travels to Hyères,* 22–25.

90 *Jefferson rebuked the slave*: Sarah Randolph, *The Domestic Life of Thomas Jefferson* (New York: Harper, 1871), 321.

91 *was "severely flogged"*: Jefferson to Reuben Perry, April 16, 1812, in Thomas Jefferson, *Thomas Jefferson's Farm Book, with Commentary . . . ,* ed. Edwin Morris Betts (Princeton, N.J.: Princeton University, 1953), 34–35, discussed in Jack McLaughlin, *Jefferson and Monticello: The Biography of a Builder* (New York: Holt, 1988), 115–16. Jefferson had engaged a man (Isham Chisolm) to chase James Hubbard, a runaway slave. Chisolm, Jefferson told Reuben Perry, "got upon his tract, & pursued him into Pendleton county, where he took him and brought him here in

irons. I had him severely flogged in the presence of his old companions, and committed to jail where he now awaits your arrival." The letter suggests that Hubbard was kept in irons pending Perry's arrival.

91 *"I hold it"*: Jefferson to James Madison, Paris, January 30, 1787, in *Jefferson Abroad,* 120.

93 *the old country of Etruria:* Walter Pater, *Marius the Epicurean* (1885; reprint, ed. Michael Levey [New York: Penguin, 1985]), 125; and Nigel Spivey, *Etruscan Art* (New York: Thames and Hudson, 1997), 80–148.

93 *Jefferson kept up:* Sowerby, *Catalogue,* 4:368.

94 *Clérisseau and Adam made the long journey:* Thomas J. McCormick, *Charles-Louis Clérisseau and the Genesis of Neo-Classicism* (New York: Architectural History Foundation and Cambridge, Mass.: MIT, 1990), 1–2, 14, 17–19, 24, 62.

94 *their "magnificent work":* Gibbon, *Decline and Fall,* 1:422 n. 129.

94 *to "make a great puff":* McCormick, *Clérisseau and Neo-Classicism,* 24, 29, 75.

94 *if the ancients:* "Let us learn from the ancients," Clérisseau said, "how to submit the rules to genius. Let us wipe out that mark of servitude and mimicry which disfigures our works." Quoted in Honour, *Neo-Classicism,* 109.

95 *makes its own laws:* "But Monticello was not only consummately designed, it was also highly personal. . . . Even though many of the decorative components of the house came from various classical or Palladian sources . . . they are brought together at Monticello, through refined adjustments in scale, into a coherent whole." Among Jefferson's models for Monticello were the ancient Roman villas, those "loosely ordered and highly individualized dwellings" about which he read in such sources as the younger Pliny's letters. William H. Pierson, Jr., *The Colonial and Neo-Classical Styles,* vol. 1 of *American Buildings and Their Architects* (New York: Oxford University, 1970), 307, 311.

95 *a nearly absolute fidelity:* In the frieze for the central (dining) room of his villa at Poplar Forest, Jefferson departed from the ancient scheme in order to intersperse ox skulls among the Apollo faces. "You are right in what you have thought and done as to the Metops of our Doric pavilion [in the Academical Village]," Jefferson wrote to William Coffee, who at the time was working on the buildings of the University of Virginia. "[M]ore of the baths of Diocletian are all human faces, and as are to be those of our Doric pavilion. [But] in my middle room at Poplar Forest, I mean to mix the faces and ox-sculls, a fancy I can indulge in my own case, altho in a public work I feel bound to follow authority strictly." Jefferson to William Coffee, July 10, 1822, in Thomas Jefferson, *Thomas Jefferson, Architect: Original Designs in the Collection of Thomas Jefferson Coolidge, Jr.,* . . . (Boston: Riverside, 1916), 72 n. How interesting to find the great progressive speaking candidly of the need to "follow authority strictly"!

95 *he incorporated:* In addition to consulting Antoine Babuty Desgodets, *Les édifices antiques de Rome: Dessinés et mesurés très exactement* . . . (Paris: Chez Ian Baptiste Coignard, 1682), Jefferson seems to have turned, in searching for models for his friezes, to a book by Roland Fréart, sieur de Chambrai, and Charles Errard, *Parallèle de l'architecture antique avec la moderne* (1650; revision, 1766; English translation, 1707). Jefferson purchased Desgodet's book in 1791, Fréart's and Errard's in 1802. Sowerby, *Catalogue,* 4:371–72, 380. See also William Howard Adams, *Jefferson's Monticello,* 109–10, 119–25, 132, 197, 198, 204; Frederick D. Nichols and James A. Bear, Jr., *Monticello* (Monticello, Va.: Jefferson Memorial Foundation, 1967), 23; Jefferson, *Architect,* 93–94; and McLaughlin, *Thomas Jefferson and Monticello,* 289–90.

95 *the soapy-smooth plasterwork:* Not really plaster, but a mixture called composite, a combination of whiting, linseed oil, hide glue, and resin, which could then be heated and pressed into shape. See Beiswanger et al., *Thomas Jefferson's Monticello,* 36.

95 *guarded by griffins:* Scholars believe that Jefferson modeled the frieze imagery in the entrance hall at Monticello—with its griffins, acanthus scrolls, and candelabra—on the frieze of the temple of Antoninus Pius and Faustina on the Sacra Via in Rome, as depicted in Desgodets, *Édifices antiques,* 110–19. That temple, however, is in the Corinthian style, and the hall at Monticello is supposed to be Ionic. The interior of Monticello, Jefferson said, "contains specimens of all the different orders. . . . The Hall is in the Ionic, the Dining Room is in the Doric, the Parlor in the Corinthian, and the Dome in the Attic." The last is a Jeffersonian pun. See McLaughlin,

Thomas Jefferson and Monticello, 289–91, 432–33; Peter J. Hatch, Lucia C. Stanton, Merrill D. Peterson, and Susan R. Stein, *Monticello: A Guidebook* (Charlottesville, Va.: Thomas Jefferson Memorial Foundation, 1997), 19; and Amanda Claridge, *Rome: An Oxford Archaeological Guide* (Oxford, England, and New York: Oxford University, 1998), 107–8.

95 *Apollo's faces:* Apollo, the sun god. See Beiswanger et al., *Thomas Jefferson's Monticello,* 24–25.

95 *In books of engravings:* Although Jefferson, in designing the Monticello friezes, consulted books by Desgodets and Fréart, it is, I think, misleading to suggest that he was drawing primarily on the example of French classicism in doing so. Compare William Howard Adams: "Even though he [Jefferson] would firmly adhere to the rules of proportion and classical design, he drew freely on classical French inspiration [for example, Desgodets] for the decoration of friezes and mantels, with their griffins, bacchanalia, and urns." *Jefferson's Monticello,* 110. But in following Desgodets, Jefferson was *not* drawing on "classical French inspiration"; when he put the Corinthian imagery of the blood sacrifice in the parlor of Monticello, Jefferson was drawing primarily on *Roman* inspiration. For he knew that Desgodets was merely copying—as faithfully and as accurately as he was able to—the details of Roman architecture.

95 *copied directly:* The imagery in the parlor frieze at Monticello is modeled on that of the temple of the deified Vespasian and Titus, which was begun after the death of the emperor Vespasian, in 79 A.D., and completed in the reign of the emperor Domitian. The remains of the structure stand near the temples of Saturn and Concord in the Roman Forum. The three columns that remain are of white marble and stand some fifty feet high; they once formed the southeast corner of the pronaos (front) of the temple. By the eighteenth century the "accumulation of rubbish" reached almost to the top of the columns; the debris was cleared away during the excavation of the Clivus Capitolinus that began in 1810. It was at this time that the architects Valadier and Camporese supervised the restoration of the columns and entablature. Rodolfo Amedeo Lanciani, *The Ruins and Excavations of Ancient Rome: A Companion Book for Students and Travelers* (Boston: Houghton Mifflin, 1897), 290–91; Kenneth Scott, *The Imperial Cult under the Flavians* (Stuttgart and Berlin: Kohlhammer, 1936), 44; and Samuel Ball Platner, *A Topographical Dictionary of Ancient Rome,* completed and revised by Thomas Ashby (London: Oxford University and H. Milford, 1929), 556.

95 *reproduced this imagery:* In reproducing the frieze imagery of the temple of the deified Vespasian and Titus in his book, Desgodets, like the great Piranesi himself, worked under the mistaken assumption that he was depicting the decoration of the temple of Jupiter Tonans ("Thunderer") in Rome, an error that has led to confusion in the scholarly literature pertaining to Monticello—for example, in Hatch et al., *Monticello,* 19. See Desgodets, *Édifices antiques,* 132–37; and Luigi Ficacci, *Giovanni Battista Piranesi: The Complete Etchings* (Köln, Germany: Taschen, 2000), 202, 712. Only in the nineteenth century did archaeologists identify the temple with Vespasian and his son Titus. See Claridge, *Rome,* 78–80; Lanciani, *Ruins and Excavations,* 288–91; Christian Hülsen, *The Forum and the Palatine,* rev. ed., trans. Helen H. Tanzer (New York: Bruderhausen 1928), pl. 12; Barbara Levick, *Vespasian* (London and New York: Routledge, 1999), 197–99; Kenneth Scott, *Imperial Cult,* 79–81; J. B. Ward-Perkins, *Roman Imperial Architecture* (Harmondsworth, England: Penguin, 1981), 72–73; and Mark Wilson Jones, *Principles of Roman Architecture* (New Haven, Conn.: Yale University, 2000), 147.

95 *The tools of ritual slaughter:* Lanciani, *Ruins and Excavations,* 288–91; Hülsen, *Forum and the Palatine,* pl. 12; and Claridge, *Rome,* 79.

95 *the emperors Vespasian and Titus:* The cult of the deified Vespasian was maintained by two orders of priests, the *sodales Flaviales,* an order of *sacerdotes,* and the *flamines.* Homer C. Newton, *The Epigraphical Evidence for the Reigns of Vespasian and Titus,* Cornell Studies in Classical Philology, no. 16 (New York: Macmillan, 1901), 94–99.

95 *the slaughtered bull:* On his visit to Arles in 1787, Jefferson would most likely have seen the frieze of ox skulls and rosettes—much like that in the dining room of Monticello—that forms a part of the facade of the ancient theater there. Though much of the theater was still unexcavated at the time of Jefferson's visit, this portion of the facade—it is level with the modern street, the rue de la Calade—would have been visible to the eighteenth-century tourist as he made his way from the amphitheater to Saint-Trophime. Jefferson seems to have mistaken the theater for what

he called "the antient Capitol of the place." Jefferson, "Notes of a Tour of France," in *Jefferson Abroad*, 160. On the antiquity of the entablature of the theater at Arles, see Wilson Jones, *Principles of Roman Architecture*, 113.

95 *Description of the sacrifice:* This composite picture of an ancient sacrifice has been sketched lightly, in broad and perhaps inexact strokes, to allow the reader to form a general idea of the nature of the ritual involved. The actual sacrificial practices of the ancient peoples varied from place to place and changed over time, and the particular obligations they entailed depended on the nature and, as it were, the demands of the god to whom the sacrifice was being offered. See Arthur Fairbanks, *A Handbook of Greek Religion* (New York: American, 1910), 100–101; R. M. Ogilvie, *The Romans and Their Gods in the Age of Augustus* (New York: Norton, 1969), 48; William Ramsay, *An Elementary Manual of Roman Antiquities* (London: Charles Griffin, 1863), 167–68; and Burkert, *Greek Religion*, 55–57.

95 *perhaps concealing the knife:* While in the Greek rite it was customary for a maiden to conceal the knife in a basket carried on her head, the Roman ritual apparently required the priest (*sacerdos*) to carry the weapon in his belt.

95 *urceus, or pitcher of water:* Lanciani, *Ruins and Excavations*, 288–91; Hülsen, *Forum and the Palatine*, pl. 12; and Claridge, *Rome*, 79.

95 *aspergillum, the device used:* ibid.

96 *the bowl, or patera:* ibid.

96 *white cap, or* albogalerus: ibid.

96 *Jefferson—the man who believed:* It is true that other neoclassical architects used similar imagery in their work; the ox skulls that Robert Adam created for his patrons in Britain are very like those Jefferson used in Virginia. But if his contemporaries worked with similar motifs, this does not make Jefferson's decision to use them at Monticello any less strange. For Jefferson, after all, was a modern man, self-consciously progressive, at times almost a caricature of the Enlightened sage. He deplored the attempts of traditionalists to preserve outmoded customs, unmeaning superstitions, the superseded relics of forgotten beliefs. And he was too independent in his thinking to have been a slave to mere fashion, the caprices of the beau monde. When he decided to put the artifacts of primitive sacrifice in the friezes of Monticello, Jefferson knew what he was doing. I should note, too, that I have not come across any other instance of a man putting images of the implements of the blood sacrifice in his living room in the way Jefferson did at Monticello, though my search has not been exhaustive.

II. VOICES

97 An evil-looking Ethiopian: Quoted in Peter Brown, *Society and the Holy in Late Antiquity* (Berkeley: University of California, 1982), 146.

97 *rice-cleaning machine:* Jefferson to William Short, Toulon, April 7, 1787, in *Papers*, 11:280; Jefferson to John Jay, May 4, 1787, ibid., 11:428; and Jefferson to John Adams, Paris, July 1, 1787, in *Jefferson Abroad*, 172.

97 *"a peep":* Jefferson to Maria Cosway, Paris, July 1, 1787, in *Jefferson Abroad*, 174.

98 *"Nay if even in the house":* Homer, *Iliad*, 22.389ff.

98 *Oh—to live with them:* Jefferson, *Literary Commonplace Book*, 9, 15, 218.

98 *An English poet:* This was William Shenstone, whose garden at the Leasowes, in Hales-Owen (then part of Shropshire), Jefferson visited in the spring of 1786. See Samuel Johnson, *The Lives of the Most Eminent English Poets*, 10 vols. (1779–81; reprint, William Milner [London: 1836]), 2:358–64; and Jefferson, "Notes of a Tour of English Gardens," in *Jefferson Abroad*, 67–68.

98 *the "earth belongs in usufruct":* Jefferson to James Madison, Paris, September 6, 1789, in *Jefferson Abroad*, 294.

98 *likens his own dead to "seraphs":* Henry S. Randall, *Life of Jefferson*, 3:545; Randolph, *Domestic Life*, 428.

98 *"each of his living and lost" children:* Henry S. Randall, *Life of Jefferson*, 1:384.

98 *dreamed of a dead friend:* Dreams, Nietzsche argued, are "the origin of all beliefs in spirits, and probably also of the belief in gods. 'The dead live on, for they appear to the living in dreams':

that was the conclusion one formerly drew, throughout many millennia." Nietzsche, *Human, All Too Human: A Book for Free Spirits* (1878; reprint, ed. Erich Heller, trans. R. J. Hollingdale, Cambridge: Cambridge University Press, 1986), 14. Proust revised the idea in order that modern, limited, secular minds could comprehend its power. The dead, Proust says, "exist only in us," that is, in our soul-worlds and dreamworlds. These worlds he compares sometimes to an ocean, at other times to a "subterranean city." The dead, Proust says, do not die "in vain": they "continue to act upon us. They act upon us even more than the living because, true reality being discoverable only by the mind, being the object of a mental process, we acquire a true knowledge only of things that we are obliged to re-create by thought, things that are hidden from us in everyday life." In rehearsing his soul-journeys to the dead, Proust described how he sailed "upon the dark current of our blood as upon an inward Lethe meandering sixfold." Proust's descriptions of his descents invite comparison with those described by Homer in the *Odyssey,* Virgil in the *Aeneid,* and Dante in *The Divine Comedy.* See Proust, *Sodom and Gomorrah,* vol. 4 of *In Search of Lost Time* (1921; reprint, ed. D. J. Enright, trans. Terence Kilmartin, New York: Modern Library, 1993), 210–29. Proust's soul-cartography invites comparison, too, with the maps made by earlier cartographers of the spirit. "I sought for myself," Heracleitus said. "Travel over every road, you cannot discover the frontiers of the soul *(psyche)*—it has a *logos*." Augustine said that "there is in man an area which not even the *spirit of man* knows of. . . . This memory of mine is a great force, a vertiginous mystery, my God, a hidden depth of infinite complexity: and this is my soul, and this is what I am. What then, am I, my God? What is my true nature? A living thing, taking innumerable forms, quite limitless. . . . For there is in me a lamentable darkness in which my latent possibilities are hidden from myself, so that my mind, questioning itself upon its own powers, feels that it cannot rightly trust its own report. Quoted in Peter Brown, *Augustine of Hippo: A Biography* (1967; rev. ed., 1969; Berkeley: University of California, 2000), 178 (emphasis in original).

98   *"The dead were held":* Fustel de Coulanges, *The Ancient City: A Study on the Religion, Laws, and Institutions of Greece and Rome* ([1864]; reprint, trans. Willard Small [Garden City, N.Y.: Anchor, 1956]), 24. Compare Propertius, 4.7.1: "The *Manes* are no fable: death is not the end of all, and the pale ghost escapes the vanquished pyre."

99   *some of these Mediterranean schemes:* Peter Brown has described a "continuum of Mediterranean sensibility that longed for invisible and ideal companions." *Society and the Holy,* 13. There were various kinds and gradations of demons; different authorities proposed different hierarchical schemes. See Ramsay MacMullen, *Paganism in the Roman Empire* (New Haven, Conn.: Yale University Press, 1981), 79. The Mediterranean notions of the demon touched upon in this chapter form a part of a larger Indo-European heritage that we do not yet fully understand. Compare the *devas* (demons) mentioned in the old Sanskrit texts and the *daevas* of the Zoroastrians with the later figure of the *diavol nero* (black demon) described in Dante, *Inferno,* canto 21.

99   *the "evil genii" . . . :* Hesiod calls demons "guardians of mortals." *Works and Days* (Loeb Library), sec. 121, 126. In Plato's *Symposium* they are called a "ministering class, midway between gods and men." *The Collected Dialogues, Including the Letters,* eds. Edith Hamilton and Huntington Cairns (Princeton, N.J.: Princeton University, 1961), Sec. 202E. In the *Cratylus,* Socrates observes that the poets "say truly that when a good man dies he has honor and a mighty portion among the dead, and becomes a daemon, which is a name given to him signifying wisdom." Sec. 398B–C. According to Plutarch, the "demigods (or daemons) have a complex and inconsistent nature and purpose." *Isis and Osiris,* sec. 361. See also Walter Burkert, *Greek Religion,* 179–81.

99   *"worser"—or "evil"—genius:* See, for example, Ferdinand's declaration that the "strong'st suggestion / Our worser genius" can put forward will never "melt / Mine honour into lust." Shakespeare, *The Tempest.* In *King Lear,* Shakespeare has the pagan duke of Gloucester declare, "You ever-gentle gods, take my breath away from me; / Let not my worser spirit tempt me again / To die before you please!" 4.6.221ff.

99   *a signal "I have had":* Plato, *Apology,* trans. Benjamin Jowett, sec. 31. See also Plutarch's *De Genio Socrates,* of which Montaigne thought highly. Michel de Montaigne, "Of Vanity," reprinted in *The Complete Essays of Montaigne,* trans. Donald Frame (Palo Alto, Calif.: Stanford Univer-

sity, 1965), 761. Nietzsche described Socrates' demon as a series of "auditory hallucinations" that have "often been interpreted in a religious sense." *Twilight of the Idols*, 41.

99   *"What did Socrates mean":* Jefferson to John Adams, Monticello, Va., October 12, 1813, in *Writings*, 1302.

99   *"nonsense" or "charlatanerie":* Such were the terms Jefferson used to condemn various kinds of (what he supposed to be) supernatural or metaphysical absurdity; the terms in this case were not directed by Jefferson at supernatural interpretations of Socrates' demon per se, but rather at the way of thinking that made such interpretations plausible. See Jefferson to John Adams, Monticello, October 12, 1813, in *Writings*, 1301, and Jefferson to Dr. Joseph Priestley, Washington, March 21, 1801, in ibid., 1085.

99   *"might readily mistake the coruscations":* Jefferson to William Short, Monticello, Va., August 4, 1820, in *Writings*, 1438.

99   *"was too wise to believe":* Jefferson to John Adams, Monticello, Va., October 12, 1813, ibid., 1302–3.

100   *"a general view of the moral doctrines":* Jefferson to Dr. Joseph Priestley, Washington, D.C., April 9, 1803, ibid., 1121.

100   his *"human excellence":* Jefferson to Dr. Benjamin Rush, Washington, D.C., April 21, 1803, ibid. (emphasis in original).

100   *the product of their own minds:* Jefferson to John Adams, Monticello, Va., April 20, 1812, in John Adams, *Adams-Jefferson Letters*, 298; Jefferson to John Adams, Monticello, Va., April 8, 1816, in *Writings*, 1382.

100   *Jefferson called "Dæmonism":* Jefferson to John Adams, Monticello, Va., April 11, 1823, in *Writings*, 1466.

100   *"When General Washington was withdrawn":* Jefferson, "Anas," ibid., 672.

100   *"suggestions" of "conscience" or "reason":* Jefferson to John Adams, Monticello, Va., October 12, 1813, ibid., 1303.

100   *"coruscations" (flashes) of individual "genius":* Jefferson to William Short, Monticello, Va., August 4, 1820, ibid., 1438.

100   *The classical idea of the genius spirit:* The cherubs, or putti, depicted in the bedroom frieze at Monticello are called *erotes* in Greek; in Latin, *cupidines;* they represent Eros, who was variously conceived, in antiquity, as a god or as a *daimon* of love. In the familiar myths Eros appears as the companion, and even the son, of Aphrodite, but he was not merely a figure of myth; he was also an object of extensive veneration, and he enjoyed the worship of flourishing cults. Readers of Plato's dialogue the *Symposium* will remember the figure of Diotima, that teacher of love who, Socrates tells the assembled company, instructed him in the esoteric arts of Eros. Diotima identified Eros, not indeed as a god or a mortal, but as a *daimon*, one of those "interpreters and ferrymen" who stand between gods and men. Plato, *Symposium*, sec. 202E. At Rome, too, the fertile or creative forms of love were thought to be inspired, and facilitated, by erotic demon spirits, those "genii" that enabled men to beget children on the nuptial couch.

100   *a little demon boy:* The putto over the fireplace in Jefferson's bedroom at Monticello appears to possess a beard. Artists, in fashioning scenes of putti at play, did occasionally depict cherubs donning masks and false beards, but excess paint may be the cause of the growth on the Jeffersonian sprite's face. Much of the frieze work in the house lies under several distorting layers of paint, and the beard may be merely the enlargement of chubby cherubic cheeks caused by a series of repaintings. For a depiction of a putto playing with false whiskers, see the frieze (c. 1788) created by Vincenzo Pacetti for the Palazzo Altieri, in Fabio Benzi and Caroline Vincenti Montanaro, *Palaces of Rome* (New York: Rizzoli, 1997), 201–2. Like the putti, the ox skulls in Jefferson's bedroom frieze, garlanded with sacrificial ribands, recall the amorous devotion of those ancient peoples who, in the performance of their rituals, offered up so much slaughtered flesh to their erotic god.

101   *Bedroom frieze imagery:* Jefferson derived the frieze imagery in his bedroom at Monticello from the temple of the harbor god Portunus in Rome, as depicted in the work of Desgodets, *Édifices antiques*, 96–104. Antiquarians once identified this structure as the temple of Fortuna Virilis, but the identification is no longer generally accepted. See Claridge, *Rome*, 253–54; and Wilson

Jones, *Principles of Roman Architecture,* 65. The order of the Roman temple is Ionic; its decoration, molded in stucco, features putti, candelabra, and bulls' skulls. Jefferson used the frieze imagery of *erotes* and ox skulls not only in his bedroom at Monticello but also in the parlor of his villa at Poplar Forest and in one of the pavilions of the Academical Village of the University of Virginia.

101 mystères littéraires: Edgar Wind, *Pagan Mysteries in the Renaissance,* 2nd enlarged ed. (New York: Norton, 1969), 3; Ioan P. Culianu, *Eros and Magic in the Renaissance* (Chicago: University of Chicago, 1987), 144–75.

101 *"character is for man his daimon":* Burkert, *Greek Religion,* 181. Like Heracleitus, Augustine of Hippo used the idea of the demonic as a tool with which to probe the niched intricacies of human character. In late Roman popular belief, Peter Brown observed, "the methods of demons were extremely crude: they would simply take on human shape to start a plague or a riot." With Augustine, "by contrast, the nexus between man and demons was purely psychological. Like was drawn to like. Men got the demons they deserved." Brown, *Augustine of Hippo: A Biography,* rev. ed. (Berkeley: University of California, 2000), 311. See also Garth Fowden, *The Egyptian Hermes: A Historical Approach to the Late Pagan Mind* (Princeton, N.J.: Princeton University, 1993), 209–10.

101 *a dialogue—with the different voices:* The presence of interior voices in the soul is perhaps a more common psychological occurrence than is generally recognized; consider, for example, glossolalia, the phenomenon of speaking in tongues. The gift of Glossolalia, according to the New Testament, was one of those gifts given to the disciples at the descent of the Holy Spirit, commemorated in the Christian churches on Whitsunday; those inflamed by this Pentecostal fire were inspired to new heights of ecstatic spiritual emotion, as demonstrated by their capacity for exalted preaching and prophetic insight.

101 *made fun of the notion:* Sebastian de Grazia, *Machiavelli in Hell* (Princeton, N.J.: Princeton University, 1989), 65.

101 *nocturnal conversations with the dead:* In the evenings, Machiavelli said, he returned to his house and entered his study,

> and at the door I take off the day's clothing, covered with mud and dust, and put on garments regal and courtly; and reclothed appropriately, I enter the ancient courts of ancient men, where, received by them with affection, I feed on the food which only is mine and which I was born for, where I am not ashamed to speak with them and to ask them the reasons for their actions; and they in their kindness answer me; and for four hours of time I do not feel boredom, I forget every trouble, I do not dread poverty, I am not frightened by death; entirely I give myself over to them.

101 Machiavelli to Francesco Vettori, December 10, 1513, in *The Letters of Machiavelli,* trans. Allan Gilbert (Chicago: University of Chicago, 1961), 142.

101 *Montaigne, in his introspective essays:* In Montaigne's imagination the memory of his dead friend Étienne de La Boétie was always present. "There is no action *or thought,*" he wrote, "in which I do not miss him." "He partook of my true image," Montaigne said, "and carried it off with him." "And the greatest man I have known in person," Montaigne wrote,

> I mean for natural qualities of the soul, and the best endowed, was Étienne de la Boétie. He was truly a full soul, handsome from every point of view; a soul of the old stamp, who would have achieved great results if fortune had willed it, for he had added much to this rich nature by learning and study. . . . If you press me to tell why I loved him, I feel that this cannot be expressed, except by answering: Because it was he, because it was I.

Complete Essays, 139, 143, 500, 752 (emphasis added).

101 *"The daemon of Socrates":* Montaigne, "Of Prognostications," reprinted in *Complete Essays,*

29–30 (emphasis added). Montaigne intimated that had his friend de La Boétie not died, the *Essays* would have taken the form of a personal correspondence with him. Montaigne's influence on Jefferson is documented in Andrew Burstein, *The Inner Jefferson: Portrait of a Grieving Optimist* (Charlottesville: University Press of Virginia, 1995), 123–24, 127, 149.

102 *Shakespeare, too, drew on the idea:* The continued vitality of the Mediterranean spirit culture as a metaphor for the perplexed intricacies of the mind is apparent in Shakespeare's Sonnet 144,

> Two loves I have of comfort and despair
> Which like two spirits do suggest me still:
> The better angel is a man right fair,
> The worser spirit a woman, colour'd ill.

Suggest here means "prompt" or "cause to be present in the mind." The demonic magnetism of the "better angel" is intimated in Sonnet 31—"Thy bosom is endeared with all hearts / Which I by lacking have supposed dead"—in which the poet professes to find his deceased lovers marvelously extant in the angelic form of the living beloved.

102 *"in council" with his "genius":* Shakespeare, *Julius Caesar,* 2.1.66. This "genius" is distinct from the ghost of Caesar, Brutus's "evil spirit." 4.3.274ff. Compare Shakespeare's blithe spirit, Ariel, in *The Tempest.* Queen Elizabeth, a student of classical literature and translator of Horace, called Lord Burghley, her chief counselor, her "Spirit," or beneficent demon. Lytton Strachey, *Elizabeth and Essex: A Tragic History* (1928; reprint, New York: Harcourt, Brace, 1956), 173.

102 *the bloody cherub:* Shakespeare, *Macbeth,* 4.1.80ff. This cherub is clearly an evil, not a beneficent, genius, its counsel supremely defective: "Be bloody, bold, and resolute; laugh to scorn / The power of man; for none of woman born / Shall harm Macbeth." See also *Macbeth,* 3.1.56–57: "My genius is rebuk'd, as, it is said, / Mark Antony's was by Caesar. He chid the sisters."

102 *the demon of Mark Antony:* Shakespeare, *Antony and Cleopatra,* 2.3.16ff.

102 *"by spirits taught to write":* See Shakespeare, Sonnet 86, one of the "rival poet" sonnets, in which the competitor poet is said to have benefited from the tuition of demonic spirits. The speaker of the sonnet proclaims himself equal, or rather superior, to this demonic challenge: neither the rival poet nor the "affable familiar ghost / Which nightly gulls [unfairly stuffs] him with intelligence" is able to strike the speaker dead, or "astonish" his verse—kill it, that is, as with a thunderbolt. It is instead, the speaker explains, the appearance of the face of his beloved in the rival poet's verse that has enfeebled his art. See Helen Hennessy Vendler, *The Art of Shakespeare's Sonnets* (Cambridge, Mass.: Harvard University, 1997), 377.

102 *secularized it in the soliloquy:* Not only Shakespeare's audience but, in Harold Bloom's reading, certain of Shakespeare's characters themselves "overhear" their own conversation: "In Shakespeare, characters develop rather than unfold, and they develop because they reconceive themselves. Sometimes this comes about because they overhear themselves talking, whether to themselves or to others. Self-overhearing is their royal road to individuation." Bloom, *Shakespeare: The Invention of the Human* (New York: Riverhead, 1998), xvii. Bloom argues that as a result of the revolution effected by Shakespeare, "[w]e all of us go around now talking to ourselves endlessly, overhearing what we say, then pondering and acting upon what we have learned." Harold Bloom, *The Western Canon: The Books and School of the Ages* (New York: Harcourt, Brace, 1994), 49.

102 *to hear a soul discoursing:* In Plato's *Theaetetus,* Socrates describes thought as the "discourse of the soul with herself." Thinking, in other words, is an "inward conversation," one that "goes on when the mind is occupied with things by itself, whatever name you give to that." *The Collected Dialogues, Including the Letters,* eds. Edith Hamilton and Huntington Cairns (Princeton, N.J.: Princeton University, 1961), sec. 189E, 196A, 187A. "I have a notion," Plato has Socrates say, "that, when the mind is thinking, it is simply talking to itself, asking questions and answering them. . . . When it reaches a decision—which may come slowly or in a sudden rush—when doubt is over and the two voices affirm the same thing, then we call that its 'judgment.'" 190A.

102 *a "science of the sepulcher":* John Ruskin, "Ariadne Florentina," in John Ruskin, *Proserpina, Ariadne Florentina, . . .* (Boston: Dana Estes, n.d.), 401. Ruskin was not the first moralist to argue that there was something sinister, even depraved, in the demonic interior dialogues of such Renaissance masters as Machiavelli and Leonardo; in composing his aspersions on the Renaissance wise man in "Ariadne Florentina," Ruskin drew on an ancient tradition, derived apparently from ancient Judaism, which held that demons were fallen angels. This notion was adopted by the fathers of the early Church, for whom the pagan gods were themselves fallen angels, demonically corrupting mankind with their myths and false truths; the idea was given its most memorable expression in Milton's *Paradise Lost.* Contemporary critics of that poem fail to get properly into the spirit of things when they present Milton's Satan, together with the other fallen angels, as a thief who cribbed from the ancient poets and orators, then catachrestically misapplied their words. "The Satanic orators," one critic has written, "build upon classical assumptions about fate, human nature, and history." Well, yes: from the point of view of a professor of English, this is perfectly true. But from another point of view, the point of view of *Paradise Lost,* it is the classical orators who build upon *satanic* assumptions about fate, human nature, and history. Milton presents Satan and the other disgraced angels not, indeed, as students of the civilization of classical antiquity but as something like the *inventors* of that civilization. Satan and his coevals are shown by Milton to have invented the pagan conceptions of time, history, and virtue; these conceptions were then handed down to men by the Olympian gods and pagan muses, demons all, who "By falsities and lies the greatest part / Of Mankind they corrupted to forsake / God their Creator." *Paradise Lost,* 1.367–69. There is a tradition that at the birth of Christ the false gods lost whatever powers God suffered them to retain before that time. See Milton, "Ode on the Morning of Christ's Nativity": "The Oracles are dumb; / No voice or hideous hum," etc. See also Sir Walter Scott, *Letters on Demonology and Witchcraft* (1830, reprint, New York: Bell, 1970), letter 2, 64–68.

102 *But Ruskin rightly realized:* If some have condemned the soul-cartography of pagan antiquity as mere *diablerie,* yet others have shown that the old maps continue to be useful, provided always that the user knows how to interpret them properly. Dante's work would have taken a different form had he believed pagan maps to be merely demonic and devoid of any greatness of spirit. Cardinal Newman said that the "Greek poets were in a certain sense prophets; for 'thoughts beyond their thought to those high bards were given.'" Newman, *Apologia pro Vita Sua,* 44. See also Ernst Robert Curtius, *European Literature and the Latin Middle Ages* (1953; trans. Willard R. Trask, Princeton, N.J.: Princeton University, 1990), *passim.* The ancient techniques of self-culture, like those of the Renaissance which derive from them, have a permanent value; but the nature and extent of their value remains a question.

102 *revised an older concept:* In this secular recasting of an older mysticism, the book came to be conceived as an inspiring demon. Milton's well-known words, carved over the entrance to the reading room of the New York Public Library, are one expression of this idea: "A good Booke is the precious life-blood of a master-spirit, embalm'd and treasur'd up on purpose to a life beyond life." A late-Renaissance expression of the same idea is found in Goethe, who argued that books possess spirits or souls: he distinguished between the "divine" core of a book and its external qualities of language, dialect, and style. *Poetry and Truth from My Own Life* (1849; reprint, with rev. trans. by Minna Steele Smith [London: Bell, 1908]) 2:131. Goethe, who called himself a pagan, was a great believer in demonic power and spoke once of the "genius" that incited him to create *Werther:* "Fortunately the genius had . . . impelled him, in the vigorous period of youth, to hold fast, describe, and with sufficient boldness and at the favourable hour, publicly to exhibit, that which had immediately gone by." Ibid., 2:166.

102 *"lively imagination, usually called genius":* Jefferson to Dr. Caspar Wistar, Washington, D.C., June 21, 1807, in *Writings,* 1181.

102 *the "mysterious mechanisms inside":* Ellis, *American Sphinx,* 101, 106.

102 *Jefferson learned how to attend:* The effect on the soul of its various "voices" has been profitably studied by the modern novelists. "Of the different persons who compose our personality," says the narrator of Proust's *In Search of Lost Time,* "it is not the most obvious that are the most essential. In myself, when ill health has succeeded in uprooting them one after another, there will

still remain two or three endowed with a hardier constitution than the rest." Marcel Proust, *The Captive,* vol. 5 of *In Search of Lost Time* ([1923]; reprint, ed. D. J. Enright, trans. Terence Kilmartin [New York: Modern Library, 1993]), 5–6. See also *The Fugitive,* in the same volume, 578–79. Of Henry James, the poet-critic R. P. Blackmur observed that he understood

> that there are within most of us those partly living other selves, those unused possibilities out of the past, those unfollowed temptations of character, which if not struck down [or, he might have added, released in creative action] will overwhelm and engulf the living self. The psychiatrist usually deals with such struggles in our day under his own abstracting terms just as the Church formerly [sic] dealt with them in the guise of exorcism, the casting out of devils.

R. P. Blackmur, Afterword to *The Sacred Fount* by Henry James (1901; reprint, New York: New Directions, 1994), 225. A different, and perhaps darker, rendering of the malignant voices of the soul is found in the novels of Evelyn Waugh. In one of these, the narrator seems to hear a malignant voice crying out, as if on some interior wireless in the mind, a "voice that had been bawling in my ears, incessantly, fatuously, for days beyond number." *Brideshead Revisited: The Sacred and Profane Memories of Captain Charles Ryder* (1945; reprint, Boston: Little, Brown, 1946), 15. The theme of depraved interior voices is developed at greater length in Waugh's late novel *The Ordeal of Gilbert Pinfold.*

102 *He learned how to* talk *to himself:* Modern poets and novelists, in transcribing these interior dialogues, have themselves drawn on the ancient Mediterranean spirit culture in their work. See, in this connection, Thomas Mann's *Doctor Faustus: The Life of the German Composer Adrian Leverkühn as Told by a Friend,* chap. 25. Mann was troubled by what he perceived to be the demonic element in art; William Butler Yeats found it suggestive. "The Greeks," Yeats wrote, "considered that myths are the activities of the Daimons, and that the Daimons shape our characters and our lives. I have often had the fancy that there is some one myth for every man, which, if we but knew it, would make us understand all he did and thought." "At Stratford-on-Avon," reprinted in William Butler Yeats, *Essays and Introductions* (New York: Collier, 1968), 107. See also William Butler Yeats, *The Autobiography of William Butler Yeats, Consisting of Reveries over Childhood and Youth* . . . (reprint, New York: Collier, 1965), 248–49. The poet, T. S. Eliot wrote, "is haunted by a demon, a demon against which he feels powerless, because in its first manifestation it has no face, no name, nothing; and the words, the poem he makes, are a kind of form of exorcism of this demon." "The Three Voices of Poetry," reprinted in T. S. Eliot, *On Poetry and Poets* (London: Faber and Faber, 1957), 98.

102 *"If ever you are about":* Jefferson to Martha Jefferson, Annapolis, Md., December 11, 1783, in *Writings,* 784.

103 *other voices, other personas:* "I think that all happiness depends on the energy to assume the mask of some other self; that all joyous or creative life is a re-birth of one's self. . . . We put on a grotesque or solemn painted face to hide us from the terrors of judgment, invent an imaginative Saturnalia where one forgets reality, a game like that of a child, where one loses the infinite pain of self-realisation." Yeats, *The Autobiography of William Butler Yeats,* 340.

12. "THE SPOT AT WHICH I TURNED MY BACK"

104 *saw the* bastides: Jefferson, "Notes of a Tour of France," in *Papers,* 11:429; Stendhal, *Memoirs of a Tourist,* 267; and Frederick Augustus Fischer, *Travels to Hyères,* 27.

104 *to the mountain villages:* Jefferson, "Notes of a Tour into the Southern Parts of France," in *Papers,* 11.429, Guizot, *L'histoire de France,* 1:66; and Frederick Augustus Fischer, *Travels to Hyères,* 36, 40.

104 *dilapidated southern farms:* Author's impressions of the Mediterranean.

104 *the terraced vineyards:* Jefferson, "Notes of a Tour of France," in *Papers,* 11:429.

105 *"for a friendly word":* Frederick Augustus Fischer, *Travels to Hyères,* 36, 40.

105 *villages bleached by the sun:* Author's impressions of the Mediterranean.
105 *"hedges of pomegranates":* Jefferson, "Notes of a Tour of France," in *Papers,* 11:429, 431.
105 *in Ollioules:* ibid., 11:431.
105 *a feeling of "rapture":* Jefferson to Lafayette, Nice, April 11, 1787, in *Jefferson Abroad,* 144.
105 *the "golden apples":*

> Almost all the flowers, the herbs, and the fruits that grow in our European gar-
> dens are of foreign extraction, which, in many cases, is betrayed even by their
> names; the apple was a native of Italy, and, when the Romans had tasted the
> richer flavour of the apricot, the peach, the pomegranate, the citron, and the or-
> ange, they contented themselves with applying to all these new fruits the com-
> mon denomination of apple, discriminating them from each other by the
> additional epithet of their country.

Gibbon, *Decline and Fall,* 1:57.
105 *"rambling through fields":* Jefferson to Marquis de Lafayette, Nice, April 11, 1787, in *Jefferson Abroad,* 143.
105 *groves of oranges:* Jefferson, "Notes of a Tour of France," in *Papers,* 11:430.
105 *the oldest of the Mediterranean resorts:* Frederick Augustus Fischer, *Travels to Hyères,* 49, 55, 58–62.
105 *studied the southern vegetation:* Jefferson, "Notes of a Tour of France," in *Papers,* 11:426, 430–31.
105 *nurseries of prophecy:* According to legend, in the ancient city of Heliopolis, on the Île de Levant, one of the islands of Hyères, a holy man from Italy had a vision. His name was Dionysius, and he later went north to convert the Gauls to Christianity. Medieval Christians knew Dionysius as Saint Denis, the first bishop of Paris and the patron saint of France.
105 *the old Roman Forum Julii:* Guizot, *L'histoire de France,* 1:66; Jefferson, "Notes of a Tour of France," in *Papers,* 11:430–31; and author's impressions of Fréjus. Antiquarians note that the father-in-law of Tacitus, Agricola, was a native of Forum Julii.
105 *used for bullfights:* "It is the Roman arena which is preserved [in the bullfight], but the bullfighter has changed since then and become a noble knight. He now fights alone, and his meaning and costume, and especially his prestige, were changed by the Middle Ages." Elias Canetti, *Crowds and Power* (1960; reprint, trans. Carol Stewart [New York: Noonday Press, 1998]), 176.
106 *It was a city of baroque:* Author's impressions of Nice; Catherine Ungar and Marcelle Viale, *Strolling through Old Nice* (Nice: Gilletta, 2001), 5, 15ff, 24ff.
106 *Nissart, a dialect cousin-german:* Ungar and Viale, *Strolling through Old Nice,* 7.
106 *Strange flowers, fruit of Africa:* Author's impressions of Nice.
106 *"quite as superb":* Jefferson to William Short, Nice, April 12, 1787, in *Papers,* 11:287.
106 *The city had much to offer:* Frederick Augustus Fischer, *Travels to Hyères,* 65; Casanova, *Memoirs.*
106 *Then he ascended:* See the excellent account in Willard Sterne Randall, *Thomas Jefferson,* 466.
106 *The roses love the Sun:* See Anacreon, Ode 44; Dante, *Paradiso* (trans. Mandelbaum), 30.124ff: "Into the yellow of the eternal rose / that slopes and stretches and diffuses fragrance / of praise unto the sun of endless spring." See also Saint Francis of Assisi, *Canticle of the Sun;* Dante, *Inferno,* 1.37ff; and Dante, *Paradiso,* 33.145.
106 *one of his favorite poets:* See Jefferson, *Literary Commonplace Book,* 8, 9, 129–30, 155.
106 *vegetable, chemical, and biological transfluxions:* Pope modeled the lines "All forms that perish other forms of supply, / (By turns we catch the vital breath and die)" on the discourse of Pythagoras in book fifteen of Ovid's *Metamorphoses:* "Nothing retains its form; but Nature, the great renewer, ever makes up forms from other forms." Ovid, *Metamorphoses: Books IX–XV,* 15.250ff (reprint, trans. Frank Justus Miller, 1916; 2nd ed., ed G. P. Goold, 1984; Cambridge, Mass.: Loeb Classical Library, 1999, 382–83.
107 *whispers to those who listen:* To "those who have intelligence, and who can love." Dante, *Paradiso* (trans. Mandelbaum), 1.118ff.
107 *"the peculiar œstrum of the poet":* Jefferson, "Notes on the State of Virginia," query 14, in *Writings,* 265, 267.
107 *these processes changed:* Jefferson was perhaps influenced in his thinking by Alexander Pope, with whose works he was intimately familiar. Pope was himself fascinated by the art that converted

base passions into beautiful things; he regarded this artistic metaplasia not indeed as an overcoming of nature but as an extension of nature's "plastic" principles into new realms. See Pope, *An Essay on Man*, 2.180ff., 3.7ff. "All Nature," Pope concluded, "is but art, unknown to thee." *An Essay on Man*, 1.289. Pope here followed Shakespeare:

> *Yet nature is made better by no mean [that is, method]*
> *But nature makes that mean [method]: so, over that art,*
> *Which you say adds to nature, is an art*
> *That nature makes. You see, sweet maid, we marry*
> *A gentler scion to the wildest stock,*
> *And make conceive a bark of baser kind*
> *By bud of nobler race: this is an art*
> *Which does mend nature, change it rather, but*
> *The art itself is nature.*

The Winter's Tale, 4.3.88ff.

107 *On the back of a mule:* Jefferson to William Short, Nice, April 12, 1787, in *Papers*, 11:287.

107 *With thoughts of Hannibal:* Henry S. Randall, *Life of Jefferson*, 1:472.

107 *"about as silky":* Jefferson, "Notes of a Tour of France," in *Papers*, 11:435.

107 *how to make Parmesan cheese:* Jefferson, "Notes of a Tour of France," in *Jefferson Abroad*, 165–66.

107 *"I turned my back":* For the reference, see Malone, *Jefferson and His Time*, 2:123.

107 *the felucca drifted:* Jefferson to William Short, Nice, May 1, 1787, in *Papers*, 11:326.

107 *"mortally sick":* Jefferson to Martha Jefferson, Marseilles, May 5, 1787, in *Jefferson Abroad*, 145; Jefferson to William Short, Nice, May 1, 1787, in *Papers*, 11:326.

108 *"Sometimes on foot":* Jefferson to Martha Jefferson, Marseilles, May 5, 1787, in *Jefferson Abroad*, 145. Descriptions of the Mediterranean coast and coastal villages are based on the author's impressions of the Mediterranean.

108 *"pheasants, partridges, quails":* Jefferson, "Notes of a Tour of France," in *Papers*, 11:442.

108 *"oil, figs, oranges":* ibid.

108 He did *"not remember":* ibid., 11:441.

108 *"If any person wished":* ibid., 11:441–42.

PART THREE: FALL

1. FIRE AND HATE

111 *"gloomy forebodings":* Jefferson to George Washington, Chesterfield, Va., December 15, 1789, in *Papers*, 16:34.

111 *He would prefer:* Jefferson, "Autobiography," in *Writings*, 98–99.

112 *"We return," he said:* Jefferson to William Short, Washington, D.C., October 3, 1801, in Lipscomb and Bergh, *Writings*, 10:286.

112 *"came on every day at Sunrise":* Jefferson to Thomas Cooper, Washington, D.C., October 27, 1808, in Lipscomb and Bergh, *Writings*, 12:180.

112 *"with child for the first time":* Lucy Ludwell Paradise to Jefferson, March 2, 1790, in *Papers*, 16:198.

112 *Genuine action is always:*

> For in every action what is primarily intended by the doer, whether he acts from natural necessity or out of free will, is the disclosure of his own image. Hence it comes about that every doer, in so far as he does, takes delight in doing; since everything that is desires its own being, and since in action the being of the doer is somehow intensified, delight necessarily follows. Thus nothing acts unless by acting it makes patent its latent self.

Dante, *De Monarchia.*

113 *was "in despair"*: Jefferson, "Anas," in *Writings*, 668.

114 *"really a stranger"*: ibid. Jefferson's statements about the assumption bargain were made much later, and they were colored by subsequent developments. Any effort to determine the exact nature of Jefferson's role in the bargain is made still more complicated by the fact that he later came to regret his efforts and tried to portray himself as the innocent dupe of Hamilton.

114 *the ascendancy of "stock-jobbers"*: Jefferson to George Mason, Philadelphia, February 4, 1791, in *Writings*, 972.

114 *There "are certainly persons"*: Jefferson to Nicholas Lewis, February 9, 1791, in Ford, *Writings*, 5:282.

114 *Charles Montague had proceeded*: Macaulay, *History of England*, in his *Works*, 4:56–59, 84–96.

115 *"machine"*: Jefferson, "Anas," in *Writings*, 666.

115 *Here he unpacked his crates*: Malone, *Jefferson and His Time*, 2:322–26.

116 *"perfect liberty" of trade*: On Jefferson's commitment to free trade, see Malone, *Jefferson and His Time*, 2:48, and Peterson, *Jefferson and the New Nation*, 304.

116 *"Let our work-shops remain"*: Jefferson, "Notes on the State of Virginia," query 19, in *Writings*, 291.

116 *carpentry, masonry, and smithery*: ibid.

116 *Husbandry, Jefferson wrote, "is the focus"*: ibid., 290.

117 *"barren & useless" activities*: Jefferson to George Washington, Philadelphia, May 23, 1792, in *Writings*, 986.

117 *He chose instead to blame*: See, for example, Jefferson's letter to P. S. Dupont de Nemours, Washington, D.C., January 18, 1802, in *Writings*, 1101.

2. Harlots and Heretics

118 *like two prize cocks*: Jefferson to Dr. Walter Jones, Monticello, Va., March 5, 1810, in Lipscomb and Bergh, *Writings*, 12:371.

119 *the "energumeni of royalism"*: Jefferson, "Anas," in *Writings*, 672.

119 *"An apostate," Jefferson wrote*: ibid., 666.

119 *his "excessive repugnance"*: ibid., 685.

119 *"It cannot be denied"*: Jefferson to George Mason, Philadelphia, February 4, 1791, ibid., 972.

119 *The "ultimate object"*: Jefferson to George Washington, Philadelphia, May 23, 1792, ibid., 987.

120 *"the great mass of our community"*: Jefferson to George Mason, Philadelphia, February 4, 1791, ibid., 972.

120 *"It would give you a fever"*: Jefferson to Philip Mazzei, Monticello, Va., April 24, 1796, ibid., 1037.

120 *He hoped that the pamphlet*: See Malone, *Jefferson and His Time*, 2:354–59.

120 *who had "originally been a republican"*: Jefferson, "Anas," in *Writings*, 671. This was enormously unfair to Adams. Even Dumas Malone, one of Jefferson's most sympathetic biographers, doubts that his hero had read Adams's *Discourses on Davila* very carefully. *Jefferson and His Time*, 2:359.

120 *"since his apostacy"*: ibid., 2:358.

120 *Their "Pharisaical homage"*: Jefferson to Dr. Walter Jones, Monticello, Va., January 2, 1814, in *Writings*, 1318.

120 *the heretical "preachers"*: Jefferson to Marquis de Lafayette, Philadelphia, June 16, 1792, in *Writings*, 990.

121 *vision of republican atonement*: The vision would receive its most enduring expression in the language of Jefferson's first inaugural address. There Jefferson spoke of the principles that

> form the bright constellation which has gone before us and guided our steps through an age of *revolution* and *reformation*. The wisdom of our sages and *blood of our heroes* have been *devoted* to their attainment. They should be the *creed of our political faith*, the *text of civic instruction*, the *touchstone* by which to try the services of those we trust; and should we wander from them in moments of error or alarm, let us hasten to regain the road which alone leads to peace, liberty, and safety.

(Emphasis added.) The language is explicitly religious; the principles of the Revolution, Jefferson said, had been corrupted by an unnamed force (the whore of Babylon, the party of Hamilton and the other heresiarchs); but a "reformation" had been effected; and the "political faith" of the revolution—a faith sanctified by the "blood" of the Revolutionary martyrs—had been restored. Americans had now to keep the "devotion" (literally, the vows to the death) of these civic saints always in their minds, that they might never again be tempted to stray from the "creed of our political faith" and the sacred "text" of civic instruction—the democratic decalogue of the Republic, the beatitudes of its orthodoxy. See Jefferson, first inaugural address, in *Writings*, 495.

121 *"high priests of federalism":* Jefferson to Justice William Johnson, Monticello, Va., June 12, 1823, ibid., 1471. Jefferson believed that Hamilton had himself been diabolically seduced—"bewitched & perverted"—by the charlatans of the Old World, the guardians of its ancient priestly and warrior castes. Jefferson, "Anas," ibid., 671. He feared that Hamilton and his followers would now use the same dumb enchantment to lull unsuspecting Americans into unvigilant slumbers. The Federalists, Jefferson said, were "itching" for "crowns, coronets and mitres," the very charms that the European magicians had fashioned to "fascinate the eyes of the people, and excite in them an humble adoration and submission, as to an order of superior beings." Jefferson to Thomas Paine, Philadelphia, June 19, 1792, ibid., 992. To erect a "tinsel" hierarchy on the European model, Hamilton had only, like the biblical wizards, to cover his sleights of hand with a sufficiently fragrant cloud of smoke and incense. "Hamilton's financial system," Jefferson said, was intended to be a mystical "puzzle, to exclude popular understanding and inquiry." Jefferson, "Anas," ibid., 666. Like the "Soothsayers, sorcerers and Wizards of the Jews"—their "Jannes and Jambres, their Simon Magus, witch of Endor, and the young damsel whose sorceries disturbed Paul so much"—the Federalists spread confusion and mystery in order to cloak their black usurpations. Jefferson thought of himself as an expert in the science of exposing these deceptive arts. He studied closely the tricks—the processions, genuflections, thurifications—of "Jongleurs, Devins, Sortileges." He exposed the false arts by which "Magi, Archi-magi, cunning men, Seers, rain makers" pretended to an ability to foretell "future events, bring down rain, find stolen goods, raise the dead, destroy some, and heal others by enchantment, lay spells etc." Jefferson to John Adams, Monticello, Va., June 11, 1812, ibid., 1262. Hamilton merely replaced this clumsy magic with a more up-to-date system of trickery—or so Jefferson contended. By affecting a deep insight into all the mysteries of commerce, the treasury secretary established himself as the oracle of American prosperity. In reports heavy with economic fate, he justified to Congress the raising up of what Jefferson called "gambling stock for swindlers and shavers," and he instituted a system of political economy that in Jefferson's view was a mechanism to filch "from industry its honest earnings," in order that speculating magicians and paper magnates might "build up palaces" for themselves and their progeny. Jefferson to Nathaniel Macon, Monticello, Va., January 12, 1819, in ibid., 1415. See also Jefferson, "Anas," ibid., 677. On the witch of Endor, see 1 Sam. 28 and Scott, *Demonology and Witchcraft*, letter 2, 49–84.

121 *The cabinet was left in charge:*

> Before the President set out on his Southern tour in April 1791, he addressed a letter of the 4th. of that month, from Mt. Vernon to the Secretaries of State, Treasury & War, desiring that, if any serious and important cases should arise during his absence, they would consult & act on them, and he requested that the Vice-president should also be consulted.

Jefferson, "Anas," in *Writings*, 670–71. See also Jefferson to Dr. Benjamin Rush, Monticello, Va., January 16, 1811, ibid., 1235.

121 *It must have been:* See Malone, *Jefferson and His Time*, 2:321–23.

121 *after the "cloth was removed":* Jefferson, "Anas," in *Writings*, 671.

122 *"Purge that constitution":* ibid.

122 *"Purge it of its corruption":* ibid. (emphasis in original).

122 *to "undermine and demolish":* Jefferson to George Washington, Monticello, Va., September 9, 1992, ibid., 994.

122 *was to be "warped in practice":* Jefferson, "Anas," ibid., 670.
122 *"hung around":* The account of this part of the April 1791 dinner is drawn from the letter of Jefferson to Dr. Benjamin Rush, Monticello, Va., January 16, 1811, ibid., 1235–36.
122 *would not have been out of place:* On Jefferson's remodeling of Puritan tropes, see Reinhold Niebuhr, *The Irony of American History* (New York: Scribner, 1952), 46–47, 70.

3. FOREBODINGS

123 *took a trip together:* Malone, *Jefferson and His Time,* 2:360.
123 *as a "translating clerk":* Jefferson to George Washington, Monticello, Va., September 9, 1792, in *Writings,* 997.
124 *"I have never enquired":* ibid.
124 *"laid the axe":* Jefferson's allusion is to Matthew 3:10: "And now also the axe is laid unto the root of the trees: Therefore every tree which bringeth not forth good fruit, is hewn down, and cast into the fire." See Richard Hofstadter's discussion of this statement in *The American Political Tradition and the Men Who Made It* (1951; reprint, with foreword by Christopher Lasch, New York, Vintage, 1974), 25.
124 *"When the vizor of stoicism":* Alexander Hamilton, "Catullus," no. 3, Philadelphia, September 29, 1792, in *The Papers of Alexander Hamilton,* 27 vols., ed. Harold C. Syrett and Jacob E. Cooke (New York: Columbia University, 1961–), 12:504–5.
124 *"Generalissimo" Jefferson:* For the reference, see Malone, *Jefferson and His Time,* 2:473–74.
125 *he had never "intrigued":* Jefferson to George Washington, Monticello, Va., September 9, 1792, in *Writings,* 994.
125 *He quietly drafted resolutions:* Or so the copy of the Giles resolutions in Jefferson's hand, now in the Library of Congress, suggests. Eugene R. Sheridan, "Thomas Jefferson and the Giles Resolutions," *William and Mary Quarterly* 44, 3rd series (1992).
126 *His "propensities to retirement":* Jefferson to George Washington, Philadelphia, December 31, 1793, in Lipscomb and Bergh, *Writings,* 9:278.
126 *"The motion of my blood":* Jefferson to James Madison, June 9, 1793, in *Writings,* 1010.
126 *As a "private man":* Jefferson to M. Odit, Monticello, Va., August 14, 1795, in Lipscomb and Bergh, *Writings,* 9:312.
126 *"I have returned":* Jefferson to François D'Ivernois, Monticello, Va., February 6, 1795, in *Writings,* 1023.
126 *He cherished "tranquillity too much":* Jefferson to George Washington, May 14, 1794, Lipscomb and Bergh, *Writings,* 9:288.
126 *Politics were, he said, "entirely banished":* Jefferson to Harry Remson, October 30, 1794, in Thomas Jefferson, *Thomas Jefferson's Garden Book, 1766–1824, with Relevant Extracts . . . ,* ed. Morris Betts (Philadelphia: American Philosophical Society, 1944), 219.
126 *"I have never seen a Philadelphia paper":* Jefferson to James Madison, Monticello, Va., April 3, 1794, in Lipscomb and Bergh, *Writings,* 9:283.
127 *"I think it is Montaigne":* Jefferson to Edmund Randolph, Monticello, Va., February 3, 1794, ibid., 9:280.
127 *he was now "totally absorbed":* Jefferson to James Madison, Monticello, Va., April 3, 1794, ibid., 9:283.
127 *His letters from Monticello:* See, for example, Jefferson to James Madison, April 3, 1794, ibid., 9:281–82; Jefferson to James Madison, May 15, 1794, ibid., 9:288; and Jefferson to James Madison, December 28, 1794, ibid., 9:293–96.
127 *He was not so "completely withdrawn":* Jefferson to Tench Coxe, Monticello, Va., May 1, 1794, ibid., 9:285.
127 *"For God's sake":* Jefferson to James Madison, Monticello, Va., September 21, 1795, ibid., 9:311.
127 *"eating the peaches, grapes and figs":* Jefferson to Maria Cosway, September 8, 1795, in Bullock, *My Heart and My Head,* 142–43.
127 *"demi-nudité misérable et hideuse":* Jean Gaulmier, *Volney: Un grand témoin de la révolution et de l'empire* (Paris: Hachette, 1959), 210–11.

127 *"living like an antediluvian patriarch"*: Jefferson to Edward Rutledge, Monticello, Va., November 30, 1795, in Lipscomb and Bergh, *Writings,* 9:313.

128 *a "retirement I doat on"*: Jefferson to James Madison, Monticello, Va., December 28, 1794, in *Writings,* 1017.

128 *Jefferson and Sally Hemings:* Contrary to popular misconception, the 1998 DNA testing about which we have all heard so much did not establish that Jefferson fathered any or all of Sally Hemings's children. The testing "did not prove Thomas Jefferson fathered Eston Hemings [or any other child of Sally Hemings], but it did place him within a group of approximately twenty-five known Virginia men believed to carry the Jefferson Y chromosome." See Lance Banning, James Ceaser, Charles R. Kesler, Alf J. Mapp, Jr., Harvey C. Mansfield, David N. Mayer, Forrest McDonald, Thomas Traut, Robert F. Turner, Walter E. Williams, and Jean Yarbrough, *Final Report of the Scholars Commission on the Jefferson-Hemings Matter,* April 12, 2001, available on the Internet.

128 *"philosophical evenings in the winter"*: Jefferson to Dr. Benjamin Rush, Monticello, Va., January 22, 1797, in Lipscomb and Bergh, *Writings,* 9:374.

128 *"My health,"* he wrote: Jefferson to James Madison, Monticello, Va., April 27, 1795, ibid., 9:302–3.

128 *"From 1793 to 1797"*: Jefferson to Maria Jefferson, now Maria Jefferson Eppes, Washington, D.C., March 3, 1802, in Jefferson, *Family Letters,* 190.

128 *"I felt enough of the effect"*: ibid.

128 *The cherry trees blossomed:* Malone, *Jefferson and His Time,* 3:238.

129 *"noise, confusion, and discomfort"*: Jefferson to Count de Volney. See also Malone, *Jefferson and His Time,* 3:326–27.

4. The Garden of Vision

130 *His name "was brought forward"*: Jefferson to Edward Rutledge, Monticello, Va., December 27, 1796, in Lipscomb and Bergh, *Writings,* 9:353.

132 *the "subtlety of your arch-friend"*: Jefferson to James Madison, with enclosure to John Adams, Monticello, Va., December 28, 1796–January 1, 1797, in *Writings,* 1040.

132 *"rejoice at escaping"*: Jefferson to Edward Rutledge, Monticello, Va., December 27, 1796, in Lipscomb and Bergh, *Writings,* 9:353.

133 *a multitude of Hamiltons:* Jefferson to Elbridge Gerry, Philadelphia, May 13, 1797, in *Writings,* 1042.

133 *as president, refused:* Jefferson, "Anas," in Lipscomb and Bergh, *Writings,* 1:415.

133 *had been touched by a "contest"*: Jefferson to William Short, Philadelphia, January 3, 1793, in *Writings,* 1004.

133 *those who had "fallen in battle"*: ibid.

133 *He drew on the language:* Jefferson's language is a reworking of an older conceit. Compare Saint Anselm, *Cur Deus Homo?*: "But, not to protract the matter further, were it not better that the whole world, and whatever is that is not God, should perish and be reduced to nothingness, than that you should make one movement of the eye against the will of God?" Quoted in Southern, *Saint Anselm,* 217.

133 *"I would have seen half"*: Jefferson to William Short, Philadelphia, January 3, 1793, in *Writings,* 1004.

133 *would "kindle the wrath"*: Jefferson to Tench Coxe, Monticello, Va., May 1, 1794, in Lipscomb and Bergh, *Writings,* 9:284–85.

134 *"I am still warm"*: ibid.

135 *the same "cunning" and "artifice"*: Jefferson to John Taylor, Philadelphia, June 4, 1798, in *Writings,* 1049.

135 *the "spirit of 1776"*: Jefferson to Thomas Lomax, Monticello, Va., March 12, 1799, ibid., 1062, 1063.

135 *He had not sinned:* See Boswell, *Life of Johnson,* 1145; and Newman, *Apologia,* 50. The conceit can, I think, be traced to Bunyan and the Bible.

135 *"suffering deeply in spirit"*: Jefferson to John Taylor, Philadelphia, June 4, 1798, in *Writings,* 1050.

136 *the "first chapter"*: Jefferson, "Autobiography," in *Writings*, 97.
136 *"the world's best hope"*: Jefferson, first inaugural address, ibid., 493. Lincoln, of course, amended the thought: "We shall nobly save," he said, "or meanly lose, the last, best hope of earth." Lincoln, annual message to Congress, December 1, 1862.
136 *"daily going into the arena"*: Jefferson to James Madison, Monticello, Va., January 22, 1797, in Lipscomb and Bergh, *Writings*, 9:368.
137 *dropping only Jefferson's nullification language*: See Peterson, *Jefferson and the New Nation*, 614.

5. TEMPTATIONS

138 *"dirty and shabby" tricks*: See Malone, *Jefferson and His Time*, 3:310.
139 *"Every man," he said*: Peterson, *Jefferson and the New Nation*, 626.
140 *Aaron Burr was on the "market"*: Jefferson, "Anas," in *Writings*, 693.
140 *"extraordinary exertions and successes"*: ibid.
140 *Hamilton came out publicly*: Letter from Alexander Hamilton, Concerning the Public Conduct and Character of John Adams, Esq., President of the United States, in Alexander Hamilton, *Papers*, 25:169–234.
141 *"honorable and decisive"*: Jefferson to Maria Jefferson Eppes, Washington, D.C., January 4, 1801, in Jefferson, *Family Letters*, 190.
142 *"Why," Burr is supposed to have said*: Peterson, *Jefferson and the New Nation*, 648.
143 *a "few choice spirits"*: For the reference, see Forrest McDonald, *Alexander Hamilton: A Biography* (1979; reprint, New York: Norton, 1982), 99.
143 ingenti virtute: Sallust, *Bellum Catlinae*, 53.6
144 capax imperii: "When an emperor discusses who is '*capax imperii*,' he announces the doom of any man he names." Sir Ronald Syme, *Tacitus*, 2 vols. (1958; reprint, Oxford, England: Clarendon, 1997), 2:485–86. See also Gibbon: "Hadrian was, by turns, an excellent prince, a ridiculous sophist, and a jealous tyrant. The general tenor of his conduct deserved praise for its equity and moderation. Yet, in the first days of his reign, he put to death four consular senators, his personal enemies, and men *who had been judged worthy of empire"*—capax imperii, that is. *Decline and Fall*, 1:83.
144 *flirted with the idea*: See Peterson, *Jefferson and the New Nation*, 623–24.
145 *a sneaky way*: See Richard Hofstadter, *The Idea of a Party System: The Rise of Legitimate Opposition in the United States, 1780–1840* (Berkeley: University of California, 1969), 136 and n. 14.
145 *"great souls don't bother"*: Henry Adams, *History of the United States*, 132.
146 *his "duty to be passive"*: Jefferson, "Anas," in *Writings*, 695.
146 *General Samuel Smith of Maryland*: Jefferson always denied the report that Smith had been authorized by him to make terms or give assurances. Ibid., 696.
146 *Federalist congressmen*: See Peterson, *Jefferson and the New Nation*, 651.
147 *"coyley refus[ed] the proffered diadem"*: Alexander Hamilton, "Catullus," no. 3, Philadelphia, September 29, 1792, in *Papers*, 12:504–5.
147 *a drab civic genius*: See the young Lincoln's reflections on the importance of "passionless" or "beaten path" virtue in the perpetuation of republican institutions. Lincoln, Address to the Young Men's Lyceum of Springfield, Illinois: "The Perpetuation of Our Political Institutions," January 1838, in Lincoln, *Speeches and Writings: 1832–1858*, ed. Don E. Fehrenbacher (New York: Library of America, 1989), 34–36.
147 *an honest man*: "Hamilton," Jefferson said, was "honest as a man, but, as a politician, believing in the necessity of either force or corruption to govern men." Jefferson to Dr. Benjamin Rush, Monticello, Va., January 16, 1811, in *Writings*, 1236. Hamilton, Jefferson said on another occasion, "was indeed a singular character. Of acute understanding, disinterested, honest, and honorable in all private transactions, amiable in society, and duly valuing virtue in private life, yet so bewitched & perverted by the British example, as to be under thoro' conviction that corruption was essential to the government of a nation." "Anas," ibid., 671.

PART FOUR: WINTER

1. AUTHORITY

151 *To the "auspices of this day"*: Jefferson, first inaugural address, in *Writings*, 492.

151 *"anxious and awful presentiments"*: ibid.

152 *"advancing rapidly"*: ibid.

152 *"transcendent objects"*: ibid.

152 *a "rising nation"*: ibid. (emphasis added).

152 *the "contest of opinion"*: ibid.

152 *the "first writer"*: Quoted in Peterson, *Jefferson and the New Nation*, 49.

152 *to "think as we please"*: Tacitus, *Historiae* (Loeb Library), 1.1.

153 *the "throes and convulsions"*: Jefferson, first inaugural address, in *Writings*, 493.

153 *"long-lost liberty"*: ibid.

153 *The "agitation" of those "billows"*: ibid., 492.

153 *Every "difference of opinion"*: ibid., 493.

153 *"We have," he said*: ibid.

153 *"as a City upon a Hill"*: John Winthrop, "A Modell of Christian Charity," reprinted in *American Sermons: The Pilgrims to Martin Luther King, Jr.*, ed. Michael Warner (New York: Library of America, 1999), 42.

153 *a "chosen country"*: Jefferson, first inaugural address, in *Writings*, 494 (emphasis added).

153 *"room enough"*: ibid.

153 *"the thousandth and thousandth generation"*: Often rendered as "the hundredth and thousandth generation." Merrill Peterson believes that "thousandth and thousandth" is correct. See *Writings*, 494, 1555.

154 *"a year of my life"*: Jefferson to Martha Jefferson Randolph, Washington, D.C., October 19, 1801, in Jefferson, *Family Letters*, 209.

154 *He went out regularly*: Peterson, *Jefferson and the New Nation*, 722.

155 *"The wine was the best"*: Henry Adams, *History of the United States*, 549.

155 *"not merely in undress"*: Quoted in Peterson, *Jefferson and the New Nation*, 731.

155 *the principles of "pêle mêle"*: Jefferson, Memorandum ("Rules of Etiquette"), in *Writings*, 705.

155 *he touched obliquely*: Jefferson told President Washington that he would not suffer his retirement "to be clouded by the slanders of a man whose history, *from the moment history can stoop to notice him*, is a tissue of machinations against the liberty of the country which has not only received and given him bread, but heaped it's honors on his head." Jefferson to George Washington, Monticello, Va., September 9, 1792, ibid., 1000–1001 (emphasis added).

155 *the "new created paper fortunes"*: Jefferson, "Anas," ibid., 685.

156 *"Jefferson's whole eight years"*: Quoted in Peterson, *Jefferson and the New Nation*, 720.

156 *governed like a moderate Federalist*: Henry Adams, *History of the United States*, 615.

156 *"accommodating trimmer"*: Quoted in Henry Adams, *History of the United States*, 418.

156 *a "temporizing rather than a violent system"*: Quoted ibid., 189.

156 *"reform the waste"*: Quoted ibid., 160–61.

156 *"If we can prevent"*: Jefferson to Thomas Cooper, Washington, D.C., November 29, 1802, in *Writings*, 1110.

156 *"how difficult it is"*: Quoted in Henry Adams, *History of the United States*, 160–61.

2. DISORDER

157 *the "loathsome steam"*: Quoted in Richard Hofstadter, *The American Political Tradition and the Men Who Made It* (1951; reprint, with foreword by Christopher Lasch [New York: Vintage, 1974]), 41.

157 *was slowly rotting*: Henry Adams, *History of the United States*, 62.

158 *"We can pay off his debt"*: Jefferson to Dupont de Nemours, Washington, D.C., January 18, 1802, in *Writings*, 1101.

158 *is "not what is commonly believed"*: Robert Harley, Lord Oxford, quoted by Jonathan Swift in Victoria Glendinning, *Jonathan Swift* (London: Hutchinson, 1998), 102.

158 *a "man of genius"*: Jefferson to James Monroe, Washington, D.C., May 1801, in James Thomson Callender, *Thomas Jefferson and James Thomson Callender, 1798–1802*, ed. Worthington Chauncey Ford (Brooklyn, N.Y.: Historical Printing Club, 1897), 39.

158 *"clear land" and a "hearty Virginia female"*: James Thomson Callender to Jefferson, Richmond, Va., September 26, 1799, ibid., 17.

158 *from "coming into my neighborhood"*: Jefferson to James Monroe, Washington, D.C., July 15, 1802, in Lipscomb and Bergh, *Writings*, 10:331.

159 *a "necessary of life"*: Jefferson to John Norvell, Washington, D.C., June 14, 1807, in *Writings*, 1178.

159 *an "ostentatious coolness"*: Callender, *Jefferson and Callender*.

159 *Xenophon and Polybius*: ibid., 5.

159 *was entitled to a remittance*: ibid., 32–34.

160 *"for the proof sheets"*: Jefferson to James Thomson Callender, Monticello, Va., October 6, 1799, ibid., 19.

160 *"Her name is Sally"*: James Thomson Callender, *Richmond Recorder*, September 1, 1802.

160 *rheumatic complaints*: Jefferson to Maria Jefferson Eppes, Washington, D.C., October 18, 1802, in Jefferson, *Family Letters*, 23.

162 *"To take a single step"*: Jefferson, "Opinion on the Constitutionality of a National Bank," February 15, 1791, in *Writings*, 416.

3. DEATH AND CHARITY

163 *Thomas Mann Randolph*: See William H. Gaines, *Thomas Mann Randolph: Jefferson's Son-in-Law* (Baton Rouge: Louisiana State University, 1966), especially 46–47.

164 *nor would he "attempt consolation"*: Jefferson to Maria Jefferson Eppes, Philadelphia, February 12, 1800, in Jefferson, *Family Letters*, 185–86.

164 *Maria gave birth again*: This was Maria's third child. Her first died, while still an infant, in 1800. Her second, Francis Wayles, was born in 1801 and lived to be eighty. The third, named for her mother, died in 1807.

164 *the mother fell sick*: Malone, *Thomas Jefferson and His Time*, 4:413–14.

164 *"lost even the half"*: Jefferson to John Page, Washington, D.C., June 25, 1804, in Randolph, *Domestic Life* (New York: Harper, 1871), 302–4, and in Lipscomb and Bergh, *Writings*, 11:31.

165 *A "north west wind"*: Malone, *Thomas Jefferson and His Time*, 4:413–14.

165 *In a "blighted" season*: Jefferson to John Page, Washington, D.C., June 25, 1804, in Lipscomb and Bergh, *Writings*, 11:31.

165 *Socrates and Jesus Compared*: Jefferson to Dr. Benjamin Rush, with a syllabus, Washington, D.C., April 21, 1803, in *Writings*, 1122.

165 *a "subject of reflection"*: ibid.

165 *"more pure & perfect"*: ibid.

165 *"gathering all into one family"*: Compare Dante, *Paradiso*, 33.85ff:

> Nel suo profondo vidi che s'interna,
> legato con amore in un volume,
> ciò che per l'universo si squaderna.
> . . . La forma universal di questo nodo
> credo ch'i'vidi.

("In its profundity I saw—ingathered / and bound by love into one single book / the scattered pages of the universe. / . . . I think I saw the universal form which the knot takes.") Adapted from the Mandelbaum translation.

165 *"show a master workman"*: Jefferson to Dr. Joseph Priestley, Washington, D.C., April 9, 1803, in *Writings*, 1121.

165 *"sent to Philadelphia"*: Jefferson to Dr. Joseph Priestley, Washington, D.C., January 29, 1804, ibid., 1142.

165 *Jefferson received the Gospels:* Forrest Church, "The Gospel According to Jefferson," introduction to Thomas Jefferson, *The Jefferson Bible: The Life and Morals of Jesus of Nazareth* (Boston: Beacon, 1989), 18.

165 *"It was the work":* Jefferson, quoted ibid.

166 *"wee-little book":* Jefferson to Charles Thomson, Monticello, Va., January 9, 1816, in *Writings,* 1373.

166 *the tradition of charity* (caritas, agape): On the "feasts of charity" instituted by the Apostles and mentioned in Jude, verse 12, see Richard Hooker: "Concerning which feasts, St. Chrysostom says, 'On stated days, they made the table common, and when the liturgical service was completed, after the communion of the mysteries, they would begin a feast, with the rich, indeed, supplying foods, and with the poor and those who had nothing being, contrariwise, invited.' *Homilies on 1 Corinthians,* 27. Of the same feasts in like sort, Tertullian [says], 'Our dinner exhibits its nature in its name. For it is called *agape,* which is, among the Greeks, love. However great the expense may be, it is reckoned a gain in the name of piety.' *Apology,* ch. 39." Hooker, *Of the Laws of Ecclesiastical Polity* (1593–1661; reprint, ed. Arthur Stephen McGrade, Cambridge: Cambridge University, 1989), 22–23.

166 *"transformed wholly into love":* Meister Eckhart's idea of the end or object of Christianity. Meister Eckhart, *Selected Writings,* trans. Oliver Davies (New York: Penguin, 1995), 147.

166 *nursed the idea:* Henry Adams, *History of the United States,* 159.

166 *the "union of all honest men":* ibid., 192.

168 *the "despicable" nature:* ibid., 427.

169 *a coward, Hamilton knew:* ibid.

169 *a dazzling summer sun:* ibid., 428.

169 *"I presume":* Malone, *Jefferson and His Time,* 4:425.

169 *"most determined Ennemies":* John Adams to Jefferson, September 3, 1816, in Adams, *Adams-Jefferson Letters,* 488.

4. TRICKS

170 *"I shall need":* Jefferson, second inaugural address, in *Writings,* 523.

171 *"the sole faculty of making money":* See the concise and illuminating discussion in Walter Berns, *Making Patriots* (Chicago: University of Chicago, 2001), 78.

171 A *"few prosecutions":* The classic account of this episode is in Leonard Levy, *Jefferson and Civil Liberties: The Darker Side* (1963; reprint, Chicago: Ivan R. Dee, 1989), 59. (The emphases in the quotations in this paragraph have been added by the author.)

173 *proposed to "lend his assistance":* Quoted in Henry Adams, *History of the United States,* 571.

174 *Virgil:* Before Aeneas could undertake the creative act of founding the state that would become Rome, he had first to descend to hell and be there initiated into the sublime mysteries of the world soul. See Virgil, *Aeneid,* book 6.

174 *Machiavelli:* The true leader, Machiavelli says, is an artist-begetter, one who shapes time and history by descending to those cisterns where the passions knot and gender in the free creativity of Eros. The lusty captain there achieves greatness by raping Fortune. For in the theory of Machiavelli, history, or Fortune, is a softly feminine creature: she longs to be taken down by the audacious young captain, made love to by him, and by his seed gotten with world-historic child. *"Fortuna è donna,"* Machiavelli says: "Fortune is a woman, and if she is to be submissive it is necessary to bat her down and knock her about." See *The Prince,* chap. 25.

174 *like Nero:* "Qualis artifex pereo!" ("What an artist dies in me!") Suetonius, *Nero* (Loeb Library), 49.

174 *This was a great blow:* See Henry Adams, *History of the United States,* 760–61.

175 *a curious interview:* Jefferson, "Anas," in *Writings,* 693–94.

175 *The "gods," he wrote:* Quoted in Henry Adams, *History of the United States,* 778.

175 *he moved to suppress:* ibid., 795.

176 *like a "crooked gun":* Jefferson to William Branch Giles, Monticello, Va., April 20, 1807, in *Writings,* 1173.

177 *"back like a child":* Henry Adams, *History of the United States,* 828.

5. Failure

178 *"cautious and shy"*: Margaret Bayard Smith, *The First Forty Years of Washington Society in the Family Letters of Margaret Bayard Smith*, ed. Gaillard Hunt (1906; reprint, New York: Ungar, 1965), 6–7.

179 *a "contest with her grandfather"*: See Andrew Burstein, *The Inner Jefferson: Portrait of a Grieving Optimist* (Charlottesville: University Press of Virginia, 1995), 252.

180 *The more fragile the vessel*: Brodie, *Intimate History*, 395.

180 *"I told him"*: "That as to the idea of transforming this govt into a monarchy he [President Washington] did not believe there were ten men in the U.S. whose opinions were worth attention who entertained such a thought. I told him there were many more than he imagined." Jefferson, "Anas," in *Writings*, 681.

180 *"he thought it a proof"*: ibid., 686.

181 *Hamilton, whatever might have been*: Hamilton to Mrs. Hamilton, May 10, 1801, and Hamilton to Charles Pinckney, December 29, 1802, in Alexander Hamilton, *Alexander Hamilton: A Biography in His Own Words*, ed. Mary-Jo Kline (New York: Newsweek, by Harper and Row, 1973), 386, 392. Hamilton *did* of course think the Constitution too weak: he believed the government it created deficient in energy, but this does not mean he wanted to pull it down. Indeed he could claim, with some plausibility, that "no man in the UStates has sacrificed or done more for the present Constitution than myself—and contrary to all my anticipations of its fate, as you know from the very beggining, I am still labouring to prop the frail and worthless fabric." Hamilton to Gouverneur Morris, February 27, 1802, ibid., 389.

181 *"glare of royalty"*: Jefferson, "Anas," in *Writings*, 671.

183 *"discords, casualties, and sufferings"*: Peterson, *Jefferson and the New Nation*, 917.

183 *Blood was spilled*: Willard Sterne Randall, *Thomas Jefferson*, 581–82.

6. Flowers

185 *He owed*: Peterson, *Jefferson and the New Nation*, 924.

185 *"under an agony"*: Randolph, *Domestic Life* (New York: Harper, 1871), 400.

185 *"from scenes of difficulty"*: Ford, *Writings*, 5:434.

186 *"Domestic life"*: Margaret Bayard Smith, *First Forty Years*, 80.

186 *The culture of his flower beds*: "He dug his garden or read and wrote, and for him both kinds of work bore the same name; both he called gardening. 'The spirit is a garden,' he said." Victor Hugo, *Les Misérables* (1862; reprint, trans. Norman Denny [New York: Penguin, 1982]), 33.

186 *"short reign of beauty and splendor"*: Jefferson's words on the subject of flowers come to life amidst the photographs of his restored garden in Beiswanger et al., *Thomas Jefferson's Monticello*, especially 125.

186 *"The Hyacinths and Tulips"*: Quoted in Beiswanger et al., *Jefferson's Monticello*, 125.

186 *"but a young gardener"*: Jefferson to Charles Willson Peale, Poplar Forest, Va., August 20, 1811, in *Writings*, 1249.

187 *"My business"*: Jefferson to William Short, Monticello, Va., October 31, 1819, ibid., 1432.

187 *"But why am I"*: Jefferson to John Adams, Monticello, Va., July 5, 1814, ibid., 1342.

187 *"documents of regal scandal"*: George Ticknor, *Life, Letters, and Journals of George Ticknor*, 2 vols. (1876), 1:36.

187 *it must evolve*: See Peterson, *Jefferson and the New Nation*, 952.

187 *"Dictionaries," Jefferson said*: Jefferson to John Adams, Monticello, Va., August 15, 1820, in Adams, *Adams-Jefferson Letters*, 567.

187 *"words going off"*: See Swift's commentary on Horace's words in Swift, *A Proposal for Correcting, Improving and Ascertaining the English Tongue* (London: Benjamin Tooke, 1712), 14–15.

187 *followed Virgil and Horace instead*: Virgil, *Aeneid*, 6.255ff. See also Horace:

Odi profanum vulgus et arceo:
favete linguis; carmina non prius
audita Musarum sacredos
virginibus puerisque canto.

("I hate the profane masses and keep them off: silence your tongues; as a priest of the muses, I sing songs never heard before to virgins and boys.") *Odes,* 3.1.

7. LOVE AND ORDER

188 Haec sat erit: See Virgil, *The Eclogues,* trans. Guy Lee (New York: Penguin, 1984), 104–07, 128 n. 71.

189 *a flour mill:* Peterson, *Jefferson and the New Nation,* 937.

189 *His new library:* ibid., 943.

189 *"truly Attic societies":* See Peterson's description of these "societies" in *Jefferson and the New Nation,* 14.

190 *"my faithful and beloved Mentor":* Jefferson, "Autobiography," in *Writings,* 4.

190 *"We are told you are becoming":* Jefferson to Maria Cosway, Paris, July 27, 1788, in *Jefferson Abroad,* 260.

190 *"academical village":* Jefferson to Messrs. Hugh L. White and others, Monticello, May 6, 1810, in *Writings,* 1223.

190 *"a small republic within itself":* Jefferson to John Cartwright, Monticello, Va., June 5, 1824, in *Writings,* 1492.

190 *"As Cato, then, concluded":* Jefferson to Joseph C. Cabell, Monticello, Va., February 2, 1816, ibid., 1381.

190 *to "pity and help":* Jefferson to Anne Cary, Thomas Jefferson, and Ellen Wayles Randolph, Washington, D.C., March 2, 1802, ibid., 1102.

191 *Her history:* Bullock, *My Head and My Heart,* 170–71.

192 *The school was set:* ibid., 193–94. Mrs. Cosway initially established a school in Lyons. Only later did she move to Lodi.

192 *"to see these children":* ibid.

192 *Historians have made fun:* Brodie, *Intimate History,* 464.

192 *"our seminary":* Jefferson to James Madison, Monticello, Va., February 17, 1826, in *Writings,* 1514.

8. DEGENERATION

193 *the "hoary winter of age":* Jefferson to John Adams, Monticello, Va., October 12, 1823, in John Adams, *Adams-Jefferson Letters,* 599.

193 *He shuddered at the approach:* Jefferson to John Adams, Monticello, Va., June 1, 1822, ibid., 578.

194 *The "life of a cabbage":* ibid., 577.

194 *"in the midst of my grandchildren":* On Jefferson's grandchildren, see the essay, "The Jefferson Family at Monticello," in Beiswanger et al., *Thomas Jefferson's Monticello,* 72–73.

194 *"cherished companion":* ibid.

194 *"essay in architecture":* Jefferson's "essay in architecture" is discussed by William Beiswanger in his contribution to ibid., 1–39.

195 *"knelt at my head":* Brodie, *Intimate History,* 459.

195 *"My own belief":* Quoted in Brodie, *Intimate History,* 430.

196 *learn to master the antique forms:* Jefferson, progressive though he was, always insisted on the importance of classical training in liberally educated minds. "The learning of Greek and Latin, I am told, is going into disuse in Europe. I know not what their manners and occupations may call for: but it would be very ill-judged in us to follow their example in this instance." Jefferson, *Notes on the State of Virginia,* query 14, in *Writings,* 273. See also Jefferson to John Brazier, Poplar Forest, Va., August 24, 1819, in ibid., 1422–25.

196 *Slavery was a lawless, disordered institution:* How Jefferson's noble, altruistic words, his liberal sentiments, his immense plans for doing good coexisted with this institution is a mystery we shall never wholly understand. One of the strangest and most harrowing documents in the whole of the Jefferson corpus alludes to the unspeakable acts of a lawless soul. It is pieced together out of the phrases of a nightmare—

> you will excuse me [the anonymous letter writer purports to inform Jefferson] the liberty when you look at my intention. I should think it a crime to listen to the base falsehoods utter'd against you without informing you of them. Mr. Brown says he slept at Monticello one night and was waked by the most lamentable cries. He looked out and to his utter astonishment saw you flogging in the most brutal manner a negroe woman.

This paper, anonymous and undated, lies among Jefferson's papers in the Manuscript Division of the Library of Congress. See McLaughlin, *Jefferson and Monticello,* 96–97, 402. Scholars do not know who the "Mr. Brown" mentioned in the paper was; nor is there any way to know whether the incident the writer purports to describe is true, or whether it is one more particle in that mass of slander and calumny that invariably accumulates around the reputation of a controversial public man. Were the concealed rites, the morbid Walpurgis-Night dances, of Monticello this dark? If they were, can they be reconciled with the fact that the master lived in his labyrinth as a man adored. Oh yes, there is abundant information that Jefferson's slaves loved him, worshiped him even, would have given their lives for him. Yet we know that extremes of degradation and veneration sometimes meet. The darkness of a slave plantation is never wholly penetrable. Washington Allston, an artist who grew up on a cotton plantation in eighteenth-century South Carolina, remembered the all-pervading deviltry in the atmosphere, the "barbaric magic and superstition" of the slaves, the "ghosts and goblins" that haunted the whites. See Richard Holmes, *Coleridge: Darker Reflections, 1804–1834* (New York: Pantheon, 1999), 54. In that disordered darkness, even an enlightened master might forget himself. Did the latent egoism in Jefferson's nature become monstrous at Monticello? Was the sacrificer unmoved by shrieks of the sacrificed? We do not know, perhaps never *can* know.

196 *replaced, in its entirety:* Jefferson, in contrast to the high communitarians, envisioned a nation in which small communities, their life grounded in the communal principles of the classical polis, would *coexist* with the Whig ideals he always cherished, the market freedoms that have their origin not in the freedom of the classical city-state but in the prerogatives of the medieval free city and in the liberties of the marketplace. The modern communitarians (Rousseau was among the first) went further than Jefferson ever wished to go; they supposed that men could replace the bourgeois order of the market town—the late Roman *burgensis*—with a social order founded on love. But such dreams rested on a misapprehension of love's capacity in a fallen world. Love requires the lover to sacrifice the whole of his heart: he consents to its being fed to his beloved, as in the poet's dream. (See Dante, *Vita Nuova,* 3.) But mortal men have not such large hearts that they can sustain the trial of many feasts; and the number of people who can partake of any one meal is limited. Christians, it is true, believe in the reality of a more comprehensive heart sacrifice, the "love of Christ, which passeth knowledge" (Eph. 3:19). In honor of it, they eat the flesh and drink the blood of the devoted heart. When, a little after the ninth hour, that great heart was given up, the Sacrifice was felt, according to Saint Matthew, as a tremor through the world, and the veil of the Temple was rent in twain. Matt. 27:46–53. See also John 3:16. At that moment even a pagan poet in hell thought that "the universe felt love." Dante, *Inferno,* canto 12. The Roman Church venerates and honors the sacred heart of Jesus, which, "out of love for men, he allowed to be pierced by our sins." *Catechism of the Catholic Church* (Garden City, N.Y.: Doubleday, 1995), sec. 2669. But although mortal men are enjoined to imitate the love which made possible the divine Sacrifice, they can never succeed in doing so.

196 *a pattern of community:* In the theory of the polis, men rise above their own *idios*—their private interest, property, and profession—and, by transcending this idiotic state, become citi-

zens and lovers. But the Hellenic polis was small in size and formed part of a system of political economy little evolved from the Bronze Age. The modern communitarians have erred in
supposing that the love that sustained the polis—and even now sustains families and small associations of men—could hold larger communities of people together in the same way. The
love that functions tolerably well as a principle of order in families and tribes loses its efficacy
altogether when men ask it to perform a universal role, and the love we bear others imper-
ceptibly diminishes across the concentric circles of affection with which we are surrounded.
We love the members of our immediate family and our closest friends with the greatest inten-
sity, but as we move beyond these intimate circles into larger ones and take into account less
intimate friends, relations, neighbors, and colleagues, our love by degrees shades into mere
fondness and affection, into collegiality and acquaintanceship, into respect and politeness, at
last into relative indifference. Jefferson understood what many progressive thinkers have
failed to see—that the project of conceiving a many-peopled polity in love is doomed to failure. Love, when it is divorced from the particular family or tribal situations in which private
individuals find themselves, degenerates into mere abstraction: the notion of a wide and public love is either meaningless or perverse. The coercive qualities inherent in love—its propri-
etary interest in the objects that it cherishes—lose their gentle and amiable character when
they are translated into a great public arena. See, on the corruption of love into a destructive
public pity, Hannah Arendt, *On Revolution* (1963; reprint, Harmondsworth, England: Penguin, 1988), 85.

196 *resisted the error:* The mirage of the progressives has in recent years assumed novel forms and
can be found, among other places, in the "civic republican" ideas that now flourish in the academy. One contemporary advocate of communitarian ideas, Suzanna Sherry, has argued that
citizens should "behave toward their country and its citizens as they do toward their families:
proud, protective, and willing to make sacrifices." Suzanna Sherry, "Responsible Republicanism: Educating for Citizenship," *University of Chicago Law Review* 62 (1995), 162. Now of
course it is true that most of us *do* love our country, but as Burke observed, our country en-
gages our affections precisely because it shelters and protects the "little platoons" in which our
love is really invested. Love of country does not require what is impossible, that we love every
thing or every person in the country. Burke famously said that he did not know the method of
drawing up an indictment against an entire people; we have no more ability to love an entire
people. In the reverse metonymy of patriotism, we seem to love the whole when in reality we
love only a part.

197 *"There is a ripeness":* Jefferson to John Adams, Monticello, Va., August 1, 1816, in John Adams,
Adams-Jefferson Letters, 484.

197 *a sure sign:* "An habitual diarrhœa of more than a year's standing, would be a very bad disease at
any age: at my age it is a mortal one." David Hume, quoted in a letter from Adam Smith,
LL.D., to William Strahan, Esq., Kirkaldy, Fifeshire, November 9, 1776, in Hume, *Essays,
Moral, Political, and Literary,* ed. Eugene F. Miller (Indianapolis, Ind.: Liberty Press edition,
1985), xlv.

197 *"the mass of mankind":* Jefferson to Roger C. Weightman, Monticello, Va., June 24, 1826, in
Writings, 1517.

197 *"spent much time reading":* Claude G. Bowers, *Jefferson and Hamilton: The Struggle for Democracy
in America* (Boston, Cambridge, Mass., and New York: Houghton Mifflin, The Riverside Press,
1925), 103.

197 *Richard Rumbold:* See Douglas Adair, *Fame and the Founding Fathers* (Indianapolis: Liberty
Fund, n.d.), p. 286. Rumbold fought in Cromwell's battles against the Royalists, and he stood
by the scaffold in Whitehall in the early hours of January 30, 1649, the day the king was
brought there to die at the hands of Parliament. Three and a half decades after the murder of
Charles, Rumbold was convicted of treason for his part in the earl of Argyll's unsuccessful effort
to raise Scotland against Charles's son, James II. In his last letter Jefferson alluded to Rumbold's
dying words, spoken just before he was hanged and quartered in Edinburgh High Street.

197 *on the threshold of eternity:* See Henry S. Randall, *Life of Jefferson,* 3:544–47.

EPILOGUE

200 *"You will see":* Jefferson to James Madison, Paris, September 20, 1785, in *Jefferson Abroad,* 35.
200 *the "fathomless abyss":* Jefferson to John Adams, Monticello, Va., August 15, 1820, in *Writings,* 1444.
200 *the "incoherences":* Jefferson to Alexander Smyth, January 17, 1825.
201 *The modern man fell in love:* See T. S. Eliot's essay, "The Metaphysical Poets," in Eliot, *Selected Essays: New Edition* (New York: Harcourt Brace, 1950), 247.
201 *the work of faith:* Compare 1 Thess. 1:2.
201 *"the sacred fire":* Coulanges, *Ancient City,* 146.
201 *the temple of Vesta:* Beiswanger et al., *Thomas Jefferson's Monticello,* 37.
202 *When he came to edit the Gospels:* Late in life Jefferson produced another and more comprehensive edition of the Gospels to supplement his *Philosophy of Jesus.* He called this work *The Life and Morals of Jesus of Nazareth—Extracted textually from the Gospels in Greek, Latin, French & English.* The abridgment is available in numerous editions.
202 *"under our democratic stimulants":* Quoted in Adams, *History of the United States,* 122. Adams believed that Jefferson failed to create so ideal a *paideia* in America; in his memoir, *The Education of Henry Adams,* Adams ironically recounts his fruitless search for education (*paideia*) during the course of a long American life. In so far as Adams did find *paideia,* he seems to have found it not in the New World but in the Old World—in Chartres and Amiens, in Beauvais and Clairvaux, not in Boston, or New York, or Washington D.C.
202 *a rich pasturage in his heart:* We have yet to come to terms with Jefferson's Hellenism and its influence on his thought. If Jefferson preferred Roman forms in architecture, he preferred Greek forms in literary art. It is true that he thought little enough of Greek contributions to political science, and he was always contemptuous of Plato; but Greek was, he said, the most "ductile and copious" language he knew, and "the Grecian Homer the first of poets, as he must ever remain." Jefferson to John Waldo, Monticello, August 16, 1813, in *Writings,* 1296.
202 kalos kagathos: Although Jefferson here embraced the ideal of *kalos kagathos,* the beautiful and the good), he rejected the idea that the untranslatable Greek notion that the pursuit of the beautiful and the ideal is the end of human life) could serve as a basis of moral conduct. The "moral sense," Jefferson said, "is the true foundation of morality, and not the truth, &c., as fanciful writers have imagined." Jefferson to Peter Carr, Paris, August 10, 1787, in *Jefferson Abroad,* 182. Yet the idea of was always important to Jefferson; and when, in the Declaration of Independence, he wrote of man's right to pursue happiness, it may be that a memory of the Greek phrase lingered in his imagination. For will not the happy life, the life rightly led, be always consecrated to some form of—to some form of the beautiful and the ideal, to what Jefferson once called the "akmé of excellence"? Jefferson to John Adams, Monticello, Va., June 15, 1813, in *Writings,* 1278. Man, Jefferson said in this last letter, had never yet reached the summit—the implication being that he must continue to strive toward it.
202 *He gave them* paideia: The life of a *paideia* statesman will be endlessly suggestive to the people he has helped to form, for such a statesman revives the moribund poetry of his civilization. In ancient Athens teachers sought to impress the poetry of Solon on the imagination of youth: in America schoolchildren study the Declaration of Independence and memorize the Gettysburg Address. To study the life and writings of a *paideia* statesman is to be initiated into the traditions of one's civilization: for such a statesman has used these traditions in his political work. Lincoln and Jefferson deliberately used archaic language from the Bible, as well as from the other fonts of Western civilization, in their oratory; the poet-statesmen of the old Greek cities deliberately used archaic language from Homer in their state-shaping work. This preference for anachronistic language is more than an idiosyncrasy of style: Werner Jaeger observed that in the Greek tradition the poet-statesman was always a teacher. Such a poet, the Greeks believed,

> could not teach unless he used the noble language of Homer, whose educational effect every Greek felt and acknowledged. . . . The poet, in fact, clothes a contemporary subject in the archaic language of Homer. . . . [Whenever] the Greeks

recast their conception of *areté* [virtue, excellence, the ideal], they quoted [the old poets], and set the new creed in the old form [provided by the earlier poets]. That is the true Greek idea of culture. Once the pattern is fixed, it continues to be valid even in later stages of development; and every innovation must adapt itself to fit it.

Jaeger, *Paideia: The Ideals of Greek Culture* (1939, 2d ed., 1945, trans. Gilbert Highet, reprint, 3 vols., New York: Oxford University Press, 1965), vol. 1, *Archaic Greece—The Mind of Athens,* 74, 89, 97. But has not the idea of culture which Jaeger describes as typically Greek become in time a universal Western one? Jefferson, the close student of the Greeks, adopted as his own the model that Jaeger depicted in his book. Jefferson used the spiritual and poetic resources of the old cultures—those of Mediterranean antiquity (see part two of this book), the Old Testament (see part three of this book), and the New Testament (see part four of this book) to fashion a new and democratic culture for America. The principal difference between the Greek and the Jeffersonian conceptions of statesmanship is that the Greek statesman worked with a political entity—the polis—that absorbed the whole of its citizens' souls. A Greek statesman like Solon could therefore lavish all his soul-shaping energy on the city, for the city, together with the souls that composed it, was a work of art—was like clay, waiting to be molded by a superior potter. The city was for the Greek

> the source of all ideal values. . . . [The] polis appears as both an exalted and a despotic power. As such, it is something very like a god; *and the Greek always felt its divinity.* . . . The polis [became] the epitome of all things human and divine. . . . The state was a spiritual entity, which assimilated all the loftiest aspects of human life and gave them out as its own gifts.

Jaeger, *Paideia,* vol. 1, *Archaic Greece,* 93, 94, 108. A Whig republic does *not* absorb the whole of its citizens' souls: it is not designed to assimilate all the loftiest aspects of human life: it does not partake of the divine: it is not a work of art. The mature Jefferson understood this; this is why, in his last years, he devoted his creative energies to those little communities, such as the family (e.g., Monticello) and the school (e.g., the University of Virginia) that *do* absorb the greater portion of their participants' souls, and so might safely be directed toward an ideal end. Jefferson, in the course of his life, drew away from the idea that a modern republic can be a nurturer of souls in the way the old Greek city was. It is doubtful whether, in the last years of his life, he would have endorsed the young Lincoln's proposal that the United States develop a "*political religion* of the nation." In proposing a "political religion" Lincoln seems to have had in mind something approaching to the old Greek ideal of a *polis* that is wholly loved and wholly loving, an emblem of the divine. (For how can one have religion without divinity?) Jefferson would, I think, have been skeptical of this idea. Divinity, he knew, has ceased to hedge the state; and the state itself has ceased to be a religious entity in the way it was for the Greek. See Lincoln, Address to the Young Men's Lyceum of Springfield, Illinois: "The Perpetuation of our Political Institutions," January 1838, in Lincoln, *Speeches and Writings: 1832–1858,* ed. Donald E. Fehrenbacher (New York: Library of America, 1989), 32.

203 *his ostensible contempt:* Jefferson to John Adams, Monticello, Va., April 20, 1812, in John Adams, *Adams-Jefferson Letters,* 298–99; Jefferson to Charles Thomson, Monticello, Va., January 9, 1816, in *Writings,* 1373; and Jefferson to William Short, Monticello, Va., August 4, 1820, ibid., 1436. Jefferson was speaking primarily of Plato, but he had also in mind orthodox Christianity, which he believed to be a form of Platonism superimposed upon the true teachings of Jesus. He said that his *Philosophy of Jesus*

> is a document in proof that *I* am a *real Christian,* that is to say, a disciple of the doctrines of Jesus, very different from the Platonists, who call *me* infidel and *themselves* Christians and preachers of the gospel, while they draw all their characteristic dogmas from what its author never said nor saw. They have com-

pounded from the heathen mysteries a system beyond the comprehension of man, of which the great reformer of the vicious ethics and deism of the Jews, were he to return on earth, would not recognize one feature.

Jefferson to Charles Thomson, Monticello, Va., January 9, 1816, ibid., 1373 (emphasis in original). See also Jefferson to John Adams, Monticello, Va., April 8, 1816, ibid., 1384 (on the "Hierophants of fabricated Christianity"). This belief that the teachings of Christ had been perverted by Neoplatonists was also held by Nietzsche, who said that Christianity was Platonism for the masses. The Protestant reformers were, to Jefferson's way of thinking, no better than the Platonizing Catholics. Jefferson deplored the "demoralizing dogmas of Calvin"; he insisted that pious Presbyterians had been persuaded to worship a "false god," a "dæmon of malignant spirit," and he expressed the hope "that there is not a *young man* now living in the United States who will not die an Unitarian." Jefferson to Dr. Benjamin Waterhouse, Monticello, Va., June 26, 1822, ibid., 1458–59; Jefferson to John Adams, Monticello, Va., April 11, 1823, ibid., 1466.

203 *a "prosaic way":* Lionel Trilling, *The Liberal Imagination: Essays on Literature and Society* (Harcourt Brace ed., 1949, 1950), iv–vi.

204 *"The earth," he said:* Jefferson to John Wayles Eppes, Monticello, Va., June 24, 1813, in *Writings,* 1280.

204 *Jefferson himself was unable:* The defects in Jefferson's understanding of himself do but confirm the truth of Proust's dictum "How little do we know of what we have in our hearts." *The Fugitive,* 641. In composing this little chapter in the moral imagination of my country, I have sometimes thought of Taine's words: "When you consider with your eyes the visible man, what do you look for? The man invisible. . . . You consider his writings, his artistic productions, his business transactions or political ventures; and that in order to measure the scope and limits of his intelligence, his inventiveness, his coolness, to find out the order, the description, the general force of his ideas, the mode in which he thinks and resolves. All these externals are but avenues converging to a center; you enter them simply in order to reach that center; and that center is the genuine man . . . the inner man. We have reached a new world, which is infinite, because every action we see involves an infinite association of reasonings, emotions, sensations new and old, which have served to bring it to light. . . . This underworld is a new subject-matter, proper to the historian. If his critical education suffice, he can lay bare, under every detail of architecture, every stroke in a picture, every phrase in a writing, the special sensation whence detail, stroke, or phrase had issue; *he is present at the drama which was enacted in the soul of the artist or writer;* the choice of a word, the brevity or length of a sentence, the nature of a metaphor, the accent of a verse, the development of an argument—everything is a symbol to him; while his eyes read the text, his soul and mind pursue the continuous development and the ever-changing succession of the emotions and concepts out of which the text has sprung: in short, he unveils a psychology." H. A. Taine, *History of the English Language,* 2 vols., reprint, trans. N. Van Laun (New York: William L. Allison, 1895), 1.5–6.

204 *"[C]ould the dead":* Jefferson, Epitaph [1826], in *Writings,* 706.

Acknowledgments

In the course of composing this book I have incurred many obligations. I have particularly to thank the following persons: Michael V. Carlisle and Michelle Tessler of Carlisle & Company, who represented the book with skill and fidelity; Bruce Nichols and Casey Reivich of the Free Press, who greatly improved the manuscript through their editing; and Matthew J. Herrington and John W. Tyler, each of whom read the manuscript and commented thoughtfully and usefully upon it. For assistance in obtaining materials in their collections, I am indebted to Jessica Tyree and the archivists of Monticello, and also to Kate DeBose of the Massachusetts Historical Society. I am grateful, too, for the help I received from Sean Bell-Thomson, Denis C. Beran, Virginia K. Beran, Henry P. Davis, Myron Magnet, William W. Morton, Jr., Adam Walinsky, Barbara J. Ward, and Sedgwick A. Ward, as well as from the staffs of the New York Public Library, the Pequot Library in Southport, Connecticut, the Hiram Halle Memorial Library in Pound Ridge, New York, and the Musée des Franciscains in the Monastère de Cimiez in Nice. I should also like to express my gratitude to M. Lambert and Mme. Lambert for the kindness they showed me and my family in the Clos des Saumanes in Provence, and to Dr. Daran and Mme. Daran for their hospitality in the Villa l'Églantier at Cannes. This book could not have been written without the sympathy and forbearance of my wife, Mary, whose help during the period of its composition I am unable adequately to acknowledge.

M. K. B.
POUND RIDGE, NEW YORK,
APRIL 2003

Index

action, power and, 131
Adam, Robert, 94, 231*n*
Adams, Abigail, 32, 33, 48, 58, 59, 62, 73
    Jefferson's correspondence with, 165
Adams, Henry, 156, 252*n*
Adams, John, 24, 25, 31, 32, 143, 144
    Alien and Sedition acts and, 134–35
    on British constitution, 122
    election of 1796 and, 132, 133
    election of 1800 and, 140–41
    Hamilton and, 132, 133, 140
    Hamilton-Burr duel and, 169
    on Jefferson, 154, 156
    Jefferson's correspondence with, 88, 99, 132,
        187, 197, 200
    Jefferson's opinion of, 119, 120, 181
    Jefferson's reconciliation with, 187
    as president, 133, 134
Adonis, 75
Aeneid (Virgil), 247*n*
African-Americans:
    Jefferson's opinion of, 38, 155
    see also slavery
Aix, 79, 80, 84, 85
Alien and Sedition acts, 134–35, 137, 144
    Callender's conviction and imprisonment
        under, 139–40, 158
Alyscamps, Les, 79
American Century, xviii
American democracy, mythology of, 136
American Revolution, 16–17, 19, 22–26, 30,
    91
    first battles of, 21
    Hamilton in, 113
    reasons for success of, 139
    Washington and, 143–44
Ames, Fisher, 157, 162, 168
Anacreon, 106
"Anas" (Jefferson), 241*n*
Anthesteria, feast of, 75
Antiquités de la France: Monuments de Nismes
    (Clérisseau), 73
antiquities:
    collectors of, 77
    Etruscan, 93

    reproductions of, used by Jefferson, 75, 77,
        78, 100, 229*n*–234*n*
Antiquities of Athens, The (Stuart and Revett), 93
Apuleius, Lucius, 98
architecture, Jefferson's interest in, 92–95, 129
    see also Monticello; Virginia, University of
Areopagitica (Milton), 152
Ariadne, 75
aristocracy, 5
    of France, 34, 35, 37, 38
Aristotle, 197
Arles, 231*n*
Arnold, Benedict, 30, 91, 225*n*
art, love and, 107
Articles of Confederation, 82, 84
askos (wine pouch), 77–78
associations and communities, Jefferson's
        thoughts on, 189–91
assumption controversy, 113–14, 240*n*
Athens, 93
    Dionysian cult in, 89
attainder, bill of, 18
Attys, 75
augurs, Roman, 151
Augustine of Hippo, Saint, 234*n*

Bacchanalia, 89
Bacon, Francis, 13, 79, 122
Bankhead, Anne Cary Randolph (granddaugh-
    ter), 195
banking, Jefferson's opinion of, 117
Bank of the United States, 114–15, 118, 156
Barlow, Joel, 76–77
Battle of the Books (Swift), 227
benevolence, 190–91, 196
Bible, 120–21, 170, 252*n*
Bingham, Anne Willing, 222–23*n*
Birth of Tragedy, The (Nietzsche), 77
Bloom, Harold, 235*n*
Bonaparte, Napoléon, 161
books, xviii, xix, 14, 37, 236*n*
Bossuet, Jacques-Bénigne, 34, 54
Boston Tea Party, 17
Boswell, James, 42
Botetourt, Baron de, 15

Bowers, Claude, xix, xvii
Browne, Sir Thomas, 87
bullfights, 105, 238n
Burgundy wines, 61
Burke, Edmund, 16, 191, 251n
Burr, Aaron, 147
  arrest of, 177
  election of 1800 and, 140, 141, 142, 145
  Federalists and, 166, 167, 168
  and Great Britain, 172–75
  Hamilton's disagreements with, 141–42,
    145, 167, 168
  Hamilton's duel with, 169
  Jefferson and, 147, 166–67, 174, 175, 176
  scheme of, 173–77, 181
  trial and acquittal of, 180, 181
  as vice president, 166, 172, 173
Burr, Theodosia, 175
Burwell, Rebecca, 10–11
Burwell, William, 179
Byrd, William, II, 7
Byrd, William, III, 8, 13–14
Byrd family, 8
Byron, Lord, 108, 144

Caesar, Julius, 122, 143, 145, 147
Callender, James Thomson, 135, 158–60, 163
  conviction and imprisonment of, 139–40
  pardon of, 159
Calvinism, 100, 136, 254n
campaigns, political, see presidential campaigns
    and elections
capax imperii, 144, 244n
capital, moving of, 113–14
cardplaying, 34
carnival, 89, 228n
Casanova, Giovanni Giacomo, 106
Cato the Younger, 143, 190
Catullus (pen name), 124
cavaliers, Virginians as, 38
Chambertin, 62, 63, 64
Chamfort, Sébastien-Roch Nicolas, 45
Channing, William Ellery, 168
Chase, Samuel, 139
  impeachment and trial of, 172
Chatham, 1st Earl of (William Pitt), 16
Chaucer, Geoffrey, 187
Chesterfield, Lord, 63, 220n–221n
Chisolm, Isham, 228n
Christianity, 252n–253n
Chronicles, 123
Church, Angelica, 56
Churchill, Winston, xx
Cicero, 10, 99, 100
Cimiez, Nice, 106
Cistercian monks, 61
Cité antique, La (Fustel de Coulanges), 98–99

Cîteaux, monastery of, 61
cities, growth of, 189, 191
civil society, 201
Clarissa (Richardson), 47, 48
classical architecture, 93
classical writers and thinkers, 73, 74, 77
  Jefferson's studies of, xix, 14, 60, 65, 71, 78,
    87–88, 92, 98, 197, 201–3, 250n,
    252n, 253n
Clérisseau, Charles-Louis, 73, 74, 93–94
Clinton, George, 156, 166, 167
Clinton family, 166, 167
Colbert, Jean-Baptiste, 34
Coleridge, Samuel Taylor, 70
College of the Dame Inglesi, 192
College of William and Mary, 4
commedia dell'arte, 228n
common sense, Jefferson's stand for, xvi
communities and associations:
  Jefferson's thoughts on, 189–91, 201, 202,
    245n–251n
  love and, 196
Confession of Petronas, The, 97
Congress, U.S., under Articles of Confedera-
    tion, 82
conscience, voice of, 102–3
constitution, British, 122
Constitution, U.S., 111, 122
  drafting of, 82–84, 227n
  Hamilton and, 113, 247
  and Louisiana Purchase, 161–62
  and presidential election by House of Repre-
    sentatives, 145n
  private interests and, 142
Constitutional Convention, U.S., 84
Continental Congress, 17, 18, 21, 24–25
Coolidge, Ellen Wayles Randolph (grand-
    daughter), 179, 195
Cornwallis, Lord, 30, 91
Cosway, Maria, 42–47, 49–52, 54, 55, 68, 74, 191
  convent school founded by, 192
  Jefferson's correspondence with, 53, 56, 58,
    59, 60, 66, 97, 127, 128, 192,
    219n–220n
  pregnancy of, 112
Cosway, Richard, 42–44, 45, 191
Côte de Beaune, 63
Côte d'Or, 61, 62, 63
country Whigs, 115
county government, Jefferson's proposal for, 190
court Whigs, 115, 147
Crèvecoeur, Michel-Guillaume-Jean de, 60
criminal code, reform of, 26
Croatia, 94

Dalmatia, 94
Danquerville, Mr., see Hancarville, Baron d'

David, Jacques-Louis, 225*n*–226*n*
Dayton, Jonathan, 173
Declaration of Independence, xx, 24–26, 36,
    160, 204
  "Creator" invoked in, 213*n*
  fiftieth anniversary of, 197
  "laws of nature" passage in, 91
deism, 91, 207*n*
Delaware, 24
Democratic Party, Jefferson's groundwork for, 137
demons (spirits), 98, 99, 101, 102, 232*n*,
    236*n*, 237*n*
Denis, Saint, 237*n*
Dennie, Joseph, 171
Desgodets, Antoine Babury, 229*n*, 230*n*
Dilettanti, 42
dinner parties, French, 72
Dionysus, 75, 77, 89, 223*n*
Discourses on Davila (Adams), 120
DNA testing, 127, 243*n*
Drouais, Jean-Germain, 225*n*
Dryden, John, 138
Dunglison, Robley, 198
Dunmore, Lord, 21
Dupont de Nemours, Pierre-Samuel, 158

Ecclesiastes, 40
education:
  and Jefferson as teacher, xix
  public, 26
Education of Henry Adams, The (Adams), 252*n*
elections, presidential, *see* presidential cam-
    paigns and elections
Eleusinian rituals, 202
Eliot, T. S., 224*n*, 237*n*, 252*n*
Ellis, Joseph, 102
Elysium, 97, 104
Embargo Act, 183–84
Emerson, Ralph Waldo, 19, 203
England, *see* Great Britain
English language, Jefferson's use of, 187
Enlightenment, the, xvi, 49, 92, 139
Epictetus, 71, 100
Epicureanism, 72, 73
Epicurus, 71, 72, 100
Eppes, Jack (son-in-law), 164, 179
Eppes, Maria ("Polly") Jefferson (daughter),
    30, 32, 54, 63, 128, 246*n*
  illness and death of, 164–65
  marriage of, 164
Eros, 107
  depictions of, 233*n*
erotic ideal, 49
Etruria, 93
executive authority, in federal government, 82,
    84
exercise, Jefferson's program of, xiv–xv, 193

Faubourg Saint-Germain, Paris, 35, 39
Fauquier, Francis, 4
Federalist papers, 113
Federalist Party, 100
  and Alien and Sedition acts, 134–35
  Burr and, 166, 167, 168
  election of 1796 and, 132
  election of 1800 and, 141, 142, 146
  French Revolution and, 134
  Gazette of the United States and, 123
  Jefferson and, 120–21, 124, 136, 137, 155,
      157, 168, 171, 241*n*
  Jefferson's inaugural address (1801) and, 153
  judiciary controlled by, 171–72
fertility myths and rituals, 74–77, 223*n*–224*n*,
    225*n*
Fleming, Will, 11
Florian, Jean-Pierre Claris de, 50
flour mill, Jefferson's, 189
Fontenelle, Bernard Le Bovier de, 199
Four Books of Architecture (Palladio), 95
France:
  Jefferson's evaluation of, 37–38, 72, 73, 215*n*
  Jefferson's travels in, 57, 58, 60–69, 70–71,
      78–81, 84–86, 88–90, 94, 97, 104–7
  Napoléonic wars of, 172
  see also Paris
Franklin, Benjamin, 24, 25, 31, 32
Frazer, James George, 77
freedom and liberty, Jefferson's dedication to, xv, 26
free trade, 116, 183
Fréjus, 105
French Revolution, 133–34, 153, 174
Freneau, Philip, 123, 124
frontier, 13, 14
Froude, Richard Hurrell, 228*n*
Fustel de Coulanges, Numa-Denis, 98

Gallatin, Albert, 143, 156, 183
Gauls, 104
Gazette of the United States, The, 123
genii, 98, 99
genius spirit, 99–102, 232*n*, 235*n*
Genoa, 107
George III, King of England, 22, 25, 44, 182
Georgics (Virgil), 96
Gettysburg Address (Lincoln), xx
Gibbon, Edward, xvi, 81, 86, 94
Giles, William Branch, 125
glossolalia, 234*n*
Goethe, Johann Wolfgang von, 48, 77, 81–82,
    88, 90
  on books, 236*n*
Golden Bough (Frazer), 77
grand tour, in eighteenth century, 81, 85, 86
Great Britain:
  American shipping and, 182–83

Burr and, 172–75
Jay's Treaty, 134
Jefferson's opinion of, 41, 72
Maria Cosway in, 54, 55, 56
Napoléonic wars and, 172
Revolution of 1688 in, 114, 115, 158
Great Seal of the United States, Jefferson's pro-
    posal for, 131
Greece:
    Dionysian cult in, 89
    spirit culture of, 98–99
Greek architecture, 93
Greek writers and thinkers, xix, 14, 252n–253n
    kalos kagathos of, 202
    paideia of, 202–3
Grenville, George, 16
grief, 92
Griswold, Roger, 167, 168

Hadrian's villa, 93
Hamilton, Alexander, xvii, 143, 144, 181
    Adams and, 132, 133, 140
    assumption controversy and, 113, 114
    blackmail of, 125
    on British constitution, 122
    Burr's disagreements with, 141–42, 145,
        167, 168
    Burr's duel with, 168–69
    early life of, 113
    election of 1800 and, 140, 145, 146, 147
    and fears of French invasion, 134
    Federalism of, 100
    Jefferson and, 112–22, 124, 125, 145–47,
        155, 156, 158, 181, 241n, 244n
    personality of, 139
    political appointees of, 124
    in retirement, 132
    Reynolds affair and, 125, 135
    Talleyrand and, 181
    U.S. Constitution and, 83, 113, 248n
Hamilton, Lady Emma, 43
Hamilton, Sir William, 43
Hancarville, Baron d' (Pierre-François Hugues)
    (Mr. Danquerville), 74, 77, 223n–224n
happiness, pursuit of, xvii
Hemings, James, 34
Hemings, Sally, 127–28, 160, 197
Hemings family, 16, 127–28, 197, 243n
Henry, Patrick, 16, 17
Heraclitus, 101
heroic virtue, 143–45
Hessian fly, 115
hierophant, 202
Historiae (Tacitus), 152
history, cycles of, 85–86
History of the Decline and Fall of the Roman
    Empire, The (Gibbon), 81, 86, 94

Homer, 14, 60, 88, 98, 190
honor, 26
Horace, 65, 187
horses and riding, Jefferson's interest in, 38, 193
Hôtel de Langeac, 33–34
Houdetot, comtesse d', 48
House of Representatives, U.S.:
    election of 1800 and, 141, 142, 145
    impeachment of judges by, 172
Hubbard, James, 228n–229n
Hugues, Pierre-François, see Hancarville, Baron d'
husbandry and craftsmanship, 116, 117, 182
Hutcheson, Francis, 217n
Hyères, 105
hypochondria, xiv, xv, 62, 68
hysteria, xiv, 62, 63

Iliad (Homer), 98
impeachment of judges, 172
impressment, British practice of, 172
indolence, xiv, 62
interior dialogues, 102–3, 235n–236n
Inventing America (Wills), xvi, 217n
Isaiah, 58, 118, 120
Italian comedies, 90
Italy:
    architecture of, 92–93
    Jefferson's travels in, 97, 107–8

Jackson, Andrew, 173
Jacobinism, 139
James, Henry, 237n
Jay, John, 145, 221n
Jay's Treaty, 134
Jefferson, Jane (daughter), 21
Jefferson, Jane (sister), 98
Jefferson, Jane Randolph (mother), 6, 10, 22
Jefferson, Lucy Elizabeth (daughter), 30, 32
Jefferson, Maria ("Polly") (daughter), see Eppes,
    Maria ("Polly") Jefferson
Jefferson, Martha ("Patsy") (daughter), see Ran-
    dolph, Martha ("Patsy") Jefferson
Jefferson, Martha Wayles Skelton (wife),
    15–16, 22, 24, 30
    decline and death of, 30–31, 92, 97–98
Jefferson, Peter (father), 3, 4, 6, 10, 47
Jefferson, Thomas:
    Adams and, 88, 99, 119, 120, 132–33, 154,
        156, 181, 187, 197, 200
    as administrator, 161
    and Alien and Sedition acts, 135, 137, 144
    antique reproductions collected by, 75, 77–78
    apathy and melancholy of, 9, 20
    apparel of, 155
    and architecture, 92–95, 129
    as artist in politics, 174
    assumption controversy and, 114, 115, 240n

Jefferson, Thomas, *(cont.)*
  bibliomania of, xiii, xix, 14, 37, 41, 48, 60, 71, 189
  boyhood and youth of, 3, 4
  breakdowns of, 9–10
  Burr and, 142, 147, 166, 167, 174, 175, 176
  Callender and, 135, 139, 158–60
  Christianity and, 252*n*–253*n*
  cities and, 189, 191
  classical studies of, xix, 14, 60, 65, 71, 78, 92, 98, 100, 106, 197, 201–3, 250*n*, 252*n*, 253*n*
  commonplace book of, 10
  conspiracy and subversion feared by, 180–81
  contemporary assessment of, xix
  Continental Congress and, 18, 21, 24
  county government proposed by, 190
  criticism of opponents by, 138
  on "Dæmonism," 100
  death as theme in life of, 10, 98
  death of, 198, 204
  deaths of children of, 92
  and Declaration of Independence, 24–26, 204
  democratic manners of, 155
  diplomatic efforts of, 83
  domestic life of, 179–80, 194, 195
  domestic policy of, 156
  dreams of, 87, 200
  economic and financial policies of, 114–18, 156, 158, 183
  education of, 4, 189–90
  as educator, xix, 203
  ennui of, xiii, xiv, xv, xx, 20, 62, 63, 64, 69, 78, 186
  entail, laws of, 26
  and exercise, xiv–xv, 193
  fall and broken wrist of, 53, 58, 80, 193
  Federalists and, 120–21, 124, 136, 137, 155, 157, 168, 171, 241*n*
  financial and economic policies of, 114–18, 156, 158, 183
  financial problems of, 40–41, 185, 188, 194, 196
  first inaugural address of, 151–54, 240*n*–241*n*, 244*n*
  flour mill of, 189
  foreign policy of, 156, 172, 183–84
  on the French, 37–38, 72
  and French Revolution, 133–34, 153
  Freneau and, 123, 124
  gardens of, 186
  as gentleman farmer, 16
  as governor of Virginia, 29–30
  grandchildren of, 179, 180, 190, 194, 195
  grave of, 204
  grief of, at wife's death, 31
  and Hamilton, 112–22, 124, 125, 145–47, 155, 156, 158, 181, 241*n*, 244*n*
  and Hamilton-Burr duel, 169
  Hellenism of, 252*n*
  and Hemings family, 127–28, 160, 197, 243*n*
  home of, *see* Monticello
  and horses and riding, 38, 193
  as host, 155
  husbanding passion of, 116, 117, 182
  ideal community proposed by, 189–91
  idealism of, 15, 138
  ill health of, 9, 11–12, 22, 23, 57–58, 107, 112, 118, 128, 154, 160, 180, 194, 197
  inauguration of (1801), 151–54
  inauguration of (1805), 170
  insomnia of, 68
  interior dialogues of, 102–3, 128, 200
  investments of, 188–89
  judiciary attacked by, 171–72
  and Kentucky Resolutions, 137
  Lafayette and, 35–36, 38–39, 120, 133
  language interests of, 187
  last days of, 197–98
  law practice of, 13
  law studies of, 10
  liberty tree invoked by, 75, 76
  library of, xviii, 187, 189
  as lieutenant of Albemarle, 15
  loans of friends guaranteed by, 188
  Louisiana Purchase and, 161–62
  on love and lust, 107
  luxury and, 20, 41, 73
  Madison and, 115, 123, 125, 126, 127, 130, 131, 136, 192, 200
  on marriage, 7, 215*n*
  marriage of, 15–16
  midlife crisis of, 58
  militia commanded by, 15
  ministerial stipend of, 40
  mockingbird owned by, 179
  moral sense of, 49, 71–72, 122
  and music and theater, 37
  mysticism of, xvi, xvii
  nail-making operation of, 189
  and national bank, 114, 115, 118, 156
  in New York City, 112
  northern trip of, 123
  novels read by, 46, 47
  old age of, 193–94, 197
  as orator, 152
  in Paris, 31–32, 33–36, 37, 42
  personal authority of, 131
  in Philadelphia, 115, 119, 121
  philosophy of, xvi, 71–72
  poetic nature of, 84–85
  power and, 131
  as president, 154–61, 166, 168, 171–72, 180, 182–84
  presidential campaign and election of (1796), 130–31, 132

presidential campaign and election of (1800), 139–47
presidential campaign and election of (1804), 167, 170
prophetic mission of, 135–37
rationalism of, 202, 203
religious and moral concerns of, 165, 166, 207n, 252n
religious tolerance of, 53
and republicanism, 119–22
retirement from presidency, 185–89, 191, 194
retirement from secretaryship of state, 126–30
in revolutionary period, 21–26, 29–30, 91
romantic episodes of, 10–11, 15, 42, 44, 46, 47, 50–56, 58–60, 68
rules and maxims of, xiv–xv, 62–63, 64, 190
Scottish philosophers' influence on, 217n
second inaugural address of, 170–71
as secretary of state, 111–12, 118–22, 123–26
sentimentality of, xvi–xvii, 46–51, 55, 68, 69
shopping and expenditures of, 40, 41, 62, 67, 188
slavery and, 7, 15, 16, 25, 38, 127–28, 196, 197, 228n
and Socrates' demon, 99
stoicism of, 20
temperament and personality of, xiv, 178
term limits supported by, 182
tombstone of, 204
Tory tendencies of, 200, 201
travels of, in France, 57, 58, 60–69, 70–71, 78–81, 84–86, 88–90, 94, 97, 104–7
travels of, in Italy, 97, 107–8
and University of Virginia, 190, 192, 195–96
U.S. Constitution and, 84, 227n
as vice president, 132–37
and violence and physical confrontation, 88, 90–92
as Virginia gentleman, 38
and virtuous leadership, 143, 144–45
war opposed by, 183
and Washington, 118, 119, 124, 126, 131, 138, 180, 245n
Whig beliefs of, 116, 117, 139, 156, 171, 200, 201
at Williamsburg, 4, 5
and wine, 61–64, 121, 122, 155, 188
as wise man, 199
women as viewed by, 10, 34, 50
Jefferson and Hamilton (Bowers), xvii
Jefferson and His Time (Malone), xviii
Jefferson Memorial, Washington, D.C., xviii
Jesus Christ, 100, 165, 166, 202, 252n
judiciary, Jefferson's assault on, 171–72
Julie, ou la Nouvelle Héloïse (Rousseau), 46–47, 48, 50, 55
Jupiter (slave), 4, 90

kalos kagathos, 202, 252n
Kennedy, John F., xviii
Kentucky Resolutions, 137
Knight, Richard Payne, 223n–224n

La Bruyère, Jean de, 73
Lafayette, Marquis de, 35–36, 38–39, 120, 133
land patents, 13
language, Jefferson's notion of, 187
La Rochefoucauld, Duc François de, 33, 73
leadership, 143, 247n
Lebanon, 93
Lee, Richard Henry, 17, 24
Letter Concerning the Public Conduct and Character of John Adams (Hamilton), 140
levees, 155–56
libel case, Pennsylvania, 171
Liber, 77
Liberalia, 77
liberalism, 203
of New England, 168
liberty, tree of, 75, 76, 77, 96, 120
Library of Congress, British destruction of, 189
Lincoln, Abraham, xvii, xx, 137, 203, 244n, 252n–253n
little platoons, Burke's notion of, 191
Livingston, Robert, 24
Livingston family, 166
Livy, 63
Locke, John, xvi, 122, 136
London, 41
Lord Dunmore's Ethiopians, 21
Louisiana Purchase, 161
Louisiana Territory, 161
Louis XIV, King of France, 34, 161, 182, 228n
love:
    associations grounded in, 191, 250n–251n
    Jesus' parables of, 202
    lust and, 107
    order and, 194–95, 196
    sentimental conception of, 49, 217n
    Whig ideas and, xvi–xvii
luxury, 20, 41

Machiavelli, Niccolò, 101, 174, 234n, 247n
McKean, Thomas, 171
Macon, Nathaniel, 87, 88
Madison, James, 31, 36, 39, 40, 58, 91, 98, 143, 145, 184
    and assumption controversy, 113, 114
    and impeachment controversy, 172
    and Jefferson, 115, 123, 125, 126, 127, 136, 192, 200
    and Jefferson's presidential campaign (1796), 130, 131
    and U.S. Constitution, 83
Maia, José da, 221n

Maison Carrée, 66–68, 73, 105
Malone, Dumas, xix, xviii, 227n
Mann, Thomas, 236n
Marbury v. Madison, 172
Marchesi, Luigi, 55
Marcus Aurelius, 100
Marius (Roman general), 80
Marius Imprisoned at Minturnae, 225n–226n
Marseilles, 88–90, 92, 97, 104
Marshall, John, 143, 171, 172
    and trial of Burr, 180
Maryland, and election of 1800, 145, 146
Mason, George, 119–20
materialism, xvi, 92
Mazzei, Philip, 120
medicine, 117
Mediterranean Sea, color of, 108
Méré, chevalier de, 73
Merry, Anthony, 155
    and Burr, 173, 174
metaphors, 76, 202, 224n
migraine headaches, 12
Mill, John Stuart, 203
Milton, John, 136, 152, 176, 236n
Mississippi river, 161
Monroe, James, 30, 143
    and Hamilton, 124–25
Montague, Charles, 114
Montaigne, Michel Eyquem de, 101, 127,
    234n–235n
Monticello, 93
    antique reproductions at, 75, 78
    British raid of, 30, 91
    building of, 15, 194
    decorative components of, 95–96, 200,
        229n–233n
    dome of, 201–2
    feudal conditions at, 37
    figure of demon boy (putto) at, 100, 233n
    Jefferson at, in 1801, 154–55
    and Jefferson's debts, 194, 196
    Jefferson's retirement to, 126–29, 185–86
    library at, xviii–xix
    nail-making operation at, 189
    originality of, 95
    and slavery, 196
    tourists at, xix
moral sense, 49, 122
    of classical writers, 71–72
Morris, Gouverneur, 146
Muses, figures of, 78
music and singing, of African Americans, 38, 155
mystery cults, 223n
mysticism:
    of eighteenth-century writers, 49–50, 78
    and fertility rituals, 74, 75

Napoléon I, Emperor of France, 161
national bank, see Bank of the United States
national debt, 156, 158
    assumption controversy, 113–14
National Gazette, The, 123
natural law, 212n–213n
nature, violence in, 91
navy, British, 182
navy, U.S., 134, 156
Nemausus, 78
neoclassical architecture, 93, 95
Neoplatonism, 253n–254n
Nero, 174
New England:
    Embargo Act's effect on, 183
    Federalists of, 168
    Jefferson's inaugural allusion to, 153–54
    morality of, 122
Newman, John Henry, 11, 228n
newspapers, 123–24, 171
Newton, Isaac, 122
New York, 24, 25, 112
    Burr and, 166, 167, 168
    and election of 1800, 140, 145
Nice, 106, 107
Nietzsche, Friedrich Wilhelm, 77, 223n, 225n,
    228n, 231n–232n, 233n, 254n
Nile river, 76
Nîmes, 66–68, 73, 78
    Jefferson's diplomatic work and visit to, 221n
Nissart, 106
Noailles, Adrienne-Catherine de (comtesse de
    Tessé), 36, 48, 66–69, 74, 78, 85
Noli, 107
North, Frederick, Lord, 17
Notes on the State of Virginia (Jefferson), 38,
    83, 107, 116
Novak, Michael, 213n
Nunc Dimittis, 198

Ode to Napoléon Buonaparte (Byron), 144n
Odyssey (Homer), 190
Old Testament, Jefferson's imagery from, 120–21,
    170
oranges, cultivation of, 105
ortolans, 108
Osiris, 76, 77, 225n

Page, John, 5, 11, 164
paideia, 202–3, 252n–253n
pain, avoiding of, 72
Paine, Thomas, 120
Palladio, Andrea, 92–95
Pantheon, Rome, 196
Paoli, Pasquale, 55
Paradise Lost (Milton), 187, 236n

Paris:
  Jefferson in, 31–32, 33–36, 37, 42
  society of, xiii, xx, 73, 215n, 222n–223n
  in winter, 29
Parmesan cheese, 107
Pascal, Blaise, 57
patriotism, 21
Peloponnesian War, 88
Pennsylvania, 24, 25
  seditious libel case in, 171
Petit, Monsieur (French servant), 33
Petitjean (servant), 70
Petronius, 89n
Philadelphia, Pa., 115
philosophy, 71–72, 117
  Jefferson's residence at, 121
Philosophy of Jesus (Jefferson), 166, 190, 252n
physic (medicine), 117
Phrygians, 75
Pickering, John, impeachment of, 172
Pickering, Timothy, 167, 168
Piers Plowman (Langland), 187
Pinckney, Charles Cotesworth, 134
pinot noir grapes, 61
pioneers, Jefferson's perception of, 14
Piranesi, Giambattista, 95
Pitt, William (1st Earl of Chatham), 16
Pitt, William, the Younger, 172
Platonism, 252n
pleasures, 73
  intellectual, 72
Plumer, William, 155
Plutarch, 20, 99
poetry, 117
political violence, 91
politics:
  artist in, 174
  Jefferson's contempt for, 20
Pope, Alexander, 104, 238n–239n
Pope, John Russell, xviii
Poplar Forest, Jefferson's villa at, 188, 229n
Potocki, Count, 74
power, action and, 131
presidential campaigns and elections:
  of 1796, 130–31, 140
  of 1800, 139–47
  of 1804, 167
Priestley, Joseph, 100, 165
primogeniture, laws of, 26
private culture, Jefferson's influence on, xix
progressivism, 203, 251n
Prospect before Us, The (Callender), 139
Protestantism, Jefferson's study of, 135–36
Provençal dialect, 67, 85, 227n
Provence, 66, 67, 73, 79–80, 85, 86, 94, 105
public virtue, 20–21, 211n

Puritanism, 136, 197
putti (cherubs), 100, 233n
Pythagoras, 71, 100

Qeb (Seb), 76

Randolph, Anne Cary (granddaughter), see
  Bankhead, Anne Cary Randolph
Randolph, Edmund, 127
Randolph, Ellen Wayles (granddaughter), see
  Coolidge, Ellen Wayles Randolph
Randolph, Isham, 6
Randolph, John (loyalist), 22, 23
Randolph, John (Representative), 172, 179
Randolph, Martha ("Patsy") Jefferson (daughter), 21, 30, 31, 117
  education of, 54
  and Jefferson's death, 98
  Jefferson's rules of conduct for, xiv, 50, 62–63, 64, 102–3
  and Jefferson's threats of violence, 90
  and Jefferson's tour of south of France, 58, 80–81
  marriage and domestic life of, 111, 163–64, 179–80, 195
  in Paris, 31–32, 34
Randolph, Peyton, 17
Randolph, Thomas Jefferson (grandson), 195
Randolph, Thomas Mann (son-in-law), 111, 163–64, 179–80, 195
Randolph, William, 6
Randolph family, 3, 4, 6, 209n
rationalism, 92, 202, 203
rebellion, necessity of, 91
religion:
  disestablishment of, 26
  Jefferson's study of, 135–36, 165–66, 250n–251n
Renaissance thinkers, 101, 102
René I, King of Provence, 80
republicanism, Jefferson's advocacy of, 119–22
Republican Party, 125–26
  Burr and, 167
  Callender and, 158
  and election of 1800, 140, 141, 142
  and election of 1804, 166–67
  and impeachment of judges, 172
  interpretation of the Constitution by, 162
  and Jefferson's inaugural address (1801), 153
Revere, Nicholas, 93
revolutionary movements, see American Revolution; Great Britain, Revolution of 1688
  in; French Revolution
  revolution of 1800, 139
Reynolds, James and Maria, 125, 135
rice-husking machine, Jefferson's search for, 97, 107

Richardson, Samuel, 47, 48
Richelieu, Cardinal, 34
Richmond, Va., 26
  capitol building for, 73
  sack of, 30, 91, 225n
Richmond Recorder, 160
rights, enunciation of, in Declaration of Independence, 26
Rights of Man (Paine), 120
Robinson, John, 16
Roman architecture, 93
Roman Catholicism:
  in southern France, 71, 73, 94
  of Cosway, Maria, 52, 54, 55
Roman Forum, 95, 230n
Roman revolution, 144
romantic disease, Goethe's notion of, 77
Romantic poets, 89
Roman writers, 14
Rome, 85
  Bacchanalia in, 89
  Gibbon's tour of, 81
  Goethe's visit to, 82
  spirit culture of, 98–99
Roosevelt, Franklin D., xvii–xviii
  roses, of Cimiez, 106
Roundhead prose and poetry, 136, 197
Rousseau, Jean-Jacques, 46–47, 48, 51, 55
Ruins of Balbec, otherwise Heliopolis in Coelosyria (Wood), 93
"Rules of Etiquette" (Jefferson), 155, 157
Rumbold, Richard, 197, 251n
Rush, Benjamin, 165
Ruskin, John, 102, 185, 236n
Rutledge, Edward, 24

sacrificial practices, of ancient peoples, 95–96, 230n–231n
Sallust, 143, 176
Sandy (slave), 15
Satan, 236n
Schiller, Johann Christoph Friedrich von, 77
Schomberg House, London, 54
Scotch-Irish settlers, in Virginia, 13–14
securities speculation, 117
Sedition Act, *see* Alien and Sedition acts
self-knowledge, philosophy of, 49
seminary, University of Virginia as, 192
Senate, U.S., trials of impeached judges in, 172
Seneca, 100, 197
sentimental literature, 46, 48–50, 68–69
  love in, 217n
sentimental sickness, Schiller's notion of, 77, 225n–226n
Set (Qeb), 76
Seven Years' War, 34–35, 161
Shadwell (farm), 3, 4, 5

Shakespeare, William, 3, 9, 29, 53, 102, 130, 151, 163, 170, 178, 193, 235n
Shay's Rebellion, 75, 82
Sherman, Robert, 24
Sherry, Suzanna, 251n
shipping, American, British interference with, 172, 182–83
Short, William, 66, 70, 72, 80, 133
Skelton, Martha Wayles (wife); *see* Jefferson, Martha Wayles Skelton
slavery, 7, 15, 16, 25, 196, 228n
  Hemings family, 127–28
  and Jefferson's threats of violence, 90–91
  and music, 38
  in revolutionary period, 21
  Volney's description of, 127
Slodtz, Michael Angelo, 68
Small, William, 4, 189
Smith, Abigail Adams ("Nabby") (daughter of John Adams), 41, 62
Smith, Margaret Bayard, 178
Smith, Samuel, 146, 173
Smith, Samuel Harrison, 178
Smith, William Stephens, 40, 41, 75, 76
Socrates, 71, 99, 100, 101
  on thought, 235n
Socrates and Jesus Compared (Priestly), 165
solitude, Jefferson's ideas on, 128
Solon, 156, 202, 203
Sorrows of Young Werther (Goethe), 48, 49, 236n
South Carolina, 24
Spain, and Louisiana Territory, 161
spirit culture, Mediterranean, 98–102, 232n–234n
Stamp Act, 16
statues, reproductions of, 78
Statute for Religious Freedom, Virginia, 204
Stendhal, 46, 65
Sterne, Laurence, 30
stockbroking, 117
Strachey, Lytton, 47
Stuart, James "Athenian," 93
Sugar Act, 16
Summary View of the Rights of British America, A (Jefferson), 17, 20, 160
  superstition, Jefferson's opposition to, xvi
Swift, Jonathan, 88, 228n
Syria, 93

Tacitus, Cornelius, 88, 152–53
Talleyrand, Prince de, 134, 181
taxation, of American colonies, 16
Taylor, John, 135
  term limits, 182
Tessé, comtesse de, *see* Noailles, Adrienne-Catherine de
Thammuz, 75

theater, 50, 90
"Thoughts on English Prosody" (Jefferson), 83
Thucydides, 88
tidewater area, Va., 4–5, 37
Tivoli, 93
Tories, xvi
    definition of, xi
    Whigs' quarrel with, 200, 201
Tott, Madame de, 60, 225n–226n
Towneley, Charles, 42–43, 55, 74
Townshend, Charles, 16
trade, 116, 184
    British interference with, 172, 183
travel:
    preparations for, 81
    regenerative powers of, 85, 86
Trilling, Lionel, 203
Tripolitan War, 156
Tristram Shandy (Sterne), 30–31
Trojan War, 88
Trumbull, John, 60
truth, searchers after, 73, 74, 77, 78, 86, 88, 94
Tuckahoe (plantation), 3
Turin, 107
Two Tickets (Florian), 50

Unitarianism, 168
United States:
    Alien and Sedition acts of, 134–35, 137, 144
    and British-French conflict, 172
    Constitution, see Constitution, U.S.
    crisis of, under Articles of Confederation, 82
    destiny of, 153
    Embargo Act and economy of, 183
    financial concerns of, 113–15
    national bank controversy in, 114–15, 118, 156

Vermont:
    and election of 1800, 145, 146
    and Embargo Act, 183
Vesta, Temple of, Rome, 201
violence, 88, 90–92
Virgil, xx, 14, 65, 88, 96, 174, 187, 188, 247n
Virginia:
    extravagance of planters of, 8
    gentry of, 4–8
    Jefferson as governor of, 29–30
    plantation life in, 37
    pseudo-aristocracy of, 38
    Randolph, Thomas Mann, as governor of, 195
    in revolutionary period, 17, 21, 26, 29–30
    and Scotch-Irish settlers, 13–14
    tobacco and prosperity of, 8
    war debts of, 113
Virginia, University of, 95, 190, 192, 195–96
virtuous action, of Americans, 19–20
Vitruvius, 94, 95

Volney, Count de, 90, 127
Voltaire, xvi, xvii

Walker, Mrs. Jack, 15
walking, xv
Walpole, Horace, 43
war, Jefferson's opposition to, 183
War Against Catiline (Sallust), 176
War of 1812, 189
Washington, D.C.:
    British sacking of, 189
    Jefferson at, 154
Washington, George, 38, 111
    Burr and, 141
    character of, 143–44
    and fears of French invasion, 134
    Jefferson and, 118, 119, 124, 126, 131, 138,
        180, 245n
    and the national bank, 118
    on southern tour, 121, 241n
Waste Land, The (Eliot), 224
Waugh, Evelyn, 237n
Wayles, John (father-in-law), 16, 40–41
Wayles, Martha (wife), see Jefferson, Martha
        Wayles Skelton
Webster, John, 157
weights and measures, Jefferson's report on, 112
Werther (Goethe), 48, 49, 236n
West, opening of, 13
Whigs, xv, xvi, xvii, 21, 116, 117, 139, 253n
    country vs. court, 115
    defects in system of, 190
    definition of, xi–xii
    in England, xii, 35, 114, 115
    expressions of, in Declaration of Indepen-
        dence, 25, 204
    and Jefferson's policy, 156, 171, 194
    and modern republic, 83, 84, 182
    Tories' quarrel with, 200–201, 201
    in Virginia, 37
Whitman, Walt, 137
Wilkinson, James, 173, 175
William and Mary, College of, Williamsburg, Va., 4
Williamsburg, Va., 4, 5
Wills, Garry, xvi, 76, 217n
Winckelmann, Johann Joachim, 77
wines:
    of France, 61–64
    served by Jefferson, 121, 122, 155
Winthrop, John, 153
women, Jefferson's views on, 10, 50
    of Paris, 34
Wood, Robert, 93
Wythe, George, 4, 10, 35, 189, 190

Yeats, William Butler, 237n

About the Author

MICHAEL KNOX BERAN was born in Dallas, Texas, in 1966. He is the author of a book about Robert Kennedy, *The Last Patrician*, and his work has appeared in *The Wall Street Journal*, *National Review*, and *The New Yorker*. A graduate of Columbia, Cambridge, and Yale Law School, he is a lawyer, and he lives in Westchester County, New York, with his wife and daughter.